TEACHING MIDDLE YEARS

DONNA PENDERGAST & NAN BAHR

TEACHING MIDDLE YEARS

RETHINKING CURRICULUM, PEDAGOGY AND ASSESSMENT

ALLEN&UNWIN

First published in Australia and New Zealand in 2005

Allen & Unwin
83 Alexander Street
Crows Nest NSW 2065
Australia
Phone: (61 2) 8425 0100
Fax: (61 2) 9906 2218
Email: info@allenandunwin.com
Web: www.allenandunwin.com

National Library of Australia
Cataloguing-in-Publication entry:

Teaching middle years : rethinking curriculum, pedagogy and assessment.

Bibliography.
Includes index.
ISBN 1 74114 673 9.

1. Middle school teaching. I. Pendergast, Donna Lee. II.
Bahr, Nanette Margaret.

373.236

Set in 11/14pt Minion by Midland Typesetters, Maryborough, Victoria
Printed by Southwood Press, Sydney

10 9 8 7 6 5 4 3 2 1

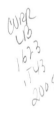

This book is dedicated to our families, who have seen too little of us during the important and challenging journey of constructing this book for and by the community of learners in the middle years. We particularly dedicate this to the young people in our families, some of whom are middle school students:

Kyrra, Bess, Blyton, Zeke and Bader
and
Jacob and Hannah

Contents

Tables

Figures

Contributors

Nan Bahr

Dr Nan Bahr is Director of Teacher Education in the School of Education at the University of Queensland. Nan helped design the first dedicated program for teachers of the middle years in Australia. Nan is an educational psychologist with interests in learning and knowledge, adolescence, and the development of resilience.

Raymond Brown

Dr Raymond Brown is a lecturer in the School of Education and Professional Studies at Griffith University, Gold Coast Campus. He came to this position after 31 years as a Years 5, 6 and 7 classroom teacher where he implemented and studied collaborative ways of teaching and learning.

Fiona Bryer

Dr Fiona Bryer is a senior lecturer at Griffith University Faculty of Education at Mt Gravatt campus. Her undergraduate and graduate teaching is focused on applied development and positive behavioural support for primary and middle school, especially on effective teacher practices for students with socioemotional risk behaviours. Her research interests overlap with these teaching interests and include participatory action research relating to positive behavioural support, implementation of recommended practice, inclusionary versus exclusionary practices, and related developmental issues in socioemotional development. She edited the *Australian Educational and Developmental Psychologist* between 1992 and 2004.

Rod Chadbourne

Associate Professor Rod Chadbourne taught in Western Australian, New Zealand, British and Canadian schools during the 1960s, began tertiary teaching at Adelaide Teachers College in 1971, and has been working at Edith Cowan University since

1973. For the past eight years has been researching, writing and teaching in the area of middle schooling.

Rick Churchill

Dr Rick Churchill is Senior Lecturer, Professional Studies in Education at the University of Southern Queensland. He has held teaching and leadership positions in middle years contexts in South Australia and Tasmania. His recent work has focused on the professional learning of pre-service and early career teachers in Tasmania and Queensland.

Terry de Jong

Dr Terry de Jong is Senior Lecturer and Director of the Middle Years Program at Edith Cowan University. An educational psychologist and academic with experience in South Africa and Australia, he teaches and researches in the areas of adolescent development; youth alienation and engagement; behaviour management; middle schooling; school improvement; and life-skills education.

Shelley Dole

Dr Shelley Dole is a senior lecturer in mathematics education at the University of Queensland. She teaches in the Bachelor of Education (Middle Years of Schooling) program. Her research interests focus particularly on promoting students' conceptual understanding of mathematics to encourage success and enjoyment of mathematical investigations in school.

John Elkins

Professor John Elkins specialises in literacy education at Griffith University and is Emeritus Professor of Special Education at the University of Queensland. He has been a director of the International Reading Association and editor of the *Journal of Adolescent and Adult Literacy* and the *International Journal of Development, Disability and Education*. He is co-editor of *Educating Children with Diverse Abilities*, and chaired the Queensland Taskforce on Inclusive Education (Children with Disabilities). His recent and current research concerns literacy and numeracy in the middle school years.

Annette Hilton

Annette Hilton is currently undertaking higher degree study in a Masters of Educational Study with a focus on middle schooling. She has nineteen years of classroom experience teaching science and mathematics, including a teaching exchange in Canada. She is currently Head of Department (Teaching and Learning) at Corinda State High School, focusing on middle years reform and Gifted Programs. She is the recipient of a 2002 Queensland Government–Smithsonian Fellowship.

Geoff Hilton

Geoff Hilton is currently undertaking higher degree study in a Masters of Educational Study with a focus on middle schooling. He has 25 years of classroom teaching experience, including a year on exchange in Canada. He is currently a Year 7 teacher at Chapel Hill State School.

Lisa Hunter

Dr Lisa Hunter has worked as a teacher and year coordinator in the middle years for thirteen years and now lectures in middle years teacher education at Griffith University. Her research has focused on transition and middle years from students' perspectives and development of schooling in the middle years in Australia and North America. Lisa works with teachers' professional development and masters coursework around middle schooling, including negotiated curriculum, integrated curriculum, student participation and voice, and social and personal education.

J. Joy Cumming

Professor Joy Cumming has expertise in learning and assessment, especially in literacy and numeracy, for children and adults. She has been a consultant to state and national governments, and international studies, in areas of assessment, benchmarks and standards, and accountability. Following formal law studies, her areas of research have extended to education assessment law.

Amanda Keddie

Dr Amanda Keddie is a postdoctoral research fellow within the School of Education at the University of Queensland. Her research interests involve gender, poststructural feminism, transformative pedagogy, social justice, and primary/middle years education.

Doune Macdonald

Professor Doune Macdonald is Head of School in Human Movement Studies at the University of Queensland. Her current research interests include curriculum reform in the field of health and physical education and sociocultural analysis of the place and meaning of physical activity in the lives of young people.

Rod Maclean

Dr Rod Maclean is a senior lecturer at Deakin University, Geelong. He lectures in Language and Literacy Education. Rod's current research is focused on language and learning, classroom discourse and academic literacies. He is currently supervising doctoral students in the areas of literary education for adults with learning difficulties and school-based materials for critical reading in English.

Katherine Main

Katherine Main has a Bachelor of Education (Honours) from Griffith University. Her honours study and current doctoral study are focused on middle schooling in Australia. Her areas of interest are teaching teams within middle schools, specifically collaborative skills and time efficiencies.

Michael C. Nagel

Dr Michael Nagel has taught for 20 years in Canada, Japan and Australia. Mike's doctoral thesis looks at how middle school students in Australia and Canada conceptualise various school experiences. Mike is also a master trainer for the US-based Gurian Institute, which focuses on neurology and gendered brain difference.

Lesley Newhouse-Maiden

Dr Lesley Newhouse-Maiden, Senior Lecturer in the School of Education at Edith Cowan University, teaches in a Diploma in Education (Middle Years). The course, initiated in 2001, aims to address community concerns for the needs of young adolescents through the education of beginning teachers specific to that age group. The team received the 2004 ECU Vice Chancellor's Award for Excellence in Teaching.

Nicola Park

Nicola Park is a practising teacher of nine years' experience in the Victorian government education sector. She is a leading teacher in the middle years at Lyndhurst Secondary College (Cranbourne, Victoria). Her research into middle years schooling has led to the development and use of a variety of models for student and teacher negotiation in classrooms. Nicola has been presenting models of negotiated curriculum through professional development forums to teachers from schools across Victoria for the past two years and is currently designing a Year 9 subject for trial at Lyndhurst Secondary College that will provide teachers and students with uninterrupted opportunity to put such negotiation into practice.

Donna Pendergast

Dr Donna Pendergast is Program Director for middle years teacher education programs at the University of Queensland. Donna was a member of the team that developed the first dedicated program for teachers of the middle years in Australia. She has played a pivotal role in key projects investigating middle school reforms around Australia, including the federally-funded MCEETYA *Middle Years of Schooling and Life Long Learning Project* and the DEST-funded *Beyond the Middle Project*. She has completed many sectoral and school-based consultancies, and provided advice to the Queensland Minister for Education regarding the middle phase of learning.

Léonie J. Rennie

Professor Léonie Rennie specialises in science and technology education at Curtin University of Technology, and is Dean, Graduate Studies at the University. Her research interests concern understandings about, and the communication of, science and technology, especially in out-of-school settings.

Peter Renshaw

Professor Peter Renshaw is Head of the Education School at Griffith University, Gold Coast Campus. He is currently working on three research projects: the first focuses on teachers' ways of understanding student 'difference' during the middle years of schooling; the second focuses on social justice and access to Information and Communication Technology tools for numeracy; the third focuses on early learning and effective educational practices in disadvantaged communities.

Leanne J. Reynolds

Leanne Reynolds managed the development of the Victorian Department of Education's Middle Years Literacy Professional Development program. She has recently been lecturing in Middle Years Literacy at Deakin University Geelong and is an educational consultant and a middle years cluster educator.

Grady Venville

Associate Professor Grady Venville specialises in science and technology education at Edith Cowan University. Grady is a teacher and researcher with experience across the primary, secondary and tertiary levels in Australia, England and Japan. Grady has published widely on curriculum integration and conceptual change and is co-editor of *The Art of Teaching Science* (Allen & Unwin, 2004).

John Wallace

Professor John Wallace specialises in science education at Curtin University of Technology, with interests in teacher learning, science teaching and curriculum integration. His most recent (co-edited) books are *Dilemmas of Science Teaching: Perspectives on Problems of Practice* (RoutledgeFalmer, 2002) and *Leadership and Professional Development: New Possibilities for Enhancing Teacher Learning* (RoutledgeFalmer, 2003).

Muriel A. Wells

Muriel Wells is currently a lecturer at the Geelong campus of Deakin University in Literacy Education for Early and Middle Years, and in Information and Communication Technology in Education. Muriel has a particular interest in the use of computer technologies in education and collaborative online projects. She is currently involved in doctoral studies researching online education.

Claire M. Wyatt-Smith

Associate Professor Claire Wyatt-Smith is Director of the Centre for Applied Language, Literacy and Communication Studies in the Faculty of Education, Griffith University. She worked for a decade as a secondary teacher, including some years as head of department (English). Her research interests focus on the relationship between information and communication technology, literacy, curriculum and assessment, as well as teacher judgement and evaluative frameworks in schooling. Claire teaches literacy and assessment courses at undergraduate and postgraduate levels.

Foreword

What happens when a traditional middle level school decides it is time to improve the learning outcomes, attitudes and behaviours of its young adolescent students? Easy—it decides to become a well-informed, highly committed, responsive middle school. But only the initial answer is easy, for the task of planning, implementing and sustaining the wide range of changes necessary to achieve this goal is the hard part. And this is made even more difficult if relevant information and reliable guidelines are not readily available.

Until now, the best available scholarly books dedicated to the middle years of schooling were those written for an American audience. While Australian schools, universities and education systems have made good use of the international literature, it is time for teachers, principals, academics and student teachers to have access to more relevant and meaningful Australian material. *Teaching Middle Years* is the first comprehensive Australian book to match and surpass the quality of many overseas publications.

This book fills an urgent need expressed by all sectors of education. It will become a text for student teachers enrolling in university courses. It will be used by schools as a reference book to guide their reform efforts. It will be used by individual teachers to enrich their knowledge and understanding of middle schooling. And it will be used by educational leaders committed to the genuine improvement of middle schooling throughout Australia.

The book is consistent with the generally accepted range of recommendations for producing successful middle years of schooling. Part 1 provides a useful context for understanding the historical developments and current thinking influencing the reform movement. It is essential reading, particularly for those new to middle schooling.

Part 2 addresses issues associated with reform in the curriculum. The authors provide an insight into the challenges confronting teachers as they leave the secure and comfortable predetermined teacher-controlled curriculum to engage students in more meaningful and relevant programs. We sense both the struggles and the triumphs experienced by those teachers who make the effort. While the book includes specific chapters on a number of key learning areas, it importantly includes advice on developing a more integrated curriculum through student negotiation. Many teachers will continue to tinker with curriculum by drawing on bits and pieces from the separate subjects, but this book encourages us to act differently by focusing more deliberately on the needs and interests of students in the middle years of schooling.

James Beane (1995) cautions us about the appearance of change:

> [A]t present, a great deal of energy is being expended in symbolic curriculum integration. Most of this has to do with simply finding some themes to serve as a context for science, mathematics, literature, and so on, or tinkering with mild correlations among several subject areas. As we have seen, such efforts are not really about curriculum integration. Instead, they are about trying to find clever ways of repackaging our own interests (p. 37).

Part 3 deals with a wide range of pedagogical issues linked with innovative practices in the middle years of schooling. There is something here for all teachers. The authors draw on recent research findings and contemporary thinking to deliver very meaningful concepts and guidelines to improve current practice. The links to curriculum and assessment reform are clearly obvious. Indeed, I found the chapters in this section to be particularly satisfying and rewarding. They challenge the status quo and lead us into new ways of managing classrooms and working productively with young adolescents.

Although often neglected or mentioned only as an afterthought, assessment is an integral component of this book. Part 4 deals exclusively with assessment issues. The authors begin by clarifying some of the common concepts and terms underlying assessment theory and practice. They then anticipate some of the challenges and key questions we all have about assessment in the middle years. But we are not left wondering about the answers. The authors proceed to enlighten us with constructive insights and comprehensive guidelines. We learn how assessment strategies are part of the ongoing teaching and learning process. We learn how to help students discover their own strengths and weaknesses and we focus on legitimate assessment criteria for a range of educational purposes. But there is much more—this chapter is a rich and productive account of assessment issues complementing the other sections of the book.

While middle schooling reform is accelerating in Australia, there is little reliable local research available to support many of these efforts. Most advocates for reform are certain about the validity of their arguments and are willing to implement their beliefs on faith. Some anecdotal evidence and a few scattered pieces of research are encouraging but much more is needed to satisfy the critics and sceptics. Fortunately, some excellent research from the United States leaves little doubt that genuine reform in middle schooling is highly successful.

In Australia, a comprehensive research agenda is needed to help direct and sustain the reform effort, and to identify which schools are seriously pursuing a critical mass of appropriate middle schooling reform. The accelerating pace of developments in recent years would suggest some schools may not be doing the 'right thing', as happened over the years in the United States. If too many 'rogue' schools appear on the list of middle schooling reform, the Australian research of the future may not be so kind to this critical reform movement. Hence, it has become increasingly important for teachers and others to have access to books such as this to guide and encourage the efforts of schools at all stages of genuine reform.

I encourage you to read this publication carefully and to share it with others, including educational leaders and the wider community. It reports on a wide variety of significant middle schooling topics and is written in a style directed towards middle level practitioners. Now is the time to be implementing developmentally responsive reform in those middle level schools that expect high academic achievements from all their young adolescents. The young people we live and work with on a daily basis deserve nothing less.

Dr Robert Hardingham
Foundation President,
Middle Years of Schooling Association, Australia;
Director, Middle Schooling Advisory Service; Assistant Dean (Retired),
Faculty of Education, Queensland University of Technology

Preface

The middle years of schooling is increasingly recognised as a crucial stage of schooling with significant consequences for ongoing educational success and future participation in society. Middle schooling reform focuses on establishing and sustaining academically rigorous and developmentally responsive educational learning contexts and experiences for young adolescents. Teachers in this critical phase need specialist preparation, as they are required to teach across key learning areas and to have the skills and knowledge to understand and manage issues related to young adolescents.

This book will assist schools, academics, pre-service student teachers and teachers in their quest to successfully develop the middle years of schooling curriculum, pedagogy and assessment to meet the needs of today's young people, in a context-specific way. The book brings together signifying practices of middle schooling by academics and school-based practitioners. It is not exhaustive in its coverage—several books would be required to document all the relevant aspects of middle schooling, such as the range of practices, policies and school-based reforms under way, and each chapter could easily be expanded into a book in its own right.

The organisation of the book reflects the cornerstone of middle schooling, that is, reform in curriculum, pedagogy and assessment. It commences with a platform about middle schooling as a site for educational reform, before addressing reform in practices grouped around curriculum, pedagogy and assessment. Each chapter concludes with questions that guide reflection of the concepts developed in that chapter. In addition to meeting editorial requirements, each chapter has been peer reviewed. The book is a collaborative effort, drawn from a range of scholars and practitioners who responded to the open call for contributions made by the editors. It fills a gap in the resources available around middle schooling, bringing together sound scholarly debate and practical applications.

Dr Donna Pendergast and Dr Nan Bahr

Acknowledgments

The editors wish to thank Joy Reynolds for her administrative contribution to this book. We also acknowledge the enthusiastic response of our colleagues who replied to the call for chapter abstracts, many of whom, given the overwhelming response, we reluctantly were unable to include. The book was initiated because of the lack of appropriate contemporary and context-relevant resources for the emergent field of middle schooling in teacher education, schooling and classroom reform in Australia. It was a difficult task to select from the excellent quality of the initial abstract submissions, and when invited chapters were received, we again reluctantly dealt with editing and in some cases the rejection of chapters based on reviewer feedback, overlap and the interests of developing a useful contemporary resource. We thank the reviewers for their insightful comments and the publishers for their confidence in this project.

PART 1

THE MIDDLE YEARS AS A SITE FOR EDUCATIONAL REFORM

1

The emergence of middle schooling

Donna Pendergast

The middle years of schooling are increasingly the focus of education reform initiatives in Australia. Evidence from around the country points to the middle years and specifically middle schooling as maturing from theoretical ponderings and tentative trials plagued by rumours of yet another passing fad, to an initiative that gives all the indications of a sustainable shift in educational approaches for young people aged from around 10 to 15 years. Middle schooling can be likened to a debutante at a coming-out ball. Like the fresh-faced, eager and excited yet naive debutante, middle schooling is taking some tentative but practised steps and is receiving plenty of attention; there is growing confidence that the benefits it promises may be turning into real outcomes. Yet, like the young debutante, there is still a long way to go to realise the full potential, to achieve maturity. There are many cues to suggest that middle schooling has 'arrived'; that it is a legitimate site for learners, teachers, teaching and teacher educators to inhabit. This chapter sets out to explore some of these signs and to speculate about what the future might hold in the reform agenda.

The emergence of middle years as an educational site

For more than a decade and a half there has been growing interest in middle schooling and in addressing the educational needs of young adolescents (a category that is challenged in the next chapter) as a distinct group of students in our schools. This is increasingly evident through a commitment to the development of policies, programs and practices that relate specifically to students in the 10–15 years age group. Middle schools are being designed and established to cater specifically for the needs of this group of students (Hargreaves & Earl 1990; Cormack 1991; Eyers 1992; Manning 1993; Chadbourne, 2001). Cormack and Cumming's (1995) report, *From Alienation to Engagement,* has been particularly influential in Australia, highlighting reform strategies for curriculum, pedagogy, school organisation and environment, as well as reinforcing the need for a multi-layered approach to reform. During 1996–97, the National Middle Schooling Project developed a 'common view of the needs of young adolescents; the principles that should guide our work with them; and the practices that are regarded as most appropriate for their positive and successful development' (Cumming 1998, p. 14).

Middle schooling is not an Australian initiative; indeed, we have had the benefit of building on a considerable body of international activity and research that has accumulated over many decades. The impetus for middle schooling in other countries, however, has been quite different to the Australian scenario. In America, for example, issues such as population growth, racial segregation and curriculum imperatives led to the development of middle school as a tier of schooling in an already three-tiered model. Claims about the success of middle schooling in America have been bold, such as that made by Lounsbury (1997, p. xi) who maintains 'the middle school movement is an educational success story unparalleled in our history. In a little over three decades the face of American education has been remade'.

In Australia, schools generally operate on a two-tier system (primary and secondary) providing a very different context for middle school reform. An important aspect of the underlying philosophy of reform in the middle years of schooling in the Australian context revolves around the provision of a seamless transition from primary schooling (which is traditionally student centred) to secondary schooling (which is traditionally subject or discipline centred) leading to more effective student learning, positive experiences in adolescence, and a desire and capacity for lifelong learning. These issues go beyond the traditional shift from the smaller primary school site to a larger secondary school. Difficulties are exacerbated by the different structures, the new relationships with teachers, the unique needs of adolescent learners, and the different emphases students encounter in the movement from primary to secondary. Abundant evidence points to the failure of traditional structures for students in the middle years. Particularly for boys, the failure to meet the particular needs of adolescent learners can manifest in disengagement from schooling, often reflected in poor achievement and behaviour. Students also believe that they are required to deal with variable teacher responsiveness. For their part, teachers must confront and deal with the consequences of student disengagement and variable work environments (Hill 1995).

However, changing school structures to reflect those more likely to be found in middle schools does not ensure that middle schooling will take place. As Chadbourne (2001, p. iii) notes, 'middle schooling refers more to a particular type of pedagogy and curriculum than a particular type of school structure'. Hence, generally speaking, middle years work has tended to focus on the convergence and transformation of curriculum, pedagogy and assessment, and to a lesser degree on organisational elements to meet the needs of young adolescents. It is not about rearranging traditional structures, but is a new concept altogether. And it is increasingly recognised that for reform to have any cogency and impact on the educational experience of students and the workplace conditions of teachers, it requires the articulation of all key aspects rather than isolated change.

In terms of curriculum, it is acknowledged that a coherent curriculum appropriate to the needs of early adolescents is focused on identified needs; it is negotiated and linked to the world outside the classroom. In addition, it is explicit and outcome based—progress and achievement are recorded continuously in relation to explicit statements of what each student is expected to know and be able to do. This leads to changing views and practices surrounding pedagogy—the way we teach these students. Classroom pedagogy must match the needs and abilities of middle year students. To be effective, pedagogy must be flexible, reflecting creative uses of time, space and other resources as well as group and individual needs. It must also be learner-centred, with an emphasis on self-directed and co-constructed learning. As the literature indicates, it must also be increasingly team focused for both teachers and learners, all of whom require supportive, ethical and challenging environments. Assessment must be relevant, authentic and connected to the life experiences of young people. Educational goals specific to the middle years must be determined. These are fundamental changes in terms of rethinking curriculum, pedagogy and assessment, not about reshaping existing practices.

In terms of school organisation, there is a need for collaboration between teachers across disciplines and year levels; there must be administrative support for change; there must be adequate resourcing at all levels—experienced teachers and support staff, supported by high-quality facilities, technology, equipment and materials; and, finally, the school must be community oriented—with parents and outside agencies contributing to productive and sustained partnerships. There are many models for middle schooling organisation which are proving to be effective, including 'pod' structures with a number of students (typically multi-aged and numbering around 70–100) with a small number of teachers who remain with the pod, typically 4–6 teachers. Teachers may 'loop', that is, stay with the same group over a two or three year period, and then start with a new group.

Table 1.1 documents a selection of reports informing the pathway of middle schooling advancement in Australia, along with a brief summary of key findings/recommendations/points of interest. This is not intended to be an exhaustive list, but a representative selection, demonstrating a growing refinement of understandings of middle schooling, and a key to some of the research that is identifiable as middle schooling from around the nation.

Table 1.1 A selection of middle schooling reports in Australia

Year, title, author	Brief description and highlights
1996 Australian Curriculum Studies Association (ACSA) *From Alienation to Engagement: Opportunities for reform in the middle years of schooling (Vols 1–3)*	• Project managed by Australian Curriculum Studies Association (ACSA). • Project was initiated in 1994 to focus on the issue of alienation during the school years of 5–8. It included field studies in schools. • The published reports included key findings and recommendations, a review of literature on alienation, and a professional development document for teachers.
1998 Barratt *Shaping Middle Schooling in Australia: A report of the National Middle Schooling Project*	• Project managed by ACSA. • Aimed to form a collective view of middle schooling in Australia. • Identified needs of young adolescents: identity, relationships, purpose, empowerment, success, rigour, safety. • Identified that middle schooling school-based practices were underpinned by the values: learner centred, collaboratively organised, outcome based, flexibly constructed, ethically aware, community oriented, adequately resourced, strategically linked. • Identified three key strategies to meet the needs of young adolescents: powerful knowledge, integrated curriculum, authentic assessment.
1999 Hill & Russell *Systemic, Whole School Reform of the Middle Years of Schooling*	• Provides a broad overview of guiding principles for the development of middle schooling. • Commonly agreed principles: based on characteristics and needs of young adolescents, holistic integrated approach to change, a sound philosophical base, partnerships with students, close

Year, title, author	Brief description and highlights
	relationships with teachers and students, collaborative teaching, flexible use of time and space, outcomes-based approach, continuity between three phases of learning, involvement of parents and community, fair and adequate share of resources, theories of change. • These general design elements were used as the conceptual basis for program designs in the Middle Years Research And Development (MYRAD) project.

2001
Chadbourne
Middle Schooling in the Middle Years
	• Commissioned by the Australian Education Union.
	• Identifies and considers key issues around middle schooling.
	• Lists the principles of middle schooling:
	  – higher order thinking, holistic learning, critical thinking, problem-solving and lifelong learning;
	  – students taking charge of their own learning and constructing their own meanings;
	  – integrated and disciplinary curricula that are negotiated, relevant and challenging;
	  – cooperative learning and collaborative teaching;
	  – authentic, reflective, and outcomes-based assessment;
	  – heterogeneous and flexible student groupings;
	  – success to every student;
	  – small learning communities that provide students with sustained individual attention in a safe, healthy school environment;
	  – emphasis on strong teacher–student and student–student relationships through extended contact with a small number of teachers and a consistent student cohort;
	  – democratic governance and shared leadership;
	  – parental and community involvement in student learning.

2002
Luke et al.
Beyond the Middle: A Report about literacy and numeracy development of target group students in the middle years of schooling (Vols 1 & 2)
	• Funded by Commonwealth Department of Education Science and Training (DEST).
	• Aimed to investigate the efficacy of programs in all states and territories for student literacy and numeracy outcomes in a range of target groups.
	• Report contains:
	  – an extensive review of middle school literature both in Australia and internationally, 1990–2000;
	  – mapping of systemic literacy and numeracy strategies including systemic site visits;
	  – analysis of the effectiveness of key literacy and numeracy teaching and learning strategies, including school visits and classroom rating using the Productive Pedagogies framework.
	• Outcomes suggest a need for: a new generation of middle years theorising, research, development and practice, with a stronger focus on engagement and demand.

(continues)

Table 1.1 *continued*

Year, title, author	Brief description and highlights
2002 MYRAD *Middle Years Research and Development Project*	• Commissioned by Department of Education & Training (DET) (Victoria) and undertaken by the University of Melbourne, 1998–2001. • Identified several strategies and practices which contribute to improvement in the middle years: primary-secondary cluster cooperation, whole-school commitment, three-year action planning, targeted ongoing professional learning, data-driven evidence-based evaluation, provision of resources and specialist support. • Recommends practices and strategies in three key areas: teaching and learning practices in the classroom, curriculum and assessment, school organisation for learning.
2005 Pendergast et al. *Developing Lifelong Learners in the Middle Years of Schooling*	• Commissioned by Ministerial Council on Education, Employment, Training and Youth Affairs (MCEETYA). • Aimed to explore practices, processes, strategies and structures that best promote lifelong learning in the middle phase of schooling. • A model was developed representing key elements: structures, cultures, curriculum, pedagogy, assessment, leadership, relationships. • A second model, a phased model of change was constructed with three broad phases: initiation, development and consolidation, linking middle schooling and lifelong learning attributes.

It is important to point out that there are many other projects/reports/ initiatives currently underway or of a more targeted nature that have not been included in the selection in Table 1.1, which is not to imply they have not made or will not make a significant impact in the field. What this selection demonstrates is a growing corpus of literature and emergent theoretical perspectives around middle schooling and hence a growing intellectual investment and commitment to the initiative. This is an area where more work needs to be done—documenting the history and emergence of middle schooling in Australia will be an important task over coming years.

Several key international publications that have influenced middle schooling development in Australia are summarised in Table 1.2.

Educational institutions at primary, secondary and tertiary level have shown active responses to the emerging middle years reform agenda, with many schools

Table 1.2 A selection of middle schooling reports influencing Australia

Year, title, author	Brief description and highlights

1989
Carnegie Council on Adolescent Development
Turning Points: Preparing American youth for the 21st century
	• Published by the Carnegie Council on Adolescent Development.
	• Regarded as groundbreaking work that suggested substantial numbers of American adolescents were at risk of being inadequately prepared to function productively as adults
	• Outlines eight interrelated elements that, when taken as a whole, provide a vision for middle schooling:
	  – creating a community for learning;
	  – teaching a core of common knowledge;
	  – ensuring success for all students;
	  – empowering teachers and administrators;
	  – preparing teachers for the middle grades;
	  – improving academic performance through better health and fitness;
	  – re-engaging families in the education of adolescents;
	  – connecting schools with communities.

2000
Jackson & Davis
Turning Points 2000: Educating Adolescents in the 21st century
	• A report of the Carnegie Corporation
	• Provides practical insights into how to improve middle years education, with a strong focus on curriculum, instruction and assessment and argues that organisational changes alone do not achieve major improvements in academic achievement.
	• Contains seven recommendations for middle schooling:
	  – curriculum: learner centred; integrated; exploratory (students' needs, interests, and aptitudes);
	  – pedagogy: interdisciplinary/collaborative teams; productive pedagogies applied; variety of activities and delivery techniques; alignment of pedagogy and assessment, i.e. authentic assessment embedded in work; higher order skills in critical thinking and problem solving;
	  – staff: knowledge of curricula areas; knowledge of development and diversity of middle school students; a genuine commitment to teach middle school students; knowledge and expertise in middle school concepts such as advisor–advisee programs, interdisciplinary teaming, and positive school climates;
	  – relationships: strong student–teacher relationships; collaborative partnerships with colleagues, parents, and other community members; pastoral care; small learning communities;
	  – democratic government: those who know the students best are responsible for planning curriculum and school organisation (i.e. school is responsive to local needs);
	  – safe environment: a safe and healthy environment where students feel comfortable taking risks; students work at own pace and experience success as part of improving academic performance; diversity is acknowledged and valued;
	  – community partnerships: Family and community partnerships to promote greater support for middle school students.

(continues)

Table 1.2 *continued*

Year, title, author	Brief description and highlights

2003
National Middle School Association
This we believe:
Successful schools for
young adolescents
	• Position paper of National Middle School Association (America).
	• Outlines eight characteristics of successful schools for young adolescents:
	  – educators who value working with this age group and are prepared to do so;
	  – courageous and collaborative leadership;
	  – a shared vision that guides decisions;
	  – an inviting, supportive and safe environment;
	  – high expectations for every member of the learning community;
	  – students and teachers engaged in active learning;
	  – an adult advocate for every student;
	  – school-initiated family and community partnerships.
	• Outlines six program elements:
	  – curriculum that is relevant, challenging, integrative and exploratory;
	  – multiple learning approaches that respond to students' diversity;
	  – assessment and evaluation programs that promote quality learning;
	  – organisational structures that support meaningful relationships and learning;
	  – school-wide efforts and policies that foster health, wellness and safety;
	  – multifaceted guidance and support services.

around Australia experimenting with the elements of reform in an attempt to address issues of disengagement and disenchantment. The various Australian state education departments along with the independent and Catholic Education sectors have responded with research and development funding, the emergence of junior secondary schools and a general positive interest in this area. Tables 1.3 and 1.4 present some initiatives from Victoria and Queensland as a means of demonstrating the type of work that is happening nationally. Some initiatives, for example for the state of Victoria, focus on projects, and some in Queensland focus on sectoral position statements.

Along with the growing body of research, projects and position statements relevant to middle schooling, there are other signs the field has come of age. The investment by universities to prepare middle school teachers is one such domain.

Table 1.3 What's happening in Victoria? Projects

Middle Years Literacy Research Project
This research was undertaken by Deakin University for DE&T, CECV and AISV and funded by DEST. It focused on literacy education in mainstream primary and secondary classroom practice in Years 5–9. The twelve case study primary and secondary schools identified critical elements of effective literacy education in the middle years of schooling.

Middle Years Numeracy Research Project
This was conducted for DE&T, CECV and AISV by RMIT University. The project was funded by DEST and involved 20 trial schools. Key findings included:
* numeracy can be measured using rich assessment tasks incorporating performance measures;
* an emergent numeracy profile can be used to inform subsequent instruction;
* there is as much difference in student numeracy performance within year levels as there is between Years 5 and 9 students overall;
* there is a significant dip in student numeracy performance from Year 6 to Year 7 which is not recovered until Year 9;
* teachers and targeted programs make a difference to numeracy outcomes in the middle years;
* action planning based on a design approach (Hill & Crévola 1997) was effective in supporting schools to improve numeracy outcomes in the middle years;
* there is a least as much difference between classes as there is between schools in numeracy;
* all trial schools demonstrated improved student numeracy performance largely as a result of a concerted focus on best practice;
* a significant number of students experience difficulty with some aspect of numeracy so early diagnosis and intervention are critical.

Middle Years Pedagogy Research and Development Project (MYPRAD)
This initiative will provide direction and support for reforming pedagogical practice in Victorian government schools. During 2003, materials were developed and trialled to support teachers to reflect on their classroom practice, develop their professional learning teams and promote whole school change. Following the successful trial of MYPRAD materials in nine clusters during 2003, MYPRAD is now being made available to all Schools for Innovation and Excellence clusters from 2004. MYPRAD is a strategy for planning and implementing change in the middle years of schooling. It provides a means by which schools and clusters can examine their teaching practices and identify key areas for improvement, develop a plan to initiate improvement and monitor change. It is based on an explicit framework describing middle years pedagogy, and a change model that reflects contemporary understandings of teacher development and school improvement. It is designed to be implemented over a three-year period.

Improving Middle Years Maths and Science Research Project (IMYMS)
This is a three-year project commencing in 2004. It is a joint project funded through an Australian Research Council Linkage grant involving both Deakin University and the Department of Education and Training. Four Schools for Innovation and Excellence clusters, representing 30 schools, are participating in the project.
    IMYMS is a strategy for planning and implementing change in the middle years of schooling. IMYMS has been devised as a means by which schools and clusters can look carefully at their mathematics and science practices and identify key points for improvement, develop a plan to initiate improvement and monitor change. It is based on an explicit framework describing effective teaching and learning in middle years mathematics and science, and a change model that reflects contemporary understandings of teacher development and school reform.

Table 1.4 What's happening in Queensland? Sector position statements

See the Future: The Middle Phase of Learning State School Action Plan
The Action Plan sets the direction, clarifies expectations and accountabilities, and commits systemic support for reforms in every Queensland state school. It requires the alignment of curriculum, pedagogy and assessment to bring greater consistency and rigour to middle years classrooms. It incorporates two stages: Years 4–5, and Years 6–9. Actions are organised around five domains: focus and accountability; curriculum, teaching and assessment; achievement; transition; and teachers (Queensland Government 2003).

Pathways for Middle Schooling: Walking the Talk. A position paper and self-audit process The Brisbane Catholic Education Commission (BCEC) position paper aims to promote dialogue about middle schooling, describe appropriate and effective practices, assist school communities to audit current practices; and to inform the development of a school action plan to assist schools to meet the needs of young adolescents (BCEC 2004).

Constructing middle school teachers

In 2002 the initial cohort of students enrolled in the first dedicated middle years teacher education program in Australia. These pioneers graduated from the University of Queensland in 2003. Since the program commenced, there has been a virtual mushrooming of middle years programs/specialisations/course electives in teacher education around the country. A search on the World Wide Web revealed a smorgasbord of possibilities for teacher education existing around Australia, including the dedicated programs listed in Table 1.5.

There are almost 20 programs that include the nomenclature of middle schooling in their title in some way. This is an astounding expansion in a period of three years, especially when the process for programs to receive accreditation through their various university hierarchies (and other stakeholders such as employing bodies and registration authorities) is considered. In addition to these dedicated programs, there are many more programs across a much wider range of institutions that offer specialisations/majors/minors/subjects related to middle schooling.

This pattern of programmatic growth heralds a new time for teacher education, and the production of new kinds of teachers. Most dramatically, this marks the shift from the traditional two-tiered approach—primary and secondary—to potentially a three-layered model—primary (early); middle; and secondary (later)—of teacher preparation. Alternatively, it could be argued that rather than introducing yet another tier we are aiming to create a seamless system. Either way, in so doing we are constructing a new kind of teacher identity, a new kind of teacher (Pendergast 2002). This heralds a new aspect of research in teacher education in Australia. Some work

Table 1.5 Dedicated middle years teacher education programs

Institution	Program title
Charles Sturt University	Bachelor of Education (K–12 Middle Schooling)
University of Western Sydney	Graduate Certificate Teaching in the Middle Years
Central Queensland University	Bachelor of Learning Management (Middle Schooling)
Queensland University of Technology	Graduate Certificate in Education (Middle Years of Schooling)
The University of Queensland	Bachelor of Behavioural Studies/Bachelor of Education (Middle Years of Schooling)
	Bachelor of Social Science/Bachelor of Education (Middle Years of Schooling)
	Bachelor of Contemporary Studies/Bachelor of Education (Middle Years of Schooling)
	Bachelor of Education (Middle Years of Schooling) Graduate Entry
	Graduate Certificate Middle Years of Schooling
University of the Sunshine Coast	Bachelor of Education/Bachelor of Science (Middle/ Senior Phase)
University of Southern Queensland	Bachelor of Education (Primary and Middle Schooling)
	Bachelor of Education (Senior and Middle Schooling)
	Bachelor of Education (Senior and Middle Schooling) Graduate Entry
Flinders University of South Australia	Bachelor of Education (Middle School) Graduate Entry
University of South Australia	Bachelor of Education (Primary & Middle)
	Bachelor of Education (Middle & Secondary) Graduate Entry
	Bachelor of Education (Primary & Middle) Graduate Entry
Edith Cowan University	Bachelor of Education (Primary & Middle Years)
	Graduate Diploma of Education (Middle Years)

Note: Sourced by web search on 18 November 2004. Inclusions based on use of middle school/ing/years in program title.

has already commenced around this area, notably that conducted by the Middle Years Team at the University of Queensland (Keogh et al. 2004) into ways in which pre-service teachers in a dedicated middle years teacher education program see themselves developing and growing as middle years teachers, and, concomitant with this, traces their emerging understandings of young adolescents in the middle years of learning. The research team is collectively known as the Woodlands Group and comprises academics involved in the dedicated middle years program. With respect to the new space for young people as learners in the middle years, the Woodlands Group (Stevens et al., under review) have conducted a historical and theoretical inquiry into adolescence, challenging four dominant discourses of adolescence: age/stage developmentalism, pathologisation, progressivism, and oppression and resistance. An alternative discourse is offered which has a complexity theory/postmodernist lens, and which highlights implications for teacher education around the shift from pedagogical content knowledge to pedagogical inquiries and curiosities, and from static questions to dynamism, recursivity and discursivity.

Other research that has commenced in the field is investigating the way in which middle years teachers construct themselves. Table 1.6 is a compilation of findings from studies about terms used by various teachers to describe themselves. The respondents were asked to provide words they would use to describe themselves as a typical middle years teacher (pre-service or in-service). The top five

Table 1.6 Top five terms used to describe typical teacher types

Teacher	Term	Frequency (per cent)
Middle years teachers* (N=48)	Tired	37.5
	Frustrated	35
	Stressed	33
	Caring	29
	Overworked	23
Middle years pre-service teachers[†] (N=61)	Organised	23
	Knowledgeable	19
	Caring	15
	Patient	13
	Creative	12
Hospitality teachers[‡] (N=117)	Organised	48
	Hardworking	41
	Dedicated	38
	Enthusiastic	37
	Creative	34
Home economics teachers[§] (N=199)	Multi-skilled	70
	Professional	43
	Organised	39
	Resourceful	35
	Practical	30

Notes: * Pendergast (2002)
      [†] Pendergast (unpublished study)
      [‡] Pendergast & Wilks (2005)
      [§] Pendergast (2001)

terms are reported based on frequency of response. This is juxtaposed with other classifications of teachers that have been similarly researched (Pendergast 2001; Pendergast & Wilks 2005). It is interesting to consider the predominance of negative valence terms used by the practising middle years teachers, when compared to other categories. For these teachers, four of the five terms have a negative valence—tired; frustrated; stressed and overworked. The other term, which is striking in its use, is the word 'organised', which was the most frequently cited term by students in a pre-service middle years program, and also by hospitality teachers. Home economics teachers used the term frequently as well, yet it doesn't appear in the top five of middle years teachers.

Complementary to this research is data around identity construction that is evident through the visual imagery in the following depictions of middle years teachers, as drawn by pre-service middle years teachers enrolled at the University of Queensland after their first practicum experience in middle school settings.

Figure 1.1 I love my job

Figure 1.2 Bag of tricks

Figure 1.3 Connecting with students

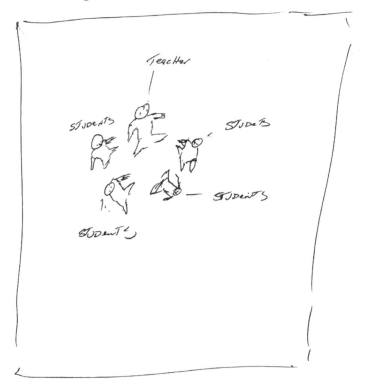

Figure 1.4 The juggler

Part of a larger study, these images provide an insight into the ways in which students are constructing themselves as middle years teachers. Figure 1.1 represents a fairly typical depiction of a teacher—desk, board, apple, pencils, books—all icons associated with teachers, along with their frustration and stress levels. Figure 1.2 suggests that middle school teachers need to be equipped with an extra 'bag of tricks', implying they are more than a typical teacher, and to a large degree this is reinforced by Figure 1.4. Figure 1.3 offers something a little different—an image of students and teacher together in circle formation, with no typical icons present. It suggests movement and a sense of cohesion. Such research is the beginning of understanding new types of teachers being produced.

The support structures for professional development of teachers, both pre and in-service, are also gradually emerging. For example, the Middle Years of Schooling Association ran the fourth annual international middle years conference in 2005. Western Australia has a dedicated state-based professional association, the Middle Schooling Association of Western Australia. Many states have network structures, such as the South Australia Middle School Network (SAMSN). And there are some dedicated professional publications, such as the Australian Curriculum Studies Association (ACSA) *Primary and Middle Years Educator*, which focuses on issues and practical ideas relating to the primary and middle years of schooling.

In support of the new construction of middle years teacher graduates from teacher education programs, there are also designated middle years teaching positions. A collection of advertisements from one state-based newspaper over two successive weekends (Table 1.7) provides an insight into the types of positions earmarked as middle school. These positions are in independent and Catholic system schools only, as government vacancies are not commonly advertised in the newspaper.

Table 1.7 Middle years teaching positions, November 2004

Job title	School description
Secondary (middle & senior), Maths/Science	P–12 Christian College
Primary/middle years teacher	P–12 Catholic College
Middle school/secondary teacher (English/SOSE)	P–12 Catholic College
Middle school teacher (Fine Arts/Performing Arts)	P–9 Christian College
Middle/upper primary teacher	P–12 Interdenominational College
Teacher specialising in middle school	8–12 Non-aligned College
Middle/upper primary teacher	8–12 Interdenominational

The rapid growth of teacher education programs, the emergence of middle schooling research agendas, dedicated publications, the establishment of professional associations and networks, designating of job descriptions—are all signs of a legitimate space for middle schooling in Australia.

Directions for the reform agenda

It is argued in this chapter that middle schooling has made a shift from an uncertain force to a major reform agenda in the first decade of this millennium. These are some of the issues and challenges that will influence the course of the reforms over coming years, many of which will be explored in later chapters of this book.

1 As a concept, middle schooling is annoyingly nebulous—it is a slippery concept. There is no single definition, no template, no formula for middle schooling. Even the terms used in the field—middle years, middle school, middle years of schooling, middle schooling—appear to lack coherence and agreed definition. This is a strength that should be articulated, along with the range of principles and practices that are to be encouraged.

2 There appear to be some commonly agreed middle school practices, but these are not exclusive to middle schooling.

3 Middle schooling reform does not exist in isolation, making it difficult to implement, explore and determine outcomes and efficacy.

4 Middle schooling is consistently constructed as being about rethinking education that meets the needs of young people in a changing world.

5 While middle schooling has achieved debutante status in terms of acceptance as a reform platform, policies, positions, their implementation and evaluation are very much in their infancy, so many educators are working on anecdotal evidence, gut feeling and good faith.

6 Middle schooling reform will affect later phase learning if it achieves its goals. Greater intellectual awakening, enhanced social connections and positive experiences and attitudes should potentially impact on the later phase with improvements across dimensions such as literacy, numeracy and intellectual engagement.

7 Middle schooling is not about implementing a three-tiered school structure. It is about a unique philosophy, with concomitant changes in pedagogy, curriculum and assessment. These changes are not about repackaging, but about a new way of doing.

8 Middle schooling means change for teachers.

9 Middle schooling is complex, site-specific and requires sustained, systemic reform. There is enormous work to be done at all levels—in the classroom, in schools, in clusters, in sectors, in systems, in government—to develop appropriate frameworks/guidelines, including supporting research, professional development and reform processes.

10 Middle schooling is here to stay—there is widespread evidence that middle schooling is a legitimate space in our education system. Regardless of this however, champions of middle schooling are required at all junctures: in schools, in systems, and especially in universities, where academic, research-based evidence is required.

Questions

1 Select one of the informing documents from Table 1.1 or Table 1.2 and investigate in detail the elements highlighted as contributing to the middle schooling movement in Australia. Consider this question from the perspective of the chosen paper—whose interests are being served by the reforms in middle schooling?

2 The newly emergent field of middle schooling has opened a new space for 'middle years teachers'. What impact is this likely to have on teacher education generally?

3 In what ways do you predict middle years teachers may differ from other teachers?

4 The young learner/young adolescent/middle years student is a new category of student that has emerged out of the middle years reform. What further work needs to be undertaken to improve teacher education programs for the needs of these 'new' student identities?

Acknowledgments

I wish to make special mention of the support provided by Joy Reynolds in locating web-based resources used in this chapter.

2

The philosophy of middle schooling

Rod Chadbourne and Donna Pendergast

This chapter identifies issues, presents perspectives and makes suggestions that middle schoolers can consider when constructing their own philosophies of middle schooling. These issues, perspectives and suggestions are structured around eight questions that middle years reformers often face. Throughout the chapter we identify our position on the issues but in a way that does not present readers with a prefabricated package. This approach reflects our assumption that middle schoolers are philosophy-makers rather than philosophy-takers.

> A thorough study of middle grades philosophy and organisation, not merely a superficial exploration, should be a main element of middle grades teacher preparation (Jackson & Davis 2000, p. 100).

The past two decades in Australia have seen considerable reform in the middle years of schooling. Many schools now publicly identify and name themselves, or a sub-school within their organisation, as 'middle schools'. For some this might be virtually a change in name only. For many others, the change involves a significant restructuring and reculturing in order to implement the philosophy of middle schooling.

The philosophy of middle schooling consists of the assumptions and beliefs underpinning the purpose, design elements and recommended practices of middle

schools. It also includes the assumptions and beliefs that support a shift from traditional schooling to middle schooling. Some of these assumptions and beliefs are
made explicit; others remain implicit. All of them are socially constructed; many of
them are contested. As with other forms of education, the development of middle
schooling is characterised by ongoing conceptual uncertainties, shifts and settle-
ments. At any one time there is unlikely to be complete consensus on all aspects of
middle schooling philosophy. And, as history attests, middle schooling is open to
cooptation by groups with different agendas, interests and ideologies. Further
complexity arises when attempts to distinguish middle schooling from traditional
schooling find that in certain contexts the differences between the two models are
less than the differences within each model. To capture some of the features, issues,
tensions and sophistication of middle schooling philosophy, we structure our
analysis of it in terms of the following questions:

- Should middle schooling be adolescent-specific?
- Should middle schooling prioritise the intellectual development of students?
- Should young adolescents be made to fit the organisation of schools or should
  the organisation of schools be made to fit young adolescents?
- What should the curriculum of middle schools consist of? What concept of
  reality should the middle school curriculum be based on?
- Should pedagogy in middle schools be teacher-centred or student-centred?
- Should middle schooling aim to help build a better society and if so what would
  a better society look like? Should middle schooling be an agent of social change?
- Is there a 'one true' or 'pure' model of middle schooling?
- Is it necessary to have a philosophy of middle schooling?

The answers to these questions in this chapter reflect our view that the philosophy
of middle schooling can be characterised as predominantly progressive, constructivist, outcomes-based, community-oriented, developmentally responsive,
student-centred, liberal reformist and contextually mediated—but neither
completely nor exclusively so.

Some of the material and propositions we present in this chapter may not
appear as 'philosophy' because they read like statements of purported fact. Philosophy, as commonly conceived, focuses primarily on what *should* be the case rather
than what *is* the case, on ends rather than means, and on purposes rather than
operations. It focuses on ideological rationales rather than scientific explanations.
It focuses on ideals, visions and values rather than everyday realities and contextual
factors. And it focuses on beliefs about what is considered to be important and

worth fighting for. However, factual statements that have not been validated by empirical evidence can often be regarded more appropriately as statements of their proponents' beliefs and world views, that is, their philosophies. This applies particularly when statements are made about the nature and construction of knowledge and reality, the nature and conditions for teaching and learning, the nature and needs of society, the nature and phases of human development, and the nature and preferred model of the school as an organisation.

In addition, we should say from the outset that we are both advocates of middle schooling and academics committed to open discussion and inquiry. The issues-based nature of this chapter represents our attempt to strike a balance between these two positions. In our view, debates within the ranks of middle schoolers (here meaning 'advocates of middle schooling') are a sign of strength, not weakness, in the development of middle schooling and a progressive society.

Should middle schooling be adolescent-specific?

> Middle level education is the segment of schooling that encompasses early adolescence, the stage of life between the ages of 10 and 15. In order to be developmentally responsive, middle level schools must be grounded in the diverse characteristics and needs of these young people. It is this concept that lies at the heart of middle level education (National Middle Schooling Association 1995, p. 5).

Traditionally, school education has been compartmentalised into primary and secondary divisions. The primary years cover three phases of development: early childhood, middle childhood and early adolescence. The secondary years cover two phases of development: early adolescence and young adulthood. The middle years of schooling cover a single phase of development: early adolescence. For that reason, middle schooling should be regarded as adolescent-specific. A stronger claim is that middle schooling should be defined as adolescent-centred, adolescent-focused, adolescent-led, rather than conceived generically as student-centred. We support that claim, within the framework of the following observations and beliefs. Student-centred education forms part of the philosophy of middle schooling but only insofar as it applies to early adolescence. The literature clearly emphasises that middle schooling should be defined as formal education that is responsive specifically to the developmental needs, interests and characteristics of young adolescents. By itself, the philosophy of middle schooling is not distinctive; it applies to students of all ages and stages. What makes it distinctive is its application to young adolescents.

The claim that middle schooling should be adolescent-specific can be challenged on a range of grounds. We list some of those grounds below and indicate our response to them in the form of counterclaims. The brevity of the claims and counterclaims leave the issues open for further exploration and debate.

- **Claim** Adolescence is an artificial, 'man-made' construct. Centuries ago adolescence did not exist; people progressed directly from childhood to adulthood.
- **Counterclaim** Adolescence exists today, regardless of whether it is biologically or socially determined. And that's a good thing. The 'absence' of adolescence centuries ago led to massive abuses of human rights.
- **Claim** Middle schoolers over-amplify the significance of adolescence; their claim that 'young people undergo more rapid and profound personal changes during the years between 10 and 15 than at any other period in their lives' ignores the magnitude of change that occurs during infancy and the menopause (National Middle School Association 1995, pp. 5–6).
- **Counterclaim** The gaining of reproductive capacity is more intensive and comprehensive than the losing of it. Virtually all 10 to 15-year-old boys and girls experience puberty whereas few, if any, men experience the menopause. Also, the changes during infancy and menopause occur outside the years of school education.
- **Claim** Adolescence is not a single entity, even as a contrived construct to categorise young people between the ages of 10 and 15. To isolate it as such stereotypes adolescence as a problem and leads to self-fulfilling prophecies that have a detrimental impact on the identities, behaviour and academic performance of young adolescent students in the middle years of schooling.
- **Counterclaim** Middle schoolers acknowledge the 'widely varying life experiences of young adolescents' and the need to promote 'a valuing of adolescence, seeing it as a rich pathway to maturity rather than a problem period to be survived' (Queensland Board of Teacher Registration 1996 p. 31). These acknowledgments counter 'victim blaming' or deficit models of adolescent development and facilitate self-fulfilling prophecies that have a positive rather than negative impact on adolescent development and performance.
- **Claim** Traditional schools have successfully served young people between the ages of 10 and 15 without constructing themselves as being adolescent-specific or adolescent-centred or adolescent-focused.

- **Counterclaim** Most young adolescents 'survive' traditional schooling, but only a few 'thrive'. To some extent, middle school reform is a response to claims that 'through Years 5–8 young people's learning either slows down, stops or even seems to go backwards . . . at a time when learning should be jumping ahead' (Stringer 1998, p. 6).
- **Claim** What do the 'middle years' refer to? What are the middle years in the middle of? Answer: The middle years are in the middle of primary and secondary schooling; that is, upper primary and lower secondary year levels.
- **Counterclaim** The 'middle years' refer to the years between middle childhood and young adulthood, that is, early adolescence. They refer to a particular stage of human development (early adolescence) that just happens to coincide currently with upper primary and lower secondary school year levels. As some recent state curriculum frameworks and the emergence of P–12 and middle schools suggests, the historical compartmentalisation of school education into primary and secondary divisions may be reaching its use-by date. As a biologically and socially determined phase, early adolescence shows no sign of having a use-by date. What are developmentally responsive middle level schools 'responsive' to? Answer: They are responsive to 'the diverse characteristics and needs' of young adolescents. 'It is this concept that lies at the heart of middle level education' (National Middle Schooling Association 1995, p. 5).

Should middle schooling prioritise intellectual development?

Let us be clear. The main purpose of middle grades education is to promote young adolescents' intellectual development. It is to enable every student to think creatively, to identify and solve meaningful problems, to communicate and work well with others, and to develop the base of factual knowledge and skills that is the essential foundation for these 'higher order' capacities. As they develop these capacities, every young adolescent should be able to meet or exceed high academic standards. Closely related goals are to help all students develop the capacity to lead healthful lives, physically and mentally; to become caring, compassionate, and tolerant individuals; and to become active, contributing citizens of [their country] and the world (Jackson & Davis 2000, pp. 10–11).

As the above passage indicates, advocates of the middle school movement emphasise that middle years curriculum, assessment and pedagogy should be based on high academic standards. Doing so, they claim, supports 'the twin towers of an education that ensures success for every student: excellence and equity' (Jackson & Davis 2000, p. 33). Despite these explicit statements of purpose and ideology, critics argue that middle schooling undermines academic rigour. For example:

> Overemphasis on the social, emotional, and physical needs of the middle school student has led to neglect of academic competencies (Bradley, in Beane 1999, p. 4).

> The most frequent criticism of middle schools is that their so-called 'child-centred' pedagogy has failed miserably with regard to academic achievement . . . and every other imaginable measure of what some critics consider to be serious and rigorous education (Beane 1999, p. 3).

> I think we should abandon the whole middle school concept. Middle schools are a disaster. They slow down the intellectual progress that kids make in elementary schools, and they effectively preclude readiness for college for many minority kids (Mitchell, in Norton 2003).

A few critics go further than claim that as a matter of fact middle schools undermine academic rigour. They make the claim that middle schoolers deliberately undermine academic rigour as part of an agenda to produce equality of outcomes. For example:

> . . . activist reformers at the middle school level soon made it clear that the middle school was not just a new educational organization, but a means to an end—that end being the implementation of massive changes meant to promote social egalitarianism . . . The goal of creating mass equality is being pursued through policies and practices implemented in many middle schools across the country . . . All these policies and practices have been working together in a systematic fashion, encouraging at many middle schools a culture of disdain and contempt for high academic achievement. This is nothing less than a declaration of war against academic excellence (Yecke 2003, pp. xix–xx).

The critics are right to suggest that middle schooling places more importance than traditional schooling does upon the development of the 'whole child'. But we believe they are wrong to claim that by devoting resources to adolescents' socio-emotional needs, middle schools forfeit some capacity and commitment for developing academic excellence. Pitting 'rigour' against 'relationships' creates a false dichotomy. Positive student–student and teacher–student relationships can increase student engagement with school tasks, which in turn leads to higher quality intellectual work. Or, as Clive Beck (1999) notes:

> If students are to feel comfortable in the class, attention must be given to the social, emotional, and even physical needs of all class members. Students will not be able to learn academically or in other ways if they feel hungry, cold, isolated, or otherwise unhappy (p. 6).

The critics are also right to claim that middle schooling embraces a reformist political philosophy that espouses social change rather than maintenance of the status quo, a point we take up towards the end of the chapter. But in our view they are wrong to claim that middle schoolers endorse the lowering of academic standards in order to achieve equality of student learning outcomes. As intimated above, the purpose of middle schooling is to 'ensure success for every student' by lifting the performance of 'all students to achieve high standards', rather than by bringing the performance of high academic achievers down to the lowest common denominator (Jackson & Davis 2000, p. 25). The assumption about human nature underlying this purpose leaves no room for middle schools to 'dumb down' the curriculum because,

> By embracing high expectations and high performance standards for every student, teachers and administrators in a *Turning Points 2000*-based school are saying, publicly, that they *believe* every student has the capacity for high-level intellectual development and that their actions will be guided by that belief (Jackson & Davis 2000, p. 227).

Three other arguments could be developed to illustrate middle schooling's philosophical commitment to raising academic standards. In skeletal form they appear as follows:

- The philosophy of middle schooling accepts most of the key principles adopted by the Coalition of Essential Schools. One principle states that 'Students should study a few essential areas deeply' (Daniels et al. 2001, p. 16). Middle schooling cautions against a curriculum that is a 'mile wide and an inch deep', supports the principle that 'less is more', and aims for deep understanding and higher order thinking.

- The philosophy of middle schooling embraces constructivism, a theory which stresses the need for all students to be intellectually challenged, experience cognitive dissonance and work within their zone of proximal development. These imperatives would not be accepted by people who wanted to lower academic standards.
- The philosophy of middle schooling embraces transformational outcomes-based education (OBE), as evident in its advocacy of integrated curriculum, 'big ideas' and enduring understandings. For example, in discussing the goals of middle school reform, Jackson and Davis (2000, p. 33) emphasise that, 'To promote excellence, high standards demand a thorough understanding of essential knowledge, require critical thinking and problem-solving skills, and encourage habits of mind that can be applied across disciplines'. Transformational OBE requires a higher level of complexity, abstraction and generality, and therefore a higher level of academic rigour, than traditional OBE (Chadbourne 2003).

There is no doubt in our minds that middle schooling is philosophically committed to academic rigour. To argue otherwise and claim that middle schooling is engaged in a war against intellectual excellence is neither helpful nor warranted. If a war must be declared, it should be a war against conservative ideologies, not high academic standards.

Should young adolescents be made to fit school or vice versa?

The underlying philosophy of reform in the middle years of schooling revolves around the provision of a seamless transition from primary schooling (which is traditionally student-centred) to secondary schooling (which is traditionally subject or discipline-centred) leading to more effective student learning, positive experiences in adolescence, and a desire and capacity for lifelong learning (Carrington et al. 2002, p. x).

Philosophy includes assumptions and beliefs not only about purposes and values but also about individual interests and rights. Part of middle schooling philosophy involves constructing answers to questions such as: What is in the best interests of young adolescents? Who determines what constitutes the best interests of young adolescents and on what basis should the determination be made? When conflicts of interests arise, whose interests should prevail?

Middle schoolers argue for a seamless transition from primary to secondary schools. They claim that traditionally the transition has been disconnected, discordant and dysfunctional. In brief, the following thinking informs their view on this matter. Primary school students are taught by one teacher in one room for a whole year. Traditional secondary school students move every '40 minutes' from teacher to teacher, room to room, subject to subject and class to class. In many cases, young adolescents find the gulf created by these differences unbridgeable. This situation is not in their best interests.

Traditional schoolers could seek to defend the lack of a seamless transition from primary to secondary by arguing that young adolescents benefit from a challenging 'rite of passage'. According to this view, young adolescents should accept the responsibility and challenge to fit into schools rather than expect schools to fit in with them. Also, after 6–8 years of primary school under a 'mother hen' classroom arrangement, young adolescents need to be and look forward to being treated more like adults than children. Depriving them of that tough initiation experience is detrimental to their best interests.

In response, middle schoolers emphasise that young adolescents make the transition from primary to secondary school at a stage when the onset of puberty requires them to cope with the most significant physical, cognitive and socioemotional changes in their lives. Being compelled by the state to attend school gives them the right to be protected from a primary/secondary transition that is unnecessarily abrupt and antagonistic to their developmental needs. Failure to provide that protection contributes to the rising rate of problems such as youth alienation, substance abuse, crime and suicide. None of this is in the best interests of young adolescents.

The contrasting views outlined above represent philosophical differences on what constitutes the best interests and rights of young adolescents, what constitutes the most appropriate form of school organisation to meet those interests and rights, and whose perspective should prevail. Middle schoolers argue that when school organisation conflicts with young adolescents' developmental needs, the school should be changed to fit the student rather than expecting the student to change to fit the school. And the school change they argue for can be summed up in one word—'community'.

A distinguishing feature of middle schools is the grouping of large numbers of teachers and students into small learning communities of about 4–6 teachers and 80–120 students. Each small community has its own name and identity; its own rooms, facilities, resources and budget; its own place and space. These structural arrangements make middle school learning communities larger than single primary school classes and smaller than large high school age-graded cohorts. To achieve the sense and substance of *community*, middle schoolers believe that their small learning communities need to develop:

- A climate of trust, openness, care, friendliness, high morale, and 'can do' optimism—rather than a climate of suspicion, secrecy, indifference, cynicism, hostility and defeatism.
- A culture that values diversity, inclusion, sharing, equity, support, cooperation, shared power and facilitative leadership—rather than intolerance, segregation, hoarding, elitism, put-downs, rivalry, neglect, domination and power-based leadership.
- A membership of young adolescents who are able to say, 'Within this community I feel that my needs, interests, values and experiences are known, understood, accepted and valued. I identify myself, and others accept me, as a respected member of this community. I feel I belong to it. I'm pleased and proud to belong to it. It's part of who I am.'

For middle schoolers, changing the school to fit the students means taking steps to establish the climate and culture of community and young adolescents' sense of positive identity with it. These steps need to be based on a clear concept of community and a firm commitment to its ideology—for example, equality of social worth, the celebration of members' achievements, and the removal of incidental and institutionalised prejudice and discrimination. These steps include being prepared to change traditional practices and move towards:

- heterogeneous classes, cooperative learning, and inclusive curriculum;
- non-competitive assessment and exhibitions of students' work;
- group building activities, pastoral care and peer support programs;
- policies to combat bullying and violence—physical, social and verbal;
- programs that promote community spirit and pride, and that prevent the development of harmful cliques, rejects and isolates.

The value that middle schooling philosophy places on building community rests on two broad assumptions. One is the belief that community enhances academic achievement by increasing the level of student participation and risk-taking in class discussions; cooperative learning; and personal growth, particularly with respect to self-acceptance and self-confidence (Beck & Kosnik 2001). A second belief is that, when built with the characteristics outlined above, small middle school communities provide a model of society we all should be aiming to develop.

What should be the middle school curriculum?

> ... we do not want to demean progress that middle-levels educators have made in trying to make better schools for early adolescents ... But among the important questions that the middle school movement has raised, it has failed to press the ultimate issue, 'What should the middle school curriculum be?'(George et al. 1992, pp. 83–4).

Some literature creates a surface impression that consensus exists on what the middle school curriculum should be—for example, that it should be integrated, developmentally responsive, negotiated, relevant, authentic, outcomes-based, explorative and challenging. However, beneath the surface there exists a rich array of issues. The discussion below presents a few of them.

Integration

Three questions can be raised with respect to advocacy for integrated curriculum in middle schools. Firstly, *Turning Points 2000* claims that the middle school curriculum must be both discipline-based and integrated, rather than one or the other. In contrast, some middle schoolers (for example, Beane) attack subject-based curriculum and recommend it be replaced by integrated curriculum. Which position should we accept, or are they both acceptable? Those who argue for a mix of discipline-based and integrated curriculum do not indicate what proportion of the school year should be devoted to each type; should it be 50 per cent discipline-centred and 50 per cent integrated, or 70:30, or 20:80, or some other ratio? These types of issues carry substance if integration is conceived as integrating material, and making connections, across disciplines. However, if integration is conceived as integrating what is learned or experienced at school with what is learned or experienced outside school, then integration can occur within a discipline-centred curriculum. When that takes place, is it valid to claim that the dichotomy between discipline-based and integrated curriculum disappears?

Secondly, advocacy for integrated curriculum often assumes that education should be 'real life', not only a preparation for 'real life', and that in 'real life' our experiences and problems are not discipline-specific. For example, Beane (1991) says:

> It is time we faced the fact that subject areas or disciplines of knowledge around which the curriculum has traditionally been organised are actually territorial

spaces carved out by academic scholars for their own purposes . . . For people other than subject scholars, such subjects are only abstract categories. When we are confronted in real life with a compelling problem or puzzling situation, we don't ask which part is mathematics, which part science, which part history, and so on (p. 9).

But is Beane right? Could he be challenged by suggesting that in real life we can often make sense of, and respond to, situations, problems, tasks and experiences in terms of specific disciplines—for example, when critiquing a film, analysing a blood sample, or calculating the odds at the casino? Also, is it not the case that much of the work in some occupations consists of subject-specific tasks?

Thirdly, is it philosophically possible for a curriculum to be both discipline-based and integrated? From Lawton's (1975) analysis of work by sociologists and curriculum theorists such as Michael Young and Philip Phenix, we can construct a framework for comparing the philosophical differences between advocates of integrated and disciplined-based curriculum. The beliefs supporting discipline-based curriculum include: that reality is discipline-based; disciplines ask different sorts of questions; children learn in a discipline-based way; and disciplines promote more economical learning, thereby assuming the existence of a fixed, external reality. The beliefs supporting integrated curriculum deny the existence of such absolutes and are typified by beliefs such as: that all knowledge is socially constructed; subject barriers are arbitrary and artificial; disciplines serve an unjust society; and the selection of curriculum knowledge should be made problematic and not taken for granted. What implications does this philosophical conflict present for middle schoolers, particularly in light of the *Turning Points 2000* recommendation that the middle school curriculum should be both disciplined-based and integrated?

Developmentally responsive, negotiated, student-based, authentic curriculum

One view of the middle schooling curriculum is that it should be developmentally appropriate and responsive to the changing physical, cognitive, and socioemotional needs of young adolescents (Lee Manning 2002). This view argues that the middle school curriculum should be student-centred or, more aptly, adolescent-centred; that the middle school curriculum should be changed to fit the student rather than the students changed to fit the curriculum. This view moves middle schooling further away from traditional schooling.

A second view, and one that moves middle schooling closer to traditional schooling, is that middle school curriculum should be a blend of student-centred and teacher-led approaches. The argument here is that teachers are agents of society as well as teachers of students, and that, as Zemelman et al. (1998) caution:

> Student-centred schooling does not mean passive teachers who respond only to students' explicit cues. Teachers also draw on their deep understanding of children's developmentally characteristic needs and enthusiasms to design experiences that lead students into areas they might not choose, but that they will enjoy and engage in deeply . . . student-centred education . . . provides a balance between activities that follow children's lead and ones that lead the children (p. 9).

Which of these two views should we accept? Or are they equally valid, to the point where middle schoolers should be free to choose between them? Is there scope within middle schooling philosophy for a third view, namely, one that argues for a teacher-led curriculum for young adolescents, at least in some circumstances?

'Authentic curriculum' refers to curriculum that students regard as relevant, real and connected to the world beyond school (Daniels et al. 2001). Newmann and associates insist that connectedness to the outside world is necessary for 'authentic pedagogy' (Newmann & Associates 1996). A similar requirement applies to 'productive pedagogy' (Education Queensland 2001). Middle schoolers could ask an important question here: would insisting that all curriculum must be authentic deny young adolescents the opportunity to pursue studies they find intrinsically interesting but of no apparent practical value or application to the outside world?

Outcomes-based curriculum

The Australian National Middle Schooling Project recommended that middle schooling practices should be 'outcomes-based' (Barratt 1998a). In doing so, it reflected the outcomes-based nature of the new curriculum frameworks developed and adopted by Australian states during the 1990s. It also predated the American *Turning Points 2000* recommendation that middle grades schools teach 'a curriculum grounded in rigorous, public academic standards, relevant to the concerns of adolescents, and based on how students learn best' (Jackson & Davis 2000, p. 32).

The four essential principles of outcomes-based education (OBE) developed by Spady (1994) are: clarity of focus, designing back, high expectations for all students, and expanded opportunities for all learners (Killen 2002). These four principles are incorporated in the philosophy underlying the middle school curriculum, as outlined in *Turning Points 2000*. The term 'standards' in *Turning Points* equates with 'outcomes' because it refers to 'agreed-upon statements of what students should know and be able to do'. *Turning Points* also advocates 'setting consistently high, public expectations for *every* student' and a 'backward design' approach to developing curriculum for young adolescents (Jackson & Davis 2000, p. 32).

The outcomes-based curriculum frameworks developed by the Australian states apply to all schools—middle and traditional, government and non-government. Middle schooling curriculum, therefore, cannot claim to be distinctive by virtue of being outcomes-based. However, of the three types of OBE—traditional, transitional and transformational—middle schooling could claim to be more philosophically aligned than traditional schooling with transformational OBE. Traditional OBE 'emphasises student mastery of traditional subject-related academic outcomes usually with a strong focus on subject-specific content', while transformational OBE 'emphasises long-term, cross-curricular outcomes that . . . reflect the complexities of real life and give prominence to the life-roles that learners will face after they have finished their formal education' (Killen 2002, p. 2). Middle schooling embraces transformational OBE by virtue of its focus on integrated curriculum, 'big ideas' and enduring understandings (Jackson & Davis 2000).

How does OBE fit in with other aspects of middle schooling philosophy? For example, is it consistent with the idea that middle schooling curriculum should be constructivist, adolescent-centred, exploratory and negotiated? OBE has roots in aspects of behaviourism; for example, behavioural objectives, competency-based education, mastery of learning and criterion-referenced assessment (Killen 2001). Middle schooling has roots in constructivism; for example, students constructing their own meanings, making choices, engaging in discovery learning and negotiating the curriculum. Philosophically, behaviourism and constructivism seem poles apart. How, then, can middle schooling incorporate OBE within its philosophy?

OBE grounds the middle school curriculum in virtually non-negotiable, state-mandated outcomes. Some middle schoolers, such as Beane, ground the middle school curriculum in adolescents' concerns about themselves and the world. Does the possibility exist here for a clash between fixed, predetermined, centrally set curriculum outcomes and student-negotiated, developmentally responsive curriculum outcomes?

Should middle school pedagogy be teacher-centred or student-centred?

There are at least three reasons why teacher-centered, whole-class instruction can and should remain part of the school day. First and most important, teachers have great things to teach . . . [secondly] because most teachers work within a mandated curriculum . . . [thirdly] as learners and as people, teachers deserve to feel safe and comfortable in school too (Zemelman et al. 1998, pp. 209–10).

Is this comment by Zemelman et al. consistent with middle schooling philosophy? Middle schoolers believe that pedagogy should be consistent with the aims of middle schooling, practised within the framework of backward design, and based on research into how students learn best. The aims of middle schooling centre on excellence and equity; that means ensuring success for *every* student. The steps in the outcomes-based backward design approach to curriculum require teachers to select outcomes, develop detailed curriculum based on these outcomes, construct assessments that allow students to show they have achieved the outcomes, and then plan instruction to prepare students to do well on the assessment. The principles of how students learn best, according to middle schoolers, are encapsulated in constructivism, authentic achievement, productive pedagogy and research on best practice. Table 2.1 lists some of these pedagogical principles and practices.

Table 2.1 Middle schooling pedagogy

Teaching principles and practices advocated by:			
Constructivism e.g. Krause et al. (2003)	**Best practice** e.g. Zemelman et al. (1998)	**Authentic pedagogy** e.g. Newmann & Associates (1996)	**Productive pedagogy** e.g. Education Queensland (2001)
• Learner-centred • Discovery learning • Cooperative learning • Collaborative learning • Peer-assisted learning • Cognitive apprenticeships • Reciprocal teaching	• Student-centred • Experiential • Holistic • Authentic • Expressive • Reflective • Social • Collaborative • Democratic • Cognitive • Developmental • Constructivist • Challenging	• Construction of knowledge • Consideration of alternatives • Disciplined inquiry • Higher order thinking • Deep knowledge • Substantive conversation • Elaborate written communication • Connections and value beyond the school	• Higher order thinking • Deep knowledge • Deep understanding • Substantive conversation • Knowledge as problematic • Metalanguage • Knowledge integration • Background knowledge • Connectedness to the world • Problem-based curriculum

The *Turning Points 2000* account of middle schooling pedagogy emphasises the need for differentiated instruction. It also identifies seventeen practices that distinguish differentiated classrooms from traditional classrooms. In essence, these seventeen practices portray differentiated instruction (middle schooling pedagogy) as student-centred, multidimensional, flexible and facilitative.

Critics of middle schooling take issue with its pedagogy. Cheri Pierson Yecke (2003), for example, claims that the driving beliefs undergirding middle school instructional practices reflect three fundamental convictions, namely: radical equity, group rights and coercive egalitarianism. She lists five of these overlapping beliefs as follows:

1 Belief in the equality of outcomes, as manifested by the decrease in rigour of the middle school curriculum, the calls to eliminate ability grouping, and the increased use of cooperative learning and peer tutoring, all of which result in the levelling of achievement.
2 Belief in questioning the value of individualism, as manifested in the drive for eliminating ability grouping (which focuses on individual effort) in favour of cooperative learning.
3 Belief in the supremacy of the group over the individual, as manifested in the drive for eliminating ability grouping (which focuses on individual effort) and increasing the use of cooperative learning and peer tutoring.
4 Belief that advanced students have a duty to help others at the expense of their own needs, as manifested in the increased use of both peer tutoring and cooperative learning.
5 Belief that competition is negative and must be eliminated, as manifested in the drive for eliminating ability group (which focuses on individual effort) in favour of cooperative learning and peer tutoring (Yecke 2003, p. 152).

The National Middle Schooling Association rebuts each of Yecke's criticisms on the website address: http://www.nmsa.org/news/critique/introduction.htm. Our response to the claims about radical equity and coercive egalitarianism appear in the next section of this chapter. Do these rebuttals and responses clear middle schooling of the charges laid by Yecke once and for all?

In addition to the concerns raised by Yecke, the philosophy of middle schooling pedagogy invites a question asked by Zemelman et al., namely, can teachers committed to 'best practice' ever 'teach' in the 'old-fashioned sense of the word' (1998, p. 209). In our view, their answer to that question applies to middle schooling. They say that it is fine for classroom work to be teacher-centred for some of the time, but the traditional balance needs to be reformed so that there is less teacher-centred and more student-centred schooling. Table 2.2 lists some conventional teacher-centred practices they recommend *less* of, and some progressive student-centred practices they recommend *more* of. Less does not mean 'none' and more does not mean 'only'. It's not a case of all or nothing, which suggests that the differences between traditional and middle schooling pedagogy should be seen as differences of degree rather than kind.

Table 2.2 Ingredients for best practice in middle school classrooms

Middle school classrooms need LESS	Middle school classrooms need MORE
Whole-class, teacher-directed instruction (e.g. lecturing)	Experience, inductive, hands-on learning
Student passivity: sitting, listening, receiving and absorbing information	Active learning in the classroom, with all the attendant noise and movement of students doing, talking and collaborating
Presentational, one-way transmission of information from teacher to student	Diverse roles for teachers, including coaching, demonstrating and modelling
Prizing and rewarding of silence in the classroom	Emphasis on higher-order thinking; learning a field's key concepts and principles
Classroom time devoted to fill-in-the-blank worksheets, dittos, workbooks, and other 'seatwork'	Deep study of a smaller number of topics, so that students internalise the field's way of inquiry
Student time spent reading textbooks and basal readers	Reading of real texts: whole books, primary sources and non-fiction materials
Attempts by teachers to thinly 'cover' large amount of material in every subject area	Responsibility transferred to students for their work: goal setting, record keeping, monitoring, sharing, exhibiting and evaluating
Rote memorisation of facts and details	Choice for students (e.g. choosing their own books, writing topics, team partners and research projects)
Emphasis on the competition and grades in school	Enacting and modelling the principles of democracy
'Tracking' or levelling students into 'ability groups'	Cooperative, collaborative activity; developing the classroom as an interdependent community
Use of pull-out special programs	Heterogeneous grouping where individual needs are met through inherently individualised activities, not segregation of bodies
Use of and reliance on standardised tests	Delivery of special help to students in regular classrooms
	Varied and cooperative roles for teachers, parents and administrators
	Reliance on teachers' descriptive evaluations of student growth, including observational/anecdotal records, conferences notes, and performance assessment rubrics

Source: Selected from research findings published by Zemelman et al. 1998, pp. 4–6.

Should middle schooling be an agent of social change?

> Thus we see the work of middle grades educators implementing *Turning Points* reforms as much more than 'school reform.' . . . At its heart, the middle grades movement is a movement in the service of social justice (Jackson & Davis 2000, p. 229).

At the level of widespread formal practice within mainstream education, middle schooling is fairly recent. As an idea, middle schooling has a long history because it is a form of progressive education. In broad terms the philosophy of middle schooling is the philosophy of progressive education. So while the term 'middle schooling' is relatively new, the philosophy is as old as progressive education itself; it has existed in the minds of some educators across the world for centuries.

Political philosophy

The difference between the political philosophy underlying traditional and progressive education, based on stereotypes, can be characterised as follows. Traditional education in Australia is politically conservative; it focuses on maintaining social control, the status quo and the social and cultural reproduction of society. Progressive education is politically reformist; it focuses on promoting social justice and social change. These stereotypes mask differences within each model of education by suggesting that they are single unitary concepts in opposition to each other. Brian Hill (1975) disturbs these stereotypes by distinguishing two types of traditional education: Education I (gradgrind indoctrination) and Education II (initiation into the most valued public modes of knowing). He goes on to distinguish three types of progressive education, namely, procedural, normative and revolutionary openness (see Table 2.3). Procedural openness advocates the acceptance of the basic political–economic values on which Australia's social structure is based. Normative openness argues for students being allowed to make up their own minds and develop in any direction they choose. Revolutionary openness contends that schools should educate students to reject the dominant value systems of a class-structured capitalist society and replace them with alternative doctrines.

The compartmentalisation of types of progressive education in Table 2.3 is not watertight, for some alternative or free schools adopt a radical ideology.

With reference to Table 2.3, most middle schools in Australia fit the liberal category (procedural openness, alternatives within schools, re-schooling). As such they are closer ideologically to Education II traditional schools than to other forms of

Table 2.3 Types of progressive education

Ideology	Open education	Alternative education	
Liberal	Procedural openness	Alternative within schools	Re-schooling
Neutral	Normative openness	Alternative schools	Free-schooling
Radical	Revolutionary openness	Alternatives to schools	De-schooling

progressive education. So, to distinguish middle schooling philosophy from traditional school philosophy on the basis that it is 'progressive' overlooks the possibility
that the differences within the various forms of progressive education may be
greater than the differences between 'liberal' progressivism and traditional education. But while middle schooling philosophy does not support the overthrow of
capitalism, it does question some aspects of the status quo. For example:

> The *Turning Points* concept challenges deeply rooted and structurally reinforced
> norms in American education that support existing social and economic inequities
> between different groups of people . . . Schools operating based on the *Turning
> Points* principles . . . represent a threat to established social and economic hierar-
> chies (Jackson & Davis 2000, p. 227).

Social justice

As a form of progressive education, middle schooling aims to contribute to the
betterment of society. It advocates that middle schools be agents of social change
rather than preserve the status quo, particularly with respect to social justice. For
example:

> Along with intellectual development, at the heart of our definition of 'middle
> grades education' is the requirement for equity in outcomes for all groups of
> students, regardless of their race, ethnicity, gender, family income or linguistic
> background (Jackson & Davis 2000, pp. 10–11).

This philosophy has come under fire. Some critics of middle schooling seem to
support a purely meritocratic model of social justice based on equality of opportunity. They accuse middle schooling of pushing an egalitarianism model of social
justice based on equality of outcomes. For example:

> Belief in reaching 'equity' by producing equality of outcomes through the levelling of achievement appears to be the sort of equity embraced by radical proponents of the middle school movement (Yecke 2003, p. 153).

> Equality of opportunity is a fundamental right in our society—but to demand equality of outcomes is nothing more than a thinly veiled attempt at imposing a socialist utopia (Yecke 2003, p. 160).

We believe in a form of social justice that represents a blend of equality of outcomes and equality of opportunity. Our thinking here is as follows. The middle schooling vision of 'success for all' and equality of outcomes does not mean each and every student should reach the same level of academic achievement. Rather, it means that the proportion of students who achieve the highest level of academic achievement within each social category should be equivalent to their proportion in the whole population of the country. That is, equality of outcomes should refer to social categories, not individual students. These categories include gender, social class, ethnicity, race and geographical location (urban, rural). Educational outcomes should be proportionately equal across these categories but can be unequal within each category.

In our view, social justice allows for some inequality of rewards (money, power, recognition) provided there is equality of educational opportunity to compete for them. However, the competition needs to be conducted on the basis of a handicap race, rather than an open race, to ensure equality of outcomes for students across, not within, social categories. Not all rewards, however, should be distributed on the basis of 'merit' and competition. Some rewards should be distributed on the basis of 'need'; that is, there are some things that people should not have to compete for.

Further considerations on middle schooling, political ideology and social change
The history of middle schooling in Australia has yet to be written. When that does occur, in all probability the type of developments quoted below will be considered. These developments suggest that a level of agreement exists among conservatives and progressives on recommended middle schooling practices. But they also suggest the lack of a common ideological basis for such agreement.

> During the 1970s, critics of traditional education came predominantly from the ranks of the 'new left', humanism, and constructivism . . . These critics condemned the regulation and rigidities of traditional education in the name of social justice,

democracy and self actualisation. Throughout this era, conservatives . . . opposed progressive education, defended traditional education and promoted 'back to the basics'.

By the 1990s, some conservatives had shifted ground and voiced similar objections to traditional education that the progressives had made two decades earlier. However, their opposition to the regulation and rigidities of traditional education was made in the name of choice, market forces and economic productivity . . . And this shift occurred within the context of moves to introduce devolution, corporate management and workplace agreements for teachers . . . Within this context it is possible to (mis)construe middle schooling as being part of a broader set of initiatives that were politically and economically motivated, rather than based on educational grounds; that is, as fitting the imperatives of management rather than the needs of young adolescents (Chadbourne 2001, p. 13).

Is there a 'one true' or 'pure' model of middle schooling?

We have witnessed many middle schools that have failed to empower young adolescents, have sustained the separate subject approach to curriculum, have resisted full inclusion, have surrendered to parents who demand tracking and ability grouping . . . and have given standardized test achievement precedence over relevant curriculum . . . while sources may vary, there is considerable consensus on what constitutes an exemplary middle level school . . . there are central principles and related practices that need to be held sacred in planning our future (middle schooling) change efforts (Doda 2002, pp. 349, 350, 354).

So far, this chapter has identified a range of specific issues related to the philosophy of middle schooling. A set of more general questions arises from variations in middle school practices across Australia. There is no doubt that such variations exist. For example, some middle schools group students into mixed ability classes; others stream them. Some middle schools include integrated studies in their curriculum; others don't. Some middle schools appoint and use teachers as curriculum generalists; others appoint and use teachers as subject specialists. Some middle schools arrange desks in small groups as their 'default' setting; others arrange them in rows. Some have open-plan buildings; others operate from a more traditional design.

From the perspective of philosophy, what do these variations in middle school practices mean? That middle schoolers lack a united philosophy? That they share a common philosophy but do not stick uniformly to it? That philosophically there is no 'one true' or 'pure' model of middle schooling? That philosophically there is a set of non-negotiable principles of middle schooling but contextually mediated factors prevent schools implementing all of them?

'One true' model of middle schooling?

The concept of a 'one true' or 'pure' model of middle schooling suggests that departures from it compromise its philosophy. Support for a pure model can be gleaned from a number of sources. One source is *Turning Points 2000* which, after proposing seven key design elements, goes on to claim that there can be 'no half measures' with the implementation of middle schooling because '. . . the goals of excellence and equity can be reached *only* [our emphasis] through comprehensive, ongoing change involving *all* [our emphasis]the design elements' (Jackson & Davis 2000, p. 219). James Beane (1999) expresses similar sentiments:

> In almost all cases where evidence is reported supporting the middle school concept, the schools involved have made dramatic commitments to the concept and moved ahead in very serious ways. Educators in such schools obviously have every right to trumpet their successes. But to use such data to defend others that have proceeded only half-heartedly is unfair to both highly implemented middle schools and to critics of the middle school concept. It is also a strategy bound to backfire since schools that have only tinkered around the edges of reform are unlikely to show the same level of effects (1999, p. 4).

Another source of support for the concept of an uncompromising 'one true' model of middle schooling comes from a perspective that sees the past and future of traditional and middle schooling as a fight for ascendancy. A thumbnail sketch of the story so far from this perspective reads as follows. In Australia, traditional schooling has been dominant since education was made compulsory over a century ago. During that time, reformers made periodic attempts to break the traditional mould and replace it with some form of progressive schooling. However, their initiatives either withered on the vine or remained on the fringe as fragile developments of marginal influence. Until recently, this pattern suggested that while educational reforms may come and go, the ascendancy of traditional schooling is destined to remain forever. Middle schooling represents a form of progressive education that challenges the resilience and dominance of traditional schooling. It has stood the test of time, having grown from strength to strength in Australia for nearly two decades now. While not yet dominant, middle schooling has become prominent; it has entered the arena as a major player with the capacity and track record to succeed where other forms of progressive education have failed.

A pluralistic model of middle schooling

In a recent interview for a national newspaper we were asked: Aren't some independent schools using middle schooling claims as marketing tools to attract students to their school? And, isn't this unethical? The journalist suggested that, at these schools, parents pay a high price for what often turns out to be an educational 'lemon'; that is, the school has a middle school structure, but lacks a philosophical and an applied understanding of middle schooling—it's just a name. Would we please comment on this? Our response went along the lines of: There is no one true model of middle schooling in Australia. Across different models, variation occurs in practices, be they focused around curriculum, pedagogy, assessment and/or organisational aspects. And the philosophy of each model is contextually mediated.

Our alternative to the 'one true' model embodies a pluralistic approach that sees middle schooling as a 'broad church'. This approach recognises the existence of numerous middle school design elements and recommended practices—but it does not regard all those elements and practices as essential and thus does not adopt the 'no half measures' policy. Rather, it allows schools to select a critical mass of these elements and practices in order to claim full middle schooling status. In doing so, it avoids the two extremes of 'anything goes' and 'all or nothing'. Also, it avoids the 'fight for ascendancy' perspective by arguing that middle schooling will break the dominance of traditional schooling not by replacing it but by reforming it. Middle schooling will do this by placing pressure on traditional education to shift ground and move toward a more progressive model. In turn, middle schoolers will need to acknowledge and accept the legitimacy of some traditional practices. This will involve making compromises to what some people might regard as the 'pure' model of middle schooling. As a result, the distinction between the old and the new forms of education will cease to exist. In its place will be a merger that is philosophically unified but operationally diverse.

Recent national research on schools implementing middle years reforms supports a pluralistic approach to middle schooling philosophy. It shows that no two schools in Australia are identical when it comes to middle schooling reforms. This raises a pressing question: How can we determine when a school has made enough reforms for it to qualify for middle schooling status?

Another point we made to the journalist referred to above is that it takes time to implement the features of middle schooling. This is confirmed in a national study (Pendergast et al. 2005) which identified three main phases for implementing reforms around middle schooling: initiation (taking 1–2 years); development (taking 2–5 years); and consolidation (taking 5–10 years). The study also identified a preferred track or pathway for implementing reforms in order to achieve consolidation in the minimum possible time (see Table 2.4).

Table 2.4 Phased model of core components for middle school reform in schools

Phase	Middle school practices
Phase 1: Initiation	• Teacher teaming • Innovative leadership • Connectedness
Phase 2: Development	• Improved alignment of curriculum, pedagogy and assessment systems • Enhanced pedagogies, especially greater intellectual challenge
Phase 3: Consolidation	• Student engagement in learning • Meeting greater diversity in adolescent needs and capacities

Is it appropriate to make claims about middle schooling if the school is at the initiation or development phase, or should it have achieved the consolidation phase before professing to offer middle schooling? In our view, schools can and should make claims about their journey into middle schooling reform—wherever they are located on the continuum—so long as the claims are clear and accurate. Doing this requires the individual/school/cluster of schools/system to have a philosophy of middle schooling and an ability to implement it.

Which perspective? A pure or pluralistic model?

Throughout this chapter we have attempted to contrast traditional and middle schooling without polarising them into philosophically watertight compartments. The outcome may have made middle schooling appear less distinctive than some advocates believe is warranted. Have we sacrificed principle and 'purity' for pragmatism and pluralism? Or are these false dichotomies anyway? The case of Ancestral K–12 School below provides middle schoolers with an opportunity to identify where they stand on the pure/pluralistic model issue. For example, what should be the External Agency's response to the 'old guard'? How much of this response would be based on philosophy? And how much would it be based on pragmatism and politics?

Recently, Ancestral K–12 School decided to restructure its traditional primary/secondary compartments into four divisions (on the same campus): K–3 (early childhood); Years 4–6 (middle childhood); Years 7–9 (early adolescence); Years 10–12 (young adulthood). It commissioned an External Agency to design the middle school (Years 7–9), in consultation with the various stakeholders. When consulted, the 'old guard' on the staff argued for the retention of streaming, subject-specialist teaching, subject-based curriculum, a separate class for intellectually gifted and talented students, age-graded classes, and a fixed timetable of 40-minute periods. In doing so, they pointed out that various middle schools in the state have incorporated at least one, and often more, of these features into their organisational design and 'If they have these things why can't we?' They also made it clear that, if appointed to the new middle school, their support was contingent upon them being left alone to teach the way they had for the past 20 years: chalk and talk, children working silently and individually, whole class lock-step instruction pitched at the middle level of student ability, teaching academically streamed classes behind closed doors in isolation from colleagues, and using the staffroom almost exclusively for social conversation rather than professional discourse.

Is it necessary to have a philosophy of middle schooling?

A philosophy of middle schooling can be developed by individual teachers, groups of teachers, individual schools, groups of schools, individual systems, and a federation of systems at state and national levels. For staff and other stakeholders at these different levels, a powerful philosophy of middle schooling can serve a variety of functions. For example, it can help them:

- construct a sense of direction, purpose and meaning;
- make choices from a menu of practices, programs and policies;
- exercise leadership, advocacy, and function effectively as change agents;
- explain and justify middle schooling practice;
- sustain commitment and maintain morale in the face of setbacks;
- help set goals for school and system development plans;
- enlighten evaluations of performance;
- enhance applications for jobs, promotion, and research and development grants.

Some people, however, question the need for and the value of philosophy. The position of Kim and Kylie Midfield outlined below provides a case in point. It invites a number of questions. For example, is the Midfields' position sustainable and justi-fiable? Could they argue that none of the functions of middle schooling philosophy listed above ever could be or should be issues for them? Could they argue that if these functions do become issues then they will be able to resolve them without a philosophy of middle schooling?

Kim and Kylie Midfield teach in a middle school, their first, and so far only teaching appointment. They reckon they do not need a philosophy of middle schooling. A husband and wife team, they pride themselves (with justification) on being people who get things done, action workers, effective classroom teachers. When asked why they teach the way they do, they simply say, 'Because it works'.

What does a personal philosophy of middle schooling look like?

Middle schoolers can be asked to provide an account of their personal philosophy of teaching young adolescents in a variety of situations, such as at meetings with colleagues and parents, in job interviews, when completing application forms for promotion and when answering questions from the media. The guidelines we give our pre-service teacher education students for writing such philosophies include the following suggestions.

*   Focus on philosophical considerations; for example, make explicit the assump-tions and beliefs underpinning statements of empirically testable principles and practices; articulate the ideologies behind the scientific theories you mention; retain descriptions of classroom realities but go beyond them to visions of the ideal.
*   Cover the range of elements that teachers should use to construct their philo-sophies of teaching young adolescents. For example, identify your concepts, beliefs, assumptions, values, visions and ideals with respect to issues raised in this chapter.
*   Illustrate and support your general statements of philosophy with examples of particular principles and practices that are frequently recommended in middle years discourse. This can involve using technical terms. If used accurately, tech-nical terms can add precision to your statement and mark you as a member of a professional community who communicates within a set of shared meanings.
*   Constantly relate the different aspects of your philosophy to the teaching of young adolescents in particular rather than students in general.

- Find ways to present your philosophy as something that is real for you, as something that you hold with conviction, as something that energises and informs your approach to teaching young adolescents, as something that is personal rather than a detached academic treatise on middle schooling.

Conclusion

On some of the issues raised in this chapter our position is explicit. On others, our position is implicit, though probably identifiable, because at the beginning we declare a commitment to middle schooling philosophy that is predominantly progressive, constructivist, outcomes-based, community-oriented, developmentally responsive, student-centred, liberal reformist and contextually mediated. We conclude with two caveats. First, the word 'predominantly' does not mean exclusively or completely; that is, it does not rule out the possibility that in some situations, at some moments in time, some aspects of traditional schooling philosophy should be adopted. Secondly, our position on the issues we discuss represents *a* philosophy of middle schooling, not *the* philosophy of middle schooling. In writing the chapter we tried to avoid presenting a 'philosophical package' that readers can simply take away and use as their own. We saw our job as asking questions, identifying issues, and making suggestions that readers might consider when constructing, deconstructing and reconstructing their own philosophy. We took this approach on the assumption that middle schoolers are philosophy-makers rather than philosophy-takers.

Questions

1 What makes middle schooling philosophy distinctive? Does it need to be distinctive? Should middle schooling be regarded as just good teaching?
2 Can middle schooling take place in traditional schools?
3 Across Australia, and the world, a variety of middle school models have been implemented. Are they all equally valid? Are there any non-negotiables?
4 Which model of society supports and is supported by middle schooling philosophy?
5 What ideological beliefs and assumptions underpin the critics' opposition to middle schooling?
6 Can middle schoolers enjoy a long and successful career, working in middle schools, without a personal philosophy of middle schooling?

3

The middle years learner

Nan Bahr

Adolescence is a problem notion, and any sense of an exact concept is undermined by the plethora of contested ideas and theories raging in contemporary literature and media. If adolescence is a murky term, then what of young adolescence? This chapter examines some of the stable and contested views of adolescence expounded in contemporary sources. Conceptions of young adolescence as a developmental stage are problematised and explored. The aim is to provide an 'interim' model for teaching the middle years' student. This model will support the development of curriculum, pedagogy and assessment; the creation of learning environments and contexts that optimise schooling for middle years students, and will give direction to the organisational structures that frame them. This interim model represents a move toward a comprehensive theory of the middle years of schooling student. That is, the middle years are characterised by dichotomy and conflict, diversity and similarity, and yet the middle years learner shares with peers unique attributes and assets that contrast with younger and older learners.

Getting started: Who are adolescents anyway?

Research and theoretical literature into adolescence is fertile and prolific, but this hasn't always been the case. Formal recognition of adolescence as a distinct place of life is first attributed to Hall, the 'father' of adolescence, in his seminal work of 1904. Hall's two-volume exposé gave rise to attention that faltered at the demise of his rather untenable recapitulation theory (Arnett 2001). Since the 1980s, specialist journals addressing all manner of aspects of the adolescent experience have emerged and have attracted prominent and gifted contributors. Indeed, the activity and interest level seems to be escalating in more recent times. All these scholars share an interest and concern for the lot of young people. But when they use the term 'adolescent', are they really referring to the same thing? Just a quick scan of this year's most prominent journals and current textbooks on adolescence shows that authors disagree on who the 'adolescent' is. They don't agree on age markers (see Table 3.1), boundaries for qualitative dimensions, or indeed whether the term is even useful (Letendre 2000). Figure 3.1 gives a graphic representation of the age spans.

The writings cited in Table 3.1 are the only empirical adolescent studies in 2004 that clearly identify an age span for their research in these key journals. Other articles published in these journals in 2004 give the mean age of their samples but no range boundaries. Unique to these articles, as opposed to texts and theoretical position papers, is the tacit assumption that their participant group aligns to some

Figure 3.1 Age ranges for adolescence in current research literature and texts

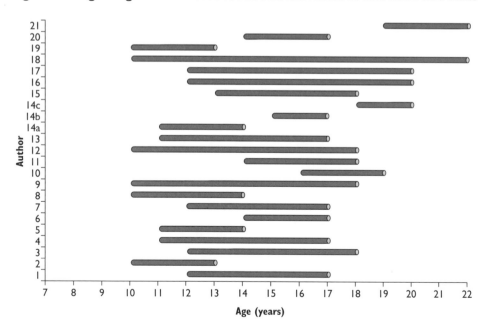

Table 3.1 Various age spans for adolescence in contemporary literature

Author by journal	Age of adolescence	Markers of adolescence
Adolescence (2004)		
1. Schettini Evans & Frank	12–17	—
2. Kuther & McDonald	10–13	Early adolescence only
3. Smith	12–18	—
4. Pinquart & Silbereisen	11–17	—
5. Allison & Schultz	11–14	Early adolescence only
6. Meyers & Miller	14–17	—
7. McCabe & Ricciardelli	12–17	—
Journal of Adolescence (2004)		
8. Engels et al.	10–14	—
9. Keisner, Kerr & Stattin	10–18	—
Journal of Adolescent Research (2004)		
10. Kvernmo & Heyerdahl	16–19	—
11. Frankenberger	14–18	—
Journal of Research on Adolescence (2004)		
12. Matthews & Conger	10–18	—
13. McMillan & Hagan	11–17	—
Author by text		
14. Rice & Dolgin (2005)	(a) 11–14 (early) (b) 15–17 (middle) (c) 18–20 (late)	Boundaries are unclear; not monolithic and uniform
15. Petersen (2004)	13–18	Bounded by rites of passage; no real age boundary
16. McInerney & McInerny (2002)		No age, just physical markers
17. Seifert & Hoffnung (2000)	12–20	—
18. Schaffer (2002)	12–20	Upper boundary bounded by work
19. Santrock (2003)	10/13–18/22	—
20. Bessant, Sercombe & Watts (1998)		No precise ages
21. Steinberg (2005)	(a) 10–13 (early) (b) 14–18 (middle) (c) 19–22 (late)	—

conventional agreement on adolescent age. They do not detail the qualitative measures for determining if participants are adolescent. It is, however, quite startling how diverse the age boundaries are. Even if we concede that the authors might simply be describing their samples, and that their participants fall somewhere within the adolescent ambit, we still do not cater entirely for the differences. There is a substantial spread of opinion shown in the comparative onset age for adolescence in these publications. If adolescence is a commonly understood term, with an agreed-upon notion of general age range, then it wouldn't be possible for a 10-year-old (paper 8, Engels et al.) and a 14-year-old (paper 11, Frankenberger) to equally be considered at the onset of adolescence without reference to qualitative markers.

Older articles and texts shy away from explicit age definition. For example, Ausubel (1954) describes physical (pubertal) and some qualitative attributes for adolescence, but doesn't delineate ages. Kimmel and Weiner (1985) also avoid clearly identifying chronological age boundaries and instead cite biological age (puberty) as the mark of onset, and social age (assumption of adult roles and responsibilities) as the transition point to adulthood. They do, however, give a ballpark range from around 10 years of age through to around 22 years. Lefrancois (1976) most strongly contests the use of age for the definition of adolescence. He argues that:

> . . . chronological age is a notoriously bad index of social, emotional and physical development during adolescence. Changes that occur during adolescence, while highly correlated with one another in terms of sequence and rate of appearance, are not nearly as highly correlated with chronological age (p. 124).

It is however, even debatable that the sequence and rate of appearance of maturational attributes are reliably predictable for social and emotional development. Further, in socially and culturally diverse environments, surely the notion of a consistent homogenous developmental progression must be stringently challenged. So, even though the term 'adolescent' is a well-worn one, adolescence as a diverse concept is not coherently characterised in the literature.

In the quest for qualitative markers, many authors write of adolescence as agony, immaturity or incompleteness (Schaffer 2002). The media have been alert to this and have expended significant effort demonising our young people and rationalising this position through reference to the rather deficit view of adolescence that often underpins the scholarly literature. The deficit view of adolescence characterises young people as lacking certain adult attributes—indeed, they are adolescent by virtue of what they are not. For example:

- Adolescents are not yet fully independent of their parents and family sanctions (Schaffer 2004).
- They are not yet cognitively complete (Giedd 1999).
- They have not yet developed a range of mature interpersonal relationships (Graber et al. 1996).

- They have not completed their personal construction of identity (e.g. Marcia 1980; Swanson et al. 1998; Selman, R. 1980).

In line with the deficit view of youth, 'adolescence' and 'adolescent' have become common usage, accepted labels for people who, in one way or another, cannot be fully considered adult. In fact, they are colloquially used to insult, to designate someone as behaving in an immature or juvenile fashion.

Although it lacks clarity, educationalists have welcomed the term 'adolescence' and use it freely. The label has provided a framework for theoretical modelling that promises 'answers' to the question of what might be best practice in schools. As a professional community we are caught between a need for clarity and a need for flow. We, like Hall and other luminary researchers, find a label useful, but we have perhaps come to a point where such a label is more misleading than useful.

Perhaps it is possible to construct a theoretical model of young people that informs without constraint. Could such a model view young people as complete? It should be able to dismantle deficit conceptions, disarm the media, and provide useful directions for schools. This kind of theoretical Nirvana will no doubt prove elusive. However, this chapter sifts through the vast research and scholarly musings about young people, and proposes a model of the middle school learner in Australia that hopefully will positively disrupt the status quo.

The need to invent a term

To appropriately construct a maturational model that assists educators of middle years learners, we must examine the purposes behind the invention of the adolescent. Hall (1904) appropriated a fairly old word, first found in written form in 1440 (Harper 2001), and fashioned a science of developmental psychology. He was responding to the unique social, political and cultural climate of his time, a period of industrial revolution. The influx of immigrant adult workers to industrialised states and the enactment of laws to protect children from exploitation in the workplace had created a new 'in-between' life phase. At the same time, psychology was finding its feet as a science and the classification of people's lives into relatively neat categories was a very attractive idea. The potential to explain behaviours by creating detailed compendiums of age-related developmental attributes was openly celebrated. But, as usual, the devil was in the detail. The Hall theory of recapitulation built on the earlier Haeckel notion of embryological recapitulation in prenatal ontogeny (1868) and proposed that human development traced a path similar to that of species evolution (Steinberg & Lerner 2004). While this idea did not hold up to close scrutiny, the classification system remained intact as a framework for developmental research.

The historical motivations for considering adolescence as a distinct phase are no longer as potent as they were. The 'in-between' category label can now be attached to those people in their late 20s who are not yet economically independent from their parents. The marketing and business industries have begun to recognise the emergence of 'kidults' or 'adultescents', a generation of people who refuse to grow up, who sustain their buying and general interest patterns from their pre-teens well into their 30s (e.g. Cameron 2004). Further, physical capability to parent is getting younger and younger; some girls as young as eight now experience menarche, compared with an average twelve years of age in the penultimate decades of the twentieth century. But these early maturing people are neither psychologically nor emotionally ready for the responsibility of raising a family (Côté 2000). They also are in-between. How useful is the concept of adolescence if it doesn't clearly distinguish between an 8-year-old and someone in their mid-20s or even 30s? The concept of adolescence may be time-stamped and already past its use-by date.

Our changing times have brought a dramatic shift in the nature of work and career. 'Working hard' has been replaced by a 'working smart' ethic, allowing people of all ages to make personal economic gains without infringement of the child labour laws that curtail certain types of employment for minors. A young, enterprising individual who makes a squillion on a venture hatched and pursued in front of a computer screen in their bedroom can be far more economically independent and 'adult' than a much older person working as an articled clerk with a law firm and still financially tied to parents. Neither person can fully be considered adolescent, or indeed adult, but to the educator they may present quite different educational needs, goals and opportunities.

In many world cultures, the concept of adolescence means nothing and has never been useful (Letendre 2000). People may transition from childhood to adulthood via some sort of rite of passage or ceremony, from then on being considered part of the adult community, with no time spent in-between. As globalisation hastily brings diverse cultures together, the meaning of adolescence becomes increasingly murky.

Steinberg and Lerner (2004) track a history of scientific interest in adolescence. They discuss the forums of the Society for Research on Adolescence, arguably one of the premier scholarly communities for research in this field. Interestingly, these forums have always been held exclusively in the United States (Steinberg & Lerner

2004). A quick search shows contributors to the society's journal are almost exclusively American. Other contemporary scholarly societies and journals for adolescence, for example the *Journal of Adolescent Research*, and *Adolescence*, have American affiliations on their editorial boards, and content that is notably American. This is true of most societies and publications on adolescence excepting perhaps, *The Journal of Adolescence*, produced by the Association for Professionals in Service for Adolescents, which has an international editorial board and an international authorship. Steinberg and Lerner (2004) have also identified an American bias in the field. Since it is clear that adolescence is a socially and culturally related notion, we must then ask if Australia is American enough for the term to be relevant here?

Eras of research and theory

Steinberg and Lerner (2004) argue that there are three stages of research into adolescence. The first two stages overlap and we are presently on the cusp of the third. The first phase (roughly the 1900s through to the 1970s) was characterised by grand theoretical models that drew on rather descriptive and anecdotal accounts of development. The second phase (the 1970s through to the early 2000s) focused on hypothesis testing and second-order applied research, and developed views on the plasticity and diversity of development. The third phase, our current venture, is characterised by a central scientist-policy-maker-practitioner organisational frame. Research in this phase 'reflects and extends the emphases on individual-context relations, developmental systems, plasticity, diversity, longitudinal methodology, and application' (p. 52). The discussion in this chapter fits neatly in the third phase. Hopefully, attempting to deconstruct the grand theories of development that have formed a foundation for the field of scholarship will have a direct and indirect impact on policy, practice and research interest, in just the way Steinberg and Lerner predict.

Deconstructing the grand theories of development

The grand theorists of adolescence include Hall (1904), Inhelder and Piaget (1958), Erikson (1963), Freud (1968), and McCandless (1970). Each has been lauded and criticised on their unique merits. Uniting their models, however, was a conception of adolescence as conforming to a linear progression in development, characterised by direct linkages and continuity and relying upon the assumption of individual development as a passive process. Researchers of Steinberg and Lerner's second era, with a rising concern for context, plasticity and diversity, have not directly challenged these fundamental tenets of the grand theorists. There exists a linear conception of development that appears to bring together otherwise quite divergent conceptions of adolescence.

Although not all ascribe to the deficit perspective (for example, Benson's developmental assets view in Benson 1997; Lerner & Benson 2003), life development, as described by these authors suggests movement towards some kind of maturational goal, in roughly a lockstep sequence. Some of the key theoretical themes are:

- adolescence as a biological event (Giedd 1999);
- adolescence as a psychosocial event (Piaget 1955; Kohlberg 1986);
- adolescence as a social construction (Bandura 1977);
- adolescence as a cultural construction (e.g. Mead 1935; Keith 1985).

A brief examination of each theme provides reference points for the construction of a new maturational model.

Adolescence as a biological event

Much discussion and theory of adolescent behaviour has centred on the 'storm and stress' theory (e.g. Hamburg 1974). Hormonal changes, growth spurts and development of secondary sexual characteristics are well-known markers for the stage, and the presumption is that such dramatic physical upheaval must inevitably impact on an individual's sense of self, and also that an individual necessarily reflects their biological programming. All manner of connections have been notionally tied between identity development, general behavioural tenor, family and peer relationships and puberty in these theories. From the biological perspective, individuals are doomed to a fairly predictable sequence of events by virtue of their maturational clock.

Recent interest in the biological template for adolescence has also considered neural development. Giedd (1999) reports that a proliferation of neural connections characterises childhood brain development; marking the onset of adolescence, and typical of the whole stage, is a dramatic rationalisation and pruning of these connections. The process is complete when the individual arrives at adulthood with a much more streamlined and less numerous set of connections than they had as children. Educationalists have already begun to imagine the ways they might assist students to the best possible outcome. Some aim to slow the pruning, preach 'use it or lose it' philosophies, and design their practices around ideas of broadened educational experiences (Fuller 2004). Others, convinced that the streamlined outcome is desirable, aim to focus students on only a small number of endeavours, hoping to force the pruning through strategic neglect of some non-essential understandings. Still others, gripped with a fatalistic view, have made little or no adjustment to their practices in the light of the new research. Any peculiar design for learning based on Giedd's research is rather prematurely developed, given that Giedd has not yet fully explored causal relationships between behaviours and neural pruning or the reciprocal.

The majority of the biologically based theories are steeped in a sense of intractable inevitability. They presume that educationalists must support, inform and cope with adolescence. Adolescents are seen homogenously and passively, and their experiences as sequentially linked and predictable. It is not reasonable to make a wholesale contestation against these biological views of adolescence. Clearly, physical and neural changes are a part of the maturational process and do deserve some professional attention by educationalists. But physicality and bodily changes are only part of the picture of who we are at any given point in our lives. They are a frame for our behaviours and self-concepts and as such are important, but models for development that are limited to physical constitution have been hotly contested in the adolescent literature (e.g. White 1968; 1994).

Adolescence as a psychosocial event

Key theorists for a view of adolescence as a psychosocial event include Piaget (1955) and Kohlberg (1986). The Piagetian approach considered cognitive development is influenced by: maturation of the nervous system; experience; intellect; and socialisation. He concurred with some of the biological theorists' ideas regarding the influence of physical maturational changes of the brain on behaviour during adolescence. The Piagetian research was pre-Giedd and so did not comment on neural pruning phenomena. However, it did consider that the natural maturational processes of the brain would have an underlying impact on the other three elements that contributed to cognition change.

Piaget (1955) argued that a formal operations stage characterises adolescent cognition. That is, the adolescent act of knowing or perceiving (12 years of age to adulthood) is qualitatively different to children (7–11 years) who are described as being typically pre-formal thinkers or in the concrete operations stage. The individual who is capable of formal operational thought exhibits a capacity for abstract logic and more mature moral reasoning. This contrasts with the earlier concrete operational thought, which is described as limited to concrete events and concrete analogies. Concrete operations include thinking activities such as classifications, hierarchies, class inclusion, relations of parts to whole and parts to parts, serialisation, symmetrical and reciprocal relationships, substitution and rules for operations. The thinking is still linked to empirical reality (that is, the actual rather than the potential, based on real experience). According to the theory, children of the concrete operational age have difficulties dealing with more than two classes, relations or dimensions at once, while adolescents in formal operations are able to make more elegant generalisations with more inclusive laws. They think formally, but only in familiar situations, are capable of abstract thought independent of concrete objects, can consider sets of symbols for symbols (for example, metaphoric speech, algebra), and can appreciate that words can have double or triple meaning. This makes them able to understand hidden meanings (for example, political cartoons). Piaget proposed that the hallmarks of formal operations were:

- thinking about thought (developing metacognition);
- going beyond the real;
- combinatorial thinking;
- logical reasoning (cause and effect); and
- hypothetical reasoning.

Neo-Piagetian researchers have interpreted Piaget's earlier work and provided some guidelines for behaviour in adolescence (Schaffer 2002). They have attempted to draw extended implications from the foundation hallmarks. For example, in the journey from concrete operational thought to formal operations, they suggest adolescents should gain an ability to grasp what might be, and therefore may appear as idealistic rebels. Further, their developing metacognitive skills might promote time spent thinking about thoughts and increase their daydreaming, which may become more positive or wishful. Their ability to look beyond the given material may give rise to pseudo-stupidity when trying to solve problems, due to a possible tendency to approach solutions at too complex a level. They should be able to appreciate symbols in literature rather than just the story line. Most importantly, their formal reasoning capabilities should provide a foundation for the development of long-term values. The Piagetian and neo-Piagetian view, while still tied to lock-step and sequential age/stage conceptions of development, did consider the individual in quite a different way to the biological theorists. Santrock (1998), in an overview of developmental theories, describes the individual, as depicted by the Piagetian and neo-Piagetian views, as a 'solitary little scientist'. Basically, they argued from a strong maturational perspective, but with maturation interacting with environmental experiences. They described the individual as cognitively active and constructivist. In schools, our legacy from the strong hold of these classic views of the child has been middle years pedagogy that has been designed on the presumption that those in their early teens were not yet capable of abstract and complex thought. As a result, intellectual rigour in the early secondary school years has floundered (Queensland School Reform Longitudinal Study 2001).

Piaget's and neo-Piagetian cognitive theory had a number of weaknesses. First, the expectation that all adults would be capable of formal operational thought in all areas of thought and knowledge was not universally founded. That being the case, the enduring question is whether older people who are not yet formal operational could be considered adult. Another point of concern centres on the development of expertise. A model that describes adolescents as cognitively unfinished does not adequately account for the observation that junior chess masters, of as little as eight years of age, can beat adults at chess (Chi et al. 1982; Chi & Ceci 1987); while contemporary theories of cognitive development, such as schema theory, provide generalisable frameworks that better explain the development of expertise and higher order thinking. These theories owe their inception to some of the Piagetian ideas, but have dismantled the potency and integrity of age/stage-based theories of cognitive development. Piaget also proposed a model for moral development that derived from the cognitive development theory. This theory, like the Piagetian cognitive development theory, typically underestimated the moral capacities of children and has lost contemporary support (Schaffer 2004).

Kohlberg's work also considered cognitive development as well as moral development (Kohlberg 1986; Schaffer 2004). His cognitive development work focused on gender identity development in young children and was criticised for underestimating the strength of early gender identity, but his moral development construct initially attracted a faithful following. In this model Kohlberg believed that moral development fell into neat, invariant stages that were sequentially ordered. The development was closely aligned to cognitive growth, but cognitive growth alone did not ensure moral development. His six-stage model was soundly criticised for its cultural and gender bias. Like Piaget, Kohlberg's theory was also contested on the grounds that he had demonstrably underestimated the morality of children (Damon 1988; Sigelman & Waitzman 1991). More recently, researchers have found that moral understanding did not predict moral conduct (Kochanska & Murray 2000), and so Kohlberg's work appears both flawed and incomplete.

These two theorists, Piaget and Kohlberg, were not the only authors advocating that psychosocial development could profitably be considered in stages linked to chronological ages. However, the criticisms their models have attracted are representative of the criticisms of other age/stage models. They almost inevitably under- or over-estimate the capacities of people at particular ages. Any model that has attempted to describe a strict template for development has drawn criticism due to the demonstrably diverse range of experiences, behaviours and capacities of people at any given age. Recent theorists like Halpern (1997) have coined the term psycho-biosocial to describe theories that consider the joint influence of nature and nurture, but this work only gives very limited attention to the social processes that contribute to maturation.

Adolescence as a social construction

In contrast to the biologically based and psychosocial or psycho-biosocial theories of adolescent development, the social constructionists asserted that development was more about social experience than age-linked hard wiring. An early, much-contested view was Watson's doctrine of environmental determinism (Watson 1913; 1925). Watson believed that people are passive reflections of their grooming by others. This notion was not popular, as it did not go far enough to describe and predict behaviour. Bandura's work, starting in the 1970s (1977), proposed and developed a cognitive social learning theory characterised by reciprocal determinism. Bandura proposed that development depended on observational learning. He described people as active and reactive, and said that cognitive development reflected a continuous reciprocal interaction between people and the environment. That is, people actively shape their environment which in turn reflects on them. The key criticism of the theory was its oversimplification of the cognitive developmental process. No account was taken of genetically endowed individual differences or the possible biological maturation impacts on development. The social construction views were almost the antithesis of the age/stage theories; in most cases they mirrored the perpetual nature–nurture controversy, and were soundly criticised for not attending to the very things that were hallmarks of the more nature-influenced theories.

A very popular contemporary theory of development is the Vygotskyan socio-cultural model. Vygotsky (1962) considered the cultural and social contextual influences for cognitive growth. He stressed that children's development was led and mediated by social dialogues with others. He proposed a process whereby social speech provided impetus for private speech, which was a key cognitive tool underpinning an individual's development. The theory described the value of skilled people leading and guiding learners based on an understanding of an individual's zone of proximal development. This process was called scaffolding. Working in the zone of proximal development was described as activity that was just beyond an individual's capacity to act independently. The skilled instructor would adapt their dialogue as the learner became more capable and the zone extended as a result. This adaptive dialogue allowed the co-construction of knowledge.

Vygotsky's theory has had a favourable reception and, as his works are progressively translated from the Russian, will attract much closer scrutiny. More recently, Rogoff (1998) has warned that the strength of Vygotsky's work lies in an assumed primacy of verbal interaction for cognitive development and that this may not be equally relevant for all cultures. While Vygotsky has found a vital middle ground between the nature–nurture extremes, this important framework for development does not yet provide specific insight to the behaviour of the middle years learner.

Adolescence as a cultural construction

Alongside the other theoretical themes has been consideration of adolescence as a cultural construction. Margaret Mead's research in Samoa and Papua New Guinea (1935), demonstrated that culture makes an indelible impression on a person's development and may indeed be a potent element for understanding maturation. Mead's cultural analysis has informed the development of biosocial theories of maturation like that of Money and Ehrhardt (1972), although theorists in this area have not provided comprehensive explanations of how the various elements impacting on development in a cultural context might interact. Mead's demonstration that some cultures do not have a discernible concept or place for adolescence between childhood and adulthood highlights the importance of ethnographic analysis when considering the nature of early adolescence and middle years of schooling in Australia.

Persistent issues

Persistent issues emerge in criticism of the key developmental theories. The most predominant are based on the nature–nurture debate as already discussed. Other seemingly irreconcilable differences of opinion include debate on whether development should be considered as:

· linear and sequential, or diffuse;
· linked to experience conforming to a principle of continuity, or discontinuity; and
· based on an assumption of the learner as active, or passive.

If development is non-linear (for example, Vygotskian theory), it is possible to imagine connections being drawn directly from one life point to another for an individual in an unpredictable way. For example, a person might have particular experiences in childhood that predisposes them to certain behaviours and understandings much later in life. A one-to-one, one-to-many, and many-to-many connection web may describe how experiential understandings may influence development at other life points. A non-linear model is attractive but doesn't enable consideration of the influence of those things we know to be linear (such as physical aging). On the other hand, the linear model, which would propose that one developmental stage necessarily leads to the next, doesn't readily account for individual, social and cultural differences.

The continuity versus discontinuity developmental debate is similar to the linear versus non-linear. In a discontinuous model the influence of any given experience may not take effect until much later. The effects of an experience may rest as a 'sleeper' for some time. Indeed, some people experience a sense of epiphany when something they experienced long ago suddenly makes sense. The discontinuous model differs from the diffuse in that it retains a one-to-one influence pattern, while the continuous model depicts development as occurring in a predictable and intractable sequence, and the learner as active versus passive debate centres on whether individuals have or have not agency in their own development.

Each of these debates has merit and utility for understanding some aspect of human development. They are irreconcilable, however, and perhaps it is futile to try and resolve the differences. Any new model for development should attempt to transcend the dichotomies.

An interim model for maturation and development

A new model for development needs to allow for the diversity of individuality as well as the conformity of social and cultural immersion. It should draw on the most productive elements of the classic theories and depict growth as both linear and non-linear; continuous and discontinuous; with influences of both nature and nurture. The developing individual should have both agency and passivity. That is, the model should embrace the dichotomies and present development holistically. Figure 3.2 crudely presents a model for development that might accomplish this. The individual is conceived as invited into a given context that is both socially and culturally framed. They bring to any life point a set of assets that are physical, emotional and cognitive. These assets reflect their wants and developmental needs,

Figure 3.2 Dynamic life path model

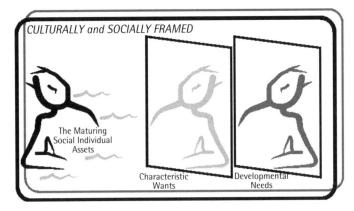

which may be both individually unique *and* characteristic or typical of those at a similar life point. The developmental needs are viewed through the characteristic wants. This is a dynamic life path model that is constantly in flux. The focus is primarily on the learner, their assets and their developmental tasks.

The individual changes and matures according to this dynamic life path model as illustrated in the next diagram, Figure 3.3. Depicted here is a person who might be typical of a middle years learner according to the middle years literature, a person with a set of personal characteristics or assets including global awareness and self-orientation, as well as the unique attributes that mark them as an

Figure 3.3 Impetus for change in the dynamic life path model

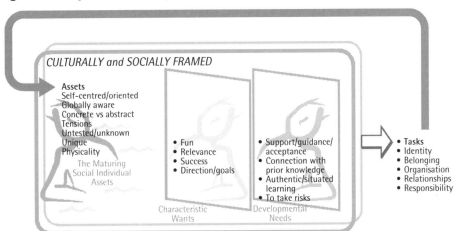

individual. The wants and needs depicted are commonly identified in the middle years literature and are not exhaustive, for in addition to typical wants and needs the individual will have unique conceptions of their own wants and needs. These will reflect their own conception of themselves and their assets. Engagement with others, with problems, with the environment, either scaffolded or naturally occurring, will alter their assets, and from there the cycle continues.

Key aspects of the dynamic life path model are:

- The superimposition of cultural and social contexts;
- The depiction of an individual as a maturing person who at any given life point is complete;
- An asset-based rather than deficit-based perspective, with assets reflected in other dimensions;
- The representation of a maturing individual adapting in response to achievement of developmental tasks;
- Allowance for learning and unlearning in maturation; and
- The dual frame for cultural and social contexts.

The adolescent, in this model, only exists in social and cultural circumstances that allow them to exist or which actually create a space for them. The stable and accepted elements of the classic biological, psychosocial, cultural and social constructionist developmental theories can be accommodated as descriptions of the driving forces behind the impetus for change.

The middle years learner: A paradigm shift

This life path model potentially liberates a new understanding of the middle years learner. We can embrace the anecdotal and consistent descriptions of our students from the coal face, which describe the shared attributes of middle years learners in our broadly similar Australian contexts. We can embrace the data available on physical maturation as giving potential insight to our middle years classrooms. We can tailor our developmental experiences for students based on our understanding of them as individuals. We can enjoy the middle years for the assets the individuals bring to us rather than entertain a deficit view of our students. We can extend and challenge our students. In short, we are empowered to take action collectively as middle years educators, individually and in teams. However, we are constantly charged with the responsibility to evaluate our own contexts for the effectiveness of our interactions with students and also the local social and cultural frames for adolescence.

Implications for the middle years educator

There are practical implications for teachers, schools, policy makers and funding bodies. First, the value of local action research must be emphasised. Resources and funding need to flow to classrooms to support the reflective, reflexive and evaluative work of teachers as they try to discern the most appropriate developmental tasks for their students. Teachers need to network with each other to provide professional support for ongoing ethnographic scanning in an attempt to characterise the shared needs and wants of middle school learners. These networks should provide a critical resource and professional development base to ensure teachers are well aware of current developmental theory and debate.

Questions

1   How is the concept of adolescence useful for middle years educators in Australia?
2   What might be a possible action research project that would inform practice across a cluster of middle years classrooms in your region?
3   Why do we still need to use the term 'adolescent' when describing middle years learners? Argue the positive.

Understanding the adolescent brain

Michael C. Nagel

In the last decade neurology has offered a great deal of insight into how the brain functions and develops. With the help of MRI and PET scans, middle school educators are able to develop a better understanding of how to engage cognitive and emotive functions more productively in an educational environment. Neurology is also offering an avenue for demystifying why some middle school students seem to have difficulty explaining their actions when doing the 'wrong' thing or indeed why they are, at times, seemingly incapable of responsible decision making. This is extremely helpful for educators and parents who often find themselves wading dumbfounded through middle school students' attempts to explain their actions. This chapter offers some insight into the neurological and biological mechanisms that impact on the adolescent brain in order to better understand what might be going on inside the heads of middle school students. It focuses on contemporary research into how the brain develops and the implications this has for those working in the milieu of middle school students' learning experiences and behaviour. The goal, however, is not to suggest that dealing with middle school students will become an easier task as neuroscientific research advances. Rather, the intent is to familiarise those who work within this particular age range that, neurologically speaking, is a time of transition, and educators would do well to rethink their pedagogical approach through understanding the adolescent brain.

It is not the brains that matter most, but that which guides them (Fyodor Dostoyevsky, 1821–81).

Being an educator in the twenty-first century should indeed be exciting. Continued advances in technology and research are adding incredible insights and opportunities for teachers to invigorate and improve on their craft. Perhaps this is most evident through the merging of neurological, cognitive and educational research. The impact of this integration is emphasised in Wolfe and Brandt's (1998) assertion that 'we have learned more about the brain in the past five years than in the past one hundred years'. Those who engage with middle school students would do well to develop their understanding of the adolescent brain, for it is during this developmental transition that the brain does some amazing things, all of which have an impact on how these students engage and/or disengage with their learning environments.

In order to truly understand what is going on inside the heads of middle school students, it is important to engage in a brief anatomical introduction of the human brain and how it develops.

Understanding the brain: Imagining the unimaginable!

The human brain is one of the most complex objects we know. LeDoux (1996) describes it as both the most sophisticated machine imaginable yet also that which is unimaginable. This part of our anatomy has long been a mystery with regards to how it functions and develops. However, with advances in technology, researchers have been able to theorise how the brain works and evolves into the marvel that it is. One of the most interesting findings in contemporary brain research focuses on how the brain communicates with itself and the rest of the human body. Wolfe (2001), a leading researcher and theorist in the area of neurology and education, believes that the foundation of human behaviour is built on the communication that exists between neurons.

Neurons are a type of brain cell that resemble bulbs, with sprouting roots called dendrites and a tail-like structure known as the axon. The dendrites are like antennae that receive information from other neurons and/or from the environment (Diamond & Hopson 1999; Berninger & Richards 2002; Hardiman 2003). The passing of information between neurons occurs via an electrical impulse through the axon, across a small gap known as a synapse and with the assistance of neurotransmitters (chemical messengers) (LeDoux 1996; Hardiman 2003;

Sylwester 2003). Synapses are electrochemical connections that occur when neurons are influenced by social and environmental stimuli (Wolfe 2001). Humans are born with over 100 billion brain cells that communicate through synapses. These structures let us become who we are, and will be, due to the fact that synapses continue to develop after birth as a result of environmental stimuli (Diamond & Hopson 1999; see also Wolfe 2001; Sylwester 1995, 2003; Strauch 2003). It is vitally important for all educators to be familiar with this neurological act of synaptic transmission, as the research suggests that it is this process which lies at the heart of learning.

Mirroring much of current pedagogical and didactic discourse, the importance of making connections between teachers, learners and content provides an interesting parallel to the brain's process of connecting and communicating. The educational act of connecting, often characterised as interpersonal, can now be seen to have a neurological foundation in that 'when axons send signals that are received by dendrites, learning takes place' (Hardiman 2003, p. 10), and many of these signals are sent as an individual responds to the environment around them through any one of their senses. The interpersonal connections that are significant for positive and stimulating educational environments also serve to enhance neural connections. In addition, the more that these types of connections are made, the faster and more efficiently the signals move and the more permanent they become (Wolfe 1998, 2001; Hardiman 2003). Many neuroscientists also believe that aspects of memory are enhanced when brain cells fire together, in that continued synaptic transmissions that are used over and over again 'get accustomed to firing together and eventually become hardwired' (Wolfe 1998, p. 63). An interesting factor adding to the importance of this hardwiring of neural circuitry is that the chemical responses that facilitate new learning also create new synaptic pathways, causing the growth of more dendrites.

With the advent of neurological research it is apparent that relevance can act to stimulate the brain's innate drive to learn and find meaning, while experiences can assist in wiring the architecture of the brain (Bransford et al. 1999; Caine & Caine 2001). In this sense enhancing middle school learning environments with the brain in mind becomes very important. This is emphasised further when we look at the neurochemical processes and structures of the brain, which indicate that emotion has a significant influence on the teaching of middle school students.

In order for neurons to 'talk' to each other, a number of neurochemicals or neurotransmitters must also be present. Neurotransmitters are chemicals secreted at the synapses that have an impact on the activity, maintenance and longevity of the synapses and neurons themselves. Among many others, examples of these chemical messengers include serotonin and dopamine. Each of these sends excitatory or inhibitory messages and fluctuates in levels depending on environmental stimuli (Carlson 2000). In other words, an individual's response to the environment and the experiences around them will affect the levels of various neurotransmitters, which in turn can have an effect on their brain and, in the context of schooling, can either enhance or hinder learning.

The structures of the brain and the maturation of those structures offer further important insights into the world of adolescent neurological development. The human brain is generally described as having three regions or layers: the cerebrum at the top, the limbic system in the middle and the brain stem, connected to the spinal cord at the bottom (Hardiman 2003). The brain stem, the region closest to the spine, is where fight-or-flight and survival responses are activated and where functions not under conscious control take place. The limbic system or central part of the brain harbours our memories and processes emotions and is home to two very important structures, the amygdala and hippocampus. Finally, the uppermost area, the cerebrum, which contains the occipital, parietal, temporal and frontal lobes, has a number of regions where thinking, consciousness and responses to environmental stimuli take place (Gurian 2001; Berninger & Richards 2002; Hardiman 2003; Sylwester 2003). In the context of middle school education and adolescence, a couple of very important new insights have emerged regarding these areas and brain function.

First, neuroscience has shown us that many aspects of brain maturation occur throughout childhood and well into the late teens and 'the most advanced parts of the brain don't complete their development until adolescence is pretty much over' (Bradley 2003, p. 6; see also Levitt 2003). We also know that during this time of maturation and development the brain goes through a number of stages whereby it constantly remodels and restructures itself, with most of this occurring during adolescence. Terms such as 'pruning' and 'plasticity' are often used to describe how the brain matures and evolves along a road towards improved efficiency (Diamond & Hopson 1999; Strauch 2003). For middle school students this process can be very profound in that the 'adolescent brain undergoes a massive remodelling of its basic structure, in areas that affect everything from logic and language to impulses and intuition' (Strauch 2003, p. 13). We also know that when this remodelling of the brain occurs, unused synaptic connections are discarded as the brain works towards becoming more efficient (Giedd et al. 1999; Sisk & Foster 2004). More accurately referred to as pruning, this period of discarding unused synapses is an important consideration for educators in recognising that adolescent development is a time of experience-dependent brain reorganisation; the adage of 'use it or lose it' is highly appropriate (Bruer 1999; Spear 2000a; Andersen 2003). Theoretically speaking, then, the educational environments middle school students are immersed in can have a direct impact on how the brain reworks its architecture.

Amid all this restructuring, it also appears that the brain actually matures from the bottom up and around to the front, which indicates that the brain stem and limbic system reach maturity sooner than areas of the cerebrum above them (Giedd et al. 1999; Gurian 2001; Sylwester 2003; Giedd 2004). Moreover, this entire process appears to occur at a different rate for males and females (Giedd et al. 1996; Blum 1997; Strauch 2003). This is very important, for educators and parents alike, for it suggests that the regions of the brain responsible for survival and emotion are in full swing before the regions responsible for logical and moral reasoning can follow suit. This helps to explain how middle school students are often at an interesting and paradoxical juncture in their lives—they can confront us with the physical and intellectual stature of an adult one minute, and act like a defiant and stubborn infant the next. The amygdala appears to play a role in this paradox.

The amygdala, a part of the brain's limbic system, has been described as the neural basis of emotion and has been the object of growing interest in most brain-referenced theories of emotion (LeDoux 1998; Berridge 2003). Shaped like an almond, the amygdala is a critical component in responding to danger as it receives information about the outside world from the thalamus and sets in motion a variety of bodily mechanisms (Conlan 1999). If, for example, the brain senses fear or stress, the amygdala acts to ensure that the endocrine system responds by sending out the appropriate hormones to raise the heart rate, blood pressure and prepare the muscles for activity (LeDoux 1998; Hardiman 2003). The amygdala is thus a very important mechanism in ensuring survival; however, it is also a neural structure that during adolescence appears to have higher levels of activity than the frontal lobes. Moreover, because the amygdala responds to stress, the research suggests that memory and learning can actually be impeded by stress. Therefore, another ramification of working with the developing adolescent brain is the realisation that a middle school student may be hotwired for emotional and risky behaviour but unable to think through the consequences of their actions. This also suggests that perhaps the most effective method of working with middle school students lies in tapping into those very emotions that are having such a profound influence on all aspects of their brain.

High on emotion

> Education is not the filling of a pail, but the lighting of a fire (William Butler Yeats, 1865–1939).

At the risk of stating the obvious, most parents and teachers know that every child is a complex mix of emotions. For many years, however, it was believed by a large proportion of researchers that emotion and cognition worked in isolation from one another and that an individual was able to learn because understanding and feeling were separate (Caine & Caine 2001). Current research suggests that emotions play an integral role in a student's ability to learn, whereby emotion and cognition are 'separate but interacting mental functions mediated by separate but interacting brain systems' (LeDoux 1996, p. 69). There is also evidence that the whole process of learning and coming to understand something is actually driven by emotion (Goleman 1995; Damasio 1999; Caine & Caine 2001). It is also the driving force of emotion that can shut down learning for middle school students. There is a growing body of research indicating that stress, fear, anxiety and other emotional responses to environmental stimuli can directly impact upon many students' neurological capacities to learn (Spear 2000a; Gurian 2001; Arnsten & Shansky 2004; Goswami 2004). Thus understanding aspects of the limbic system becomes a vitally important component of working with middle school students.

As noted earlier, the areas of the brain responsible for emotive and survival responses (the limbic system and areas of the brain stem) mature and develop sooner than the areas responsible for thought processes and logic. Specifically, the prefrontal cortex, the area of the brain implicated in behavioural inhibition and the ability to control emotions and impulses, is the last area to mature. It undergoes major changes throughout puberty and is the most important neural region for thinking through the results of one's actions or the responsibilities attached to those actions (Lewis 1997; Giedd et al. 1999; Casey et al. 2000; Spear 2000b; Giedd 2004). Simply stated, the prefrontal cortex sits just behind the forehead and acts like the brain's chief executive officer. As this area matures, the ability to reason better, develop more control over impulses and make better judgments also matures. Furthermore, this pathway of neurological maturation is also why, at times, educators may need to act as their middle school student's prefrontal cortices and carefully monitor the 'freedom' that these students tend to move towards; too much responsibility and independence may not necessarily be in the best interests of the adolescent brain or the student.

A second important factor, which may appear somewhat contradictory to the points and suggestions made above, is that while the adolescent brain may not be able to weigh up certain consequences before acting, there is also some neurological merit in allowing for risk-taking and risky behaviour. Ponton (1997) suggests that risk-taking provides middle school students with an opportunity to shape their identity and acts as a natural impulse needing to be channelled in a positive fashion. Neurologically speaking, research suggests that a link exists between risk-taking behaviour and levels of dopamine in the brain.

Dopamine, as noted earlier, is a type of neurotransmitter between synapses. Dopamine also seems to play a role in an individual's novelty and reward seeking, motivation and feelings of 'well-being' (Kalivas et al. 1993; Dellu et al. 1996; Strauch 2003). New experiences, especially those with some element of risk, thrill or degree of danger, may actually influence dopamine levels which in turn can produce feelings of intense pleasure. Berridge (2003) signals the euphoric properties of dopamine by stating that 'dopamine has often been referred to as the brain's pleasure neurotransmitter'. Sylwester (2003) notes that Parkinson's disease and difficulties with maintaining attention on tasks have been linked with low levels of dopamine, while exceedingly high levels are evident in those individuals who suffer from schizophrenia, Tourette's syndrome and obsessive-compulsive disorder. For those working with middle school students, it is significant to note that the amount of dopamine present in the brain appears to rise during adolescence and begins to decline as adulthood approaches (Lewis 1997; Koepp et al. 1998; Spear, 2000b). Furthermore, for the developing middle school brain, risk-taking appears to facilitate further increases in dopamine levels, which in a cyclical fashion may predispose middle school students to further risk-taking due to the sense of pleasure associated with thrill seeking (Strauch 2003). This is not to say that all middle school students will indulge in exceedingly risky behaviour. The roles of hormones and other neurotransmitters such as serotonin also influence risk-taking.

Serotonin, like dopamine, has received a great deal of research and experimental attention over the last decade. Serotonin plays a role in the control of eating, sleep and arousal, as well as the regulation of pain and various moods (Carlson 2000). Serotonin has also been recognised as an important chemical in the processing of emotions and can act as a calming mechanism (Gurian 2001; The Society for Neuroscience 2002; Nagel 2003). Researchers associate high levels of serotonin with high self-esteem and social status (Sylwester 1997). Conversely, low levels of serotonin have been linked with impulsivity, risky behaviour, anger, hostility and suicidal tendencies (Mann 1997; McEwen & Seeman 2003). A key point for middle school educators to consider regarding serotonin is that stress, especially chronic stress, can inhibit the brain's production of serotonin and simultaneously impair the cognitive function of the prefrontal cortex (Hardiman 2003; Arnsten & Shansky 2004). Moreover, it appears that levels of serotonin in the brain decline temporarily during adolescence. From a purely scholastic standpoint, this suggests that a middle school student who is stressed is a student whose ability to learn may be impeded. There is increasing recognition that efficient and constructive learning cannot take place when a learner is experiencing fear and/or stress (Goswami 2004). This is an important point for all middle school stakeholders to consider when looking at school discipline and behaviour management strategies, the relationships that exist between teachers and students, and how even seemingly benign practices like unclear directions for performance might escalate stress levels in the already emotionally charged mind of a middle school student. Add the influences of a pubescent hormonal tidal wave and the emotions once again surface as pivotal considerations in working with middle school students.

There are a number of hormones that influence and are influenced by the brain. There is also evidence to suggest that hormones take on a more powerful role in parts of the brain, with greater activity occurring in the limbic regions than other areas (Strauch 2003). Moreover, the amygdala and hippocampus have a very strong connection and influence on the prefrontal cortex (Goswami 2004). The amygdala in particular, and as noted earlier, plays an important role in processing emotion and influencing the prefrontal cortex. In a stressful situation, the amygdala sends a signal for a wave of hormones, predominantly cortisol, to surge through the body; once secreted into the bloodstream these hormones can last for hours (Hardiman 2003). In a middle school context, the impact of this is that when students become stressed they are unable to use the higher, thinking part of the brain and revert to using those areas of the lower brain responsible for coping and surviving. Only after a stressful period diminishes and students feel secure again can learning occur. Research also suggests that exposure to too much cortisol and other stress-related hormones for too long can impair factual memory and, in extreme cases, damage parts of the brain (Goleman 1998; Sapolsky 1999; Sylwester 1994, 2003). Further-more, the developmental passageway middle school students find themselves travelling en route to adulthood is also marked by how the brain reconstructs itself during adolescence.

From birth, the brain is busy setting up connections or synapses that seem to develop in fits and starts followed by periods of consolidation (Diamond & Hopson 1999). Early in life the neural connections of a child come to outnumber those of an adult, then around the age of seven the brain starts to discard or prune synaptic regions that are seldom used. This allows the brain to refine itself and become more specialised and efficient. The important point here is that the greatest influence on what the brain maintains and what it decides to discard is found in an individual's own life experiences and environment (Diamond & Hopson 1999; Strauch 2003). As a result, the experiences that are provided throughout childhood are very important, but arguably become increasingly so during adolescence, when synaptic pruning may cut back as much as 10 per cent of the brain's grey matter, with some smaller regions losing as much as 50 per cent (Sowell et al. 1999). Thus a middle school student who is constantly dealing with stress may find learning anything very difficult. Neurological researchers refer to continued diminished capacity to learn due to sustained stress as 'downshifting', and some suggest that students are often locked into this mode of thinking due to standard educational practices that repeatedly, and quite often inadvertently, raise stress levels (Caine & Caine 2001; Hardiman 2003). Synaptic pruning set in a middle school context therefore suggests that curriculum, learning experiences and educational environments would do well to ensure that they are well structured, positive, current, relevant, stimulating, safe and emotionally appealing.

Finally, if we add all the neurological insights noted above to the wealth of environmental stimuli available during puberty, it is little wonder that middle school students are prone to be highly charged emotionally and unable to explain their actions when their behaviour appears inappropriate. In other words, there are very good reasons why middle school students might be engaged in activities deemed questionable by the adults around them. This is also a very good reason why middle schools should offer pedagogy which maintains a high degree of relevance within environments founded on emotional well-being.

Educating with emotions in mind

> There can be no knowledge without emotion. To the cognition of the brain must be added the experience of the soul (Arnold Bennett, 1867–1931).

There is little denying the role emotions play in the learning process. Some researchers and authors even suggest that emotions are actually the 'gatekeepers' to learning and that they drive the learning process, aspects of memory and attitudes towards tasks (Damasio 1994; Sylwester 1995; McGeehan 2001). Arguably then, in the social milieu that exists in any school setting there should be a concerted effort to ensure that the emotional environment enhances rather than inhibits the learning environment. A fundamental consideration in any desire to enhance the emotional climate of a classroom or school exists in the relationships that exist between students and teachers. This is not to say that relationships have not been given due consideration in the past, but it is now possible to link science to something which has generally been taken for granted as a commonsense approach to working with young people.

Much of what is attributable to emotional well-being in a middle school context focuses on the provision of a safe and supportive learning environment. A key consideration of such an environment is founded on the notion that students appear to thrive when they feel that the teachers care about them personally (McGeehan 2001). This is very difficult to achieve if, for example, the teacher–student relationship is frequently adversarial or confrontational. In such scenarios the limbic system and the brain stem initiate the types of emotional triggers and/or fight-or-flight responses outlined earlier in the chapter. Often the end result is misbehaviour or withdrawal, but it most certainly is not learning (Jensen 1998; Tomlinson & Kalbfleish 1998). In order to foster positive relationships, middle school educators should look to plan activities that build team spirit and mutual understanding while providing clear procedures in order to eliminate embarrassment resulting from unintended misbehaviour—class meetings, posting of agendas and assessment criteria, as well as developing strategies for conflict resolution assist in facilitating team spirit and a sense of community (Gurian 2001; McGeehan 2001).

Another important consideration regarding emotion and learning focuses on the use of experiential or active learning and the significance of content that is relevant to the learner. In this sense, emotions can be used to enhance learning. Experiential and active learning experiences, especially those that are novel, can physically change the brain's architecture by causing the brain cells involved with cognition to sprout new dendrites and consequently increase synaptic communication between neurons (Bruer 1999; Diamond & Hopson 1999; McGeehan 2001; Hardiman 2003). When these pathways are used repeatedly they become more efficient and we can identify that learning has occurred. Moreover, experiences that are rich in sensory input and are relevant to the interests of the students offer greater opportunities for sparking dendritic growth and memory retention than experiences derived from a reliance on worksheets and textbooks (Brandt 1999). In their separate, yet complimentary work on emotion and neurology, Damasio (1994, 1999) and Schacter (1996) provide detailed elaboration on the connection between experience, relevance, emotion and memory. In laypersons' terms, the more intense and interesting an experience, the more students will attend to it and the more it becomes embedded in memory. Furthermore, if the information received by students is deemed as irrelevant and showing no useful purpose in life, the less likely is it that it will become encoded in their neural circuitry. Wolfe (2001) comments succinctly on this point: 'sustained attention on something that you can't figure out or that makes no sense is not only boring, it's almost impossible' (p. 84). In a middle school context, tasks and activities that students see as relevant will engage their emotions in a positive sense which, in turn, will enrich their learning.

There is ample research to suggest that positive emotions can contribute to higher order thinking and long-term memory. Howard (2000) and Glenn (2002) note how laughter produces chemical changes in the brain resulting in increased production of neurotransmitters that enhance memory and alertness, and boost the body's immune system. Researchers have also found that music, visual arts, drama and movement act as key contributors to shifts in brain wave patterns and the release of various neurochemicals, resulting in a more activated and stimulated brain (Campbell 1997; Sylwester 1997; Wolfe 2001; Hardiman 2003). Understanding that both negative and positive emotional experiences impact on the neural networking which is arguably at the foundation of learning provides middle school educators with a sound foundation for examining their own practice and facilitating a lively, safe and supportive environment that connects with the real world of the students. This type of understanding can act as an impetus in reforming middle school didactics and pedagogy towards eliminating that sense of being 'boxed in' and 'bored'. Finally, designing learning experiences that are premised on relevance and a capacity for students to form personal and emotional connections can ultimately increase opportunities for enriched neural activity, long-term memory and work to eliminate a perception of being 'brain dead'. Indeed, in coming to terms with contemporary neurological research, middle school educators are well placed to re-invigorate and re-engage the young minds they work with.

Questions

1   Much of brain research shows the consequences of extremely poor or often atypical environments and stimulation on brain development. It also appears that sensory-enriched environments stimulate positive neural development. With that in mind, how might middle schools invigorate their practice to ensure a continually stimulating learning environment?

2   When middle school students are stressed, fearful or insecure, the limbic system's response can prevent the brain from learning. The daily events or encounters in unsympathetic school environments might push students into a survival or emotive response superseding their ability to effectively engage with learning. How might structures and/or situations that spark stress or fear be overcome in a middle school context? How do middle school educators go about identifying and alleviating these factors?

3   In relation to the question above, how might middle schools design their pedagogical experiences to ensure that emotions and brain stimulation might be engaged in a positive sense?

5

Producing resilient middle school students

Lesley Newhouse-Maiden, Nan Bahr and Donna Pendergast

This chapter explores the nature of resilience. It asserts that teachers, schools and families share a central role in the productive construction of protective factors and assets during the middle years, and proposes approaches to the development of proactive whole school programs for resilience development in the middle years.

Research suggests that people who are emotionally resilient, courageous and hopeful are more likely to succeed now and in the future. In the face of difficulties or hardship, resilient people are able to bounce back (Fuller 1998, 2002; Cefai 2004). The types of attributes that appear to reduce vulnerability show a striking alignment to the developmental tasks being nurtured during the middle years (Newhouse-Maiden 2002). Research that points to resilience as a competence rather than a naturally occurring quality (e.g. Super 2000) would suggest that the middle years of schooling is a time of unique opportunity for teachers and schools. Deliberate educational action targeting the competencies that promote resilience is possible, and arguably ethically demanded, in the middle years of schooling. Full exploitation of the opportunity to provide all students with the necessary protective attributes must become fundamental to middle schooling philosophies.

As middle years students characteristically move into the challenging stage of young adolescence they search for identity, for an understanding of themselves as having independent and multiple identities; they develop toward more formal operational thought, and toward a personal understanding of more adult relationships; they may develop an internal locus of control, and hone their organisational skills. These are significant contributors to the protective attributes of resilient people.

Establishing friendships with peers and gaining more independence from parents are important aspects of their social development at this time; so too are choice of subjects and career pathways. Growing uncertainty about the future, the ready availability of alcohol and drugs, powerful media messages, divorce, socio-economic adversity, and violence in relationships, all serve to increase children's vulnerability and exacerbate the healthy achievement of these life tasks. But resilience competencies reach beyond the immediate world of the middle schooler. A person who has a well-constructed set of life skills and attitudes emanating from quality middle schooling is more likely to cope in the face of negative personal events through their whole life. In this way middle schooling is inextricably connected to each life point of the individual. Given that it is rarely possible to accurately predict which individuals are likely to be exposed to life-defining risks, it behoves middle years educators to design resilience building programs for all, not just those nebulously identified as being 'at risk'.

Since the definitive work of Bronfenbrenner (1979) and Super (1980, 1983, 1990), there has been renewed interest in how the sociocultural context influences both the personality and life-career development of an individual (Newhouse-Maiden 2002). Super (1990), like well-known theorists Erikson and Havighurst, accepted the biological heritage of temperament as the predisposition of personality to behave in certain ways, and the genetic endowment of 'general and specific aptitudes' as the bases for the child's active construction of knowledge about the world and self-schemes through the process of adaptation to the environment (p. 49). Super also emphasised the importance of positive 'structures of opportunity' created by key figures within the individual's family, school and community for healthy career and personality development. Researchers of resilient children and youth have highlighted the importance of 'protective factors' or 'assets' where the most significant and consistent are connectedness to parents and school (Withers & Russell 2001). Therefore, not only do middle years students develop key attributes or 'protective factors' for lifelong impact on resilience, schools and parents are key influences in the process.

There is scant theoretical guidance for the design of school-based resilience building programs in the middle years. However, Super's (1990) research suggests that an individual is the 'socialized organizer of his/her experience' (p. 221) and Newhouse-Maiden's (2002) modification of Super's Life-Stage Life-Space Rainbow

Model of Life-Career produces a more gender-inclusive representation (Jaggar & Rothenberg 1993). This model highlights the situational and personal determinants that may affect an individual's accomplishment of developmental tasks at each life stage. Thus, any program with an explicit objective to foster resilience-protective factors will need to exploit and respond to the situational and personal circumstances of individuals, and refer to immediate and future life-roles.

Contested terms

The literature on resilience is somewhat diverse and emerges from disparate fields of endeavour (including psychology, social work, medicine, sociology). Although recently there has been a sense of convergence there remain some distinctive differences in the meaning and discussion of resilience and vulnerability. To clarify, in this chapter we refer to resilience as the ability to bounce back or recover quickly from setbacks (Fuller 1998, 2002; Cefai 2004) and as 'manifested competence' in the context of significant challenges to adaptation or development (Masten & Coatsworth 1998, p. 206). We draw from research of high-risk children and families that has constructed resilience as the development of competence, the maintenance of positive adaptation and effective coping by individuals despite adverse experiences (Garmezy 1987; Egeland et al. 1993; Luthar et al. 1997). We conceive resilience not as a childhood given, but as a process where this capacity develops over time in the context of person–environment interactions (Brendtro et al. 1990; Egeland et al. 1993).

Associated concepts are competence and vulnerability. Masten and Coatsworth (1998, p. 206) define competence as 'a pattern of effective adaptation in the environment'. We accept this, but add that competence is a set of applied skills, combined with the knowledge required to select and monitor the application of those skills to desired effect. Vulnerability is the flip-side of resilience. A person is vulnerable when multiplicative and additive circumstantial and personal factors serve to heighten susceptibility to negative developmental outcomes when exposed to risk conditions (e.g. Gerard & Buehler 2004). Vulnerability is increased in the absence of 'protective factors' or resilience attributes. A person succumbs to negative pressures when circumstances outweigh their conception of their own abilities to cope (e.g. Frydenberg 2002). Therefore, as we argue here, resilience and vulnerability as competency-framed attributes are targetable educational objectives.

The concept of 'at risk' is also contested in the literature. The term is often used in policy documents to identify students for special programs and funding

(Dryfoos 1990, 1993, 1998) and has become a catch-all phrase for children with a wide range of problems. In the present context we propose 'at risk' more generally as the potential for not enjoying a satisfying and fulfilled adulthood, perhaps leading to social maladjustment, injury, harm or death.

Being at risk is a concept of vulnerability. Many risk factors have been identified in the literature that may contribute to negative outcomes for young people (Batten & Russell 1995; Withers & Batten 1995; Withers & Russell 2001; Frydenberg 2002). There are intrapersonal risk factors within the individual, as well as risk factors within the peer group, the family, the school and the community. Withers & Russell (2001, pp. 14–17) provide an elaboration of personal and situational risk factors which are useful for producing individual and group needs assessments for at risk middle school students, a summary of which is presented in Table 5.1.

Table 5.1 Needs assessment of students at educational risk

The individual	The school	The family	Community and societal factors
Psychosocial, physical and behavioural factors	Situational factors: • school organisation • curriculum • school climate • professional development	Structure, functioning and socioeconomic status	• Extreme poverty • Anti-social community norms • Demographics • Aboriginal and ethnic groups

There are longer term repercussions of cumulative adversity, where educational failure can in turn influence adjustment in work and health related outcomes. This perpetuates the cycle of poverty, and communities become second and third generation unemployed. This dimension of lifelong learning has added to our vision of middle schooling as a vital stage in the process of reclaiming communities to becoming creative and productive, where parents, teachers and educators both mentor and learn alongside middle school students (Cumming 1996; Freire 1996; Hargreaves et al. 1996; Csikszentmihalyi 1997; Epstein et al. 1997).

Protective factors
Research on resilience reveals substantial potential for augmenting the understanding of processes affecting at risk individuals. Many researchers have argued that the resilience of the individual ought to be viewed as the 'outcome of the operation of

protective factors' (Withers & Russell 2001, p. 23). There is growing evidence to support the premise that a reduction in individuals' vulnerability to risk factors can be achieved by strengthening protective factors, such as family and school connectedness. The major psychosocial factors among less privileged individuals that have served to produce a protective network to counterbalance adversity include:

- Emotionally responsive caregiving, which has been found to mediate the effects of high-risk environments and to promote positive change in children who experience poverty, family stress, and maltreatment. In particular:
  – parental educational aspirations for their child are significantly associated with educational resilience;
  – high expectations of their children;
  – good parenting quality helps in preventing anti-social problems;
  – encouraging their children's participation in the family, school and community;
  – intervention programs targeting parent involvement are a key to improving their children's academic success.
- Relationships with other caring adults contribute to successful emotional and intellectual adaptation of children.
- Early tutoring programs produce improvements in behaviour as well as reading.

We argue that resilience has a personal competence dimension, an environmental support dimension, a preventative dimension and a remediation dimension that incorporates a sense of 'resilience as process' that can be enhanced. However, there is a need for training for all stakeholders, and a need for pro-social bonding to significant others in family, school, peer group and community (Resnick et al. 1997; Dryfoos 1998; Masten & Coatsworth 1998; Withers & Russell 2001). Other researchers caution that protective factors and processes that modify the impact of adversity are context-specific and their influences should be studied in the context in which they operate (e.g. Piko & Fitzpatrick 2004).

Personal determinants: Characteristics of resilient individuals

One of the central questions identified in the literature on resilience and the development of competence is whether there is something unique or special about those people who have overcome adversity in extreme situations to achieve competence when others have floundered. Power (2000), like Benard a decade earlier, made a strong statement about resilient young members of a caring community. She, in fact, expresses both the hoped-for outcomes and the life-span career progress of such individuals, namely that they:

- know 'that they belong';
- know they 'possess the personal traits and skills that will help them contribute to their home places now and in the future';
- recognise they are 'capable of doing needed, capable work';
- locate themselves in relation to the community's definitions of a 'model member';
- aspire to 'achieve respected adult status'; and
- can identify 'means of reaching that goal' (Porter 2000, p. 211).

These are nurturable characteristics, and as such present middle schooling education professionals with a set of specific challenges for the design, development and implementation of resilience development programs.

Developmental tasks: Links to competence and resilience

The middle years are characterised by particular developmental tasks that are the key to resilience development. Therefore, it is possible to specifically target and assist students toward resilient attributes, skills and behaviours. In the current climate of inclusive education, it is important to accept that developmental tasks reflect universal human phenomena, as well as more culturally or historically specific tasks. Within the individual, the self-domain is the most common task area, first in the form of self-differentiation from the environment and later in terms of identity and autonomy (Masten & Coatsworth 1998).

By middle childhood we would expect students to conduct themselves in a way that, though rule-governed, reflects respect for self and others, with moral responsibility for their own behaviour. Academic achievement is an important domain of success for children in our society; it continues to be important in adolescence, with the quality of expected performance continually rising. Getting along with other children becomes a salient domain by middle childhood, initially in terms of peer acceptance and later in terms of developing friendships.

As students mature into adolescents they develop through a process of setting personal goals by comparing their individual motives with age-graded developmental tasks and role transitions. In order to realise their goals they construct 'plans by considering different institutional opportunities in relevant domains, such as school, work, peer relationships, and society in a broader context—developmental standards and beliefs concerning age-appropriate behaviour provide an eventual basis for new self-definitions and identity' (Nurmi 1993, p. 169). Any agenda for targeted educational practice to improve resilience must work alongside the students' own agendas for the middle years and complement their capacities.

First, during early adolescence individuals experience erratic influences on their sense of self due to the physical maturation process. Change in stature and physical bulk, the development of secondary sexual characteristics, and the influences of hormonal surging and associated drives, provide a complex canvas for the development of specific personal competencies. However, these developments also provide a point of reference for exploration of personal agency in the light of diversity.

Second, the development to more formal operational thought, simply described as the ability to grasp what might be, provides a foundation for the development of long-term values. The move from concrete reasoning is often characterised by the demonstration of pseudo-stupidity; the tendency to approach a problem at too complex a level; thinking about thoughts; an increase in daydreaming and more positive/wishful thoughts; and by appreciation of symbols in literature rather than just the story line (e.g. Matter 1982). This provides educators with an environment conducive to the examination of hypothetical circumstances. This allows middle years students to practise and develop a set of strategies and a suite of learned behaviors to deploy at times of heightened risk.

Third, the development of identities though rationalising identity conflict, and balancing the need for belonging and conformity against the developing sense of an independent self, is a frequently reported key task for the middle years (e.g. Jackson & Davis 2000). A strong sense of self feeds the sense of agency required for a personal conception of competence. This is a fundamental resilience asset.

Fourth, the middle years student is moving from childhood, where society arbitrarily imposes age-equivalent relationships through contemporary schooling structures, to adulthood where relationships between people are bounded by shared interests and objectives. Their experience of a change in the breadth and nature of the interpersonal relationships they are establishing beyond the age cohort will set the frame for all future relationships. Strong interaction with positive and relevant adult role models beyond the immediate family will have a potent influence on the development of resilience (Bandura 1986).

Next, during the middle years, students are challenged to organise an increasingly complex set of personal stuff (including time, materials, obligations). The availability of personal strategies for management become central to the sense of personal integrity through adolescence. Often, organisational skills are developed by each individual through trial and error, and yet the ability to manage competing demands is a key protective factor mitigating against vulnerability. These skills can be explicitly taught and practised in schools, and concrete thinkers can develop their skills through demonstration of successful practices employed by others.

A model for producing resilient middle school students

We assert that resilience building in the middle years is a key responsibility for teachers, parents and the wider community. It is impossible to identify those young people who are going to be beset by trials and tribulations, so the programs must include everybody. That is, resilience is an attribute that needs attention in all middle years students, even those who appear to be developing smoothly.

A useful model that focuses on asset building, in which the individual actively develops competencies and resilience within the life spaces of the school, family and community, has been developed by Withers and Russell (2001). This all-encompassing coalition is an important way of representing the integrated nature of achieving resilience in young people.

Characteristics of exemplary programs

Educating for resilience

Currently, there is a strong climate for school reform in Australian, British and American schools based on the principles of the Health-Promoting School model and on building sound relationships with significant others. This is coupled with a desire to find ways to move middle years students from alienation to engagement, particularly Indigenous youth. The more progressive minds have focused on re-inventing education for young adolescents and for communities to 'live well' in a changing world. A systems approach is favoured where there is a 'willingness to share power' in a system based on 'reciprocity and sharing rather than control' (Benard 1991, p. 24). This will require a change in attitude towards power relation-ships within the family, school and community. In this regard it will be important to build links between families and schools and between schools and communities to create a 'network of protection' for all students. It will also require the implemen-tation of planned prevention and intervention strategies to build protective factors into the lives of all children and families.

Factors influencing successful implementation of resilience and safe passage programs: benchmarking

Dryfoos (1998) has identified success factors when implementing programs for building resilience that are sustainable and replicable. Table 5.2 sets out bench-marks for evaluating the potential of a program to make a positive difference in the lives of middle school students and the community. Success factors are presented at

Table 5.2 Success factors at the individual, family and community levels of implementation

Individual level	Family level	School level	Community level	Additional sustainability factors
Early intervention	Parental involvement	Educational achievement	School location in the community	Evidence of success
One-on-one attention—creative shepherding	Reaching across generations—volunteer mentors	Effective principals	Community outreach	Charisma of leader/s
Developmentally appropriate		School-based community agencies	Community responsiveness	Encouragement of local control
Youth empowerment—community problem-solving		On-site facilitators to train teachers and youth workers	Community police	Legislation → state and federal initiatives
		Social/life skills training—'increased dosage' → greater intensity and sustainability	Safe havens	Political savvy
		Group and individual counselling	Incentives and entrepreneurial approaches	Foundation blessings
		Community service	Multi-agency, multicomponent programs	Attention to training
			Food—sustenance plus caring	Marketing the program
			Availability of residential care	National youth organisations
			Intensive and long-term involvement in the program	University involvement
				National research organisation links
				Disseminating findings, e.g. conferences, journals, www sites
				Intuitive appeal
				Responsiveness to special groups

a range of levels, from individual, to family, school and the community. Finally, additional sustainability factors are considered.

Principles for resilience building

It is within the context of schools that have adopted middle schooling philosophy and practices to 'create a climate of intellectual development and a caring community of shared educational purpose' (Jackson & Davis 2000, p. 24) that we now recommend a number of principles for resilience building:

- Avoid promoting achievement goals, instead develop a system for acknowledging the achievement of mastery goals in all areas of endeavour.
- Provide for the development of positive self-concept through opportunities for the development of self-knowledge, particularly of strengths and weaknesses. This allows students to reinforce their strengths and to not despair at their weaknesses.
- Provide an environment that encourages an internal locus of control. Students need to be able to select paths, plan actions and accept the consequences of their own actions in a supportive context.
- Explicitly develop communication and self-help skills. Provide students with opportunities to practise and develop these in a multifaceted way to a high level of skill.
- Encourage a high activity level but not to the exclusion of discretionary time. This promotes the development of personal management skills.
- Practise cognitive skills. Explicitly teach problem-solving strategies, scaffolding support, providing scalable worked examples to problems and training in the application of metacognitive processes.
- Discuss coping strategies. Use opportunities that arise as object lessons for application of the strategies or concrete understanding though vicarious observation.
- Proactively establish social networks that cut across age cohorts.
- Expose students to support networks and practise engaging in them through role plays, research activities and community-based activities.
- Provide opportunities for the sanctioned development of a personal relationship with a positive role model with full regard to the maximisation of the influence of a model. The influence of a role model is increased when the student perceives positive consequences for the continued relationship, and when the role model:
  – is perceived as attractive (physical and emotional);
  – holds social power (over reward and punishment);

- is perceived as high status;
- is competent (in areas of shared interest);
- is nurturing (perceived concern for observer);
- exhibits a high interaction level (degree of contact, energy of contact);
- is similar (real or expected commonalities) (Bandura, 1986).

Schools that are able to establish processes to maximise the potential of relationships between middle school students and their role models will be making a potent contribution to the development of lifelong resilience.

Conclusion
The goal of producing resilient young people is a challenge and opportunity for the field of middle schooling. Current literature suggests that we have a growing capacity to achieve this desirable goal, but that it depends on the integration of a range of key factors across a range of contexts, including within the school environment.

Questions
1 Explain the relationship between competence and resilience in empowering middle school students to become effective learners, citizens and well-balanced productive individuals.
2 Why is it important to establish a whole school community approach to addressing potential 'risks'?
3 In what ways do middle schooling philosophy and practices meet the criteria for empowering the development of resilience and allied social, emotional, moral, cognitive, language and physical competencies in the students?
4 How would you begin to establish a whole community school approach to foster resilience in middle school students? What would be the role of each stakeholder?

6

Researching the middle years

Katherine Main and Fiona Bryer

The research so far done on middle schooling has revealed poor technical implementation of middle school practices and poor conceptual understanding of the
vision of responsiveness to the developmentally appropriate learning of Years 6–9
students. Poor implementation has contributed to the weak, negative and confus-
ing evidence which has, in turn, contributed to the reactive blaming of middle
schooling for the failure of robust organisations to emerge from the reform
process and for the unconvincing data that has been reported from various trials.
Analysis of educational research and its role in school reforms helps to explain
some of the difficulties encountered by middle school proponents in implementing their vision. Future research efforts need to be focused on the implementation
process, the barriers to and facilitators of successful reform, and the way to
advance the interests of Years 6–9 students as the priority for implementing
middle school practices. Australian researchers need to address ways to bridge the
gap between the conceptual vision of a developmentally targeted education
programming for Years 6–9 students and the everyday complexities of education
for participants in this reform.

A research agenda is outlined here, in which starting points are set for research
on practice that will be beneficial for Australian middle schools. The model
considers practices recommended for middle schooling in terms of criteria for

field-useful middle school practice (acceptance, effectiveness and sustainability) and in terms of participants in middle schooling (teachers, students and the community).

Field-based investigation of middle school practice is central to genuine acceptance by the school community, to authentically effective practice across the school system, and to the sustainability of middle schooling as a truly viable and valuable option in Australian education. Educational research of all kinds is more a field-based enterprise between researchers and teachers, administrators, policy makers and curriculum designers rather than an abstract, intellectualised monologue: much metatheoretical talk about theory is disconnected from practice in the field. Particularly with respect to research on middle schooling, there is a wide gap between theory and practice: the everyday reality of middle school teaching and learning experiences have rarely met the ideals and ideologies behind the middle schooling vision. In a sense, research-based mediation between the theory and practice of middle schooling has not been necessary to proceed with implementation, but its absence has left the gap unbridged.

There has been a poor record of success behind middle schooling and its standing as a major, comprehensive effort of educational reorganisation (Anfara 2004). The literature is at a point where Swain (2004) has stated that failures in middle schooling over the last 30 years are attributable not to the vision but to the conceptual misunderstandings and methodological weaknesses in the delivery of middle school programs to Years 6–9 students. Much middle schooling innovation has acquired only a hazy awareness of the holistic conceptualisation of this form of education and has established only broad goals with open-ended objectives. These conceptual and methodological limitations have been attributed to much middle school research having been based on relatively little substantial data or conceptual analysis (Evans 2002). Australian literature has by and large followed the American trend to generate much background filler and, moreover, to deploy the internationally recognised educational habit of 'tinkering' with recommended practices (Hargreaves 1997).

Middle schooling has encouraged individuals to work 'together for the good of the whole as well as the good of the individual' (Hunt et al. 1998, p. 222). This reorganisation was intended to provide a metaphorical developmental bridge between the primary school focus on the child learner and the secondary school focus on the learning of subject matter. However, the bridge over the ideal-to-actual practice gap requires more extensive preparatory research on the meaning of middle schooling, more resource investment in pre-establishing practice-useful outcomes, and more team research in partnerships with critical friends. Teacher researchers need to identify, document and systematically work towards a related series of explicit, measurable, achievable, realistic and targeted objectives in order to facilitate 'smart' outcomes for the middle school learner. Teaching and learning partnerships among a community of learners involved in the implementation of middle schooling practice have also being translated into recent recommendations for action research; (Weller 2004; Caskey, in press). Yet many educational researchers have been criticised as 'dilettantes' (Bessant & Holbrook 1995) whose conceptions of school are too poor to warrant investing resources 'into understanding and changing schools' (Sarason 1996 p. 14).

Anfara (2004) has argued that implementation is the key to outcomes for student social and academic performance and that middle schools have some control over implementation. Because empirical evidence indicates low fidelity to the middle school reform (Carnegie Council of Adolescent Development 1989; National Middle School Association 2003), one strategy for further research is to obtain more evidence of how the reform affects schools. Anfara, however, has recommended the focusing of research on implementing practices that improve outcomes in teacher quality of life, school climate and student supports which, in turn, mediate student outcomes (academic, behavioural, socioemotional).

Recommended practices developed from evidence-based theory need to be feasible (acceptable to the field), measurable (effective for student outcomes) and contextually relevant (sustainable within local resources, which include training). In the effort to deliver major reforms tailored to local contexts, there have been compromises made to the complex and time-consuming process of introducing transformational changes to middle schooling (Ames 2004). With too little scholarship and information gathering, the immediate drive to implementation has fostered simple solutions, externally developed models and a counterproductive reversion to education as a conservative force for the status quo rather than a revolutionary force for change (Fullan 2001). The main roles of educational research have been defined as radical societal change, practice improvement, policy formulation and knowledge production (Winch 2002). Future middle school research should address these four aims, in order to: increase acceptance and support in the learning community and the wider community; strengthen effectiveness of recommended teacher practice in local contexts; clarify policy issues such as training and certification that affect sustainability; and enhance theoretical understanding of the middle schooling alternative(s) as a developmental approach to building student competence.

Implementation

There has been increasing acceptance of middle schooling across different sectors of Australian education. That is, some schools are implementing middle schooling programs; some universities are offering specialised teacher training in middle schooling; and some researchers are inquiring about the student benefits of middle schooling. Thus, it is becoming a prioritised school reform. Implicit in this acceptance is an assumption that not only is this change worth doing for Years 6–9 students but also that local primary and secondary schools can accommodate these changes and that locally trained teachers can implement them. Further implementation of middle schooling practices needs to be grounded in clear educational outcomes for students, teachers and the community.

Efforts must be made to maintain the momentum of the growing professional consensus to accept this reform and to respond positively to tentative policy changes and administrative interest and priority. Practitioners, in particular, embarking upon middle school innovation need to understand what the existing knowledge base is and how they can apply it to their local setting. Similarly, they need to understand what the existing federal, state and district policy support for a middle phase of schooling actually provides and how existing policy affects the conditions for practice. Finally, they need to understand what the introduction of a middle school experience can achieve for community and societal goals and how they can work systematically towards specific objectives with broad middle school goals.

Middle schooling is acquiring status as a way to improve school image and performance, to attract students and to assure per capita funding (Kellett & Nind 2003, p. 20). Documentation of how middle schooling comes to acquire this status as a preferred change in an Australian school needs to examine how individuals in a school become engaged in a problem-solving exercise in organisational change. Some research needs to be directed to school-to-school decisions to introduce a middle school program. What is the problem that the school faces? (Does this school want to overcome negative attitudes and disengagement among disadvantaged students in their preparation for senior school? Does the school want to augment its positive influence on child development?) How does the school decide to use middle schooling to solve this problem? What actions to involve staff flow from this decision? These research questions mirror more general issues for middle schooling research. How does the way in which a school community engages in this problem-solving process affect the alignment between theory and practice to better serve student interests? In what way does educational research typically work between theory and practice to bring them into better alignment?

The decision to reorganise schooling to create this change involves three elements: (a) discovery of information about middle schooling; (b) selection of the kind and amount of change that will produce an efficient and effective outcome; and (c) acting to undertake selected changes (Argyris 1970; Stacey 1996; Sytsma 2004). In particular, key research issues in studying problem solving are, first, the quality of conceptual and empirical information used to prioritise this change and to define and solve the existing problem (Evans 2002); secondly, the selection of the level of system change (for example, improved efficiency of specific practices in the existing system versus changed practice effectiveness arising out of a transformed system); and thirdly, the commitment to replace present behaviour and habitual practice (for example, restricted to current leadership and staff rather than transferred across staff changes). In middle schooling reform, as in much educational reform, there have been issues about informed consent by participants, which is an important precondition to all research. Teachers who engage with and commit to a choice to make changes have often done so without either making a free and transparent decision to introduce a middle school program or auditing the information used by school agents to justify change and its relevance to the surrounding community it serves.

Middle school initiatives in this country might yet fall victim to the 'boom-to-bust' cycle that often occurs with educational reform (Slavin 2004, p. 1). If middle schooling in Australia is to be considered more than a marginal, faddish and ad hoc activity, then local academic and practitioner researchers must work together to refine local knowledge of middle schooling and to improve evidence-based support for various signature features of middle school practice (Hunt et al. 1998; Jackson & Davis 2000). The history of educational reform of practice, the current standing of educational research, and the international standing of middle school research within educational research, are all framing issues for this examination of the evolving research enterprise within Australian teacher practice and for recommendations about research directions.

Research-based criteria for useful practice change, moreover, must consider issues of the acceptability, effectiveness and sustainability of middle school practice. High values and mundane ease of everyday use can influence acceptance of new practice; creativity and energy of teacher input rather than responsibility for student output can affect assessment of effectiveness; uncontrolled and multifaceted forces that are hard to study determine sustainability. Getting teachers to adopt and make sustained use of practices in new ways of thinking about teaching and learning faces many barriers beyond our current knowledge (Davis & Florian

2003). Problems in teacher implementation of middle school practice are viewed as mostly system-related (Anfara 2004; Swain 2004).

A more general concern for educational research is the emphasis on the individual teacher as the change agent. This model, which has worked well as a vehicle for professional development and reflective practice, has focused on documentation of practice and testing of teacher assumptions against class data. The characterisation of the self-empowered teacher with a moral purpose and passion (Fullan 2003) can be applied to changes in the efficiency and effectiveness of current work practices. Innovations of first-order change, however, are more common and more successful than second-order changes in the fundamental way in which an organisation works (Kellett & Nind 2003). 'For most teachers, daily demands crowd out serious sustained improvements' (Fullan & Hargreaves 1991, p. 118). Elmore (1996) also argued that a key flaw in many reform efforts is to rely solely on teachers who are highly motivated and emotionally connected to the reform. Implementation of middle school has relied on individual teachers and teaching teams to drive practice change in school-specific situations, which may account for the present doubts (Anfara 2004) and 'blame the reform' distortions of middle schooling (Swain 2004, p. 1).

Valuing the 'new': Research on educational change

Research is an inherent but often a shadowy and pursuing appendage of the ubiquitous process of educational change, renewal and future orientation. It can be an afterthought to the immediacy and motivating urgency of change anticipated, initiated and in progress. Education is apparently dynamic, developing and open to new experiences and opportunities rather than static, matured and closed. Yet historically it has functioned as a reproductive rather than an adaptive system. Because change is a process that can succeed or fail (McKinney et al. 1999) or even flounder in uncertainty, indecision and unreached goals (Weller 2004), researchers must work to generate evidence that supports, guides and facilitates the change process (in other words, to research the ongoing action of change and to document the engagement of all participants in the change process).

When reform challenges the status quo in education, then research should test and challenge the benefits of the new status quo. Often, however, it provides only a critique of the speed of change. The search for the 'new' in education has been linked to failure to accumulate a coherent body of evidence-based theory and to validate practice effectiveness. It can be argued that the reform process has habitually used a wholesale impetus to change to provide momentum for change and that, when practitioners exhaust their personal resources and commitment to change, the system will tend to regress to conventional practice (Elmore 1996).

Throughout the 1960s and 1970s, education became less authoritarian in teacher behaviour, less reliant on memorisation for pedagogy and less narrowly classical in curriculum. However, evaluation of some of the major school reforms of that time (such as open classrooms, ethnic integration and cooperative learning) demonstrated that reform of one unit of a school's ecology often caused unintended consequences and negative side-effects in other aspects of schooling, with students and teachers not always prospering in a reformed teaching and learning environment (Gump 1980). Holistic investigation of how each area of a reform impacts on other areas of a school's ecology is essential.

Middle school research on Australian practice

Middle school research has reflected overarching problems identified in educational research (Anfara et al. 2003). 'Positive' assumptions about the benefits of a middle phase of schooling, with little empirical basis, have propelled its continued implementation. After more than 30 years of research on middle schooling in the United States, this piecemeal and ad hoc approach to research, dissemination of practice and review of implementation has resulted in inconclusive findings (Anfara et al. 2003).

Much of what has been reported of schools embarking on a middle schooling program has been descriptive commentaries of 'how' various aspects of middle schooling have been implemented across different sites. Hunt et al. (1998) noted that middle schooling had been viewed as a vehicle to inspire and lead change in the entire K–12 curriculum. Increasing criticism has been levelled at middle schools as being the '"weak link" in the K–12 education chain' (Anfara 2004, p. 2). Recent American research across various topics in middle schooling has noted pressure on educational districts to abandon their middle school models or to substitute basic structural regrouping for middle school practice (Swain 2004). However, Anfara et al. (2003) caution that the 'inconclusive nature of middle school research should not be adopted as a rationale for inaction or refusal to move forward in improving middle level schools' (p. 2).

The seven recommendations outlined by the Carnegie Corporation (Jackson & Davis 2000) can accommodate most of the various listings of signature practices, or practice indicators, for exemplary middle schools. 'Recommendations for creating exemplary middle schools that would be responsive to the needs of young adolescents and result in improved academic and socioemotional development' (Anfara 2004, p. 2) have been published, reconfigured and republished by many professional organisations in the United States and in Australia. These indicators, listed in detail in Chapter 1, continue to provide a coherent framework for middle school researchers to implement, contextualise and evaluate middle school organisation and practice.

These recommendations provide guidance and support for the generation and identification of practices for schools implementing middle school programs. With the implementation of these recommendations is an expectation that those schools adopting a middle schooling philosophy will be different. Unsurprisingly, noticeable differences between the ideals and the actual practices of middle schools are evident due to the tensions between an educational vision and the day-to-day realities of educational reform.

Research agenda for Australian practice

To date, the middle schooling phase in Australia has been sustained by teacher enthusiasm, some student-centred values, relatively little training and minimal research support. Research efforts need to be engaged at the point of practice implementation, in order to ensure that conditions for implementation are favourable and do not continue to repeat historical errors in research on reform processes.

Table 6.1 presents an outline for a research agenda to guide further study of the implementation of middle school practice. Research can be directed to a range of middle school practice topics in terms of practice criteria (acceptance, effectiveness and sustainability) related directly to recommended practices for middle schooling. Research can be directed to the same range of topics in terms of participants engaged in practice use, but participation-related topics are also related to intermediate variables for good practice (Anfara 2004). These intermediate variables concern teachers (their quality of life and job satisfaction), students (their in-school supports, resources, and stresses), and school climate (learning community), which is extended in Table 6.1 to include the wider community.

It can be seen in Table 6.1 that some recommended practice indicators, such as training, are shared vertically across criteria for teacher acceptance, effectiveness and sustainability. Some practices (such as informed consent and relationship quality) are shared horizontally across stakeholders but at different levels of criteria. A number of indicators (including improved student outcomes), which are explicit respectively to teachers and students, are also critical factors for other indicators that affect sustainability, such as community support and policymaker support (Baker 2003).

Table 6.1 Research agenda for middle school practice

	Teachers	Students	Community and school as community
Acceptance	Informed consent: choice to teach Access to training Awareness of benefits Supportive leadership	Informed consent: voice Learning based on students' interests, preferred teaching and learning styles and assessment models	Informed consent: involvement in consultation process
Effectiveness	Relationships: • teacher–students • teacher–teacher • teacher–others Access to training Essential skills: • curriculum and pedagogy • sense of efficacy • alternative classrooms	Relationships: student–student; student–teacher Curriculum: • exploratory • safe environment • autonomy	Relationships: • school–parents • school–community Ongoing community partnerships demonstrating a democratic ideology
Sustainability	Teacher support is derived from improved student outcomes in both affective and academic domains Access to training Leadership Avoiding labels such as 'experimental' or 'rigid orthodoxy'	Improved student outcomes occur in both affective (behavioural and socioemotional) and academic domains	Policy support is derived from improved student outcomes in both affective and academic domains

Acceptance

The rationale for middle schooling has provided the basis for some acceptance of reform by teachers, students and community stakeholders. In this approach, smoothing the transition between the primary and secondary divide would provide a more developmentally appropriate educational experience for middle school students. For teachers, acceptance of this rationale for reform has been uncritical. However, its acceptance has been conditional on their confidence that they can be effective within this environment (that they have adequate training or relevant experience), their commitment to teach in this age group (10/11–14/15 years), their awareness of potential benefits for students and their reliance on supportive school leaders.

Informed consent is a problematic issue for acceptance of middle school practice. The non-voluntary nature of teacher transfers can result in teachers with no training being placed in a middle school and teachers with appropriate training being placed elsewhere. For students and for the community, acceptance has been a neglected issue, although several of the *Turning Point 2000* indicators (Jackson & Davis 2000) are addressed to environmental climate for learning, democratic practices and community outreach. Middle school reform has been skewed to teacher-centric changes that are focused on changes in teacher practices for curriculum, pedagogy and staffing rather than on holistic changes in the school system and its organisation. Students 'voice' has been muted in directing how and what they learn. Many students and their parents continue enrolment in the local school following changes in school organisation, but others may choose to attend another school in another catchment area if they fear the change or to discontinue enrolment if they become dissatisfied. Students and community stakeholders can 'buy into' the reform when the school undertakes an inclusive consultation process. Acceptance of reorganised practice by these stakeholders might not involve an understanding of the benefits to students and the community and thus needs further investigation. Acceptance by teachers cannot be assumed to generate good practice, which must also be investigated and established.

Effectiveness

The strength of middle school reform can be measured by the effectiveness of practice indicators in delivering outcomes. Improved relationships between students, teachers, administration, parents and the community appear to be a key issue, a signature feature, for the effectiveness of a middle phase of schooling (Jackson & Davis 2000; Brown 2001; Hill et al. 2001). Yet teachers have generally not been trained in either how to develop or maintain effective relationships with colleagues, in working towards middle school goals (relevant from curriculum integration to school climate), or in how to develop and maintain the complex pastoral and mentoring relationships recommended for responsive practice with middle school students. There is little published evidence of either training or research on relationships in middle schools in Australia. As an integral indicator of reform that affects all stakeholders, the complex web of relationships within middle schooling warrants investigation.

Another teacher-centric indicator of the effectiveness of a middle school program is the breadth of teachers' knowledge of the curriculum, effective pedagogical skills, and interpersonal and communication skill levels; the absence in regular teacher training of these indicators has been challenged (Buckingham 2003). These indicators actively contribute to teachers' sense of job satisfaction. Teachers who have been trained in these indicators can feel confident and competent working within a middle schooling framework, being able to teach across all key learning areas and able to communicate effectively with students, teachers, administration staff and parents. Teachers' skill levels on these indicators are directly related to curriculum delivery for students and whether the program is authentically responsive to students' needs. Teachers' sense of competence and confidence may be challenged when they have not been specifically trained to teach across all areas of the curriculum (particularly high school trained teachers) or to teach an integrated curriculum. Furthermore, teachers can find it difficult to feel competent and confident when teaching a dynamic, free-wheeling curriculum that is responsive to students' immediate needs. Main (2003) reported that teachers in one middle school felt that they were not 'in control' and, indeed, were 'flying by the seat of their pants' for much of the time (p. 67).

Sustainability

The middle school movement in the United States is undergoing a 'reinvention' (Beane 2001) at a time when the movement has acquired some prominence in Australian education. Sustainability is an issue of school-wide capacity for self-assessment and continuous improvement. It requires strong leaders with the shared conceptual vision and an informed commitment to middle schooling, teachers who are specifically trained and want to work with middle school students, and a systematic research agenda that it is able to collate and disseminate data supporting the change. The major challenge to the sustainability of the middle school movement, however, is its ongoing failure to gain universal acceptance as 'best practice' for effectively educating middle school students. This has in turn fuelled the continuing lack of trained staff, weak leadership, and inadequate reporting of benefits for students in both the affective (behavioural and socioemotional) and academic domains.

Australian researchers must learn from the US lesson in order to avoid the 'boom-to-bust' cycle. The effectiveness of the reform has been questioned when policy-to-practice implementation has focused on issues such as rigid orthodoxy (Williamson & Johnston 1998), organisational rather than pedagogical change (Beane 2001; Dickinson 2001) and an imbalance between emotional development and academic rigour (Reisling 2002). To be acceptable, effective and sustainable, the reform model must be implemented as a holistic reform that seeks to incorporate the interrelated elements, noted in Chapter 1, recommended by Carnegie (Jackson & Davis 2000; Swain 2004). Middle schooling is a 'framework, along with a set of structures, tools and processes designed to facilitate change' (Ames 2004, p. 141) rather than a reform 'model' to be implemented as a foolproof recipe. Program design must be encouraged to explore some middle way between highly experimental and highly orthodox implementation in order to expect a bright future.

Conclusion

The purpose of research into the implementation of middle schooling practice in Australia is not to establish if a good or inferior job of reform has been done. Its purpose is to identify what teacher skills and competencies will be most responsive to the needs of Australian middle school students. Teachers can, and must, play an important role in the research agenda for middle schools. Teachers as researchers of their practice have been targeted specifically in a new volume in the series, *The Handbook of Research in Middle Level Education*, announced by the National Middle School Association in the United States (Caskey, in press).

Questions
1   How do schools ensure informed consent from teachers, students and community stakeholders when considering implementing a middle school program?
2   Discuss the effects of teacher training and differences in teacher training on student outcomes.
3   Identify an area that would be suitable as an action research project within a middle school classroom.
4   What are the benefits of teacher-as-researcher or teacher-in-partnership-as-researcher for middle schooling practice?
5   Discuss the practice indicators of acceptance, effectiveness and sustainability for community members involved in a middle school.
6   Evaluate an Australian study on middle schooling and its value in terms of change for the practice criteria of acceptability, effectiveness and sustainability.

CURRICULUM
PRACTICES FOR
THE MIDDLE YEARS

7

Literacies and multiliteracies

Rod Maclean

Students face special literacy challenges in the middle years as a result of changing reading and writing demands and as a result of a lessening of their engagement in the school system. In order to support students to rise to these challenges teachers need to design units of work and activities that integrate print, sound, illustration and visual design, that are purposeful, engaging and relevant, and that lead students to critique and transform their social worlds. Within the context of these units, skills and strategies must be taught at the point of need to help students to achieve their immediate goals and also help them to be more independent readers and writers.

As students approach the final years of primary school their world broadens. They develop interests in sports, hobbies, popular culture, the Internet and, later on, romance and the world of work. They are increasingly able to sustain and pursue activities without support from adults. Corresponding to this change in interests is a broadening of the ways they engage with literacy. Students read and write to please themselves rather than others, and they learn how to choose their own reading materials. The range of difficulty they can manage increases as they develop strategies for coping with challenging materials. They begin to be able to sustain engagement with longer books or to write longer texts that cannot be completed at a single sitting (Szymusiak & Sibberson 2001). They learn to read selectively to locate information, rather than having to begin at the beginning and keep going to the end. Students learn to see their writing from the reader's point of view and to write in interesting and informative ways for a wide audience.

But the middle years are also a problematic time for literacy learning. Achievement in literacy for many tends to plateau or go backwards, and the gap between good and poor readers grows ever wider. Many learners disengage from literacy, and do not read and write even if they are able to. The reasons for these problems are varied. Some students who read successfully in the early years are unable to cope with the increased demands of middle years literacy. Schools are often out of step with the needs of students during early adolescence (Kiddey & Robson 2001a). The reading and writing tasks typically encountered in secondary classrooms are more fragmented and less interesting than in upper primary school (Green 1998). Many lessons do not have a purpose which is clear to either the students or the teacher, and have no direct connection to students' backgrounds or interests. There is a lack of intellectual depth, challenge and rigour, and a lack of the focused teaching of skills and strategies which students need to complete the tasks set for them (Hargreaves et al. 1996).

This chapter outlines teaching approaches to help students rise to the challenges of middle years literacy. Using the multiliteracies approach as an organising framework (New London Group 2000), the chapter brings together a range of perspectives on middle years literacy. I begin by looking at the 'what' of literacy, asking what aspects of literacy typically are difficult for students in the middle years. A key feature of modern texts often ignored by teachers is the integration of words, images and design that is characteristic of the students' everyday reading and viewing of websites, games and magazines. The second part of the chapter looks at the 'how' of literacy teaching. I examine the design of teaching activities and units of work that allow students to read and write in enjoyable, relevant and purposeful ways, that allow them to critique and transform texts and that support them to become independent learners.

What aspects of literacy challenge students in the middle years?

In the middle years a knowledge of spoken language is no longer sufficient to support reading and writing, as students come across words and linguistic forms that are specialised to written language. Writing in the content areas is especially difficult because it increasingly deals with general classes of objects such as 'lungs, work, gills, muscles', and with abstract objects such as 'work, energy, fuel'. This abstraction makes it hard to visualise what is being talked about and thus makes the writing hard to understand.

The increasing complexity of sentences also makes writing more difficult to understand. In the sentence below, which was written for a child audience, there are at least five separate ideas linked by complex grammatical relationships of comparison ('Like all other creatures'), definition or qualification ('creatures which live on dry land and which get their oxygen from the air'), and purpose ('to let the oxygen in'):

> Like all other creatures which live on dry land and which get their oxygen from the air, we have to keep a permanently moist surface to let the oxygen in (Miller & Pelham 1983).

Processing complex sentences challenges students' ability to pay attention to grammar as they try to keep the start of the sentence in mind while making sense of the end. Techniques like sentence rewriting and sentence combining, where simple sentences are rewritten into more complex ones, and complex sentences rewritten into simpler ones, can help students come to terms with sentence complexity.

Another challenge for students in the middle years is the use of paragraphs. In early writing a sentence usually can stand on its own because it conveys a complete idea. With more complex texts, however, a sentence is often insufficient to tell everything there is to say about an idea. Sentences do not stand on their own but are organised into paragraphs that elaborate an idea or topic. One useful strategy to teach students how to write paragraphs is bundling. Students brainstorm ideas relating to a topic and then everyone writes their own sentence on individual strips of paper. The group sorts these sentence strips into bundles that deal with related subtopics. The bundles are then rewritten by the group into paragraphs. Bundling is particularly useful for teaching report writing. Paragraph structure can also be taught by sequencing activities in which students sort cut-up sentences from a paragraph back into the original sequence.

In their reading and writing students have to think about the relationship of one paragraph to another and about the relation of one sentence to another within the paragraph. They have to be able to identify the topic of a paragraph and to use their knowledge of paragraph structure to identify important ideas and organising themes.

The reader has to work out how one paragraph relates to the next. Unlike many early years texts, where one thing happens after another, middle years texts are more likely to be organised by abstract relationships such as:

- Classification: What kind is it? What subtypes are there?
- Qualities: How does it look, feel, smell, weigh, sound? What size and shape is it?
- Composition: What parts is it made of?
- Function/performance: What does it do? How does it behave?
- Cause/effect: How does it work?
- Problem/solution: How can we fix it?
- Evidence/support: How do we know?
- Compare and contrast: What is it like?
- Definition: How is it defined?
- Rule/example: What's an instance of the generalisation?

Students find it much easier to understand factual writing if the text offers clues to help the reader identify the underlying relationships and if they have been taught to identify these clues. An effective way to improve students' comprehension is therefore to help them to detect the underlying relationships between paragraphs that organise texts.

Narratives become more complex and demanding in the middle years as students begin to read longer novels and 'chapter books' that employ more 'literary' techniques, books where the authors make the readers work harder. Authors give only indirect clues to character traits and leave readers to form their own opinion. Larger numbers of characters are introduced and extensive use made of dialogue. Readers may have difficulty keeping track of which character is speaking or thinking at a particular time; they also have trouble coping with flashbacks and with shifts between subplots. Teaching techniques like plot graphs, character profiles and the use of response journals can help students come to terms with these challenges.

Awareness of language also helps students to read actively. Readers begin to recognise how the author manipulates points of view to encourage them to feel sympathy for a character. Other techniques used to influence readers can also be highlighted, like stereotyping, the representation of characters as included or excluded, use of emphasis or omission to present some events as important and others as unimportant, and the representation of some cultural values as normal and natural and others as strange and unusual. Analysis of advertising, where these techniques are often used in a blatant way, is good for this purpose, and students are often already sophisticated in their approach to advertisements.

Increasing their awareness of the 'author's craft' also allows students to use these devices in their own writing. They begin to use plot devices like suspense, quests, puzzles and misunderstandings to make their own writing more interesting. They begin to recognise how writing is given a concrete sensory impact by the use of metaphor and similes, and by poetic devices such as alliteration, rhythm, repetition and rhyme.

In one sense the knowledge demands are not as great for writing as for reading, as students are not expected to write texts that are as sophisticated as the ones they read. On the other hand, writing demands a more precise knowledge than reading because it is a productive or expressive activity and a lack of knowledge is immediately evident in mistakes. As written texts become increasingly remote from spoken language patterns students can no longer rely on their instincts about what is right and wrong, and have to call on explicit knowledge of language in order to write correctly and effectively.

Knowledge of text types or genres is a helpful way of improving students' awareness of written language. Text types or genres are characteristic ways in which texts are organised to achieve particular purposes. Knowledge of the features of text types or genres helps students adjust their writing to different audiences and purposes. It also helps them to identify elements that need revising where texts do not achieve their aims. Students of writing need knowledge of a wider range of text types or genres in the middle years, including expositions or arguments, reports, descriptions and explanations (Education Department of Western Australia 1997; Wing Jan 2001). Middle years students also need to know about spoken language genres such as reports, interviews and debates (Allen 1994). Factual genres much more frequently include visual elements like photos, illustrations, icons, diagrams and full colour design.

Increase in the number of texts that combine a range of mediums is one of the reasons why literacy educators now refer not just to singular literacy but to plural literacies or multiliteracies. It is no longer sufficient for students to learn to communicate just through writing. They must be expert in a range of mediums, including spoken language, sound, body language, film, illustration, online and digital or electronic texts. And they must control these literacies not only singly but in combination, thus displaying what Lemke (1998) calls 'metamedia literacies'. In the design of a PowerPoint slide, for example, students control the combination of print, layout, illustration, colour, animation and sound.

As a result of technological change, visual literacy has become an integral part of literacy learning. Students need to be aware of how images and visual designs are organised, how they present themselves to the viewer, and of how types and styles of visual design match types and styles of written text. 'Organisation' (Lemke 1998) relates to the layout of text and images on the page through principles of framing and balance, foregrounding and highlighting, and repetition and contrast. It includes the grouping and separation of elements on the page. Students need to be aware of the conventions governing placement on the left of the page to indicate familiar information (such as the placement of menus on a web page) and the use of the right to indicate unfamiliar information. They need to be aware of the convention that the top of the page includes the most highly valued information and the bottom the less highly valued information, and also of how the reader's or viewer's eye is directed over the page, whether in a left-to-right linear way, as for a page of print, or in a circular, spiral or zigzag way, as for an illustration (Kress & Van Leeuwen 1996).

'Orientation' (Lemke 1998) concerns the way in which the viewer is related to the visual elements on the page or screen. Viewers take note of whether the gaze of an illustrated character is directed within the frame or outside the frame. Is eye contact made with another character or with the viewer? Point of view is important as a way of indicating power relationships. Does the viewer see the scene depicted from above as a superior, from below as an inferior, or at the level of an equal? Is the viewer involved with a scene depicted frontally or disengaged from a scene shown obliquely? The viewer is addressed in a more indirect way by the contrast between realistic and non-realistic images. Realistic images or colour photographs indicate truth, immediacy and authenticity. They appeal to the senses. Non-realistic images in which detail is obscured or the colours are muted, such as diagrams, icons or line drawings, connote a scientific or abstracted perspective. Greeting cards are an item familiar to children that can be used effectively to make these points. They use a wide range of styles of illustration. Teachers can ask why some cards use photos and others illustrations. Why do some use full colour and others muted colour? Why do some use line drawings and others more complex images? (Kress & Van Leeuwen 1996).

In linking visual and written elements within a text students need to be aware of what kinds of visual elements belong in particular genres. For example, explanations and instructions are linked to labelled flow diagrams that illustrate the steps in a process. Descriptions and reports are linked to cross-sections or cutaways which show the internal structure of an object, or to maps or bird's-eye views which show the layout of an object in space. Recounts or diary entries or observations may be linked to time lines or story maps (Moline 1995). Persuasive or argumentative writing is linked to graphs providing evidence for an argument or to photographs which persuade by appealing to emotions. Narratives are linked to illustrations which use a range of techniques to indicate character, setting and action. Narrative is also reinforced by change or contrast from one image to the next on successive pages of a book, for example (Anstey & Bull 2000).

How to teach literacy in the middle years

While the range of aspects of literacy that students learn increases markedly in the middle years, there are also changes in the way in which literacy is taught and learned. Although many teachers retain a whole group/small group/whole group structure to organise the literacy session, the use of this structure varies markedly (Fountas & Pinnell 2001). Students become more independent and in control of their literacy learning. Teachers negotiate tasks with students rather than just assigning them. Students make their own choices about what texts to read, and write, from a range that includes children's literature, information books, magazines and websites. Teachers need to be able to assist students to find texts that will engage them by staying informed about children's books and electronic texts. A feature of literacy teaching in the middle years is the importance placed on use of texts for 'real' purposes—purposes that students perceive as relevant to their lives. Students should be reading, writing, speaking, listening and viewing with real audiences for authentic purposes that engage and enthuse them.

Effective middle years teaching creates a community of learners. Literacy is used as a means of developing the class as a community with shared rules and values and a shared history of common experience. This goal is achieved by class meetings, by class conflict resolution, and by establishing one-to-one communication between all members of the class. Success in literacy is linked to a sense of self-worth and of acceptance within a social group. Students work together on shared reading and writing tasks, they support each other's reading and writing through peer conferencing, and they write for each other as audience and read each other's work. Students engage in joint projects and activities that require them to write and read with each other and for each other. Students also participate in broader literate communities. They write and read about family, community and school events, and within online peer communities.

One way to build the classroom as a literate community is to base units of work around 'authentic' or service learning. In authentic learning students read or write for real purposes that have to do with their schools or communities. For example, Komesaroff and Morrison (2002) show how the literacy curriculum can be related to authentic uses of literacy for real purposes within the social world of a school. Students are given responsibility for tasks such as ordering playground equipment, helping to organise the school camp, preparing items for newsletters, inviting guests to the school and writing thankyou letters.

In service-learning students use literacy to mediate a relationship with a community organisation. Lyons (personal communication) describes a service-learning module focused on the RSPCA, in which students read and write about the RSPCA as a means of introducing them to a community service volunteer role with the organisation. Stowell (2000) describes service-learning roles in which young people organise to help out in nursing homes for the elderly.

It is important to engage students with books and other texts that they find personally meaningful and enjoyable. There is a range of programs aimed at achieving this goal, including literature-based programs (Nicoll & Roberts 1993), silent reading, literature circles (Samway 1996; Daniels 2002). These programs have in common that they assist students to make their own book choices, allow time in class for extended free reading, and encourage sharing of books within small groups.

Students can also be engaged in purposeful reading by the WebQuest model (Dodge 1998). WebQuests are structured online tasks set around books or other texts that specify a set of purposeful, achievable and interesting tasks related to the reading. They include an introduction, a set of information sources embedded as links within the web page, a clear set of steps to follow, and advice on how to organise and present information learned as part of the quest. Examples of WebQuests based on Australian books for primary age children can be found at the Younger Readers' WebQuests site (www.patterson_lakes-ps.vic.edu.au/html/webquests/htm) (Weymouth et al. 2001).

Teachers should also engage students with texts by helping them find topics that they feel passionate about. The teacher can do this by sharing her or his own passions with the class (Harvey 1998) and by encouraging students to share and catalogue their own interests. Harvey suggests this be done in a writer's notebook. Students over time write down the things they want to find out more about and share their lists with each other. Current events or chance happenings can also spark off a desire to know more. Students need to be encouraged to follow up their initial interests, as they do not know what is going to interest them unless they are exposed to a range of topics and texts to get an idea of what is available. Regular attention to news sources such as newspapers and television can help promote this wish to find out more. Other sources of ideas for writing topics include community events, peer culture 'crazes' and family travel experiences or histories (Harvey 1998).

Student interests can be used as a starting point for inquiry learning in which students are reading and writing with the goal of answering a question that interests them. Inquiry learning begins with a tuning-in process in which students explore an issue with a view to finding personally interesting questions. They then accumulate information relevant to answering the question, sort out the information and draw conclusions from it, communicate the conclusions to an audience, and then decide on further action that follows from the conclusions. Within this framework teachers can negotiate elements such as task requirements and assessment criteria, the use of workbooks or reflective journals, and procedures for documenting inquiry processes and presentation of results. In inquiry learning the setting of a question or problem gives the students a motivation and a goal for their work, and creates a meaningful way of linking activities together. This puts students in control of the process of learning as they seek to accomplish their goals.

Another kind of inquiry approach is to have students examine the literacies used in their own communities. Myers and Beach (2001) suggest that educators link the teaching of literacy to participation in students' own 'social-worlds' of peer groups, school and sports, family and romance, community and workplace, and online or virtual worlds. A social-worlds approach relates literacy to students' own interests and allows them to see literacy as relevant to their own lives. Students are positioned as researchers of their own language. They enjoy assuming the role of experts and explaining to their 'ignorant' teachers the literacy of text messaging or of popular online role-play games. They also enjoy assuming the role of critic by spotting flaws and inconsistencies in these popular texts and documenting the commercial interests at stake in them.

Another meaningful context for reading and writing in the classroom is preparation for a presentation or performance of some kind. Osborne and Wilson (2003) describe a project in the Torres Strait which provides an excellent example of a multiliteracies approach. Students had to create a 30-second radio commercial to raise awareness on diabetes. In order to do this, they had to research diabetes from a range of sources. They then worked with a drama consultant to develop a script for the commercial. Students drew creatively from a range of cultural and linguistic resources including Yumplatok, the local language, and from familiar television programs.

An important feature of multiliteracies teaching, and indeed of all the approaches to unit design outlined here, is that they involve not only participation in literacy practices. Students must also be made aware of the techniques and devices that authors and artists use to manipulate and influence their readers and viewers. This awareness helps protect students from the commercial interests that lie behind the production of powerful and seductive literacies. Critique undermines the authority of the writer and puts the reader on the same level. It forces readers to clarify their own values where these are opposed to those of the writer.

Critique is also necessary to help students to make the next step, which is to become text producers who themselves use texts for significant purposes. Students use critique as the basis for action and transformation. Transformation occurs when students take a text and make it their own by adapting it for their own purposes. Transformation also involves mixing a range of text types and language resources to create new meanings. For example, in preparing their radio commercial the Torres Strait students (Osborne & Wilson 2003) did not just copy a 'conventional' way of doing commercials familiar to them from their own radio listening. They took this text type as a starting point and used it as a basis for improvising a text that they felt comfortable with. These students did not want to speak like a radio announcer. They wanted to present themselves in ways that were consistent with their own identities as members of an Indigenous community. To do this they had to make use of ways of writing and talking from the media world but at the same time bring their own voice or identity to the task by using local ways of talking. Only when they developed their own way of speaking and writing could they learn to control the language of the radio commercial effectively. Dyson (2003) draws on the popular music metaphors of sampling and remixing to describe this process in which children draw on community, school and popular culture resources to create texts and literacies that are personally meaningful to them.

Explicit teaching of literacy

While some people are able to learn literacy simply through exposure to meaningful and enjoyable uses, most students need overt and explicit assistance in order to learn. Students need to be taught specific skills and strategies (Kiddey & Robson 2001b).

A skill is an ability that is required for performing a task. In order to understand a long novel, for example, one has to have the skill of remembering who the characters are and what their names are (as well as many other skills). Fluent readers and writers are generally not aware of the skills they are using. Their focus is on the meaning.

A strategy, on the other hand, is a consciously applied way of achieving goals or solving problems. Strategies help learners to become more independent, and they are generally applied when there is some sort of breakdown in the reading or writing process. For example, when I realise that I am not understanding a book because I cannot remember who a character is, I go back and reread the page where that character is introduced. Strategies are only needed when there are barriers to reading or writing fluently, enjoyably and thoughtfully for a wide range of purposes. The reading or writing that can be done consciously using strategies is slow and clumsy. Once strategies are automated they keep on developing to become more flexible and efficient; at that stage they stop being strategies and become skills.

It is important to distinguish literacy-learning strategies that are used by learners to solve problems and to make them independent in their own reading and writing from literacy-teaching strategies that are used by teachers to help students learn. To avoid confusion here I reserve the word 'strategy' for students and refer to teacher 'activities', 'techniques' or 'approaches'.

Activities for teaching reading strategies have three main types of purposes. They aim to help students:

* check up on their own understanding of what they are reading, to detect any failures, and to remedy or fix up any problems;
* read more actively, constructively and purposefully, to generate their own interpretation or representation of what they are reading and to vary their reading according to their purpose; and
* read more critically, so that they do not just accept what is on the page but question the author's motives and attempts at manipulation.

The goal must always be to help students learn to apply their own learning strategies independent of teacher assistance. There is no point in students learning strategies if the strategies do not make them more independent as learners and as readers and writers.

Before teaching strategies it is important to establish through careful observation and, if necessary, diagnostic testing that students have a genuine need. Many good readers have already developed their own effective strategies and do not need explicit teaching.

Explicit teaching of skills and strategies should occur in the context of engaging and purposeful uses of literacy. Students should understand that the purpose of the literacy teaching is not just for them to learn more about literacy but also a means of enabling them to achieve their goals.

Applying a learning strategy takes effort and time. Students should always be allowed to make their own cost/benefit assessment of strategy use. In order to allow students to make an informed decision teachers should always clearly identify the purpose of a strategy. Students should be encouraged only to use a strategy when the benefits outweigh the costs. This is a personal judgment and will differ considerably between students.

In teaching reading and writing strategies, there are a number of general guidelines to follow:

- establish/negotiate a purpose and context of activity which facilitates the task;
- activate background knowledge of the topic;
- explain the purpose of the strategy and why it is important;
- discuss examples of the text type and talk about its uses in school and the community;
- model the task and text with the whole class;
- collaboratively make processes and requirements of the task explicit;
- have students do the task with peer and/or teacher support, in both whole-class and small-group settings;
- empower students to make their own decisions about what strategies they find useful and what they do not find useful;
- collaboratively establish assessment criteria;
- have students perform the task independently; and
- have students assess their own performance using the criteria (Marshall 1999; Edwards-Groves 2003).

These guidelines help ensure a staged, scaffolded transition from teacher-supported use of the strategy to its independent use. If these guidelines are followed, students will be able to understand the purpose of the strategy and make their own decisions about its usefulness.

Edwards-Groves (2003) describes a teaching framework for explicit literacy instruction that conforms with these guidelines. The teaching session begins with an introduction in which background knowledge is activated, connection is made to previous learning, students are introduced to tasks and instructions are given, the purpose of the session is established and the rationale for the teaching focus is explained. The second stage is 'elaboration', in which the skills or strategies that are the focus of the session are explained, modelled and demonstrated to the students. The second stage provides the students with more detailed knowledge about subject matter and about the steps they need to follow in order to complete set tasks. 'Soloing' may also be used at this stage, as when one student completes a task with teacher assistance as a model for other students. The next stage is 'practice', in which students complete set tasks independently and with teacher support. In this stage students apply the strategies or skills they have learned in the actual process of reading and writing, listening and viewing. The final stage is 'review', in which students and teacher jointly summarise what they have learned and reflect on the learning process, and in which students express in their own words what they have learned and how useful it is to them.

Teaching literacy strategies

A fundamental difficulty for many middle years students is that they do not understand the purpose of reading. Their previous experience may have disposed them to see reading as a matter of reading words. They may not realise that they are supposed to get meaning from the text. They are 'fake readers' (Tovani 2000, p. 5). They can decode the words efficiently and read out loud well, but they do not understand how to make sense of what they are reading. Students may not understand that their job as a reader is to relate what is in the pages of the book to what they know already, and they may not recognise the knowledge they have that is relevant to understanding a text. Much of the background knowledge they need in order to understand what they are reading is itself acquired through reading. This sets off a vicious circle in which the less they read the less they are able to read and the further they lag behind their peers.

Similar problems occur with writing. Young students tend to write as if they were talking to someone. They find it difficult to write a sustained, coherent text over several sittings. When asked to write at length they produce rambling stories or journal entries, where each writing session begins a new episode, and where there is no overall structure to the writing. One reason for this is that young students find it difficult to plan. Another problem is that they find it very difficult to break into what they have already written to make revisions. If they have to revise something they tend to just rewrite it, unless the changes are superficial matters of spelling, grammar or punctuation.

To overcome these problems students need to set goals for their writing just as they do for their reading. They have to generate content goals for what they are going to write, and structure and purpose goals for how the text is to be organised. They generate goals for the effect the text will have on the audience, and process goals for how they will go about writing.

Goal setting can be taught using a range of teaching techniques such as graphic overviews (Morris & Stewart-Dore 1984), 'frontloading' (Wilhelm 2001), What I know, what I want to know, and what I learned (KWL) charts (Ogle 1983; Vervoorn & van Haren 2002), brainstorming (Osborn 1963), concept mapping (Novak 1977), top-level structures, structured overview, diagramming, data charts and Venn diagrams (Morris & Stewart-Dore 1984; Creenaune & Rowles 1996; Dumbleton & Lountain 1999a, 1999b, 1999c; Marshall 1999). These techniques have in common that they create graphic-based representations of the structure and/or content of a text that can be used to help students make predictions and set reading goals. The techniques can also be used in writing to help students set goals and generate plans. The graphic nature of these tools helps students integrate visual and print-based literacies.

Another kind of problem that students have with longer texts is that they cannot remember events, characters and settings from one reading to the next. They need to keep track of key features of the text they have read already in order to make sense of what is to follow. One way to do this is to help them visualise the content of the text, including the setting, key events and characters. Imaging makes a text much easier to understand and remember. Harvey and Goudvis (2000) suggest ways of teaching visualising by having students draw and compare their images of key events in a text. This can be extended to discussion of non-visual images: 'I see . . ., I hear . . ., I can feel . . ., I smell . . ., I can taste . . .' (p. 104).

Writers of middle years texts try to make things interesting for readers by leaving gaps for them to fill in and by leaving the story open to a range of interpretations. Many middle years students struggle when not everything is spelled out for them, and when they have to fill in the gaps themselves. Students need practice and support in reading between the lines in order to make sense of a text. For example, the appearance of the main character in a story might not be described because the reader sees the world through his or her eyes. A good way to teach inferencing is to have students retell the story from a different point of view. Suddenly it becomes necessary to say what the main character looks like. Students then have to search through the text to look for clues about his or her appearance.

A further key strategy that students need to control is comprehension monitoring. Readers monitor their own comprehension by keeping track of whether they have understood what they are reading and whether they have achieved their reading and writing goals. It is a common experience for all readers to reach the bottom of the page and realise that they have been reading the words without taking in the meaning. But some readers do this all the time without realising that they have a problem. They have to be shown how to check up on their own under-standing using techniques like self-questioning (Raphael & Hiebert 1996). Another way to teach comprehension monitoring is for the teacher to 'think aloud' (Wilhelm 2001) while monitoring her own comprehension of a modelled text. Wilhelm suggests that 'think alouds' can be used to teach a broad range of reading strategies such as predicting, inferring missing information, linking the text to personal experiences, visualisation, comprehension monitoring, and fixing up comprehension failures. Think alouds can also be used to model planning and revision processes in the teaching of writing.

Another version of the think aloud strategy is reciprocal teaching (Palinscar & Brown 1985; Maloney 1993; Pullela 1993; Begg 2001). In reciprocal teaching the strategies of setting a purpose or generating a question, summarising, predicting and clarifying confusion are modelled by the teacher in a think-aloud process as students read a short text. These strategies are taught to students in simplified form as part of a routine. Once students have mastered the routine they can take it over for themselves. Within a small group they take turns in developing independence by modelling use of the strategy for the other students in a process known as 'soloing'.

Text coding can also be used to teach reading and writing strategies (Harvey & Goudvis 2000). In text coding, following a teacher model, students use Post-it notes to label sections of a text with simple codes. Coding can be used to teach compre-hension monitoring when students label comprehension failures. It can also be used to teach students how to make connections between the text they are reading and their own experience. Coding can also be used in the teaching of writing by way of annotating parts of a student's text that need revision.

A major problem many students experience after reading is in summarising and identifying what is important. Readers may fail to understand because they focus on concrete details that grab their attention and ignore the important ideas. This is a special problem when the main idea is not explicitly stated in a text but has to be inferred by synthesising information from a range of paragraphs. One way to teach this skill is by the technique known as 'get the gist'. Students summarise the content of a text or paragraph they have read in a single sentence. Retelling is also useful for improving students' comprehension of the gist or main ideas of a text. A student is asked to retell the content of a narrative or information text to an audi-ence. The technique works best when the student is retelling material that is unfamiliar to the audience for a genuine purpose. The retell may be spoken, written, enacted or visual, and ideally the medium should be changed between original text and retell—for example, when the original is written, the retell is a dramatic enactment (Johnston 1997; Brown & Cambourne 1988; Hoyt 1999).

Conclusion

Only by working on several parallel fronts can teachers meet the challenges of middle years literacy. Teachers design units of work and activities that integrate print, sound, illustration and visual design, that are purposeful, engaging and relevant, and that lead students to critique and transform their social worlds. Within the context of these units, skills and strategies are taught at the point of need that help students to achieve their immediate goals and that also help them to be more independent readers and writers.

Questions

1   Literacy achievement in the middle years has been described as 'problematic'. Identify and investigate a data source that provides evidence of the tendency for middle years students' literacy achievement to plateau or to go backwards— a good starting point is your state or territory Education Department or equivalent.

2   What literacy initiatives specific to literacy are underway in your state or territory?

3   Literacy and numeracy achievement are often used as benchmarks to determine the effectiveness of middle years reform. Why are these aspects of schooling considered to be so significant for middle years students?

8

Numeracy

Shelley Dole

Promoting numeracy is a high priority in the middle years to ensure students are sufficiently prepared for life beyond the compulsory years of schooling. Numeracy is inextricably linked to school mathematics, and issues associated with the teaching and learning of mathematics impact upon numeracy. In this chapter some of these issues are described, and a brief summary of approaches to numeracy provided. As numeracy links to real life situations, I begin with a little scenario to provide a context for the discussion that follows.

A numeracy scenario

A party of seven is dining on tacos and burritos at the local Mexican restaurant. Towards the end of the evening the bill for the meal arrives, totalling $198. It is picked up by the closest diner, and then passed to the next person, accompanied by the words, 'You work it out. I was never any good at maths.' All other diners then focus on the bill, asking how much it is, and performing various mental actions, including estimating that each diner must pay between $20 and $30 (because 7 × $20 gives $140, and 7 × $30 gives $210); surprise that the bill is so high; acceptance that the bill is appropriate; annoyance that less food was eaten by one party member, but the expectation of all paying the same is the norm for the group; fear of being asked to calculate how much each person must pay. As one party member finally decides to take out her mobile phone to divide 7 into $198, another party member is mentally rounding the bill to $200, multiplying 2×7 to get 14, which is then changed to $140, which is subtracted from $200. Focusing on the remaining $60, seven-times tables are then recalled (7×7 is 49—too low; 7×8 is 56—okay), with $8 added to $20. Upon reaching this figure, the mental calculator announces that all must contribute a bit more than $28, further suggesting that all pay $29 to leave a tip. At this same moment, the mobile phone user announces that all must pay $28.29, or $28.30, to cover the bill.

How real to life is this, and what does it say about numeracy in the middle years of schooling? The situation likely resonates with most adults as it is a typical cultural practice in our society. Before discussing this scenario in relation to numeracy in the middle years of schooling, take a moment to consider who is the most numerate of the party. Clearly, one member had the strategies, skills and disposition to mentally divide 7 into $198, and to contextualise the result to ensure the total bill was covered, and even provide a tip. However, what of the diner who used the calculator on her mobile phone? Is this person any less numerate because the instinct was to reach for technology? Or what of the person who thought the bill was too high, or the one who thought it was fair? Are they any less numerate because they did not perform any calculation to split the bill, but obviously contextualised the bill to the situation and to their experiences and expectations? And the two who 'passed' on contributing anything to solving the problem—are they innumerate because their reactions were a combination of avoidance and fear?

The questions posed here are for the purpose of defining the term 'numeracy' and the phrase 'being numerate'.

Numeracy and being numerate

In similar vein to discussion and debate over definitions of literacy being more than reading, writing and spelling, definitions of numeracy encapsulate considerably more than arithmetic. Once the focus of extensive discussion and debate, numeracy is now generally accepted as application of mathematics as required in the real world. Although this is a rather simplistic and nebulous definition, richer descriptions are available, ensuring that sufficient breadth, depth as well as specificity are given to the term. For example, the definition put forward by the Australian Association of Mathematics Teachers (AAMT) in 1997 described numeracy as thinking, reasoning, cross-curricular, context-based, as well as incorporating mathematical skills and concepts:

> To be numerate is to use mathematics effectively to meet the general demands of life at home, in paid work and for participation in community and civic life. In school education, numeracy is a fundamental component of learning, performance, discourse and critique across all areas of the curriculum. It involves the disposition to use, in context, a combination of: underpinning mathematical concepts and skills from across the discipline (numerical, spatial, graphical, statistical and algebraic); mathematical thinking and strategies; general thinking skills; and a grounded appreciation of context (p. 15).

From an international perspective, the Organisation for Economic Cooperation and Development (OECD) (1999) described numeracy as:

> . . . the individual's capacity to identify and understand the role that mathematics plays in the world, to make well-founded mathematical judgements, and to engage in mathematics, in ways that meet the needs of that individual's current and future life, as a constructive, concerned and reflective citizen (p. 41).

In 2000, the Department of Education, Training and Youth Affairs (DETYA) provided a definition of numeracy as follows:

> Numeracy, like literacy, provides key enabling skills for individuals to participate successfully in schooling. Furthermore, numeracy equips students for life beyond school in providing access to further study or training, to personal pursuits, and to participation in the world of work and in the wider community (p. 10).

Rather than in the form of a succinct definition, the term numeracy has also been described through detailed descriptions of separate elements that collectively comprise numeracy. For example, Wilkins (2000) stated numeracy comprises 'mathematical content knowledge, mathematical reasoning, understanding the social impact and utility of mathematics, understanding the nature and historical development of mathematics, and mathematical disposition' (p. 405). Recently, Zevenbergen (in press) described numeracy in terms of it being transdisciplinary, realistic, a sense (in relation to mathematical ideas and concepts), a disposition, and consisting of core skills. (Intentionally, Zevenbergen listed core skills last in her summary.)

Foremost in definitions of numeracy is an emphasis on the application of mathematics in life situations. In this sense, definitions of numeracy must be continually revisited to ensure students are sufficiently numerate for an ever-changing and technologically advancing society beyond compulsory schooling. With new technologies, numeracy for future worlds requires considerable imagination. A futures-focused view of numeracy is assurance that numeracy definitions will continually evolve (Noss 1998), and therefore the word numeracy is an elastic term (Doig 2001).

Numeracy, mathematics and the middle years of schooling

The study of mathematics is regarded as the foundation for numeracy (DETYA 2000), and this is reflected in the goals of school mathematics. As proposed by the Australian Education Council in 1990, the goals of school mathematics are to promote students' appreciation and engagement in mathematics, where students see mathematics as meaningful, relevant and culturally embedded; and where they have skills and confidence to apply mathematics to everyday living, decision making and problem solving. In light of such a vision for school mathematics, the question is whether there is a need for such a term as numeracy, when the stated goals of school mathematics share many themes similar to those contained within definitions of numeracy.

The vigorous debate engaged in by educators, academics, policy makers, professional organisations and teachers over definitions of numeracy and what it means to be numerate has resulted in general awareness that the onus on numeracy development is not only within the mathematics classroom, but also beyond, into all other curriculum areas. Like literacy, the development of numeracy is the responsibility of all teachers (AAMT 1997; DETYA 2000). One of the key aspects of numeracy that does, however, relate directly to the teaching and learning of mathematics, is the importance of having a positive disposition to using mathematics. Consider the scenario presented at the beginning of this chapter. Two of the party members clearly indicated reluctance towards solving the mathematical task confronting the group. Such negative feelings can only be a result of school mathematics, and mathematics anxiety, aversion and fear as an unfortunate by-product of school mathematics is well documented in the literature (e.g. Maxwell 1988; Hembree 1990; Meyer & Fennema 1992; Dossel 1993).

Assisting mathematics-anxious students to overcome their fear of mathematics, and focusing on reducing the incidence of such fear, must be the responsibility of teachers of mathematics. However, in the middle years of schooling, school mathematics, and thus the development of numeracy, is challenged by students' disposition towards the study of mathematics, and often schooling in general. The middle years literature describes adolescence as a time where students undergo immense physiological, social and emotional development and growth. Adolescent behaviour in the classroom is typified by words and phrases such as disengagement, disinterest, and disruptive behaviour.

Taking 'typical' adolescent characteristics into account, consider the following description of a traditional mathematics classroom as described by Battista (1999): 'Every day is the same: the teacher shows students several examples of how to solve a certain type of problem and then has them practise this method in class and in homework' (pp. 426–7). Such instructional approaches can readily be seen to lead to student disengagement, disinterest and disruptive behaviour, most probably exacerbated by a large majority of the class feeling confused about a subject that lacks meaning, giving rise to further feelings of frustration and boredom. Alarmingly, visits to some middle years mathematics classrooms indicate that such a traditional approach to mathematics instruction still occurs. To promote numeracy, teachers of mathematics need to consider their approaches to instruction to ensure students develop rich conceptual understandings of all mathematics topics, thus ensuring a solid foundation for numeracy is laid.

A further factor impacting upon mathematics instruction in the middle years is the wide variation in students' performance and achievement in mathematics. In a comprehensive study, Siemon et al. (2001) found that typically, in any one middle years classroom, there was as much as a seven-year gap between the highest and lowest performing students. With such a range in performance, catering to the needs of all is difficult.

To promote numeracy, mathematics in the middle years needs to be reconsidered. In the next section, new approaches to mathematics and numeracy in the middle years are described. The positive and negative aspects of each are discussed.

Approaches to promoting numeracy

A range of strategies have been successful in promoting numeracy in the middle years.

Withdrawal

One of the common approaches to 'promoting numeracy' is to withdraw students from the regular mathematics classroom and provide them with a program to promote knowledge and understanding of 'the basics'. Such programs may be structured as self-paced modules and individualised programs. Typically, instruction is via drill and practice exercises and completion of endless worksheets. A major national study into literacy and numeracy programs for at risk students in the middle years found that this was the approach to numeracy in many cases (Luke et al. 2003), with such programs being questioned in terms of their effectiveness in promoting numeracy required for life beyond school, and their relevance to the life worlds of adolescents (Dole 2003).

The withdrawal approach appears to be predicated upon a belief that numeracy is about computational skills (O'Brien 1999), and a belief that a 'back to basics' approach is what is required to improve numeracy. Battista (1999) describes the folly in this approach by using a medical analogy:

> How would you react if your doctor treated you or your children with methods that were 10 to 15 years out-of-date, ignored current scientific findings about diseases and medical treatments, and contradicted all professional recommendations for practice? (pp. 425–6).

The withdrawal approach does suit some learners, however, as they begin to experience success through repetitive practice of algorithmic procedures with consequent reduction in mathematics anxiety. But in a withdrawal mode, the individual is missing out on the mathematics lessons being undertaken by the rest of the class. Thus, being selected for withdrawal classes often becomes a perpetual state of schooling for mathematics instruction.

Another way of catering to the mathematical needs of students in the middle years is to stream classes; that is, to allocate students to particular classes based on performance on a particular measure or series of measures. Zevenbergen (2003a) highlighted the impact of such school practices on students depending upon the stream to which they were allocated. Students in the lower stream openly admitted that they were in the 'dummy' class, and expressed feelings of low self-esteem with respect to their potential achievement in mathematics. These students also presented more challenging classroom behaviours (disinterest, disengagement, disruptive behaviour). Although potentially a beneficial means for promoting mathematics understanding through a better paced curriculum, the reality often is that, once 'classified', students find that movement between class groupings occurs only infrequently, and that instruction in the bottom stream typically reverts to a 'skill and drill' program.

Whole-school approach

Whole-school approaches to middle years have been found to be most successful in promoting learning outcomes in general (Luke et al. 2003). A whole-school approach to numeracy has been found to be successful for learners in the middle years, particularly those deemed at risk (e.g. Perry & Howard 2000; Fletcher et al. 2001; Perry & Fulcher 2003). The features of such programs are their alignment with middle years philosophy—meaningful activities linked to the life worlds of the students, mathematical skill and conceptual knowledge development embedded in life-related problem-solving tasks, group work, encouragement of student discourse, together with a team approach to planning and teaching. The programs also include professional development workshops for teachers and support from management through allocation of school resources to support team planning and collaboration. Such approaches align recommended approaches to mathematics teaching in Australia (e.g. Australian Education Council 1990) and in the United States. In summarising recommendations for mathematics instruction as proposed by the National Council for Teachers of Mathematics (NCTM) in the United States, Schoen et al. (1999) stated:

> [that] instruction should be focused on student investigations of substantial mathematics problems; that the classroom teacher should act as a stimulant, sounding board and guide in that student problem solving; that students should be encouraged to discuss mathematical ideas and discoveries with classroom mates and with that; that the classroom activity should include frequent challenges to students to develop justifications for their ideas and discoveries; that students should be encouraged to use calculators and computers in their mathematical explorations (p. 446).

In whole-school approaches to numeracy, teachers are in a position to reflect more critically upon their practice, to question the positive and negative aspects of traditional methods, while trialling new ideas and strategies.

Integrated curriculum

Middle years principles advocate an integrated curriculum. With respect to mathematics, the promise for students is that the study of mathematics may occur in a repackaged and more palatable form. As stated by Brennan and Sachs (1998), 'an integrated curriculum gives multiple pathways to different traditions and bodies of knowledge, even for those who might not usually "fit" themselves into those disciplinary areas' (p. 21).

An integrated approach underpins the New Basics reform (Education Queensland 2001), currently being trialled in schools in Queensland, where rich tasks are the focus of investigation by students, necessitating an integrated and team-based approach to be undertaken by teachers. New Basics sits comfortably within middle years philosophy and principles in that it involves students in authentic tasks designed to link to their life-worlds, encourages students to take control of their own learning, focuses on promoting integrated and connected knowledge, and necessitates group work and collaborative problem solving. Critics of an integrated approach typically bemoan a 'watered down' curriculum with little focus on discipline knowledge through breakdown of traditional subject demarcation lines. An integrated approach, as advocated by New Basics, is intensive of teachers' time, and this leads to resistance from teachers (Zevenbergen 2003b).

An integrated curriculum has the potential to provide students with a new avenue for developing mathematical understanding and thus to develop confidence, but an integrated curriculum that is designed to promote numeracy requires high levels of teacher expertise. Expert teachers of mathematics are those who can create rich learning environments to optimise deep knowledge and conceptual understanding, where students can apply their knowledge to solving authentic and real tasks. Such teachers are those with high levels of pedagogic-content knowledge (Schulman 1986; Ball 2000) who know the content matter of their subject, together with effective ways to teach it. To ensure an integrated curriculum meets the numeracy needs of students in the middle years, expert teachers of mathematics are required.

Reframing classroom practice

To promote numeracy through the teaching of mathematics requires new approaches in the mathematics curriculum. As whole school numeracy, and an integrated approach require considerable collaboration and support, individual teachers can consider new ideas and approaches to teaching mathematics in their own classrooms without necessarily having to work with others. Woodward (1999) described how one teacher, who was placed with the remedial mathematics class, implemented changes to his traditional way of mathematics teaching with positive results. The beginning point for this teacher and his class was an investigation into the popular music enjoyed by his students, with the purpose of assisting students connect understandings of common fractions, decimal fractions and percentages. The students were asked to conduct a class survey to gather data of favourite bands, and then report their findings on a spreadsheet. Through entering formulae, the data were converted to common and decimal fractions and percentages, which could then be analysed by the students. From this data, the teacher then repackaged typical textbook questions to promote further understanding, such as: 'What if the 12 students that I asked were representative of all Marshall students? There are 720 students in the school. How many would like Pearl Jam?' (pp. 76–7). The students undertook further investigations, including an analysis of McDonald's fries and their packaging, in which they analysed the number of fries per different size packages, and determined what the effect would be if three extra fries were added per serve. This investigation led the students to conclude that such a practice would lead to substantial decrease in profits, which they calculated would amount to tens of thousands of dollars over the year in a number of restaurants. As a result of this investigation, students developed valuable knowledge and understanding of business practices, as well as important numeracy skills.

The sobering message from this story is that although the teacher knew he needed to take a new approach to teaching, 'like many other teachers in charge of mainstreamed remedial classes, wasn't sure how to go beyond the textbook' (Westwood 1999, p. 76), and had to work it out for himself. Professional development of teachers to promote numeracy clearly remains an ongoing need.

Critical numeracy
New approaches to mathematics in the middle years are appearing more frequently in schools and classrooms. The key to such approaches, as highlighted above, is to begin with students' interests. Some of the more obvious starting points are mobile phones, part-time employment, banking, drug awareness, fitness and healthy lifestyles. Through investigations that link to their life worlds, students are in a position to critically analyse their worlds, and thus develop critical numeracy skills. Critical numeracy, like critical literacy, is to use mathematical skills and knowledge to make informed decisions, to become aware of underlying and covert messages that may be enveloped in mathematical terms, text, diagrams, and/or jargon (interpreting data as presented in a variety of modes in our society is an obvious example here), and to act accordingly. Critical numeracy is linked to the notion of empowerment and, beyond basic skills, this must be the goal of numeracy programs. As stated by Ernest (2000):

> . . . complex mathematics is used to regulate many aspects of our lives, e.g. our finance, banking and bank accounts, with very little human scrutiny and intervention once the systems are in place. Only through a critical mathematics education

can future citizens learn to analyse, question, challenge these systems that can distort life chances and reduce freedoms (p. 85).

The Chance and Data strand within the mathematics curriculum (as proposed by the Australian Education Council 1990), is one of the major avenues through which to promote critical numeracy skills. Developing an awareness of how statistical information can be manipulated to add different emphases, depending upon the point a person is trying to make, provides students with analytical skills through which to question information presented. This aspect of critical literacy is sometimes referred to as statistical literacy, and is seen as a major component of numeracy for a 'data-drenched' society (Steen 1999).

Statistical literacy means taking a critical view of information, rather than simply accepting it at face value. Some simple ways to promote students' statistical literacy skills is to take a set of data and manipulate it in various ways to present different messages. For example, a set of seven daily temperatures recorded over a week (23, 18, 22, 19, 24, 26, 17 degrees) can be graphed to show minimal change in weather over the week, or quite varied change in temperature, depending upon the ways the axes are set up. To show minimal variation, the scale on the temperature axis would be small, perhaps marked at 10 degree intervals (see Figure 8.1). To show wide variation, the scale would be large, perhaps marked at 1 degree intervals (see Figure 8.2). In the first instance, the resulting line graph would show a slight change in the line across the week, but basically indicating a steady temperature; the second graph would show an extremely erratic line, zigzagging across the graph.

Figure 8.1 Daily temperature graphed to show minimal variation

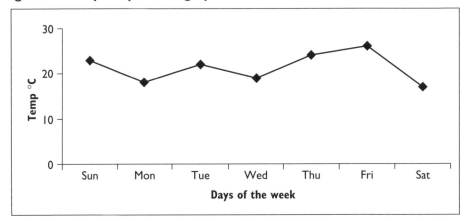

Figure 8.2 Daily temperature graphed to show wide variation

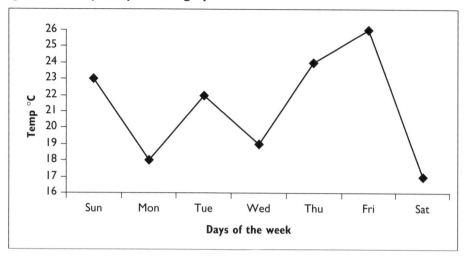

Graphs are extremely powerful in presenting particular messages as they provide a ready image of the data. Another example of a way to manipulate data representation on a graph is to truncate the axis to indicate a large difference, when in effect there is probably a minimal difference. Consider a graph representing government funding for an initiative, say in Education. In one year, the figure could be $80 million. In the following year, the figure could be $70 million. By truncating the money axis to begin at $60 million, rather than zero dollars, and scaling the axis in $5 million, a bar graph will show a significant drop in funding in the second year as the first amount of funding has not been represented to scale. See Figure 8.3 as representation of this.

A further example of manipulating graphs to convey particular messages is the use of pictures, or symbols, to provide a distorted image of statistical information. Consider a graph that uses the image of a piggy-bank to represent savings (Figure 8.4). In the first image, a plump piggy-bank is drawn to match the height of the mark on the vertical axis that indicates savings ($2 million). The second pig's height is double the height of the first pig on the savings axis, and represents $4 million. But even though the second pig's height is only double the height of the first, the overall image presented is of a pig (savings) actually four times the size of the first pig.

This technique can be analysed through investigations into scale drawing, with a preliminary investigation into what happens to the area of a square, for example,

Figure 8.3 Government spending

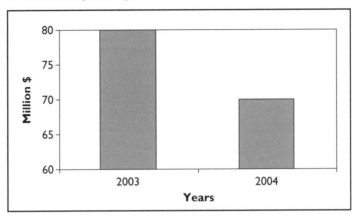

Figure 8.4 Savings

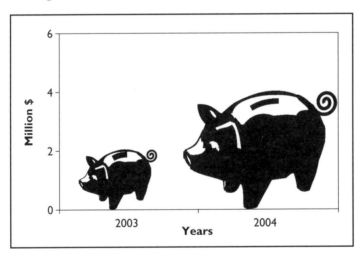

when the side lengths are doubled. An understanding of scale factors assists in distorting picture graphs to show a particular message.

The above three methods for representing data are just a few of the ways to alter the impact of information. Analysing advertisements is another way of promoting students' statistical literacy. Common phrases used in advertising campaigns, such as 'Ninety-nine per cent of women agree . . .,' can be questioned. How many women were interviewed? If the sample consisted of 18 women, how representative is the claim, and would it be possible to attain a measure of 99 per cent? 'Rapid headache tablets work twice as fast': twice as fast as what? Do we know how fast other headache tablets work? 'Laboratory tests prove . . .': if this is the result in concentrated form in a test-tube, what does this mean for consumer use? 'Ninety-nine per cent fat free . . .': what about sugar content?

In many mathematical investigations in the middle years, collection of data is integral to the investigation, thus providing a platform for the development of critical numeracy skills. An example of a real investigation undertaken by students in the middle years is a study into the school tuckshop. The impetus for this investigation was the students' view that the school tuckshop did not sell a wide enough range of food, with the result that many students were breaking school rules and buying food at a shop across the road. The students developed surveys to determine what food most students would prefer. They also conducted interviews with staff, and with tuckshop management. They collated the data and developed an argument for the tuckshop revising its menu. In their final report, they took into account costs to tuckshop management to increase the menu and provide greater choice. Students also visited a range of websites to find information on nutritional value of particular foods and food combinations. As a result of their investigation, the tuckshop menu did alter, and there was a consequent decrease in students leaving the school at lunchtime. From this investigation, the students became aware of the need to have supporting evidence on which to base their claims for change. They also developed an awareness of the nutritional value of particular foods, which resulted in their creating a series of posters to display around the school and near the tuckshop, outlining the nutritional value of the foods sold through the tuckshop.

Another investigation undertaken by a group of students in the middle years was in response to teachers' concerns about the amount of food wastage being witnessed every day. The school brought in a rule that all uneaten food, as well as food wrappings, must be taken home each day. To promote students' awareness of wastage, and of the nutritional value of food, a lunchbox audit was conducted for a week, in which students analysed their lunch in terms of its representation on the food pyramid categories (fruits and vegetables, grains and nuts, meats, dairy, fats and oils), and also rated the packaging of their lunch through a rubbish scale. The rubbish scale assigned units to particular pieces of packaging, with recyclable material having the lowest score, and prepackaged containers the highest score. Students also investigated the costs of prepackaged containers of food, which led to broader investigations of pollution, recycling, buying in bulk, and consideration of the time and efficiency factors that influenced decisions about single-serve portions. From this investigation, students developed an awareness of consumerism, and began to discuss nutrition and recycling in a broader sense.

In another investigation, students from an inner-city school explored a real situation impacting upon them daily, which was how they travelled to and from school. The difference in this investigation to others of a similar nature was that the students considered school travel from the perspective of city bus routes and peak-hour traffic, which they experienced on a daily basis. The majority of students from this particular school lived in locations at a considerable distance. Their investigation included traffic surveys of numbers of passengers in the buses and cars that passed the school gates, surveys of students' transport methods, analysis of bus routes in accordance with the majority of students who attended the school, and the adequacy of bicycle tracks from various locations to their school. The students also measured traffic noise through assigning levels of noise pollution to traffic at different times of the day. This extensive investigation also led to research into fossil fuels and air pollution, and alternative modes of transport. From council data bases, the students located information about population increases in the city, road usage increases in and around their schools over the last decade, and proposals for new transportation routes. This investigation also extended to the study of energy, particularly the production of electricity and the cost of running various electrical appliances around the home. Over the course of the investigation, students collected newspaper articles on new road proposals, and followed government and council discussion on the future of roads to address peak-hour traffic delays that were a daily occurrence. The costs of transportation and use of fossil fuels allowed students to develop greater awareness of their place in the world, and the impact of such usage upon the environment. Their discourse became peppered with suggestions for reducing energy consumption, and they began to question the efficiency of the methods by which they travelled to and from school. In one instance, the students mapped out a new bus route to increase efficiency for the greatest number of pupils in the school, supporting their proposal with evidence based on their research findings.

In a simpler investigation, middle years students analysed the well-known fairy tale of Rapunzel, the princess who was taken by a witch as a child and locked away in a tower with no doors. The only way into the tower was through a window at the top, which posed no problem for the witch, who flew there on her broomstick. A prince riding through the forest heard Rapunzel singing and, realising her plight, set about rescuing her. Rapunzel's hair had grown to an extraordinary length over the years, and she used this to allow the prince to climb up the tower. The investigation posed to the students was to determine how high the tower was, how long Rapunzel's hair was, how many years it would take for her hair to reach this length, and hence determine Rapunzel's age. This investigation resulted in students presenting their findings through visual means, primarily using graphs and/or scale drawings. Although not a real-life situation, through investigating Rapunzel the students developed awareness of persuasive devices used in texts. Another linked investigation involved students interrogating a film showing a bank robbery in which the robbers escaped with an undisclosed sum of money. Through simulation and role play, the students determined the approximate amount of money that could fit into a sports bag, and its approximate mass. From these calculations, they explored the probable distance an average-sized 'bank robber' could run from the crime scene with that amount of money. Such investigations provided a basis for developing referents with which to analyse particular information presented in movies, films, books and the like, with students frequently making comments like: 'As if that could happen!' A further investigation using stimulus from information presented in the media was the birth of septuplets to an American family. From reading the newspaper report, the students were charged with the task of determining how many nappies would be required before these babies became toilet-trained. The students quickly realised that they were dealing with large numbers, and started calculating the cost of disposable nappies compared with cloth nappies. The issue of disposable nappies led to investigation of disposal of such, which resulted in consideration of the environment. Again, the nature of this investigation can be questioned in terms of its relevance to the lives of students in the middle years, but being provided with opportunities to apply mathematical skills and knowledge to interesting situations provides greater chance for numeracy development.

Who is numerate?

Returning to the scenario presented at the beginning of this chapter, who is numerate? The answer, of course, is that all members of the party may be numerate, but to varying degrees. It may appear that the person who mentally split the bill equally is the most numerate, as this person clearly has the necessary skills and confidence. Yet the person who reached for the mobile phone also demonstrated numeracy required in a technological world. Those who avoided the situation may have the skills, but clearly do not have the confidence. And this is a cause for concern, although it appears to be an overly acceptable state of being in our society. As stated by Battista (1999):

> Many adults readily confess, 'I was never any good at mathematics' as if displaying a badge of courage for enduring what for them was a painful and useless experience. In contrast, people do not freely admit they can't read (p. 426).

In saying this, however, we must not reduce numeracy simply to the ability to perform calculations and literacy to being able to read. Numeracy is a state of being along a continuum; clearly, however, confidence is a strong determining factor in a person applying mathematics skills to life situations.

Numeracy benchmarks

To measure school numeracy, the Australian government has mandated that all students in Years 3, 5 and 7 will undertake a standard numeracy (and literacy) test. The tests have been developed to measure the degree to which students in each of these year levels reach National Numeracy Benchmarks (Curriculum Corporation 2000). For numeracy, benchmarks have been developed for three categories: number sense, measurement and data sense, and spatial sense. A list of the numeracy benchmarks is available at the web address: http://cms.curriculum. edu.au.numbench/bench.HTM. The numeracy benchmarks detail the mathematical skills and concepts that are expected of students in each of the three targeted year levels, and thus assist teachers in planning and preparing for numeracy teaching. Descriptions of the numeracy benchmarks are accompanied by further information for teachers that elaborate the benchmarks, and discuss the conceptual basis for them. This information is not only geared to teachers of mathematics, but also to teachers of all subject areas to further support planning for numeracy across the curriculum.

With the advent of the national numeracy benchmarks, the term 'benchmark' has become associated with specific, demonstrable mathematics skills in context. However, 'benchmark' has been prominent in mathematics education literature prior to its new accepted use in Australia. In the mathematics education literature, benchmark is generally used to refer to a personalised referent from which a person can make mathematical judgments. For example, many people use their body to estimate other lengths. Common body benchmarks include knowing that the width of the little finger is approximately 1 cm; that the length of the foot is approximately

30 cm; that a handspan is approximately 20 cm and the width of the palm approximately 10 cm. Some people can relate the measurement of one metre to the distance from the ground to almost their hip. Such benchmarks provide a means to contextualise a situation in the absence of a measuring device. Other benchmarks relating to number include those that assist in determining the size of a collection, such as knowing how large a group of 10 is, a group of 100, and so on. Some people acquire this ability through experiencing particular settings. Attending a major sporting event at a stadium is a way of considering the capacity of the stadium and estimating the number of people in attendance. For example, the Melbourne Cricket Ground has a capacity of approximately 90 000. Attending a major sell-out sporting event there enables a person to experience the size of this number. When smaller crowd numbers are reported in the news, this benchmark can be recalled to provide a basis for contextualising the situation. Other common number benchmarks relate to strategies that assist mental computation. For example, determining a 10 per cent discount on an item priced at $59.90 through rounding to $60 and then dividing by 10 is the application of per cent benchmarks. A further example is mentally estimating that the cost of two items marked at $72 and $35 will give a total of around $100 (plus a bit more) because 3 and 7 make 10. In this case, 10 is used as a benchmark, and readily seeing combinations to 10 (e.g. 1 + 9, 2 + 8, 3 + 7 and so on) provides a solid benchmark for application in the real world. Other examples of real world benchmarks include being able to estimate the time required to undertake particular activities, being able to approximate travelling distances, being able to visualise arrangement and location of objects in the environment, being able to estimate the amount of space an object takes up, and so on.

To promote the development of benchmarks requires a lot of immersion in real situations. The role of the teacher is to draw upon students' life experiences to enable them to contextualise mathematical information within their own personal life-frames. The measurement and spatial examples described above can be assisted through a mathematics curriculum that requires students to become active participants in a range of investigations. For example, to promote the development of a benchmark in relation to the length of one metre, classroom activities can include those where students are actively measuring one-metre lengths and locating familiar objects in their environment that have lengths of one metre. To promote visualisation of objects in space, students can arrange and rearrange collections of items, stacking them and calculating their arrangements. A trip to the supermarket to conduct observations of how particular items are stacked on shelves can promote visualisation skills.

For number benchmarks, students need to be immersed in activities where they are constantly analysing numbers. For example, when they perform any sort of calculation, they should be encouraged to consider whether the answer could possibly be correct, and to give reasons as to why or why not. They need to develop personal checking mechanisms whenever they work with numbers from which they can gauge the reasonableness of their solutions. They need to see numbers in a variety of ways (for example, knowing that 24 is 20 + 4, but is also 14 + 10). Such traits are referred to as number sense in the mathematics education literature. Number sense is defined as an 'at-homeness' with numbers (McIntosh et al. 1992). In the middle years, aspects of number sense include knowing the effect of operating on numbers, having a sense of the relative size of numbers (particularly those beyond 100 000), seeing numbers in flexible ways (for example, that 100 is 90 + 10; 250 is one quarter of 1000), and using a range of strategies when operating with numbers (using a process of rounding and adjusting to calculate, for example, 203 − 68) (Reys 1994).

When considering the national numeracy benchmarks and the term benchmark in a general sense, measures to determine the degree of proficiency with which a person can apply benchmarks take on two different meanings. The national numeracy benchmarks are tested through a pen-and-paper test; other benchmarks, which may or may not relate to the national benchmarks as they are usually personal to each individual and their experiences, often cannot be assessed until the person is in a real-life situation requiring such skills. This highlights the difficulty in assessing numeracy, which in turn relates to the difficulty in defining the actual skills and knowledge required for numeracy in an individual's life.

Conclusion

Numeracy in the middle years is more than good mathematics teaching. It is undertaking real investigations to develop skills, knowledge and dispositions for success beyond school. Numeracy at a whole school level has the promise of a shared vision and common goal, with numeracy development the responsibility of all teachers. Numeracy has its foundations in school mathematics, and issues associated with teaching and learning school mathematics have been highlighted in this chapter. Teachers of all other key learning areas also have a responsibility for promoting numeracy in the middle years. All teachers in the middle years must work together to support and strengthen numeracy growth and development, and this can be assisted by calling into play the 'tremendous energy, creativity, idealism and passion that characterises adolescent young people' (Barber 1999, p. 9).

Questions

1   What would be your reaction to presentation of the bill at the Mexican restaurant evening as presented at the beginning of this chapter? Analyse your reaction to assess your level of numeracy.

2   Compare your own mathematics education to what you have seen in schools today. How many classrooms do you feel actively promote numeracy? Describe the factors that you believe are present in the classrooms to promote or hinder numeracy development.

3   Consider the suggestions for developing numeracy in the middle years of schooling. How real are they to students in this stage of schooling?

4   Is numeracy different from mathematics? Discuss.

5   All teachers are teachers of numeracy. What are the implications of this statement for beginning and experienced teachers, and for mathematics teachers and teachers of other disciplines?

6   How important for numeracy is a positive disposition to mathematics?

9

Bodies and minds

Lisa Hunter and Doune Macdonald

Young people are physical (as are adults) and their physicality plays a large part in who they are and who they can become. Much research has shown the middle years of schooling to be an important time assigned to identity development and physical development while also a time when many young people become less physically active and less engaged in learning at school. There is a danger that with current reforms claimed to be, or heralded as, 'middle years reforms' we risk reinscribing some of the previous problems of traditional schooling by trying to develop the minds and control the bodies of students in their middle years. Alternatively, middle years reform could be an opportunity to revisit some of the taken-for-granteds that underpin schooling, such as Cartesian dualism, and shift to practices that take into account learning as embodied and social. This chapter reviews current research around physical activity, physical education and physicality in order to locate the place of the physical in kids' lives and learning experiences. We want to encourage those who interact with young people in the middle years to consider this research more broadly in schooling, not just in areas that focus explicitly on the physical, such as physical education. We offer suggestions for curriculum development that would take into account this current research and relate it to the middle years of schooling.

The current social, cultural, economic and technological contexts of young people in schools provide complex, unique and challenging circumstances. Particular circumstances in these 'new times' are impacting on schooling in ways that we do not yet fully understand. Globalised economies impact on the nature and possibilities of work and demand new skills of the learner. Information and communication technologies have transformed most workplaces and new kinds of literacies or 'multiliteracies' (The New London Group 1996) are required. In a world of increasing uncertainty and challenge to traditional ways of doing things, organising our lives, and interacting with nature (including our own bodies), young people choose to keep their options open, in turn adding to uncertainty, heightened risk and increased anxiety (Giddens 1991; Mackay 1993).

Research from epidemiology, the biophysical and sociocultural movement sciences, and cultural studies highlights new patterns and issues associated with young people and physical activity, physical education and physicality in these new times. Here we review the following patterns and issues: physical activity engagement and the contemporary political and media response; dominant ways of understanding the physical and ways in which the physical is overlooked; and finally, teaching the physical in ways that promote learning for all students. We conclude that contemporary research provides signposts for good practice that involves the young person being viewed as an embodied self and an active participant in broad-based physical activity contexts. For the work of middle schooling to be supported and successful in increasing student engagement in learning, we *must* attend to physicality across the curriculum as a way to reconceptualise young people and learning.

Physical activity engagement patterns and contemporary responses

The benefit and importance of physical activity that is regular and fun has been well documented. Cavill et al.'s (2001) review of research in health-enhancing physical activity for young people confirms that physical activity *in particular forms* enhances psychological well-being; self-esteem (particularly in disadvantaged groups such as those with learning difficulties); and social and moral development. Physical activity also has the *potential* to decrease obesity and overweight, and chronic disease risk factors (such as metabolic syndromes). Young people should be physically active daily, or nearly every day, through activities associated with transportation, play, sport, physical education and recreation, as well as undertaking at least three sessions a week of moderate to vigorous levels of exertion. This advice comes at a time when more young people than ever are not being physically active, particularly girls (Trost 2003). They are walking to school less, and reducing their participation in organised sport. It is strongly suggested that young people should take part in regular physical activity to optimise physical fitness, current health and well-being, and growth and development; develop active 'lifestyles' that can be maintained throughout adult life; and reduce the risk of chronic diseases of adulthood such as osteoporosis.

The mounting evidence that habitual physical activity positively influences quality of life is connected to enjoyment playing a central role in this relationship. Berger et al. (2002) suggest that physical activity and exercise exert strong influences on one's perception of self. For the most part these are positive influences, but beliefs about gender appropriateness and conceptions of ability have powerful negative influences on beliefs about competence. While the links between self-esteem, identity construction, and mood states such as anxiety and depression are complex, when physical activity is properly used it provides positive benefits to physical self-esteem and facilitates advantageous forms of motivation. However, there is a corresponding caution to increasing the level of physical activity. When used inappropriately it can have negative effects on self-esteem and motivation, and ultimately on participation and engagement. Body image is instrumental in fostering certain behaviours and attitudes to exercise, diet and health. Eating disorders and excessive exercising are often consequences of negative body image. Like physical self-esteem, body image can be influenced by the experiences young people have in sport and physical activity contexts. The fact that many young people have negative experiences related to physical activity and their bodies within school, makes problematic current curriculum and pedagogical practices, as contributing to an undermining of self-esteem in some young people.

School-based physical activity and health work have been present in Australian schools since as early as 1903 (Kirk 1998), in forms of organised exercising, physical and health education, disease control, sport, dental and nutritional programs. Positive school-based physical activity experiences are particularly important for young people from low socioeconomic, minority and rural backgrounds who have reduced access to community-based physical activity due to limitations in terms of money, parental encouragement and transport (e.g. Brown et al. 2001; Wright et al. 2003). The ease of accessibility to young people via schools is argued as a reason to maintain these practices, as noted by Prime Minister John Howard, who 'blamed lifestyle and lack of physical activity in schools for the alarming statistic that 28% of girls and 27% of boys were overweight or obese' (Cole 2004). This prime ministerial response is part of a current media storm around issues of physical activity and childhood obesity. With the Coalition's 2004 election policy promising 'at least two hours of physical activity per week for children in primary and junior high school' (Karvelas & Tobler 2004, p. 13) and Labor's call for a limit on 'junk food' advertising, the language of crisis and cries for urgent political action have captured the federal agenda.

We suggest there is a danger in using physical activity in schools to solve the nation's health problems (Gard & Wright 2001; Gard 2004). As Gard reminds us, 'Lots of things being taken up in schools could be damaging to kids because the focus of physical activity is on body weight . . . I think there are lots of dangerous possibilities to come out of this and we will be picking up the pieces in 10 years' (cited in Karvelas & Tobler 2004, p. 13). Two topical examples are the misuse of physical fitness tests and weight measurements (body mass index, BMI) in school programs. Armstrong and Biddle (1992) argue against fitness testing, given that there are no tests suitable for use in the school environment or that provide valid and objective measures of fitness. Further, fitness testing can be a major contributor to negative attitudes towards physical education (Luke & Sinclair 1991; Armstrong 2002). In similar vein, nutritionists working with diet and weight issues call for content and pedagogies that focus upon health rather than weight or BMI, with a view to engaging rather than alienating young people. Too many young people in the middle years of schooling find it difficult to accept the change in their body weight and composition that is represented by a healthy increase in their BMI. The extreme behaviours that many adopt result in nutritional inadequacies and disordered eating.

Despite schools' and teachers' good intentions in working with issues associated with physical activity and nutrition, the use of 'popular knowledge' rather than knowledge informed by the research can prove to be not only ineffective but also potentially detrimental to student learning and growth (Macdonald 2002; Macdonald & Hunter 2003a, 2003b). For us to respond responsibly in the middle years there is cause to tease out how teachers and students understand and interact with knowledges surrounding physicality, in particular in relation to young people and learning.

Ways of understanding the physical

Although the most valued aspect of schooling is arguably academic 'knowledge about', with certain knowledges prioritised over others, healthy lifestyles and responsible citizenship are nevertheless increasingly included in the goals for schooling. Contemporary views on the body in schools tend to perpetuate a dualism of the mental and physical, of theory and practice, and rely heavily on knowledge generated through the biophysical sciences. Such knowledge not only results in knee-jerk responses to health issues, it also plays into the positioning of physical activity and health as an individual responsibility.

There seems to be a 'commonsense' view that schooling is about educating the mind while at the same time taming the body. This is reflected in the promotion of academic subjects (e.g. senior maths) over practical subjects (e.g. senior drama), in the 'superiority' of cognitive word-based communication (e.g. reading and writing) over other forms of communication (e.g. visual, movement), and in the coupling of 'serious learning' with stationary individual deskwork in classroom settings rather than with physically active work incorporating movement and the body. The underlying assumption being played out in such learning environments reflects that of Cartesian dualism, also referred to as a mind/body dualism and credited to the seventeenth-century philosopher Descartes. Following Descartes and the Enlightenment, rational thought and the intellect have become privileged over other aspects of human nature such as spirituality, emotions and the body. This dualism is partly responsible for student disengagement with schooling in their middle years, when many issues relate to their bodies and relationships with others, including bullying and disconnection with healthy lifestyles (Hunter 2002), and student control, for example through behaviour management, seating, timetables, and even when one may urinate. The irony is that although we privilege the mind, it is the body that has become a central concern in our commodified/capitalist culture (Bunton & Burrows 1995) and a medium for good citizenship (Young 1971, 1998).

The privileging of particular knowledge bases is born out in the Health and Physical Education (HPE) curriculum, which draws largely on biophysical and epidemiological knowledge bases (such as exercise physiology, biomechanics, motor learning, health promotion) that position the body as a biological, bio-mechanical machine that is knowable, and on which predictable changes can be made through practice, training and testing. Further, the application of these knowledge bases is traditionally linked with organised sport. This way of knowing the body alienates some students both from their bodies and from other ways of knowing their bodies, sometimes accessible through subjects such as dance, art, music, manual arts and activities such as tai chi and sport massage.

It follows that if a young person can learn to care for their body/machine, in so doing they are taking individual responsibility for their health and thereby decreasing the likelihood that they will be a burden on the state. In other words, through the education system young people are now expected to become healthy (good) citizens who are informed about risks to their health, self-regulating with regard to their own health practices, and critically reflective of health practices in general (Tinning & Glasby 2002). Students must become lifestyle managers (Peterson & Lupton 1996) in these 'new times' that are characterised by manufactured uncertainty. In this 'risk society' (Beck 1992) the individual is required to constantly monitor healthy body 'inputs' such as good diet and exercise, and to avoid unhealthy products such as tobacco, alcohol and fast foods. Such monitoring feeds into and reinforces the 'cult of the body' (Petersen 1997).

The dominant discourses of biophysical science thus need to be balanced by the appropriate study of the sociological, philosophical and cultural aspects of physical activity, bodies and health, in and beyond the HPE curriculum. Other ways of thinking about issues of mind/body expose contradictions and/or blind spots in the ways in which physical activity, bodies and health are understood. As a good deal has been learned about the social construction of the body—the body as commodity; the body in consumer culture—and about how, in Western societies, the dominant culture is one in which health, self-identity and consumption are increasingly entwined, it is important to make these understandings a priority in what young people do in schools. Recent research with students (Glover et al. 1998; Hunter 2002), supported by middle schooling literature (Beane 1993, 1997a; Barratt 1998b) indicates just how important learning about, and for, personal and social issues is to students' engagement with learning.

Teaching the physical

We have argued against the mind/body dualism and called for a balanced knowledge base to be brought to how the physical is understood. Knowledge generated in the fields of skill acquisition and pedagogy offer in the study of the physical important ways to enhance young people's growth, development, learning and inclusion in the physical culture.

Research suggests that learning by doing at an early age is fundamental to the quality of skill acquisition (Behets 1997). The best time for teaching motor skills is in the pre-primary and primary years, the optimal 'age of readiness' being 5–6 years of age (Blanksby et al. 1995). Young people in their middle years of schooling should continue to be exposed to a variety of physical activities, with specialisation, if it is to occur, generally happening after the age of 13 or 14 years. Further, research in the area of learning physical activity suggests that while the practice of a skill can be optimised through the blocked or repetitive practice of that skill, in the longer term the lack of adaptation required by blocked practice impedes skill development and its applications. This thinking has informed the extensive use of approaches to teaching and learning that develop skilled sequences of movements (for example, gymnastic or dance routines, participation in a game of tennis) rather than isolated skill development.

In physical education settings two pedagogies, Teaching Games for Understanding and Sport Education, highlight student-centred, context-based approaches to teaching and learning. Through the constructivist lens of situated learning, Teaching Games for Understanding has been shown to increase students' learning and rigour in a range of game-like physical activities by starting with the tactical dimensions of the game rather than learning a set of discrete, game-related skills and drills. Similarly, Sport Education seeks to engage young people as players, coaches, managers, scorers, trainers in units of work that involve student-managed competition with a view to better aligning physical education to the sporting community of practice (Kirk & Macdonald 1998).

Moving from sport to the aesthetic, dance educators also argue for constructivist pedagogies that balance both structured and unstructured/creative movement experiences to provide students with the confidence and space to enjoy dance (Gard 2004). Gard and others highlight that dance is a distinctive art form with a potential to serve as both a form of movement and a medium for learning; and as a space for personal inquiry, aesthetic critique, cultural challenges and the understanding of embodied identity. By presenting sequential and open-ended tasks and learning cues, Chen and Cone (2003) found expert teachers in dance were able to help students 'generate divergent original movement responses and refinement of dance quality and expression, which are critical thinking elements' (p. 169).

Other pedagogical approaches such as cooperative learning (Dyson 2002), negotiated curricula (Beane & Brodhagen 1995), developing responsibility through physical activity (Hellison 1995), and violence prevention (Wright 2001) have impacted upon HPE and classrooms more generally. Cooperative learning requires students to develop communication and interpersonal skills that are enacted through appropriate physical gestures (for example, speaking, listening, waiting). These same cooperative skills are self- and group-monitored in social responsibility programs. Using an organised physical activity (for example, karate or basketball) as a medium for learning, small groups of students work together to progressively adopt behaviours that are socially responsible (such as sharing, assisting, praising and leading).

In problem-based pedagogies and integrated curricula, whether in a classroom, pool, outdoor education setting or gymnasium, young people are encouraged to engage with personal, social and environmental issues that are important and meaningful to them (Macdonald 2004), and which have a significant physical dimension. Authentic problems that engage young people in 'real' tasks such as the construction of an artefact or a community-based project provide important opportunities for them to develop life skills that are physically, intellectually, socially and emotionally engaging. Similarly, integrated curricula, consistent with the philosophy of middle schooling, can develop physicality in association with numeracy, literacy, musicality, citizenship and the like. Indeed, within the heuristic of Gardner's (1993) multiple intelligences, musical, spatial, bodily kinaesthetic and interpersonal intelligences are recognised as integral to holistic learning. We argue that these pedagogies, employed within and beyond traditional HPE contexts, offer significant and generative spaces in which 'physical' learning occurs.

While acknowledging that some young people have positive experiences in HPE and school, and healthy attitudes to physical activity and their bodies, many young people still graduate from our schools oppressed by the tyrannies of elitism, sport and cult of the body. Some educators are now arguing for an education system that pays closer attention to the problematic kinds of 'body work' (Armour 1999) that characterise 'typical' classrooms and HPE classes. The practices resulting in the marginalisation and alienation of young people from school have included a lack of personal meaning, lack of control, isolation and a lack of opportunity for young people from different groups, such as those with disabilities. Other reasons why young people can become alienated in activity and sporting contexts relates to the hegemonic masculinities manifested through sexism, homophobia and elitism. Some of these alienating factors, alongside aspects of youth and risk cultures, have led to increased participation in non-traditional, alternate, often unstructured sports such as skateboarding, inline skating, and 'x' sports.

If most of what occurs in school HPE focuses strongly on traditional sport, health as individual work, and physical fitness, while ignoring other concerns relevant to young people such as relationships, gender, sexuality, the pedagogical relationships between students and teachers, and the interaction between pleasure and learning, alienation will continue. To redress this problem a good deal of research within the field of HPE has been directed towards issues associated with differentiating between groups of people on a range of differing bases. Examples are presented in Table 9.1. Much of this research indicates that the understanding of equity and inclusion is still poor, and the resultant practices are limited, within HPE specifically and more broadly within schooling. There is also an indication that the teaching of, and with, difference within a class is at best difficult, and at worst ignored. There is much here to also inform what is happening in the broader middle school curriculum, particularly when we think of learning as embodied.

Table 9.1 Issues and key research

Issue	Key research
Gender	Reay 2001; Penney 2002
Sexuality	Portman & Carlson 1991; Leahy & Harrison 2001; Sykes 2001
Social class	Tinning 1990; Shilling 1993
Disability	De Pauw & Doll-Tepper 2000; Fitzgerald & Jobling 2004
Race	Daiman 1995; Harrison 1995; Sparks & Verner 1995
Age	Tinning & Fitzclarence 1992; Hunter 2002
Physicality	Kirk 1997; Shilling 1993
Religion	Zaman 1997; Kahan 2003

Learning as embodied

The concept that learning is embodied challenges the mind/body hierarchy that comes from theory developed in the sixteenth century. Unfortunately this theory is now mistakenly regarded as common sense, and underpins much of how we work in schools. It is not, however, difficult to conceptualise a person as a whole being where thoughts, emotions, muscles, organs and relationships work together in the form of an individual in order to learn. Helpful concepts such as habitus (Bourdieu 1977), somatic mind (Fleckenstein 2003), and embodied subjectivity (Grosz 1994) attempt to capture a more holistic concept of a person, as well as taking into account the individual's interaction with society rather than as a totally separate entity. Learning occurs via senses and is processed within the individual in various ways. Learning happens by going into the flesh and is then demonstrated through the flesh. It is not helpful to think of the body as separate and inferior to the mind. The material body is also a symbolic representation of many things, such as gender, race, social class, ethnicity, size, etc.—socially constructed categories used to understand who people are. Unfortunately these 'boxes' stop us from recognising the complexity of every person and the positive differences between people. We learn who we are through, with and because of our bodies, and much of this goes on at school. Recognising that learning is 'embodied' means we need to consider:

- what students learn, physically and symbolically, about themselves in our schools;
- the many different ways in which they learn;
- what is learning and how do we notice it? (For example, do we ask students to communicate answers about social justice or do we expect to see them act more justly?); and
- the curriculum of young people in their middle years to incorporate ways of knowing about, by and for their bodies, both materially and symbolically.

When students spend so much time trying to understand themselves, their peers, their world, and their place in the world (Beane 1995, 1997a; Hunter 2002), and how this is about their physical and symbolic body, we owe it to them to pay attention!

Conclusion

Education and schooling are charged with ensuring good health for our young people although in often ad hoc, narrowly conceptualised or ill-defined spaces in the curriculum and the general life of the school. Where responsibility is posited with school principals and teachers who are not fully aware of contemporary and broad-based research in the field of physical activity and health, inappropriate or alienating practices may ensue. In saying this we acknowledge health problems associated with sedentary lifestyles and problematic eating patterns in our young people. Much has been researched and written about the problematic but assumed positive relationship between physical activity, fitness, sport and health (see for example, Tinning 1990; Trost 2003; Hunter 2004) and the negative effects of individualistic, competitive and fitness-oriented HPE programs (see for example, Kirk & Colquhoun 1989; Gard & Wright 2001; Evans et al. 2004). Further, as noted in the introduction, young people are physical and their bodies play a large part in who they are and who they can become. For us to deny this and continue to see students in their middle years of schooling as minds to work with and bodies to be controlled, and young people as 'unfinished' or 'deficient', 'hormones on legs', 'between childhood and adulthood', will only further their alienation and disengagement with current practices, structures and philosophies in schools. Our positions have implications for curriculum and the practices and education of teachers in the middle years. We implore all educators to re-evaluate how they see the physical and, in physical activity and HPE contexts, to take on board contemporary knowledge that provides pathways for engaging and inclusive practices.

Questions

1   What are the different ways we think about the physical?
2   What does the research tell us about physical activity engagement and young people in their middle years of schooling?
3   How have you learned to be physical? What values have you embodied?
4   What are some practices you could use in your teaching to pay attention to the broad range of issues associated with being physical for young people?
5   How might HPE specialists become a productive part of any middle years team?
6   How might HPE be reshaped as a subject or key learning area to acknowledge the broader agenda of physicality that students indicate are important to them?

Acknowledgments

Sections of this article come from previous work between the authors, Professor Richard Tinning and Dr Trish Glasby. Dr Lisa Hunter was employed at the University of Queensland, Schools of Education and Human Movement Studies at the time this chapter was prepared.

10

Integrating the curriculum

John Wallace, Grady Venville and Léonie J. Rennie

Integration is a widely promoted middle school curriculum reform strategy. In this chapter we draw on our observations of Australian middle schools to propose some new ways of thinking about integration. In the first section we describe and exemplify six different forms or types of integration—synchronised, cross-curricular, thematic, project-based, school-specialised and community-focused. The second section looks at the various knowledge interests, or ends-in-view, that may be pursued in integrated teaching. Three interests, the technical, the practical and the critical (Habermas 1971) are used to analyse two case examples. The third section describes our theoretical stance on integration, based on what is termed a 'worldly' curriculum perspective (Venville et al. 2002). A worldly perspective is one which recognises the legitimacy and importance of the various forms and interests, and the need for an appropriate balance among them. This perspective is also pragmatic, acknowledging the contribution of technical or disciplinary knowledge in solving practical problems and the importance of sometimes acting critically to resolve personal and community needs. We also propose an integrated and worldly teaching framework involving five intersecting elements. Finally, we acknowledge the challenges faced by teachers and summarise our ideas about how teachers can work towards incorporating integrated curricula into their practices.

In one form or another, curriculum integration is firmly on the middle school reform agenda. In Australia, and internationally, there are calls for more relevant middle school curricula that reach across and beyond traditional subject boundaries. The reform agenda is driven by new ways of thinking about knowledge and knowing, and concerns about an increasingly diverse (and often alienated) middle school population. An integrated approach, it is argued, places the learner at one with nature; entwined and implicated in local and global conditions, large and small (Davis et al. 2000). Such curricula should focus on big curriculum ideas, based on problems or issues of personal and social significance in the 'real' world (Beane 1996). These big curriculum ideas should form the organising centre of the middle school curriculum with other components linking or jigsawing into them. Under an integrated approach, students are provided with opportunities to engage with and make sense of those ideas in learning communities, to problem solve and, importantly, to act thoughtfully on their new understandings.

While these broad arguments and components form a useful framework for curriculum planning, teachers are still faced with the practical challenges of incorporating these new interdisciplinary forms into their classroom communities. The challenges, according to Shulman and Sherin (2004), are fourfold:

- devising, adapting and planning instruction around big curriculum ideas;
- jigsawing interlocking subtopics or disciplinary-based concepts into the larger ideas;
- bringing together subjects (and teachers) with different curricular traditions; and
- implementation of the new curriculum in (classroom) communities of learners.

We believe that these four challenges permeate the deliberations of teachers and others concerned with middle school curriculum change.

In this chapter, we draw on our own work with schools to explore the range of ways that teachers meet the challenges of integrating the curriculum. We describe our observations of curriculum integration in practice using a conceptual framework involving two dimensions, which we call forms and interests. The term 'forms' refers to the type, style or particular means of scoping and sequencing the curriculum around the big ideas referred to above. 'Interests' refers to the end-in-view or goal of teaching, be it subject understanding, problem solving or political action. These two dimensions, we argue, are different but complementary. One form of integration, for example, a thematic form, may involve multiple interests depending on the instructional sequence and the emphasis and interests of the teacher and students at the time. Alternatively, a particular curriculum interest may be achieved by adopting a number of integration forms. We describe and provide examples of several forms and interests of integration in Australian middle schools, show how these fit within what we call a worldly perspective on integrated practice, and how they might address the challenges of implementation.

The forms of integration

In this section we describe and exemplify six forms of integration based on our observations of middle schools over the past several years (Venville et al. 1999). While these six forms are broadly sequenced from subjects taught 'separately' to subjects taught 'together', it should be emphasised that no particular hierarchy is intended in this ordering. Neither is it suggested that these forms exhaust the possibilities for integration. Each form has in common a set of big ideas (admittedly some bigger than others) around which instruction is organised. Under each form of integration, we provide an explanation and a brief snapshot of integration in practice.

Synchronised approach

Synchronised approaches involve the teaching of similar content and processes in separate subjects across the middle school. Under this approach, there is a correlation between elements of the middle school curriculum that remain separately taught, although often at similar times. This is an example of an interdisciplinary approach where the connections are planned in advance and made clear by the teachers. Typically, it involves teachers from different subject areas identifying points of connection between pre-existing topics, explicitly drawing the links and teaching in a similar manner, sometimes using common tasks or assignments. These points of connection can include both big and small curriculum ideas. Examples include the concept of hypotheses in science and mathematics, graphing in mathematics and social studies, and design in clothing and technology.

> The middle school mathematics and science teachers at Duncraig Senior High School collaboratively developed concept charts to identify where integration could occur. Every six or seven weeks, or about twice each term, the Year 8 mathematics teacher involved her students in an integrated mathematics and science investigation. Examples of such investigations included pendulum motion and a road traffic investigation at a local street intersection, with students developing a hypothesis, a procedure and evaluating their final assignment. The science and

mathematics teachers used the same framework for designing and writing up investigations. Another example of linking the two subjects was the synchronised teaching of chi square analysis in mathematics and Punnett square problems in genetics.

Cross-curricular approach

A cross-curricular approach to integration involves the incorporation or harmonisation of broad skills, concepts or attitudes across separately taught elements of the middle school curriculum. While this approach has some commonalities with a thematic approach, it differs in that it is generally more fundamentally embedded across the curriculum. A cross-curricular issue will generally serve as a lead motive or *leitmotif* for teaching and learning. These big ideas are often about important life skills such as literacy, numeracy, critical thinking, problem solving and computing, or behavioural skills such as working cooperatively and resolving conflict.

At Wananami Remote Community School, English, as Standard Australian English (SAE), is taught as a second language. There is a LOTE program which teaches Ngarinyin, the Indigenous language of the area, which, although spoken among adults in the community, is generally not known by the children, even though they have the cultural background for this. The home language, which is usually their first language, tends to be Kriol. All of the integration between subjects in the middle school (Years 8–10) was done via language. Rather than linking the separate subjects explicitly with each other, the middle school teacher (whose training is in languages) tied up all other subjects through language. In science, during classwork on space, students looked at the Hale-Bopp comet and linked it with the stories of the Wandjina (Wandjina Gorge is some distance away). They discussed time and space, its vastness and where humans fit. The students found this difficult but their reactions were interesting in terms of how they placed themselves in time and space. The students also made benches out of local natural wood, using photography to record the sequence of work. This project was also linked with language, as the trees had both Ngarinyin and English names. Specialist words used in design and technology and photography became list words in English and the procedure for building the benches was written up as one of the genres in English. As in other classes, most of what was done related to language one way or another.

Thematic approach

A thematic approach to curriculum integration usually involves linking various middle school subjects into a particular theme or common point of focus. The theme is usually selected in advance by groups of middle school teachers to run for a set period, perhaps a term or a semester. Typically, the disciplines are taught separately in different classrooms, with teachers and students expected to make the connections back to the theme. Sometimes classes are brought together for a culminating thematic event, such as an excursion. Under this form of integration, the thematic connections are often well planned and explicitly made, other times they are incidental and result from opportunistic teaching moments. Either way, thematic approaches provide occasions for middle school communities to share some common language and understandings around some multidisciplinary big idea. Examples of possible themes include differences, decision making, the Olympics, relationships, systems, communication, popular culture, cooperation, Earth and people, and resources.

> The middle school (Years 7–9) at Ballajura Community College was configured into several multi-learning teams, each team consisting of six teachers and 160 students. Teachers in each team collaboratively planned integrated modules of work for a term around a common theme. One such theme was called 'My Heritage', incorporating such concepts as mathematics and culture, famous Australian scientists, food and culture, changing attitudes to health, biographical writing, family trees, and culture and the arts. For the most part, subjects were taught separately, although occasionally classes were combined for the teaching of certain concepts. There was also considerable sharing of resources and ideas. The culminating focus of the module was a theme day, designed to highlight the term's activities. Visitors from the wider school community and the school administration were invited to the theme day and students exhibited individual and group work and developed activities related to the theme. In the case of the heritage module the theme day was Anzac Day, incorporating a remembrance service, student plays, story and poetry readings from the First World War, and a morning tea prepared by the students and served to guests.

Project-based approach

A project-based approach involves the deliberate organisation of the middle school curriculum around a project or series of projects in which the subject boundaries are blurred. Integration in this form is seen as a culminating event requiring the application and assembly of an array of knowledge and skills that might come from different subjects. This is an interdisciplinary approach where the subjects are interconnected beyond a theme or issue, and where the connections are explicitly made and understood by the students. Often, project-based approaches are organised around the technology process of design, make and appraise, with links particularly to science, mathematics, engineering and materials. However, projects may also centre on other fields, such as food, the arts, social studies, health, English and Languages Other Than English (LOTE), among others. Examples of big project ideas are playground design, family histories, school productions, healthy lifestyle campaigns, raising small animals and bridge-building activities.

Swanbourne Senior High School used a technology-based project to integrate science, mathematics and technology with a Year 9 student cohort over a 12-week period. The project brief required students to 'design and produce an electric powered vehicle that can climb a gradient on the standard test track faster than anyone else's'. The students were taught separate discipline-related material by their subject teachers and provided with 'common' time to work in groups to design, make and evaluate their models. The technology research component involved traction options, materials and construction techniques, motor mounting options and power transmission systems. The science research component investigated friction, gears and pulleys, torque and power transfer, and how scientific trials influenced the students' choice of traction, gearing and drive options. In mathematics the research component examined the effects of changing variables on standard Lego model hill-climbers and recording, presenting and analysing group results from the time trials. The project culminated with a 'formal' competition between groups.

School-specialised approach

Under this approach to integration, a middle school (sometimes in concert with the primary and senior school) adopts a long-term curriculum commitment to a particular specialisation. This approach does not rely for its survival on the enthusiasm and interest of individual teachers, but rather embeds the specialisation into the staffing and infrastructure of the school. School specialisation (and the accompanying big idea/s) is intended to permeate the life of the school. The specialisation is likely to be a subject in its own right, have explicit links to other subjects, and involve related school-wide activities at various points in the school year and throughout the middle school. Examples of school specialisation approaches to integration include horticulture and performing arts.

South Fremantle Senior High School, a coastal high school, developed a marine studies specialisation over a decade. Marine studies was taught as a component of other regular subject courses in the middle school years (Years 8–10), drawing on a school-based resource and textbook written by the teachers. Each of the 'core' subject areas taught one specified unit of marine studies to each year level each year. For example, Year 8 students studied weather and oceans in society and environment; dangerous creatures, seawater properties, pests and seabirds in science; boating in technology and enterprise, and water safety and snorkelling in physical education. Year 9 marine studies students studied coastlines, trashing the sea and shipwrecks in society and environment; waves, currents, tides and seawater quality in science; fishing, fisheries and food from the sea in technology and enterprise; and first aid in physical education. Where appropriate, English and mathematics teachers also referred to the theme, for example, writing essays on a marine topic.

Community-focused approach

Community-focused approaches to integration are those that reach out beyond the school into the broader community. They often involve a futures component, where middle school students imagine better ways of doing things and seek to harmonise their own needs with those of the community. Community-based approaches are similar in some respects to project-based approaches, in that they bring the disciplines together to tackle or 'solve' some problem or issue. However, community-based approaches have the potential to be more transdisciplinary, starting from a real-life community problem, rather from within one or other discipline. A big idea such as water, for example, could be examined from a community perspective, considering such influences as social, political, economic, media, global, environmental and technological. Ideally, a community-based approach goes beyond a theoretical consideration of a problem, involving also some individual or concerted action on the part of students, such as tree planting or writing letters to the local media.

The middle school mathematics and social studies teachers at Armadale Christian College initiated a joint community-based project on the world's north–south inequities. The project was conducted over a three-week period including a total of 30 lessons (four social studies lessons and six mathematics lessons per week). Students worked in groups to collect, analyse and display data comparing the resources and environment of one developed and one developing country. Analyses included various statistical treatments such as mean, mode, median and standard deviation, as well as qualitative comparisons. The students were required to present their data in both graphical and descriptive forms. They were asked to conjecture about the implications of their findings and consider ways of contributing positively to the north–south dialogue. Findings were reported in the form of portfolios.

The interests of integration

The notion of curriculum interests draws heavily on the work of Habermas (1971), who distinguished among the interests of the empirical-analytic sciences, the hermeneutic-historical sciences and the critical sciences. These three sets of interests are often referred to as the *technical* interest, concerned with rule-like regularities; the *practical* interest, concerned with relating and communicating; and the *critical* interest, concerned with political action. Habermas also referred to two aspects of the practical interest, the personal (making personal meaning of situations) and the problem-solving (resolving practical problems).

Here we illustrate the different interests by reference to two middle school cases, one an illustration of community-focused integration and the second an example of the project-based form. The first case, described in more detail in Lloyd and Wallace (2004), involved a class of Year 9 middle school students in a long-term study of fresh water ecology and the fresh water needs of South Australian residents. The second case, described in detail in Venville et al. (2000), involved students designing, constructing and evaluating the performance of a solar-powered boat.

Technical interest

The technical interest in curriculum integration refers to the need for students to come to a better understanding of the techniques, ideas and concepts behind the topic. It involves a serious engagement with the canons of knowledge in the various subjects, attending to the interest of knowing how the world works from various disciplinary standpoints.

In the fresh water ecology case, wetland management was a major focus. As Lloyd and Wallace (2004) explained, the middle school students became involved in a scientific study of aspects of the nature of water, water quality (chemical and biological), types of micro- and macro-invertebrates, aquatic plant life and macro-fauna, and ecological aspects such as energy transfer. Students also examined the consequences of land clearing on water salinity, the effects of degrading riparian zones, the effects of altering food chains, the problems associated with introducing exotic species, and the effects human lifestyles can have on wetlands. Associated concepts included social phenomena such as the nature of human communities and political institutions, the economics of water supply and water conservation, and the technical requirements of preparing environmental impact statements.

In the solar-powered boat example, three Year 9 teachers collaborated to synchronise and integrate the content and teaching processes in the three learning areas of science, mathematics and technology. One of the components of the project required students to tabulate the current, voltage and power for several circuits for various solar cell combinations. As Venville et al. (2000) explained, during science, students were taught the concepts of current, voltage, resistance and power, and circuitry. They were asked to set up their circuits and test with a multimeter the cells in series, in parallel and in combination of both series and parallel. During mathematics, the students were taught how to read a sun chart for latitude 32°S (Perth's latitude) so that they could work out where the sun would be at the appropriate time on the final testing day. In technology, the students were introduced to design and construction techniques, properties of materials, and the importance of testing and evaluation.

While the nature of these examples may seem self-evident, the reality is that choosing the appropriate depth and breadth of technical treatment is not always easy. While science teachers, for example, may feel an obligation to teach the detailed physics, chemistry or ecology of water, these aspects may not always be essential for a good understanding of the broader topic of wetland management. Moreover, a science teacher's view of what is important technical knowledge is likely to be different from that of a social studies teacher or of a student. As Shulman and Sherin (2004) point out, the direct connection between the content taught and the bigger idea is not always apparent, particularly at the beginning of a topic. Many questions remain. How much (and what kind of) technical knowledge? Who decides? How does this knowledge jigsaw into the bigger curriculum idea?

Practical interest

The practical interest refers to the manner in which students make personal sense of the topic at hand, how they solve problems and communicate their ideas. The emphasis here is on personal and communal sense making, finding the links between and across different discipline areas and with students' worlds, testing new ways of doing things, and working with others.

The water quality topic presented many possibilities for exploring the practical interest (Lloyd & Wallace 2004). Students considered the past, present and possible future use of wetlands and rivers, including Indigenous and European use. Water management practices by local officials, the views of environmental advocates, and media and government reports were also examined. Students considered the societal, environmental and technological impacts of various water-management strategies. Futures wheels and cross-impact matrices were used to assist students to develop a personal and arguable rationale about water use in their local setting.

The practical interest was also evident in the solar-powered boat example, where students worked with peers to make links between technical knowledge and practical problem-solving situations. According to Venville et al. (2000), this practical interest was particularly evident at three critical decision points in the boat's construction, namely hull design, circuit design and solar cell orientation. In designing the hull, students employed scientific and technological principles to build a stable boat capable of carrying a load of solar panels and a motor, and being propelled at optimum speed. Students were also required to use their scientific understandings to test various series and parallel circuits to help them decide on a configuration to provide their motor with maximum power output. Drawing on their mathematics understandings, students also needed to decide on the most suitable mount for their solar panels so that the optimum angle to the sun could be achieved on the testing day.

In each of the above examples, there was ample evidence of discussion, sourcing alternatives, debate, disputation, justification and testing of ideas. The practical interest is also a place where the solutions and traditions offered by the technical interest are tested against one another. In the solar boat project, for example, students found that technical scientific and mathematical knowledge did not always offer easy solutions to the messy practical problem of boat design. Frequently, it was the methods of technology, with its practical traditions of design, make and appraise, that provided a way forward. This observation speaks to another of Shulman and Sherin's (2004) challenges, that of bringing together subjects (and teachers) with different curricular traditions.

Critical interest

The critical interest involves questioning current practices, considering how those practices may be changed, and taking personal or political action to achieve changes in the status quo. The emphasis here is on examining the taken for granted, achieving consensus and finding a balance between personal, community and future generational needs.

This interest, according to Lloyd and Wallace (2004) is about shared decision making. In the water quality example, students developed ideas about how they could make a difference and devised strategies and action plans for getting there. This was a shared and collective task based on an informed view of the issues they had studied. Actions included writing an article for a local newspaper, producing a display for the school library, and getting involved with a local action group or the school 'Waterwatch' or 'Frogwatch' programs. However, as Lloyd and Wallace

(2004) point out, the extent of student involvement was not the greatest concern. Rather, the critical interest was about students contributing meaningfully and tangibly towards a better future for themselves and for others.

The critical interest is less evident in the solar-powered boat example. However, one could imagine a critical component involving students in discussions and actions around alternative energy sources, such as solar power, and the emissions caused by diesel-powered boating and shipping. Alternatively, students could investigate and consider their own possible futures in science and technology, including careers in marine or electrical engineering, or some aspect of boating as a hobby.

In pursuing the critical interest, we are faced with the continuing problem of linking the interest with the big curriculum ideas. Some big ideas, particularly environmental ideas such as wetland management or social concerns such as ethnic conflict or abortion, have obvious critical components. Indeed, some commentators (for example, Wilson 1998) argue that the curriculum should be largely guided by these big critical issues facing humankind, including arms escalation, overpopulation, the greenhouse effect and endemic poverty. However, there is also strong justification for incorporating big ideas that lend themselves to a more technical or practical treatment. These ideas could be technological, as in the solar boat project, mathematical, historical, literary, artistic or otherwise. As we have illustrated in the various forms of integration, some ideas are bigger than others, and some strategies for implementing those ideas are bolder than others. The choice of idea and strategy depends on the context, experience and the needs of the community of learners.

A worldly perspective on integration

Often the literature depicts curriculum integration as having a distinct and separate structure compared with traditional discipline-based subject approaches to curriculum. A strong temptation is to postulate two paradigms, a discipline-based paradigm and an integrated paradigm, situated at either end of a continuum. Some authors propose a curriculum structure based on this model, with different 'degrees' of integration at different points along the continuum; moving gradually into higher degrees of integration as more connections are made between subjects. The terms multidisciplinary, interdisciplinary and transdisciplinary are derived from this approach, and each of the different forms referred to earlier could well be categorised in this way. The concern with this approach is twofold. Firstly, it presupposes an integration hierarchy, where some kinds of integration are better than others, and where teachers' progress to 'superior' forms may be measured. Secondly, it assumes a particular view of knowledge itself, where integrated knowledge is said to stand separately from other discipline-based forms of knowledge.

Our view is that curriculum integration embraces many forms and many interests. We call this a worldly perspective on integration (Venville et al. 2002), which we believe reflects a holistic or unitary view of knowledge. This perspective recognises the legitimacy and importance of the different curriculum forms and interests and their contributions to knowledge. We acknowledge, for example, that disciplinary or technical knowledge interests present powerful tools for representing and understanding the world and for solving practical and critical problems. But a worldly perspective also invites teachers and students to view the curriculum from whole to part, with big issues, concerns or interests becoming the organising framework rather than serving as illustrations of disciplinary concepts.

To elaborate, we draw on the work of Lloyd and Wallace (2004) to propose an integrated and worldly teaching framework involving five intersecting elements:

- selecting the topic around a big curriculum idea;
- eliciting students' prior understandings;
- learning about the way the world works (the technical interest);
- making personal sense and solving practical problems (the practical interest); and
- acting thoughtfully to find harmony between personal, community and future generational needs (the critical interest).

These five elements could form the basis for a sequential 'topic plan', but are more appropriately used as referents for curriculum planning. An elaboration of each element can be found in Table 10.1. The first element is the big idea itself. As we have illustrated in the several forms of integration described earlier, big ideas can range from overarching themes, issues or projects, such as conflict, narrative, poverty, genetic engineering or Aboriginality, to important interconnecting links between subjects, such as computer or graphing skills, writing genres or critical thinking. Selection of big ideas will be guided by middle students' needs in terms of life-skills and interests, and important community issues, both local and global.

Eliciting students' prior knowledge is the second element. The focus here is to examine students' backgrounds, experiences and understandings with respect to the big ideas contained in the topic. This helps to identify and define the topic as perceived by the students. The aim here is to acknowledge students' viewpoints, establish the topic as an important area of study and provide a foundation for topic planning. Various teaching strategies can be used to elicit students' prior understandings, including brainstorming, futures imaging, and stating and critiquing viewpoints.

The third to fifth elements of a worldly perspective involve attending to the various knowledge interests, the technical, the practical and the critical. As we have seen in the examples described above, the balance among these three will depend largely on the nature of the big idea or topic. Some ideas will lend themselves to a greater emphasis on the critical (for example, community-focused), others on the practical (for example, project-based), etc. Generally speaking, however, the various interests should be seen as building blocks in integrated teaching and learning. Firstly, students' opinions and understandings about the big ideas need to be informed by a solid foundation of technical knowledge; that is, knowledge about how the world works from various disciplinary standpoints. Secondly, students need to make sense of, and test out, new understandings by undertaking practical inquiry and problem-solving activities. Finally, students act on their new understandings by seeking ways of balancing personal, community and future needs. Each of the three interests is guided by the kinds of curriculum questions and teaching strategies proposed in Table 10.1.

Conclusion

Theoretically, curriculum integration holds considerable potential for middle schooling because it is focused around interesting and important big ideas that promote wholeness and unity rather than separation and fragmentation. Practically, integration is beset by several enduring curriculum challenges. These challenges, described by Shulman and Sherin (2004), include those of selecting appropriate big ideas, jigsawing the disciplinary 'bits' onto these ideas, bringing separate subjects together and implementing effective teaching strategies. Even the most accomplished teachers, we believe, are challenged because they are asked to do different things with the disciplines, learn new kinds of pedagogical content understandings, and often work outside the dominant disciplinary culture.

In seeking a practical resolution of these challenges, in this chapter we have argued for a moderate or pragmatic approach to integration encompassing a variety of forms and interests. In each of the examples provided, the choice of integrating idea, the means of jigsawing, the 'separateness' or 'togetherness' of the subjects, and the teaching strategies selected, were derived from the needs of

Table 10.1 A teaching framework incorporating a worldly perspective on curriculum integration

Curriculum element	Curriculum focus	Curriculum questions	Forms of integration	Strategies
Big idea	Selecting the topic	What life skills do students need? What issues are of immediate concern to students? What are the big local/global issues?	All forms	Mapping existing curriculum documents, identifying community issues and current affairs, surveying students and parents
Prior knowledge	Eliciting students' prior understandings	What are students' backgrounds, experiences and understandings?	All forms	Brainstorming, elicitation, futures imaging, critiquing viewpoints
Technical interest	Learning about the way the world works	What essential technical knowledge will best prepare students?	All forms	Direct instruction, reading, field trips, practical activities
Practical interest	Making personal sense and solving practical problems	What kinds of (guided) inquiry will help students to make sense of the idea?	Potentially all forms, particularly project-based, thematic and cross-curricular	Guided inquiry, experimentation, problem solving, creative writing, model building
Critical interest	Acting thoughtfully	What kinds of actions are appropriate for this group of students?	Potentially all forms, particularly community-focused and school-specialised	Community projects, letter writing, debates, theme days

the individuals involved, the purpose of the curriculum and the nature of the school setting. Moreover, our perspective on integration—a worldly perspective—recognises the legitimacy of the different knowledge interests and the need to find an appropriate balance among those interests. This kind of approach recognises the practicalities of curriculum change and the challenges faced by teachers. We believe that it also provides a promising way forward for middle school teachers to test their own ideas about incorporating elements of integrated curricula into their practices.

Questions

1   The word 'integrate' is derived from the Latin *integrare*, which means 'make whole'. How does this influence your own understanding of the meaning of the term 'curriculum integration'?

2   Think about an example of curriculum integration from your own experience as a student or teacher in a middle school setting. Which of the different forms best describes your experience?

3   Think about another example of curriculum integration from your own experience that included a balance of the technical, practical and critical interests. Describe how this worked.

4   Provide a critique of the notion of a worldly perspective as outlined in this chapter. What are the advantages and disadvantages of thinking about integrated curricula in this way?

5   Generally speaking, this chapter offers pragmatic rather than radical curriculum examples and solutions. What is your own position on middle school curriculum change?

6   Choose one of Shulman and Sherin's (2004) four curriculum challenges and propose a possible response to the challenge.

7   Sketch out a brief plan of an integrated topic using the framework proposed in this chapter.

Acknowledgments

We thank the teachers and students from the schools referred to in this chapter for inviting us into their classrooms and allowing us to observe and describe their work. School names were used in the research with the permission of the teachers and principals.

11

Negotiating curriculum

Lisa Hunter and Nicola Park

The negotiation of a curriculum between students and teachers can happen at a number of levels—from the students' selection of an assignment topic through to their input into the whole school curriculum. Research suggests that students' learning is more effective and rewarding if they have a 'voice' in and ownership of aspects of the curriculum and the teaching/learning process. This chapter explores the concept of negotiation and democratic schooling through curriculum, pedagogy and assessment. After identifying the ideas and practices that relate to negotiation we discuss the levels and spaces available for negotiation. One curriculum model illustrates how a curriculum might be negotiated before we describe in more depth a specific example taken from practice. We finish with some of the issues that might be worth consideration by those entering into negotiation.

Negotiation: What is it and what has gone before?

With a focus on democratising schools, civics and citizenship education, and an upsurge in interest in schooling for the middle years, it is important to be able to discuss student perspectives as the basis from which negotiation in action may be taken, both for and by students, so that they have an input into framing their own futures, rather than being passive recipients of an education created by adults and adult perspectives of students.

We argue for students' role in the learning environment (class/school) to be shifted from that of 'educational or learning object (that is, treated by the teacher, professionally or pedagogically, as an object which learns) to the [student] as co-inquirer' (Young 1992, p. 88) through democratic processes that include negotiation.

Roberts (1998) asks, 'What should we do as teachers when we find out that students' questions about themselves and the world are specific and deep and the school curriculum, by comparison, is broad and narrowly delivered?' Do we, as experienced eductors, impose topics of study for our students, or do we choose to support them to wonder at the world, to find responses to their own questions about the local and global issues, and to build their skills of active citizenship? Along with those who focus upon schooling for the middle years in Australia, negotiated curriculum, students as researchers, democratic classrooms, joint curriculum design and student networks, we would extend Roberts' challenge to include supporting students in researching and designing their own curriculum and influencing the various levels of their education.

We suggest that, through the use of negotiation by and for students, within the classroom and school environment, a greater awareness of the complexity and diversity present would inform adult decision makers at the very least, but that shared, informed decision making between all stakeholders should be the ultimate goal. As the idea of democratic schooling and student participation underpins a number of other negotiation-related 'initiatives' within schools, it is useful to firstly explore these to realise that many of these ideas have already been practised, although brought to the fore currently through the middle schooling movement.

Student networks

Student forums, school parliaments and student councils are becoming more prolific and vocal within schools as well as on a state and national level. Organisations such as the Professional Association of Student Representative Council Teacher/Advisors (PASTA) have also emerged to support programs of student participation, representation and leadership. Unfortunately, Mellor (1998) reports an air of cynicism among students concerning their political participation:

> For most of them there is no point in trying to participate and get involved in influencing decisions . . . it will get them into trouble with administrators and teachers, have them offside with some of their peers, create havoc within classrooms where they should be doing real school work, distract them from their exams, and it's a waste of their time anyway, because schools don't want students to be part of any

real decision making . . . they are not convinced they will be listened to by their seniors (p. 5).

Despite this disturbing, yet unsurprising perception (and the reality within schools), practical successes have also been reported (see for example, Holdsworth 1999) where students have taken on roles with various degrees of responsibility and power.

Democratic classrooms

The meaning and use of the word 'democracy' is presently ambiguous and surrounded by rhetoric within political as well as education circles. But this is not something new. In 1916, Dewey was speaking about democracy and education. Nearly a century on, the coupling of the two words might seem to be an oxymoron. Learning about democracy (as opposed to practising it) has been firmly situated in the English and Social Studies curricula in Australia, both in the past (Hepburn 1983) and again in the new curricula (e.g. Queensland School Curriculum Council Study of Society and Environment Syllabus 1999). At the national level the *Discovering Democracy* kit (Curriculum Corporation 1998) was launched in schools as a response to government perceptions that our students are not well enough informed in government, democracy and citizenship. It is still questionable as to whether the theory of democratic schools and classrooms has moved any closer to practice. Pearl and Knight (1999) go so far as to submit that democratic classrooms are necessary to ensure students become responsible, informed citizens and effective problem solvers in order to respond to the wider problems of the world.

Beane and Apple (1995) propose that democratic schools involve two lines of work: democratic structures and processes to allow for all stakeholders to participate in the process of decision making (and change the conditions that create inequity), and a democratic curriculum, where 'official' and 'high status' knowledge is not taken as truth but recognised as 'socially constructed, that it is produced and disseminated by people who have particular values, interests, and biases' (p. 13). This suggests the need for supporting teachers and students to construct their own curriculum rather than following centralised and academicised handing-down of knowledge.

Negotiated curriculum

Boomer (1982) and Boomer et al. (1992) write about the concept of negotiating the curriculum between teachers and students, a concept that has received widespread attention throughout Australia since 1978. The focus is on teachers and students negotiating the content and processes/strategies of what is to be learned 'to teach children to discover themselves as learners' (p. 7). Boomer (1982) points out that this is only made possible through a change in belief by teachers from one of teacher-planned curriculum to that where student interest is engaged, that is, teacher- and student-planned curriculum:

> Student interest involves student investment and personal commitment. Negotiating the curriculum means deliberately planning to invite students to contribute to, and to modify, the educational program, so that they will have a real investment both in the learning journey and in the outcomes. Negotiation also means making explicit, and then confronting, the constraints of the learning context and the non-negotiable requirements that apply (p. 132).

Middle schooling

Much has been written under the banner of middle schooling in Australia (ACSA 1993, 1996; Berkley 1994; Barratt 1997, 1998a, 1998b). This literature focuses on alienating schooling cultures and curriculum, with a plethora of words such as 'democratic', 'student-centred', 'authentic' and 'negotiated' describing the suggested shift required in schooling. Within this paradigm it is important to address the notion of students' perspectives so that authentic voices may be heard and therefore allow negotiation and democratic processes to occur in the construction of curriculum.

Presuming that a democratic approach to curriculum making *is* valued, it would seem wise to explore the perspectives of the students involved, as well as those of the teacher, before moving to the next step of negotiation. Cothran and Ennis (1997, 1998), Hunter (2002), Lemos (1996), Parker (1996), and Raviv et al. (1990) present findings where the perceptions of teachers with regards to values, goals or the learning environment were different from those of their students. Ultimately, this can result in incongruence in desired outcomes, conflicting values and unparallel pathways in decision making between teacher and students. Ignoring the diversity within the student group may further isolate those whose values are different from that of the teacher.

Waxman and Huang (1998) investigated student perceptions of their learning environments through the use of questionnaires and found that, in general, middle school classes had less favourable perceptions of their learning environment than did either elementary or high school classes. Unfortunately, the first step to under-standing student perspectives and/or perceptions is often not even attempted, teachers' assumptions overriding more solid ways of knowing where the students are at.

Students as researchers

It would seem logical that educational institutions such as schools would support the evaluation and reconstructions of knowledge through students exploring their own lives and connecting this with what is regarded as 'known'. Much has been documented to the contrary, with students reporting school to be boring and alien-ating. Kincheloe and Steinberg (1998) suggest that 'students as researchers gain new ways of knowing and producing knowledge that challenge the common sense views of reality with which most individuals have grown so comfortable' (p. 2).

Those familiar with Beane's work (for example, 1990a, 1990b, 1991, 1993) would recall his attempts to address this problem through a thematic approach to curriculum based upon the worlds of the students. In this curriculum the students help construct the content and processes of their curriculum using their own lives and interests as a base.

Students at an early age are very inquisitive, but are often 'educated' to become passive recipients of information. To re-induce students to become researchers, teachers play an important role. Kincheloe and Steinberg (1998) envisage student researchers to be autobiographical inquirers exploring their identities, explorers of the nature of experience, analysing experience in the classroom, as cultural studies researchers examining the power of contemporary popular culture, researching their own academic experience. They propose that critical student research:

- moves students to the critical realm of knowledge production;
- focuses student attention on thinking about their own thinking;
- creates an analytical orientation toward their lives;
- helps students learn to teach themselves;
- improves student ability to engage in anticipatory accommodation;
- cultivates empathy with 'others';
- negates reliance on procedural thinking; and
- improves thinking by making it just another aspect of everyday existence (pp. 240–41).

Kincheloe and Steinberg point to negotiation as an action, and negotiated curric-ulum as a particular process used for curriculum construction, providing opportunities for students to make choices about what they learn, how they learn it and how this can be assessed. Often teachers and schools respond to this need by giving students some choice in how they present their work and an opportunity to use a variety of learning styles. However, while this provides students with some choices about *how* they will learn and be assessed, it rarely creates an opportunity for students to choose *what* they will learn or to participate in the broader educational game. It is this opportunity for students to negotiate and therefore actively participate in the construction of pedagogy, curriculum and assessment at various levels and in different spaces, from the meanings attributed to 'ways of knowing' to the decision-making processes and practices of schooling, that we need to include in our classrooms to really be able to say we are negotiating the form and substance of curriculum.

Levels and spaces for negotiation

Previous work around teaching styles, for example, Mosston and Ashworth's (2002) spectrum of pedagogical styles (see Table 11.1), have attempted to explore the different pedagogical relationships between teacher and student. While the many ways of depicting these differences could be explored, it is more appropriate here to realise that there are different levels and spaces available for negotiating the broader definition of curriculum (that which goes on in schools) as well as the more specific aspects of the planned and enacted curriculum in classroom practice.

Another way of understanding this might be represented by the continuum in Figure 11.1. At one end of the continuum, as at level A in Table 11.1, there is little

Table 11.1 The spectrum of pedagogical styles

A = Command style
B = Practice style
C = Reciprocal style
D = Self-check style
E = Inclusion style
F = Guided discovery style
G = Convergent discovery style
H = Divergent discovery style
I = Learner-designed individual program style
J = Learner initiated style
K = Self-teaching style

Source: Adapted from Mosston & Ashworth, 1992.

negotiation, with the teacher making most, if not all, of the decisions around curriculum content, pedagogy, assessment. In differentiating the power relationships between teacher and student we can then move to the other end of the scale, which might be thought of largely as self-teaching, where the learner has developed the skills of independent learning and the metacognitive skills of learning how to learn. While Figure 11.1 and Table 11.1 are simple representations of a continuum, it is important to remember also that these categories are constantly overlapping, and that you might see a number of different levels of negotiation in an effective classroom at any one time.

All too often our schools are still strongly working at the teacher-directed level with little or no attempt to encourage other pedagogical relationships. This is not to say that any particular level is 'good' or 'bad', however. It is more useful to think about what work is being done through the process of style or through the level of student negotiation allowed for. If the intention is to help students become independent learners, and for them to be able to 'live democracy', they need opportunities to practise the ways of doing this. Sadly, when teachers attempt to move away from the less-negotiated space, it is often without spending the time for students to learn how to negotiate, make decisions and be democratic. The activity fails and so does the teacher's faith and motivation to keep working in this direction. Students are also a part of this failure. As a teacher meets with a new group of students, it is often a mistake to attempt the more negotiated aspects when all the students have known is teacher-direction. It is vital not only that the appropriate levels of negotiation be used according to the learning experiences that are to take place in the class, but also that we are constantly working towards developing all levels if we are to achieve the benefits of the different positions students might take in curriculum making, decision making, research and knowledge creation. The

Figure 11.1 Negotiated curriculum continuum

Teacher-directed	Teacher-directed	Teacher/student	Teacher/student	Student
Negotiated curriculum	Content Student assessment choices	Negotiated assessment choices	Negotiated content & assessment choices	Curriculum
Absence of facilitated student choice				Teacher
				Learning

continuum takes teachers and students along a journey of negotiation, moving from teacher-directed curriculum towards student-negotiated curriculum, where the teacher takes on the role of facilitator rather than director. The continuum recognises the need to sometimes move back toward teacher-directed tasks, and provides a step-by-step approach to help both teachers and students to become comfortable with the process of negotiating the curriculum, rather than being thrown in at the deep end. The aim of the continuum is to steer teachers towards the use of a model for negotiating the curriculum that has been adapted from the Beane/Brodhagen (1995) model. The student outcomes and teacher and student engagement that result from this approach inspire many teachers to adopt it in their middle years classrooms.

Much of the current work focusing on reform in school curriculum recognises the importance of the interrelationship between curriculum, pedagogy and assessment. All three spaces are seen as inherently related. For there to be reform one must consider all three spaces as potential sites of negotiation while attempting to build the larger commitment to democratic schools and student participation. The Beane/Brodhagen model is perhaps the best-known model of integrative curriculum with teacher teaming and authentic assessment located in the middle years literature, so we will describe it before considering what it might look like in practice. As with all models, it acts as a guide and will not look the same between schools or even classrooms. However, aspects of the model are recognisable in their many forms, shaped by the context of the school. Hence it is imperative that we also discuss some of the issues that might need to be considered when working with such a model.

The Beane/Brodhagen model of negotiated curriculum

James Beane and Barbara Brodhagen have worked in education, and more specifically in the middle years movement in the United States, both theoretically and practically for over 30 years. Beane (1990a, 1993, 1997b, 2004a, b) continues to ask us to consider: 'What should be the middle school curriculum?' and to answer: 'What is the purpose of the middle school curriculum?' While there often seems to be an ambiguous and at times contradictory set of purposes, Beane maintains the concept of 'democratic education' to be of utmost importance, while still recognising the tensions and investments between those promoting democratic education in middle schools and the descendants of the original junior high advocates, the developmentalists, vocationalists, classical humanists and social reformers.

The model we propose would incorporate some if not all of the pedagogical styles of Mosston and Ashworth (1992) and move about the continuum, but with an emphasis towards the development of student decision making. Essentially, through the notion of an integrative curriculum related to the students' lived worlds and constructed from their interests and needs, an outline and then specific curriculum is negotiated between members of the class. Common themes at the intersection of students' 'self' and broader 'world' questions become the curriculum program for the class. Examples of students' self and world concerns that have been constructed as curriculum themes are illustrated in Figure 11.2.

These themes are created through a process that requires prior work to be done as a class with a focus on relationships, group work and classroom climate. Then, working through the five steps below, the themes are developed and voted upon, with more in-depth planning carried out by students and teachers for more specific questions and activities.

1   What concerns or questions do you have about yourself?
   a. Individuals construct their own list
   b. Groups identify common questions
   c. Class constructs a common list.
2   What concerns or questions do you have about your world?
   a. Individuals construct their own list
   b. Groups identify common questions
   c. Class constructs a common list.

Figure 11.2 Sample intersections of personal and social concerns

Early adolescent concerns	Curriculum themes	Social concerns
Understanding personal changes	Transitions	Living in a changing world
Developing a personal identity	Identities	Cultural diversity
Finding a place in the group	Interdependence	Global interdependence
Personal fitness	Wellness	Environmental protection
Peer conflict and gangs	Conflict resolution	Global conflict

Source: Adapted from Beane (1993, p. 61). Used with permission from the National Middle School Association.

3   Identify themes where self and world questions overlap for the group.
4   Vote on themes.
5   Develop sub-questions for themes adopted.

Through finding themes and planning with the students you work towards bringing together personal and social concerns underpinned by personal, social and technical content and skills, as well as the concepts of democracy, dignity and diversity.

Adapting the Beane/Brodhagen model of negotiating the curriculum

It is good to have a model or framework to work from when attempting something new, but it is important to be able to adapt it to suit both teacher and the students. The nature of the teacher–student relationship, the structures within a school, the parent community and the nature of the students themselves are all reasons to be adaptable and flexible when implementing proposed change. The following example of adapting the Beane/Brodhagen model of negotiating the curriculum comes directly from the work that Nicola Park, one of the authors of this chapter, has done with her own middle years classes, and through the work she has done with other teachers and schools which have taken on some of the negotiation tools she has developed. The adapted model (Figure 11.3) is presented as a 10-stage guide with an explanation of some of the changes and further variations to the original model following. It builds upon the model discussed in the previous section and the five steps that relate to Figure 11.2.

Figure 11.3 Negotiating the curriculum project development: Ten stages

> **Negotiating the curriculum—project development**
>
> **Based on the Beane/Brodhagen model**
>
> **STAGE 1 Personal questions**
> Working individually, students brainstorm a list of questions they have about themselves.
>
> **STAGE 2 Finding common personal questions**
> Students in small groups share their questions about themselves and decide which of these are 'common' questions. Common questions are recorded on a large group sheet titled 'Shared Personal Questions'.
>
> *(continues)*

STAGE 3 World questions
Working individually, students brainstorm a list of questions they have about their world.

STAGE 4 Finding common world questions
Students in small groups share their questions about their world and decide which of these are 'common' questions. Common questions are recorded on a large group sheet titled 'Shared World Questions'.

STAGE 5 Finding themes
Small groups consider ways in which some of their personal questions may be connected. The words or ideas used to connect these questions become possible themes. This is repeated for the world questions. In their groups, students create a 'World Themes' sheet and a 'Personal Themes' sheet, and record their ideas for themes, listing the relevant questions under each one.

STAGE 6 Sharing themes
Small groups come together to share their ideas of themes for study. The 'Theme' sheets can be posted around the room for all students to look at and compare. Students then reconsider the themes to remove repetition or overlap.

STAGE 7 Connecting questions to themes
Students look over the common questions, deciding which questions belong to which of the new themes they have identified and agreed on. Each question should be linked to a theme. This is done separately for personal and world themes/questions.

STAGE 8 Selecting themes
Using coloured sticky dots, students nominate (vote for) their top three preferences for study by placing a dot on each of the three themes they most wish to include in the curriculum. This creates a very good visual, helping the students to understand why some themes have been included and others excluded. Most popular themes are identified and time is negotiated for working on one or more themes as a whole group and/or for individual assignments.

STAGE 9 Selecting student research questions
Each student selects the theme/s and question/s they wish to include in their own negotiated curriculum project. A negotiated learning agreement is used to clarify this process for each student.

STAGE 10 Unit planning
The themes and questions selected by students can be used as the basis for unit planning and to help teach particular skills, knowing that the theme used is one that the students should be engaged in. Time should be set aside for the presentation and sharing of all student work.

Following these ten stages enables teachers to negotiate the curriculum with students in such a way that the end result comes from within the students and their beliefs and understandings about their worlds and their sense of curiosity and inquiry. These are powerful tools for teachers and students to be sharing. This tool for negotiation can be used to determine the curriculum for a term or longer, or can be used to help the students design their own negotiated curriculum project. This becomes an independent task that is self-guided and fulfils a negotiated learning agreement (Figure 11.4) that the teacher and student form together. It is from this model that students complete work that sees them focus on and enjoy a valuable learning journey full of inquiry and discovery along the way, rather than being forced to concentrate on the importance of a final answer to their questions.

It is important to always explain to students the purpose behind the ten stages of negotiation shown in Figure 11.3, so that they understand the importance of their contributions and the impact the final result will have on them. It is worth discussing with students the school's efforts to engage them in their learning, and why the teacher sees value in seeking their input into the curriculum.

In Stages 1 through to 4, the term 'questions' (rather than 'concerns') has been used quite deliberately. Students can consider their personal being and their world without necessarily drawing on what concerns them. It is common, however, for students (and teachers for that matter) to list questions that arise from concerns they have. It is still recommended by these authors, though, not to dwell on the term 'concern' for middle years students, giving them the opportunity to also explore the positive elements of their personal and world curiosities.

Another way in which this model has changed from the Beane/Brodhagen model is Stage 5: Finding themes. Instead of linking personal and world questions together through themes, it is suggested that the two remain separate. This makes the process less complicated to follow. It also provides meaningful time to discuss and work on personal interests, separate from world interests. If the aim of the negotiation is to have the students complete the individual negotiated curriculum project, then this is an important division to make because it helps the student to clarify the objectives and requirements of the project.

Ultimately, students will draw up an agreement that sets out for them a self-directed research project on question/s they have about their world and their personal lives. Herein lies the importance of having explicitly taught research and reporting skills (and within this, reading and note-taking skills) through quality teacher instruction. The teacher can then spend time facilitating the learning involved in the project and help organise access to resources, guiding students

Figure 11.4 Suggested format for a negotiated learning agreement

Student name _____

Home group _____ Teacher _____

Students in (*class/team name*) have negotiated their curriculum for term ___. They have raised questions about the world and their own lives that are relevant to them. The team has voted on themes under which these questions can be researched. This process of negotiating the curriculum results in individual agreements being drawn up between students and teachers.

This agreement is to be undertaken by all students in the team. It will be worked on during class time on (*day or periods and time allocated*). The presentation of all work will occur on (*date*).

The due date for completion of this agreement is _____

Student signature _____

Parent signature _____

Teacher signature _____

1. As a team member of ___, I agree to research one question for each of the two world themes I choose. □

2. As a team member of ___, I agree to research two questions for the one world theme I choose. □

3. As a team member of ___, I agree to research one question for the personal theme I choose. □

World themes	Question to be researched	Resources to be used	Method of presentation

Personal theme	Question to be researched	Resources to be used	Method of presentation

Student signature _____ Teacher signature _____
_____

Teacher comments & suggestions

_____
_____

towards an exploration of their questions, rather than a definitive answer. Where such skills need to be further taught or developed, the teacher is now aware of a suitably engaging theme to work under to teach these skills.

If the teacher chooses not to use the model for the purpose of developing individual negotiated curriculum projects, then the aim is to select themes to teach towards, incorporating a variety of integrated skills. The theme can remain constant, while the key learning areas or core subjects become 'ways of seeing' that theme. Either way, the opportunity for negotiation has been offered and used authentically to a high degree, promoting engagement and a meaningful learning opportunity for the middle years student.

Conclusion

The negotiation of a curriculum, whether at the level of teacher and student for curriculum content, pedagogy or assessment, or more broadly between students and teachers in school decision making and practices, requires a focus on our philosophies of schooling. Promotion of practice in democratic processes requires a range of pedagogical approaches that allow students to develop skills/knowledges around learning to learn and the construction of knowledge. This chapter has explored the concept of 'negotiation' and democratic schooling through curriculum, pedagogy and assessment by identifying some of the ideas and practices that relate to negotiation. We discussed the levels and spaces available for negotiation before outlining a model that demonstrates how a curriculum might be negotiated. This is illustrated by an example from one school's practice, leading into some of the issues that might be worth considering by those working with negotiation. We invite students and teachers or schools to participate in some or all of the spaces available for negotiation and welcome stories of experiences in such ongoing practices. It is a new space for many teachers to enter, no doubt one with many pains and pleasures, but what lies at the heart of negotiation is a respect for those in the learning space and a goal of learning as action. Furthermore, the fulfilment and engagement for teachers who take this challenge makes it hard to revert back to a more traditional, teacher-directed model of pedagogy.

Questions
1   Why negotiate in middle years classrooms?
2   What are the differences between negotiation and the negotiated curriculum modelled by Beane/Brodhagen?

3 To what extent have you 'negotiated' as a teacher or student? What were the effects of this?

4 How might teachers and students negotiate in the classroom or school?

5 What are the difficulties associated with negotiation?

6 Why might it be necessary to make a gradual move towards negotiation as suggested by the continuum?

7 What considerations are necessary to enact a Beane/Brodhagen negotiated curriculum?

PART

3

PEDAGOGICAL PRACTICES FOR THE MIDDLE YEARS

12

Learning collaboratively

Raymond Brown

This chapter examines the characteristics of collaborative learning in the context of the middle years of schooling. Classroom practices associated with individual representation, comparison, explanation, justification and validation are examined in order to explore the collective construction of knowledge and the nature of classroom norms that allow collaborative activity to take place. An episode of student talk collected in a Year 7 classroom that has (as its goal) a culture based on collaboration, the collective construction of knowledge, and the explicit negotiation of classroom norms of participation, is examined in order to illustrate the nature of knowledge construction within a collaborative classroom. Year 9 students' reflections on these norms and practices are reported in a fashion that shows the long-term effects of participation in collaborative classroom activities on students' identities as learners.

For over a decade I have, in collaboration with others, been exploring how to reconstitute everyday classroom practices in the middle years of schooling using a sociocultural perspective (see Vygotsky 1978) as a tool to generate collaboration between students and between students and teachers and to critically reflect on collaborative activity as it has emerged. Learning occurs in social partnerships and mediated relationships with others and is therefore an interpretive activity. Such activity is embedded in collaborative relationships that sustain students' movements beyond established competencies by continually mediating their engagement in authentic, ongoing inquiry.

Unlike cooperative learning that brings students together to share their understandings and then sends them off to construct individual products in response to a task, collaborative learning requires students to come together with the specific goal of co-constructing a group response (for example, representation, solution, understanding, interpretation) to a task.

To promote collaboration, students within these classrooms are often permitted to arrange their own groupings and to move in and out of areas of high student density within the confines of the learning environment. Such movement is important because it promotes learning through allowing students' understandings to meet and to be shared (Roth 1995). In order to maximise engagement, teachers within collaborative classrooms are rarely situated at the front of the room arranging the affairs of students' lives. The collaborative classroom requires the teacher to participate with students in the organisation of spaces, times and activities within the classroom. This organisation may require the teacher to guide student activity within a small group, support student-led activity at a work centre, monitor the thinking and sharing of dyads of students, and to introduce new concepts at a whole-class meeting, all within the time-frame of a single learning session.

Although a collaborative classroom is more than the sum of its parts, certain features provide a framework for identifying activity within a collaborative classroom. According to Palincsar and Herrenkohl (2002), for students to be classified as collaborating they must be contributing to and helping others to contribute to the group's effort by sharing ideas and representations; justifying and explaining ideas and representations; working to understand others' ideas and representations; and building on each others' ideas and representations. Such collaborative activity can, according to Hatano and Inagaki (1991), facilitate the collective construction of knowledge previously deemed beyond the epistemic capabilities of individual students, and may take a number of forms.

One form of peer learning that utilises the above framework is reciprocal teaching (Palincsar & Brown 1984). Reciprocal teaching can be considered a form of collaborative learning because it requires students to reach a consensus about the meaning of texts. In simple terms, reciprocal teaching requires a participant in the reading process to read a section of text, summarise its content, ask questions about the text, clarify difficult words within the text, and predict what the next section of text to be read in the group will be about. As common understandings are reached within the group and competencies in using reading comprehension strategies develop, the teacher 'fades' direct involvement in the activities of the group and adopts a role where the level and type of intervention is guided by an ongoing diagnosis and evaluation of students' levels of participation.

Taking another approach to designing a model of collaborative learning, Scardamalia and Bereiter (1991, 1994) constructed a computer-supported intentional learning environment (CSILE) to bring about learning in the classroom. The model uses classroom-based networked computers as a database and memory bank to support students' collaborative inquiries. Within a CSILE classroom, the learning process begins with students developing questions and curiosity about social and physical phenomena. They then suggest strategies for gathering evidence and finding solutions that adhere to scientific criteria for coherence and logic. Solutions are then constructed, contested and elaborated via the technology of the computer so that ideas, representations and points of view are stored on the computer memory and able to be regularly evaluated, examined for gaps, added to or, if need be, reformed by others. In this way, the students are assisted by the technology of the computer to build new understandings in collaboration with others.

One model of collaboration that I've used that employs many of the characteristics of reciprocal teaching and computer-supported intentional learning is 'collective argumentation' (Brown & Renshaw 2000). Collective argumentation is designed to extend the range of speaking opportunities available to students in the classroom. To achieve this, collective argumentation is organised around a key word format that requires students to represent a task or problem alone, compare their representations within a small group of peers, explain and justify the various representations to each other in the small group, reach agreement about a possible solution or solution path within the group, and finally present (validate) the group's ideas and representations to the class to test their acceptance by the wider community of their peers and the teacher.

Although teachers in the middle years of schooling often recognise the merits of collaborative learning, they rarely implement the technique according to the requisites of pre-set models such as collective argumentation (Lopata et al. 2003). Such models promote not only the attainment of intellectual quality, but also positive interdependence, individual accountability, face-to-face interaction and group process (Johnson et al. 1984).

But—why should students individually represent their ideas about a task before engaging in cooperative activity with others?

Generalising ideas through individual representation

When students complete a brief written response to a text, or a solution to a problem, or an evaluation of the efficacy of an experiment, they are more likely to participate in any discussion that follows (Gaskins et al. 1994). Requiring students to commit ideas to paper or to some other medium provides them with a resource that they may use to ask questions of others, share ideas with others, and self-monitor their understanding.

Summarising, rephrasing and re-representing have been referred to by O'Connor and Michaels (1996, p. 76) as 'revoicing'. Teachers within collaborative classrooms are likely to employ revoicing quite often as they attempt to incorporate students' contributions into the discourse of the classroom. By revoicing and naming a particular student as the author of an idea, the teacher positions the student in relationship to other participants in the discussion. In this way students may acquire shifting understandings within the classroom discourse as they are required to either assent to or challenge ideas or representations accredited to themselves or to other speakers in the class.

Revoicing also raises dilemmas about the individual and collective authorship of ideas. Insight and understanding within the collaborative classroom arise from the orchestration of difference—the effective composing and recomposing of different voices that produce a performance that is appreciated and accepted as valid by the group to which the speaker is presenting. For many students their individual and group representations will be a 're-authoring' of past events that have been transformed through experience and insight. Integral to the collaborative learning process, therefore, is the notion that 'my ideas' are made up in part of 'your ideas' and 'our ideas'. However, although students need to be facilitated in their learning through the efforts of their peers and other resources, they need also to be made aware that to revoice another's contribution without reference to its source can be seen as copying, as illegitimate appropriation (see Brown 1998).

Relating students' ideas through comparing and explaining

Comparing representations with others and explaining ideas to others takes learning from the individual plane to the cooperative plane, and allows students to see what is the same and what is different about their ideas and interpretations. For some students it can be a challenging experience as they note and attempt to interpret dissimilarities between ideas and representations. Such challenges can help students learn by making them view concepts from different perspectives (Feltovich et al. 1996). For other students comparing and explaining can be an affirming activity as they see congruence between ideas and representations. Within most classrooms, however, students operate within a social system that has well-defined notions of authority. This means that when comparing and explaining ideas, students may simply converge on a representation or an explanation that is recognisable as being authoritative rather than on a representation or explanation that represents their understanding (Hubscher-Younger & Narayanan 2003).

Relating students' ideas through justifying and agreeing

Learning in a collaborative classroom occurs in social partnerships and in mediated relationships with others as students and teachers engage in ongoing inquiry (Renshaw & Brown 1997). Such a process involves the gathering and sharing of evidence that satisfies disciplinary constraints associated with coherence and logic. Requiring participants in the learning process to justify their ideas enables students to become conscious of others' ideas and points of view by allowing processes of thought as well as products to become visible, and encourages cognitive change to occur through peer critiquing and guided participation in the collaborative process. In this way, the talk generated through justifying ideas and representations provides participants with models of the thinking process that encourage students to question, evaluate and inquire so that consensus can be attained through understanding, rather than through convergence on an authoritative classroom representation, style or reputation.

Before agreement can be stated, each member of the group must be able to explain some aspect of the representation or idea being negotiated; if they cannot do this, there is an obligation for that student to seek clarification and a reciprocal obligation for the other group members to provide assistance. Through this collaborative process, all members of the group are provided with opportunities to develop more sophisticated understandings of lesson content than any one of them could have achieved as an individual. In order to ensure that all group members access these opportunities, it is important that each group be required to validate their group's idea or representation through a whole class discussion that is embedded within norms that relate students to other knowledge-producing groups that operate outside the context of the school classroom; for example, engineers, environmentalists and journalists.

Making ideas public through whole-class validation

Group presentations of their representations and ideas focus on students representing their co-constructed understandings to the other members of the class for validation, and challenges them to rephrase their ideas in terms familiar to the class; defend their thinking from constructive criticism; and when required, reassess the validity of their thinking. Such public presentations of group work permit students to engage with the conceptual content of a lesson at their level, employing their own prior experiences, preconceptions and language in a fashion that distributes the nature of their knowing across a group rather than in a fashion that focuses on any one individual.

Students' participation in the discourse that accompanies group presentations requires overcoming obstacles ('walls') to learning. According to Schoenfeld (1988), obstacles to learning in a middle school classroom revolve around the beliefs that:

- using knowledge, for example mathematics, to explain, prove, discover or invent has little to do with problem solving;
- a good student can solve a problem or complete a task in five minutes or less;
- school subjects, such as mathematics, are studied passively, with students accepting solutions to problems from teachers or textbooks rather than expecting that they can make sense of the solution process for themselves; and
- learning in school is 'an incidental by-product to "getting the work done"' (p. 151).

To help overcome these obstacles, the presentation of students' work to the class needs to take learning from the collaborative to the communal. This requires that the students who make up the audience for group presentations be actively engaged in the validation process. Audience engagement needs to centre on asking inquiry ('why' and 'how') type questions about the group's ideas and representations, and on the provision of constructive criticism of the substance rather than the surface features of the group's ideas and representations. In order for this to happen in a fashion that assists students to become aware of alternative interpretations, possible misconceptions and possible refinements to their own understandings, it is important that the whole-class talk that embeds group presentations be guided by norms that reflect what Bereiter (1994) refers to as the 'quasi-moral commitments' (values) of adult knowledge communities. In this way, confidence building can occur through the process that is supportive and constructive.

Negotiating values of participation in the collaborative classroom

In adult knowledge communities (for example, those belonging to scientists, mathematicians or historians) the community is shaped by commitments to advance mutual understanding, to frame ideas in ways that evidence may be brought to bear, to expand the basis for discussion and to open ideas to critical perspectives from within and without the community (Bereiter 1994). The interactions of individuals within those communities are driven by the intellectual courage to revise one's beliefs, the honesty to change a belief when there is good reason to do so, the wise restraint necessary to not change a belief without serious examination, and the intellectual humility to accept the inadequacy of ideas (Lampert 1990). Engagement as adult scholarly activity may thus be said to be premised on an understanding that critical comment on each member's work is expected, that individuals confront each other as equals and as participants, and that correctness, truth, plausibility and their counterparts are to be found through the discourse of collaborative inquiry (Seixas 1993).

However, the level of commitment by students in a local classroom to the processes of collaboration differs from that manifested in an adult knowledge community. For one thing, the breadth and depth of knowledge of the local class community is limited by comparison to that exhibited in adult communities. The challenge for the teacher and the students at the local classroom level, therefore, is to set in place in some authentic way, selected aspects of those commitments that characterise the collaborative activities of adult knowledge communities.

One way of achieving this is to negotiate with students a 'class charter of values' (Brown 2001). These charters usually reflect social virtues of engagement, courage, humility, honesty, restraint, persistence and affirmation, and together with a pre-set format (for example, represent, compare, explain, justify, agree, validate) guide activity and participation in the collaborative classroom at both the small-group and whole-class level. Table 12.1 provides an example of a class charter of values negotiated by the teacher and students in a collaborative Year 7 classroom.

Over the years, each class of students that I have been involved with has negotiated its own charter of values in accord with the perceived needs of the class and the school at the time. Each charter has provided a tool that the teacher and students may employ to establish and maintain a classroom climate where students are encouraged to display the *courage* required to state their ideas and opinions to others, the *humility* necessary to accept that their ideas may not always be adequate,

Table 12.1 Class charter of negotiated values

Name of value	Negotiated definition
Respect	To consider other people's ideas without putting them down.
Honesty	To tell someone truthfully what you think of their ideas and not cover up.
Concentration	Stay on task and give your full attention.
Active listening	Think about what the speaker is saying.
Sharing	Give other people your ideas and give others a chance to give their ideas.
Courage	Don't be afraid to participate and to express yourself.
Participation	To take your place in your group's activities.
Humility	To accept when you're mistaken and to accept the class's decisions.
Wise restraint	To stand up for yourself, but in a reasonable way.

the *honesty* essential to giving accurate feedback and reports, the *restraint* integral to maintaining social cohesion, the *persistence* required to pursue ideas and views in the face of opposition and the *generosity* necessary to affirm the achievements of others.

The teacher's role in the collaborative process

Besides having an active role in negotiating a class charter of values with the students, the teacher has an active role throughout each phase of collaborative learning. The tasks of the teacher include:

- *allocating* management of the task completion process to the group;
- *facilitating* peer co-operation by reminding students of the norms of participation (turn-taking, listening, etc.);
- *participating* in the development of representations and explanations (especially for those students who find it difficult to 'get started';
- *modelling* particular ways of constructing arguments;
- *facilitating* class participation in the discussion of the strengths and weaknesses of a group's co-constructed representation or idea;
- *introducing* and modelling appropriate language; and
- *providing* strategies for dealing with the interpersonal issues (for example, peer domination or submission) that may arise when working with others.

Teacher participation in the activities of the small groups involves an online assessment of student progress. The teacher should listen and observe before challenging students to engage in and demonstrate different types of representations, explanations and justifications.

After participating with students at the small-group level, the way that the teacher orchestrates the communication of small-group activities to the whole class becomes important. The teacher already knows what the groups have been doing and thus is better able to orchestrate the communication of the small-group presentations to the whole class. For example, group presentations may be sequenced from those that display concrete representations and understandings of the task to those that reflect more sophisticated understandings and the use of abstract symbols, signs and other representational systems.

This orchestration of group presentations is important for the progressive building of understanding over time and provides students with multiple opportunities to participate in the whole-class discussion that follows presentations at levels that suit their evolving levels of understanding. In managing the reporting process in such a fashion, the teacher can traject students' learning towards higher levels of sophistication by rephrasing, paraphrasing and re-representing the contributions of particular groups; drawing connections between contributions; referring to previous problems or tasks; and recalling the ways in which similar situations were approached in the past. In this way, the teacher is positioned to be the 'agent for the collective memory' of the class (Renshaw & Brown 1997) and can create for students a sense of systematicity and continuity in their work so as to ensure that the ways of knowing and doing that are emerging in the local classroom are connected to the ways of knowing and doing adopted by adult knowledge-building communities.

When such connections are made, powerful changes can occur in students' learning. The following section provides an example of student learning as evidenced in a group presentation in a collaborative Year 7 mathematics classroom.

An example of student learning in a collaborative classroom

Once students become accustomed to engaging in a collaborative learning process, quite powerful changes can occur in their approaches to knowing, doing and valuing mathematics. An example of such change occurring is provided in Cath and Tracey's solution to finding the area of three concentric circles contained within a square. Although not provided to the students, the radii of the circles from smallest to largest were 2 cm, 4 cm, and 6 cm respectively.

Cath and Tracey operated in a Year 7 inner-city classroom. The class consisted of 15 female and 11 male students along with their teacher. This class of students had been involved in a year-long study (see Brown 2001) that employed collective argumentation to bring about collaborative learning in the classroom. That is, they regularly worked in groups of their own choosing to represent a problem, compare their representations with each other, explain and justify their problem solutions to each other, reach consensus about a problem solution, and to present their group's solution to the class for discussion and validation.

Before the study commenced, Cath and Tracey both described themselves as high-ability mathematics students who frequently achieved good results in the subject, but liked mathematics only sometimes. Cath and Tracey had attended the school since Year 1 and were not considered by any member of their class as liking mathematics more than they did. Like their peers, Cath and Tracey had not previously participated in any collaborative form of classroom learning for any sustained period. Figure 12.1 is a reproduction of Cath's and Tracey's solution to the problem as represented for the class.

Cath and Tracey's representation of a problem solution to the class provides, from the outset, a complete picture of the group's thinking about the problem space—a picture that provides the class with a record of thinking that the group, in argumentation with the class, can correct, modify, retract and replace. As can also be seen in Figure 12.1, Cath and Tracey are not only working with the conventional rule for finding the area of a circle ($\pi \times r^2$), but have co-constructed their own

Figure 12.1 Cath and Tracey's solution to the area problem

Cath and Tracey's Problem Solution

Smallest Circle
Area
$= \pi \times r^2$
$= 3.14 \times (2 \text{ cm}^2)$
$= 12.56 \text{ cm}^2$

Square Number Pattern
12.56 cm^2 x **4** = 50.cm^2
12.56 cm^2 x **9** = 113.04 cm^2
12.56 cm^2 x **16** = 200.96 cm^2

Middle Circle
Area
$= \pi \times r^2$
$= 3.14 \times (4 \text{ cm}^2)$
$= 50.24 \text{ cm}^2$

Largest Circle
Area
$= \pi \times r^2$
$= 3.14 \times (6 \text{ cm}^2)$
$= 113.04 \text{ cm}^2$

approach to finding the areas of the circles. In short, this approach centres on seeing a relationship between the radii of circles that are multiples of 2, the area of a circle with a radius of 2 units, and the areas of the circles to be found. The group found that if the radius was a multiple of 2, then they could find the area of its circle by multiplying the square number, which corresponded to the ordinal position of the multiple, by 12.56 square units—the area of a circle with a radius of 2 units. For example, if the radius of the circle was 6 units, the third multiple of 2, they could multiply the third square number (9) by 12.56 square units to find the area of the circle—113.04 square units.

We enter the classroom discussion about this approach to finding the areas of the concentric circles where Cath and Tracey are presenting their ideas to the class (see Table 12.2).

Table 12.2 Cath and Tracey's presentation to the class

Cath	We discovered that the area of the middle circle was 50.24 cm² which is a multiple of the area of the smallest circle. We then looked at the smallest and largest circles to see if there was a relationship and found that the area of the largest circle, 113.04 cm², is a multiple of the area of the smallest circle.
Tracey	We had to check whether our theory—that when the radius of a circle is a multiple of 2, its area will be a multiple of the area of a circle with a radius of 2 centimetres—works. We saw that the area of the middle circle had an area 4 times the area of the circle with a radius of 2 centimetres, and that the area of the largest circle had an area 9 times the area of the circle with a radius of 2 centimetres. So the areas of the circles were going up in line with the square numbers.
	(points to the representation on the blackboard)
	The area of the circle with a radius of 2 centimetres was 12.56 square centimetres. The area of the circle with a radius of 4 centimetres was 4 times that of the smallest circle and the area of the circle with a radius of 6 centimetres was 9 times that of the smallest circle.
	So we had a pattern of square numbers, the areas were going up in line with being timesed by the square numbers.
	So to check our theory, we extended the pattern and predicted that the area of a circle with a radius of 8 centimetres would be the area of a circle with a radius of 2 centimetres times the next square number, which is 16.
	So we predicted that the area of this circle would be 200.96 cm². When we checked this prediction by using the rule (area of a circle = π times the radius squared), it worked. We actually predicted the area of a circle with a radius of 8 centimetres.

Source: Brown & Renshaw (2004).

In the whole-class discussion that followed the group's presentation, Les (another student) wanted to know why Cath and Tracey had used this method when all they had to do was use the rule. Cath explained that it was a challenge for them and that they had just tried to find a relationship between the circles by using trial and error (see Table 12.3).

When asked by a student what the group had learnt by doing the problem this way, both Tracey and Cath replied: 'We learnt that if you understand relationships, you can use your understanding to predict answers to other problems.'

In the above example, learning occurs at two levels. Firstly, it occurs at a level where students' inventive ideas (for example, that, 'the areas were going up in line with being timesed by the square numbers') may be interwoven with the conventions of mathematics (area of circle = $\pi \times$ radius^2) by employing salient elements of a conventional approach to scientific investigation (theorising, hypothesising, testing). Here, it is the practices of mathematics that dominate as Cath and Tracey set about proving their prediction 'that when the radius of a circle is a multiple of 2, its area will be a multiple of the area of a circle with a radius of 2 centimetres'.

Secondly, learning occurs at a more personal level where students' individual approaches to doing mathematics are interwoven with the more flexible representation systems employed by adult mathematicians. In the discussion of Cath and Tracey's presentation Les refers to issues related to challenge, persistence and discovery ('Why did you use this method when all you had to do was use the rule?'). Cath and Tracey's response refers to using challenge ('it was hard work') persistence ('we were just about to give up'), and discovery ('we discovered it using trial and error') to find patterns and relationships to understand mathematics. These utterances relate to the aesthetic elements of the investigative process and to the flexible representation systems that expert mathematicians (mathematics professors, graduate students in mathematics, etc.) have available to them (Silver & Metzger, 1989). The everyday and the mathematical perspectives are both present in this aspect of the discussion. Les is upholding the everyday/pragmatic view of school mathematics

Table 12.3 Cath and Tracey's responses to Les's question

| Cath | It was hard work, but then we found a relationship and it worked, the pattern worked! |
| Tracey | We discovered it using trial and error and when we were just about to give up, Mr Brown came along and helped us to keep going. |

Source: Brown & Renshaw (2004).

that revolves around the principle that you only do what you have to. Cath and Tracey are beginning to talk within a set of mathematical assumptions—they make general claims ('that when the radius of a circle is a multiple of 2, its area will be a multiple of the area of a circle with a radius of 2 centimetres') and appeal to experimentation ('we had to check whether our theory . . . works') and empirical evidence ('when we checked this prediction by using the rule, it worked'). They are beginning to consider the conditions and dispositions (the scholarly norms of the mathematical community) that might enhance their growth as mathematicians—a position later supported by Cath in response to another student's question: '. . . we may be children, but we are still great mathematicians ready to discover or invent a new rule'.

Cath and Tracey's presentation to the class illustrates that participating in a collaborative process that extends from individual representation, through cooperative engagement in group work to communal validation can have powerful effects on student learning at a number of different levels. Collaborative learning in this classroom was not facilitated simply by placing students in a group and asking them to work together. It emerged from the shared experiences of the class over time and from the means (the pre-set format and the charter of values) they employed to help represent and communicate their understandings.

But—what happens to these students when they move year levels within an institutionalised schooling system?

Beyond the walls of the collaborative classroom

Fortunately I was able to track the progress of Cath and Tracey and their peers as they progressed through Years 8 and 9. In Year 9 I asked them to respond to a questionnaire comparing their learning in Year 7 with their learning in Year 9. (For a description of the questionnaire and a detailed analysis of students' responses, see Brown, 2001).

In simple terms, the questionnaire asked these Year 9 students to reflect on the collaborative learning process (which the students referred to as collective argumentation) that had taken place in their Year 7 mathematics classroom and to compare that process with the ways they were learning mathematics in their Year 9 classrooms. In general, the students were overwhelmingly positive about the collaborative learning process that they had participated in during Year 7 and quite negative about their participation in their Year 9 mathematics classrooms.

These recollections imply that the Year 7 classroom these students participated in fostered an awareness that mathematical problem solving can be an enjoyable collaborative process in which ideas are generated, compared, explained and evaluated in interaction with others—an awareness that is still in evidence two years after participation in the process.

Students' recollections of doing mathematics in their collaborative Year 7 classroom are very different to their perceptions of doing mathematics in their Year 9 classrooms. Statements about finding different ways of solving a problem, knowing my way of solving a problem, and arguing about and discussing ideas, seem to have been superseded by statements which refer to being told how to do problems, listening to teachers' explanations, and learning from textbooks. This implies that the teaching–learning relationships in their Year 9 classrooms requires these students to participate in classroom cultures where the teacher and the textbook are to be viewed as the authority in the teaching–learning enterprise, and that students are expected to accept this authority without argument or discussion.

How then did Cath and Tracey and their classmates cope when it came to doing mathematics in these classrooms? Their responses to questions that asked whether working collaboratively in their Year 7 classroom facilitated or constrained their participation in their Year 9 mathematics classrooms throws some light on this issue.

Student responses imply that participating in a collaborative learning process in Year 7 has assisted Cath, Tracey and their classmates to develop a view of themselves as being capable of making effective use of whatever skills and understanding they possess to engage in learning mathematics in Year 9. However, in these Year 9 classrooms, knowing seems to be restricted to a curriculum where students are required to study mathematics passively, compliantly and individually, and to master sections of subject matter in a short period—a teaching–learning relationship where it may be hard for students who have experienced collaborative ways of knowing 'to get back into the swing of things'.

Conclusion

Collaborative learning in the middle years of schooling is not facilitated simply by placing students in groups and asking them to work together. The benefits to students' learning of participation in a collaborative process originate from the partnerships established in the classroom between teacher and students over an extended period of time. The effort to translate these partnerships into long-term learning benefits for students requires from the teacher a commitment to a particular type of teaching–learning relationship with his or her students. Within these relationships participants employ a pre-set format (for example, represent, compare, explain, justify, agree and validate) and negotiate norms of participation (for example, a class charter of values) to establish a classroom learning environment in which students are provided with regular opportunities to use speech in collaborative activities with others, to adopt different roles within the discourse of the classroom, to change the ways in which they relate to each other and to their teacher, to participate in the decision-making processes of the classroom, and to view participation in the activities of the classroom as being for everyone—regardless of perceived ability.

In sum, students, in the process of reaching consensus on an issue of common interest, may operate in student–teacher dyads, peer groups, or in whole-class modes of participation, often accessing more than one mode of operation in any one learning session. The essence of collaborative learning in the middle school classroom is students coming together to co-construct understanding through representing, communicating and validating ideas and points of view. Collaborative learning in the middle school, therefore, must provide students with the means to engage with knowing and doing in ways that will traject them along pathways conducive to lifelong learning. Collective argumentation is offered here as one of many collaborative models of learning that communities of teachers and students may employ to make such pathways visible to students—one of many models of collaborative learning that may assist in transforming teaching and learning in the middle years of schooling.

Questions

1   What are some of the implications of collaborative learning for classroom teaching in the middle years of schooling?
2   What possible conflicts can you see between classroom cultures that promote collaborative learning and those that promote traditional approaches to teaching and learning?
3   What practical things might classroom teachers do to support collaborative learning?
4   At a meeting of parents, how would you explain the importance of implementing collaborative approaches to teaching and learning in the middle years of schooling?

13

Higher order thinking

Annette Hilton and Geoff Hilton

As schools move to implement middle years reforms, teachers must develop an understanding of the developmental needs of middle school students, and how to adapt or adopt practices that will best cater for these needs. The intellectual growth of middle school students must be acknowledged and supported by matching students' dramatic changes in thinking ability with increased expectations of what they can achieve. The inclusion of higher order thinking skills as a middle schooling practice, in conjunction with other pedagogies, will greatly enhance the prospect of meeting middle school students' developing cognitive needs.

Educators must be aware that factors from beyond the school, in the school and in the classroom can affect the successful development of higher order thinking. Rapid advancements in science and technology will improve understanding of brain function with consequent advancements in understanding of how best to promote higher order thinking in middle school students.

Higher order thinking was identified by Lingard et al. (2001) in the Queensland School Reform Longitudinal Study (QSRLS) as one demonstration of the intellectual quality of student performance. From this survey the Education Queensland Curriculum Implementation Unit (2002) published *Productive Pedagogies*, which included as its first pedagogy higher order thinking.

When implementing middle schooling reforms, teachers, schools and school systems must identify practices that appropriately address the unique needs and characteristics of students in this stage of schooling. Middle school students' characteristics are evident in their physical, social, emotional and intellectual development (Education Queensland 2003). According to Beane (1993), sensitivity to middle school students' needs is only part of the reform package. It is also necessary to consider what is important for students to learn. Thinking skills and knowledge should be learned and used in an integrated way, rather than in isolation from one another. Scott (1997) suggested that successful middle schooling provided opportunities for students to use multiple intelligences, feel extended and academically challenged, and reflect critically when engaging in learning tasks. The deliberate development of higher order thinking skills is one link in a complex chain of curriculum, pedagogy and assessment that can better address the learning needs of students in the middle years of schooling. The Carnegie Council (1989) highlighted the lack of recognition of the intellectual ability of middle years students when they reported an unfounded assumption that middle school students were not capable of critical or complex thinking. The Centre for Collaborative Education (2000) stated that the intellectual characteristics of middle school students included:

- moving from concrete to abstract thinking;
- intense curiosity with a wide range of intellectual pursuits;
- high achievement when challenged and engaged; and
- ability to be self-reflective.

Suggestions for how teachers could support these characteristics include a focus on complex thinking skills. The first step towards achieving this requires an understanding of the importance of higher order thinking. Any discussion of higher order thinking must begin by distinguishing it from ordinary thinking.

The nature of thinking

All human beings think, but thinking can occur with different levels of complexity. Definitions of thinking can be complicated. Lower order thinking requires routine or simplistic applications of prior knowledge (Newmann 1988). Cognitive scientists have defined thinking as problem solving, which begins with perception and recognition, followed by a search for connections. Then, data are retrieved and transformed, and lastly, progress towards problem resolution is assessed (Geertsen 2003). Higher order thinking incorporates much more.

The nature of higher order thinking

Higher order thinking challenges students to expand the use of their minds. The Education Queensland Curriculum Implementation Unit (2002) defined higher order thinking as the transformation of information and ideas in order to synthesise, generalise, explain, hypothesise, or arrive at some conclusion or interpretation. O'Tuel and Bullard (1995) noted ongoing confusion in defining higher order thinking. Several authors have attempted clarification by restricting higher order thinking to Bloom's (1956) analysis, synthesis and evaluation (Hopson et al. 2001/2002). However, Braggett (1997) maintained that this definition excluded some higher order thinking skills important for middle school students and added critical thinking, relationships, predicting, hypothesising, problem solving and reflective thinking.

Ultimately, it is important that educators focus on the value of higher order thinking rather than being overwhelmed by the definitional debate that continues among theorists. Some general, broader definitions of higher order thinking may be useful. An easy and workable definition has been offered by Geertsen (2003), who summarised the debate by identifying higher order thinking as an appropriate umbrella term for all types of extraordinary (not ordinary) thinking. He went on to say that higher levels of thinking are distinguished from ordinary thoughts by the amount of control exercised by the thinker and the degree of abstraction required.

Why teach higher order thinking skills in middle schools?

Throughout history, and in many facets of life, higher order thinking has been an attribute that enhanced an individual's possibility of success. The better hunters in a tribe, the better players in a team, the better employees in an organisation are those with that something extra. Many hunters, players and employees may have the basic skills to perform the required task, but the standout members of these groups are those who can analyse, synthesise and evaluate the circumstances in which they find themselves. It is their higher order thinking skills that give them the advantage. Unfortunately, it is not possible to say that schools always identify the better students by their higher order thinking skills. Instead, success is often measured by students' ability to reproduce knowledge, rather than by their ability to create their own (Renzulli 2000). As children grow, their capacity to learn thinking skills increases. However, the QSRLS (Lingard et al. 2001) found low levels of intellectual demand across schools. The stories that abound of great achievers in our society who were underachievers at school bear witness to incorrect judgments of student ability. Reis (1998) argued that some students who underachieve do so because the level of thinking required provides so little challenge that they choose not to participate as a matter of principle. She suggested that there is a need to address the mismatch between students' abilities and the thinking opportunities provided in the classroom.

Linking higher order thinking to other signifying practices of middle schooling

Higher order thinking is one of a number of signifying practices associated with middle years reform. It can be viewed as a link between these practices. Without higher order thinking, the other signifying practices are weakened and cannot be successfully implemented. Conversely, without the other practices, teaching and learning of a wide range of higher order thinking skills cannot be embedded in middle years schooling.

Traditional practices in schools have been described as desk-oriented, with teaching often based around a textbook, and directed at one level, usually the middle ability range (Braggett 1997). The signifying practices associated with middle years schooling attempt to address these concerns by providing alternatives in which students are more actively engaged in learning. According to Forte and Schurr (1997), an exemplary middle school program emphasises the use of higher order thinking skills. Problem and performance-based learning, independent projects, cooperative and collaborative learning, and curriculum integration and negotiation are examples of alternative practices designed to encourage active learning and higher order thinking. Other authors have advocated the use of research tasks as a means of empowering students to learn new knowledge and skills, develop higher order thinking, and learn about themselves (George et al. 1992; Kincheloe & Steinberg 1998). Kincheloe and Steinberg suggested that when students engage in research, they engage in the cognitive act of deconstructing and reconstructing their own experiences, and use metacognition and critical thinking to create new meaning. When such activity is missing from the classroom, students are deskilled because they are exposed to busy work and rote learning, which require no reflection.

While many of the significant pedagogical practices of middle schooling support the development and teaching of higher order thinking, the current organisational reforms being promoted by policies such as the Middle Phase of Learning State School Action Plan (Education Queensland 2003) are also necessary to address possible constraining influences. These influences on the development of higher order thinking exist on a number of levels, beyond school, within the school and within the classroom.

Influences on teaching higher order thinking

Beyond the school

Middle years reforms have been seen as a grassroots movement (Carrington 2004). As education systems remodel to incorporate these reforms, they and society as a whole must redefine the expectations of systems, teachers and students. Educational systems need to do more than prepare students to be cogs in the machinery of commerce (Jalongo 2003). The modern world needs citizens who are competent at handling information, can continually solve problems in creative and collaborative ways, and can communicate these solutions. Higher order thinking plays a major role in fulfilling these societal needs. Unfortunately, there are societal barriers to the development of higher order thinking skills in students. For example, the governments of some countries, to determine funding allocation to schools, have introduced high-stakes testing. This often hijacks the curriculum, as schools retreat to drilling students in knowledge reproduction in order to maintain funding and avoid being labelled a failing school. Renzulli (2000) referred to this attitude as the 'ram, remember, and regurgitate' model (p. 152). He suggested that this is evidence of top-down policy making without regard for the needs of students, or for the need to develop higher order thinking skills to prepare students for productive futures in an ever-changing world. High-stakes testing, and too often school-wide block testing, requires teachers to place emphasis on content. This forces teaching to become subject-centred, and students to rote-learn facts and procedures. Little time is left for depth of thought. This approach is in conflict with the student-centred approach needed by middle school students. While society, government or education systems continue to have such priorities, real, system-wide development of higher order thinking will not occur.

Within the school

The way a school is organised can affect the teaching of higher order thinking. For example, many secondary schools have lesson blocks from 40 to 70 minutes in length. Students may only study a particular subject two or three times each week.

Higher order thinking takes time. When it is confined to isolated lessons, the types of problems and the range of thinking skills which students can use are restricted (Sparapani 1998). Teachers also need time to plan experiences that provide opportunities to learn and use higher order thinking skills. Often teachers have limited time or must plan alone because there is no common planning time. Administrators, through timetabling initiatives, can help facilitate the implementation of higher order thinking. Common planning time allows teachers to collaborate, differentiate the curriculum, and discuss appropriate pedagogies for a single group of students. It also allows teachers of different subjects to plan integrated curriculum or multidisciplinary strategies, which provide interconnected, authentic contexts in which students can further use higher order thinking skills.

The teaching of higher order thinking at the school level can be influenced by resourcing and school policies. Higher order thinking often leads students in diverse directions. This requires access to a range of resources, including information and communication technologies (ICTs). If resources are inadequate to support the learning, student interest and teacher enthusiasm are likely to diminish quickly. Not all learning or higher order thinking is best suited to the classroom. Schools with excursion policies that restrict or impede teachers from providing such experiences also restrict potential for students to experience a full range of higher order thinking opportunities.

Middle schooling reforms provide opportunities for schools, particularly traditional secondary schools, to address the factors that influence the teaching of higher order thinking. For example, block scheduling in which students are with the same teacher for an extended period of time or have the same teacher for more than one subject, provides students with more time to engage in active learning and problem solving, and consequently to develop deeper knowledge. Individuals differ in the type of thinking they find challenging—a problem that challenges some students may not be a challenge for others. Having more regular classroom contact with fewer students allows teachers to develop a better understanding of the needs of individuals. Teachers who deal with large numbers of students may have little opportunity to analyse the prior knowledge, experiences and thinking skills of individuals.

In the classroom

While it is common for the teaching of higher order thinking to be constrained by systemic imperatives and school structures, teachers' attitudes remain the most powerful influence. Teachers must believe that students want to think—and it takes time and energy to develop learning experiences that require students to think critically or creatively. It is often easier to tell students the answer, and move on (Sparapani 1998). According to Newmann (1988), studies of high school classrooms showed that students engaged in low levels of cognitive work and acquired knowledge without being challenged to use it. If the dominant classroom discourse involves the teacher presenting information to students, higher order thinking is unlikely to occur, since that requires students to be actively engaged. Teachers who value thinking skills do not simply dispense knowledge. They allow students to work productively with knowledge.

Other classroom-based middle school reforms provide opportunities for the development of higher order thinking. For example:

- Thematic teaching and integrated curriculum show students the interconnections across disciplines and allow opportunities to engage in experiences requiring higher order thinking.
- Constructivist pedagogy links learning to students' interests, prior knowledge and learning strategies.
- Authentic assessment allows for a variety of assessment instruments such as performance-based tasks that are more relevant to students; and more reflective of practitioners' work in the field.
- Cooperative learning supports higher order thinking because students must discuss and defend their opinions and ideas when they work with other students.
- Homerooms allow teachers to create a learning environment that values thinking and thoughtfulness by providing stimulating physical surroundings and celebrating the products of students' learning.

Middle school students are more likely to be engaged when their learning is challenging and relevant to their needs and interests. It is very important that this unique developmental stage is considered when planning programs for students in this age group. Recently, researchers have found that a great deal of change occurs in adolescent brains during this time, as discussed in Chapter 4. The teaching and integration of higher order thinking skills is a vital pedagogy to support cognitive development of middle school students.

Adolescent brain development and higher order thinking

Adolescent brains differ from adult brains, neurochemically and anatomically, and in terms of activity levels (Fuller 2003; Wolfe 2003). A number of dramatic changes begin to occur in the brain in early adolescence. An understanding of these changes and their impact on learning and thinking can help teachers to better cater for middle school students. It can also help students to understand the changes that are occurring and respond accordingly. When students learn about brain development, they more clearly understand the influences of such choices as nutrition, physical activity, sleep patterns and substance abuse (Caskey & Ruben 2003).

Between the ages of nine and ten years, prolific synapse development occurs. This is followed by synaptic pruning, which takes place until puberty. When synaptic pruning occurs, the brain removes certain connections to allow it to function more efficiently. Several authors have referred to this period as the time to use it or lose it (Caskey & Ruben 2003; Fuller 2003). The brain grows by retaining connections that are most used and losing those that are not. According to Clark (2001), connections can be formed or maintained if stimulation is provided through learning experiences that require higher order thinking.

The consequences of such extensive brain development can include difficulty discerning important information, motivation and attention problems, risk-taking and mood swings. This does not mean that middle school students are not capable of complex thought. Several authors have suggested a range of strategies to help students develop cognitively during this period. For example, middle school students often display poor cognitive performance in situations such as timed examinations. Fuller (2003) suggested that during this time project-based assessment might be more appropriate. Caskey and Ruben (2003) extended this idea, adding that such learning experiences help students to form complex neural connections through higher order thinking processes. According to Wolfe (2003), the brain is the only body organ that develops as a result of outside experiences. The implication for teachers and students is that appropriately challenging activities will assist the brain's development. The brain deconstructs experiences as they enter the brain and reconstructs them when remembering. The more connections the brain has developed, the more effective the thinking and learning will be. Wolfe went on to say that unless middle school students are provided with in-depth understanding of concepts, and a physically and psychologically safe learning environment, they would be unable to use what they have learned in the world beyond school.

Self-reflection for teachers of higher order thinking

Rather than asking how middle school students could learn about particular subjects (a subject-centred approach), Stringer (1997) suggests that teachers should ask how these subjects could help students learn (a student-centred approach). This demonstrates an immensely important shift in thinking and a vital step in middle years reform. From this step, higher order thinking practices can be initiated.

A study by Torff (2003) found that as teachers develop from novice to expert, their classroom practices change, from content-rich, curriculum-centred and higher order thinking-lean, to content-lean, learner-centred and higher order thinking-rich. Focusing students' learning experiences on their needs and interests rather than on the facts and knowledge of the subject or discipline, is a significant aspect of middle schooling reform. While this constructivist approach is the basis of new syllabuses, teachers must do more than change the content they teach. They must recognise that students need to learn content that is meaningful and, at the same time, learn skills to use the information for a range of purposes. Without higher order thinking skills, the content students learn is little more than a collection of unrelated or irrelevant facts.

The expert teachers in Torff's (2003) study utilised much more higher order thinking and learner-centred pedagogies than did the novice group. He also identified a third group which he referred to as experienced teachers. This group had gained experience in the classroom and through professional development, and had some skills and strategies that reflected this. Despite their experience, they had failed to develop expert skills with respect to such strategies as the use of higher order thinking. This is evidence that the shift from novice to expert does not happen automatically. Teachers can be resistant to changing their classroom practices despite professional development programs. According to Torff, this desired change in teachers requires time and persistence in addition to cognitive and metacognitive engagement.

Developing higher order thinking skills

When students develop their own knowledge through higher order thinking processes, there is an element of uncertainty and outcomes are not always predictable (Education Queensland Curriculum Implementation Unit 2002). To facilitate the engagement of students in higher order thinking, teachers must de-emphasise some of the more traditional approaches of convergent, right/wrong, yes/no, factual thinking. Paul (1992) asked a series of questions about the teaching of thinking to challenge teachers. For example, are teachers willing to rethink methods; learn new concepts; bring rigour to their own thinking; and be an example of what their students must be? Teachers must also overcome some prevalent misconceptions about how thinking skills can be developed. Costa (1985) emphasised that:

- learning how to think does not happen automatically;
- students do not learn to think critically by themselves; and
- asking students to think about something does not develop thinking skills.

Some debate then arises as to how thinking skills should be taught. Should they be developed in isolation, taught as part of the wider curriculum, or taught as a combination of these methods?

To aid the teaching of thinking skills, several models have been developed. Bloom (1956), through his Taxonomy of Cognitive Development, defined a hierarchy of thinking skills from knowledge, comprehension and application to the accepted higher order thinking levels of analysis, synthesis and evaluation. Other more contemporary influences on the teaching of thinking skills include:

- De Bono (1995), who developed the Six Thinking Hats framework that teachers and students can apply across the curriculum, though he suggested that initially, the skills be taught explicitly. Students become familiar with the Six Thinking Hats and learn to apply different perspectives to their thinking, leading to different possible solutions to questions posed. Other strategies developed by de Bono to assist thinking skills are Plus, Minus and Interesting (PMI), Other Peoples' Viewpoint (OPV), and CoRT Thinking.
- Gardner (1993), who through his Theory of Multiple Intelligences highlighted the diverse thinking strengths that a person may have, has encouraged teachers and students to value varying forms of intelligence as valid and human.
- Buzan (2000), who developed Mind Mapping as a way of representing thoughts and plans in graphic form, taking advantage of new understandings about the brain and memory. Mind maps are representations of what he calls radiant thinking.

To further assist teachers of thinking skills, some innovative tools have been developed. For example, Bloom's levels of thinking can be cross-referenced with Gardner's multiple intelligences to create a planning matrix that caters for all styles and levels of thinking. Software such as *Inspiration* has allowed for the simple and clear depiction of thoughts and plans through concept mapping, tree diagrams and flow charts. Incorporating these frameworks and tools into thinking classrooms is an excellent method for teachers to scaffold the development of higher order thinking in students.

The notion of scaffolding is important in assisting students to develop higher order thinking. Vygotsky (1978) defined scaffolding as the support structure for learners engaged in activities just beyond their independent abilities. Just because thinking is inherent in the structure of the brain, this cannot be used as an argument against making students conscious of their thought processes and practising to improve them (Sylwester 2000). One cannot just think, but must think about something. Therefore it is essential to integrate academic content with the teaching and learning of higher order thinking skills (Matters 2004).

A practical example: teaching higher order thinking through class/group discussions

Since higher order thinking skills could be applied to any teaching and learning situation, it would be impossible to give examples pertinent to all circumstances. However, O'Tuel and Bullard (1995) presented a very helpful framework that could guide the development of higher order thinking skills across the curriculum. This framework has three steps—the teaching of, for and about thinking skills.

Teaching of higher order thinking occurs when a specific thinking skill is taught and students have the chance to practise it. This involves explicit teaching through guided practice. For example, during discussion, thinking about other people's viewpoints and being able to articulate personal thoughts, in an appropriate way, requires the higher order thinking skills of analysis and evaluation. To help students achieve this, specific higher order thinking skills can be taught and practised prior to the discussion. Some of these skills, with associated sentence starters, are shown in Table 13.1.

The benefits of this can be contrasted with what happens if these skills are not taught. Cam (1995) stated that people who were unpractised at thinking skills often rejected alternatives out of hand, showed themselves to be unimaginative, were dogmatic and inflexible, and did not make the most of their opportunities.

After some thinking skills and ways of expressing ideas have been taught, students move on to integrating these skills into broader activities. Teaching for higher order thinking occurs when an activity requires the use of the skill but the skill is not the focus of the lesson. Once students have developed familiarity with some of these discussion skills, teachers can encourage their use at any time. This may not always lead to comfortable situations for the teacher. When students begin to think critically about what they view, hear or read, and when they have the skill

Table 13.1 Cognitive organiser to guide students' higher order thinking skills during class/group discussions

Skill	Sentence starters
Stating and defending points of view	I believe . . . My point of view is . . . I still maintain that . . .
Concurring with or expanding ideas	I agree with . . . I would like to add . . . In addition I would like . . .
Contradicting others' points of view	I disagree with . . . I strongly oppose . . . I believe this is unfounded . . .
Noting self-contradictions of speakers	Previously you stated . . . You have contradicted your previous . . . You seem to have changed your . . .
Re-evaluating one's own point of view	I see what you are saying . . . I have reconsidered . . . I still firmly believe . . .

and confidence to articulate their thoughts, a sedate and accepting group of knowledge recipients is replaced by an inquiring, dynamic group of thinkers.

Teaching about higher order thinking gives students opportunities to practise metacognition that allows them to evaluate their thinking. With targeted questioning a teacher can help students think about their own thinking. Cam (1995) illustrated some excellent examples of this type of questioning/prompting (see Table 13.2).

Table 13.2 Examples of teacher prompts to assist students to think about their thinking

Thinking skill	Teacher prompts
Considering alternatives	Does anyone have a different idea? How else could we look at this?
Keeping your bearings	Does that help us with the problem we are looking at?
Appealing to criteria	Why (by what criteria) do you say that?
Seeing implications	What is being implied here? What could happen if . . . ?
Consistency	Can you say both that and that?

Source: Selected from Cam (1995). Used with permission from Hale & Iremonger.

At the conclusion of any discussion students can be asked to reflect on the thinking skills used, and on the success of the group and individuals at using these skills. Finally, at the end of any discussion, students can be asked to articulate reasons why they have changed or maintained their point of view.

Assessment of higher order thinking skills

Assessing higher order thinking is not an easy task. Proponents of teaching thinking skills in isolation from the main curriculum cite ease of evaluation as a major advantage to their method, as it does not get lost in the broader agenda. The fact that this approach does not relate to students' broader curriculum or middle schooling philosophy and therefore has little authenticity would seem to outweigh any assessment advantage. Dede (as cited in Hopson et al. 2001/2002) suggested that assessment must become more complex, to measure higher order thinking rather than simply measuring regurgitated facts. A more authentic assessment method is the development of criteria sheets, which scaffold and assess students' thinking skill development in the broader context of an integrated curriculum. Hurley and Weldon (2004) pointed out that this assists students in taking ownership and responsibility for their thinking and learning.

In the preceding example of classroom discussion, assessment could occur in a number of ways. Firstly, as part of the overall process, the teacher could monitor performance using a checklist, taking note of the speaker and the skill used. Over a number of discussions, this tracking method would soon reveal patterns of participation and development of higher order thinking skills used by the speakers. Secondly, since students must reflect on their own participation in the discussion, as well as that of others, self-assessment and peer assessment are possible. Students could track their own performance by indicating on personal cognitive organisers when they used particular skills. Again, over time, patterns of their own performance would be revealed to them. Finally, an example of student self-assessment might be through reflections on conclusions reached in the discussion, and on how thinking and ideas were reinforced or changed.

With the broader use of higher order thinking in classrooms, comes an increased need to develop methods for its assessment. Hopson et al. (2001/2002) have called for more research into how changes in student performance in higher order thinking are measured.

What do students think about higher order thinking?

Students are reported to acknowledge the efforts of teachers to engage them in higher order thinking. In an American middle school survey by Meece (2003), improved positive motivation and greater academic engagement were reported when teachers used learner-centred principles, which included higher order thinking. The Middle Years Research and Development Project (Department of Education and Training Victoria 2002) found students felt motivated to learn, valued understanding their work and felt in control when they were given time to explore and understand new ideas while they were learning to think.

Conclusion

In our rapidly changing world, middle school students are faced with an increasing array of knowledge sources and technologies. This fact, coinciding with the relatively recent identification of early adolescent characteristics by the Carnegie Council (1989), creates an imperative to fully exercise the intellectual capabilities of middle school students.

For schooling to have relevance to these students, and for them to be informed participants in the real world, their intellectual engagement at school must match the increasingly sophisticated and complex nature of their thinking. The development of higher order thinking must be facilitated on many levels, from societal expectations to individual classroom practices. Higher order thinking is a pedagogy that can contribute to the requirement of increased intellectual demand on middle school students.

Questions

Ordinary thinking questions: reproducing knowledge from within the chapter

1   What is higher order thinking? Give a practical definition suitable for use by classroom teachers.
2   How does higher order thinking complement the other signifying practices of middle schooling?
3   In the chapter, discussion skills were used to illustrate the teaching of, for and about higher order thinking. What other strategies could be used to develop higher order thinking?
4   Identify possible barriers to the implementation of higher order thinking beyond school, and within schools and classrooms. What can classroom

teachers do to enhance the development of higher order thinking skills in students despite influences beyond the classroom?

5   What modern developments are occurring that will change the way in which higher order thinking is taught and understood in the future?

Higher order thinking questions: going beyond the information presented

6   Consider adolescent brain research. Give examples of classroom strategies for teaching and using higher order thinking that are compatible with brain research findings.

7   Reflecting on your own practice, give examples of higher order thinking strategies that you have used with students.

8   As an educator, how can you use higher order thinking in your own practices to make you a better educator?

14

Teacher–student relationships

Amanda Keddie and Rick Churchill

Mutually respectful student–teacher relationships are central to improving educational experiences in the middle years. As much research continues to confirm, teachers relating well to their students remains one of the most significant factors in generating positive academic and social outcomes. Developing these sorts of relationships, however, necessarily involves problematising the traditional power inequities that exist between teachers and students. This chapter explores this premise and identifies ways that teacher practice, through a tendency to be mobilised around relations of domination and control, can constrain learning outcomes by suppressing students' sense of legitimacy and agency. Drawing on data and findings from two Australian studies, we bring these issues to life through detailing students' concerns about their relationships with their teachers. Given '[t]he first imperative of some teachers when teaching boys appears to be "controlling" rather than teaching them' (Lingard et al. 2002, p. 4), our focus in this chapter is on boys' experiences of schooling in the Middle Years. We do not wish to silence or marginalise girls' experiences, but the boys' voices featured here are most useful in making visible the constitutive nature of authoritative and coercive school and classroom relations (Davies 2000). As an issue of power and control, we explore these relations within the context of boys' investments in dominant constructions of masculinity. Drawing on the dimension of Supportive Classroom Environment, within the Productive Pedagogies framework (The State of Queensland 2001), the chapter concludes with a discussion of a number of ways in which schools might take these issues forward to establish more genuinely equitable and positive student–teacher relationships.

Adam's story

Adam is twelve years old and in Year 6. He hates school. Actually he would like to 'get rid of all the teachers'. 'Really dumb stupid rules' are what Adam hates most about school—like being sent to time-out for 'a week or something' if you're late for lining up or if you forget your hat or if you check your email when you aren't supposed to or if you hang around with your friends in big groups. Adam thinks that the teachers get 'cut over the smallest little things' like when Mr B. (Adam's classroom teacher) goes 'psycho' just for talking in class or 'when we have fun'—or when Mr R. (Adam's school principal) wrecks all the outside games with his 'crap rules'.

Adam doesn't care about the usual consequences for breaking the rules: time-out or being sent to the office. 'I just go to sleep . . . it does nothing . . . they can't win.' Indeed, Adam loves to 'play the teachers'. One time he and about 30 other kids tried to construct a human pyramid on the oval with about '20 people on the base and . . . about ten other people . . . on the back'. When the third row was 'gonna hop on', several duty teachers approached. Adam and most of the group responded by performing the Maori haka in a threatening way, and when the teachers 'came after them' the whole group ran in different directions. Adam laughed and said it felt 'really cool' because the teachers couldn't 'get any of them' and could not punish them because there 'wouldn't be enough time-out seats to put us all on'.

Other games Adam plays to outsmart his 'high and mighty' teachers involve defying the school's rules. Instead of going to music class, Adam and his friend Tim sometimes hid in the school grounds for the duration of the music lesson, returning to their regular class group at the 'appropriate' time. On another occasion Adam delighted in smuggling into school sixteen cans of Coke hidden in his backpack (Coke is banned at school). He smirked when he told me that he and Tim secretly drank the whole sixteen cans during lunchtime and had to visit the toilet all afternoon to 'wash their hands'. Adam also tells the story about his friend Wolfie. Apparently Wolfie hit a T-ball over the school fence and through a window of a private house near the school grounds. The school charged Wolfie's mum to replace the broken glass. Apparently also, Wolfie was 'the wrong guy to mess with because he is like a computer genius and he put a firewall up and went and deleted all of the teachers' files.' Adam explains 'Cos like anything that we do wrong, the teachers put it on the computer and Wolfie went and deleted everyone's files so they had absolutely nothing against us. So I've only like been on time-out my entire life now about 12 times.'

Adam also plays the teachers by acting dumb to get out of schoolwork. He doesn't want to be seen as a smart kid—they are 'just a bunch of nerds and computer junkies'. For example, when his class did a unit of work on mechanics, Adam (who works on his dad's farm and knows a lot about mechanics) acted dumb because 'you get extra work if you're smart'. He said that he was proud when he got all the answers wrong because he had copied them from the 'dumb kids' and that he had 'won' because Mr B. didn't think he was all that bright.

Many of the teachers couldn't stand Adam because of his 'smart mouth' and his 'defiant' and 'surly' nature. Adam was regularly reprimanded and put on time-out or sent to the office as punishment for this defiance and his unwillingness to adhere to the school's rules. Mr B. thought that Adam's 'strong will' and tendency to 'fire up' meant that he had to be 'pushed' and 'shoved' a bit to get his work done. Mr B. also thought that Adam's tendency to fire up was what brought on opposition from the other teachers.

Power, control and authority

Boys' experiences of schooling

Adam's story brings to life how teacher attitudes of control and domination can work to constrain educational outcomes, and highlights the importance of positive teacher–student relations. Consistent with key research in this area (Martino & Pallotta-Chiarolli 2003), Adam seems to be disengaged from and constrained by authoritative school cultures that he doesn't understand, and frustrated by the lack of agency and control he has over his school life and the lack of connection and mutual respect that characterises his relationships with his teachers and principal. It seems that Adam understands his teachers' authority as predominantly relating to keeping him in his place rather than having any reasonable or functional purpose. We can see that these relations of power are counterproductive with Adam because they seem to amplify his resistance and reinforce his investments in control and domination.

Issues of power, control, fairness and oppression seem to be particularly dominant themes in our work with boys in the middle years. Adam's story certainly resonates with the voices of other boys in our research (see Keddie & Churchill 2004). Here we find that many boys, like Adam, express their negative feelings in terms of how the student–teacher relationship positions them with a lack of power and control over what happens in their school lives, and express their concern about what they see as being unfairly treated by their teachers. For example, Adam's frustration at his school's crap rules and his teacher going psycho at him for the smallest things are reflected in the following comments from other boys in terms of what they say they dislike about their teachers:

- 'They get up you if you sharpen your pencil if he or she is out of the class and they see you out of your chair.' (Year 5)
- 'They keep you in for no reason at all.' (Year 6)
- 'They're mean, too loud.' (Year 6)
- 'They keep a close watch on you if you do something small that's wrong and then they blame you for something that you didn't do.' (Year 7)
- 'They're very impatient and angry and they can be mean and unforgiving and give bad judgment.' (Year 7)
- 'When other people play up in class and we all get punished for what other people have done.' (Year 7)

A sense of unfairness and constraint is particularly strong in these comments and seems to be associated with the boys' resistance to the way their teachers' use of authority and power works to position them with a lack of agency. The comments certainly point to a lack of connection and mutual respect in the student–teacher relationship. As in Adam's story, these boys express frustration at the policing and enforcement of rules and punishments they appear to perceive as designed predominantly to put them in their place. Moreover, this sense of powerlessness seems to amplify their defiance and opposition towards their teachers.

The boys' voices illuminate their opposition to what they see as the prescriptive, irrational and authoritarian ways that some of their teachers wield their power over them. Drawing on Davies (2000), these teachers seem to be 'shaped to read and interpret behaviours within a set of discourses that rob students of power and thus the possibility of agency' (p. 164). Certainly it is clear that Adam and other boys we have surveyed read these discourses in this way—as oppressive and as rendering them powerless. Further, our research with teachers (see Keddie 2003; Keddie & Churchill 2004) also suggests that, through their belief that boys are naturally active, boisterous and high-spirited (and essentially different to girls), they consider that firm levels of control must be established before they can meaningfully engage in 'teaching'. Such assumptions about boys' resistant or disruptive behaviours, as somehow an inevitable result of their biological make-up, remain pervasive in schools and are well documented (Davies 1993; Kamler et al. 1994; Gilbert & Gilbert 1998; Lingard et al. 2002). Indeed, as Adams and Walkerdine, suggested nearly 20 years ago, and a suggestion that still holds true (Keddie 2003), boys are almost expected to be 'challenging' and to misbehave: 'The high-spirited child is traditionally regarded with affectionate tolerance. Boys will be boys. A boy who never gets up to mischief, it is suggested, is not a proper boy' (Adams & Walkerdine 1986, p. 26).

In moving beyond essentialist assumptions about boys' behaviours, it is seen as imperative for teachers to understand how the social processes of schooling, and in particular teacher practice, can work to endorse and perpetuate boys' resistant behaviours. To these ends, in attempting to construct relationships with boys that reflect mutual respect and social support, we must understand issues of masculinity construction and, more specifically, issues of power and masculinity.

Issues of masculinity

Issues of power, control and authoritarianism are key elements within the masculinities literature and are positioned as particularly significant in understanding how narrow versions of masculinity are endorsed through teacher practice (Davies 1993; Martino & Pallotta-Chiarolli 2003). Research in this sphere highlights the associations between the ways teachers model authority and power and the maintenance of students' disruptive and resistant behaviour. Here we need to recognise many boys' investments in dominant or hegemonic constructions of masculinity mobilised around power and control.

Adam's story, for example, highlights his emotional investments in hegemonic masculinity and how he draws on these investments as a means of self-legitimation and agency. This is evident, for example, in his struggles to 'outsmart' his teachers through his continual attempts at undermining and challenging their authority. In this sense, Adam's adversarial relationship with his teachers—his acts of resistance and subversion—can be seen as associated with his sense of successful masculinity as synonymous with power, control and domination. Against this backdrop, we can understand Adam's behaviour as a manifestation of his attempts to manage and negotiate his sense of self as 'successfully' masculine within the dominating and controlling structures and practices of official schooling. Here we might interpret Adam's efforts to subvert and sabotage formal school cultures and practices as generating from an 'excessive deprivation of a sense of powerfulness' (Davies 2000, p. 164). The contradictions and tensions between the discourses and power relations of hegemonic masculinity, on the one hand, and being positioned as student within the discourses and power relations of official schooling, on the other, seem to leave Adam with very limited spaces for managing and maintaining his sense of masculinity. To be recognisably and laudably 'masculine', Adam appears compelled to refuse (what he interprets as) the imposed and coercive structures and practices of schooling through calculated performances of subversion and sabotage (Davies 2000).

Drawing on Davies' (1993) work, we can see that models of teacher authoritarianism reflect some of the more negative aspects of hegemonic masculinity, and in this sense can be associated with how Adam takes up his way of being male in his wish for control, agency and power. Ironically, his dominating and controlling behaviour may be legitimised and sustained by the very same behaviour modelled by his teachers in their attempts to control him (Clark 1993). This parallels with key work which illustrates how teachers' oppressive uses of power (such as the rigid policing of rules, the use of 'put-downs' and the enforcement of punishments) work to reinscribe and reinforce relations of control and domination and invariably incite further student resistance (Lingard et al. 2002; Martino & Pallotta-Chiarolli 2003).

It is argued that prescriptive, systematic and controlling strategies work to privilege the rational and instrumental over the relational and affective, and in this regard may perpetuate violent cultures through ignoring or devaluing the world of emotions and feelings, and actively denying irrational experiences as aberrational (Fitzclarence & Kenway 1997; Fitzclarence 2000). Rationalising behaviour through individualising and pathologising, and controlling through repressive measures, they argue, defines students' identities clinically within conservative, narrow and incomplete paradigms.

Teacher–student relations characterised by control and domination are seen as hindering boys' academic and social outcomes. Lingard and his colleagues (2002), for example, associate teacher authoritarianism with generating students' disengagement from, and rebellion against, school cultures. This rebellion is very much evident in Adam's story through his adversarial 'playing' of the teachers and can be seen as constraining both his social and academic outcomes. Certainly Adam's sense of resistance to being controlled by school structures and practices seems to incite his desire for rebellion and risk-taking—clear in his subversion of the school's crap rules—but this resistance also works to constrain his academic work, not least because he is generally disengaged from school, but more explicitly, for example, when he acts dumb to get out of schoolwork.

Issues of authoritarianism and control and their negative impacts on the relationships between teachers and their male students have perhaps their greatest significance when considering their pedagogical implications (Lingard et al. 2002; Keddie 2004). Much of the research which examines the sociopolitical power dynamics of boys' enactments of masculinity (Alloway et al. 2002; Martino & Pallotta-Chiarolli 2003; Keddie 2004), positions teachers facilitating boys' exploration of their personal experiences of what it means to be 'masculine' as central to enhancing academic and social outcomes. Through pedagogies that connect with boys, the aim here is to broaden understandings and enactments of masculinity to be more inclusive and accepting of difference and diversity (Alloway et al. 2002). Part of this process necessarily involves critically analysing, questioning and problematising essentialist and hierarchical constructions of masculinity as associated with power, control and domination, and reworking these constructions to be more inclusive of difference and diversity. One would also think that a critical part of this process would also involve positive and generative, rather than authoritarian and controlling teacher–student relationships (Alloway et al. 2002).

In understanding why relations of control and authority continue to be key characteristics of much teacher practice (Martino & Pallotta-Chiarolli 2003), it is important to acknowledge the impact of broader sociopolitical contexts. Such teacher practice has been linked to the regimes of efficiency driving the processes of Australia's globalised economy (Lingard 2003). In the sphere of education, these regimes have resulted in greater managerial responsibility devolved to schools within a competitive framework (Lingard 2003). A deregulated environment of competition, reduced funding, and the pressure of 'market advantage' has spawned a culture of performativity.

This culture of performativity has resulted in an obsession with academic results and the measurement of specific aspects of education (principally, easily quantifiable and measurable literacy and numeracy outcomes), and has narrowly defined success and achievement (Mahony 1999). These narrow definitions have been foregrounded as the most important measures of school effectiveness, while social outcomes have been sidelined and perceived as somehow less significant than measurable academic outcomes (Pallotta-Chiarolli 1997). Despite the wide acceptance at school level of the importance of supportive environments and relationships, formal accountability measures are invariably reduced to academic performance alone. By extension, in a context where market forces are increasingly driving school priorities, classroom environments are characterised by an over-emphasis on management, basic skills and narrowly defined understandings of success and achievement (State of Queensland 2001). Against this multi-layered backdrop, we can see how these forces interact with expectations in teacher culture to perpetuate authoritarian and controlling teacher practice.

A way forward

The voices and stories of this chapter help us to recognise the importance of positive teacher–student relationships in addressing the educational needs of boys in the middle years. Issues of behaviour management and, more specifically, strategies of control and authority, are undoubtedly the central considerations here, particularly given that males continue to 'make up an overwhelming proportion of students experiencing disciplinary problems' (Commonwealth of Australia 2003, p. 4). The concern here, to reiterate an earlier point, is '[t]he first imperative of some teachers when teaching boys [which] appears to be "controlling" rather than teaching them' (Lingard et al. 2002, p. 4). Most critically, 'controlling' constructs around domination and authority remain a key characteristic of teacher practice and are a particular concern when considering issues of masculinity.

Against this backdrop we call for professional learning communities in schools to critically 'evaluate the ways in which power relations and constructs around domination and authority are being played out and systematically legitimated within school structures and classroom practice' (Martino & Pallotta-Chiarolli 2003, p. 208). In presenting such a statement we accept that those who want teachers 'to succeed at new kinds of teaching must understand that the process of change requires that teachers have time and opportunities to reconstruct their practice through intensive study and experimentation' (Darling-Hammond 1997, p. 223). The lessons of decades of school improvement and teacher change initiatives (see, for example, Fullan & Miles 1992; Louis & Marks 1998) make us mindful of the complexity of the processes necessary for the conception, implementation and institutionalisation of pedagogic change, with these processes being especially critical when the proposed change involves the degree of personal and professional risk that attaches to moving away from pedagogies grounded in control and authority. The scope of this chapter does not extend to the detail of specific strategic approaches for professional learning communities of middle school teachers, but attending to such process issues would be crucial to the potential outcomes of any attempts to change teacher practice on a schoolwide basis.

With such caveats in mind we look at one avenue for moving beyond constructs of domination and authority in the following, which draws on the Supportive Classroom Environment dimension of the Productive Pedagogies framework, to articulate a way forward. After a brief explanation of the framework, we identify key strategies for enhancing social as well as academic outcomes through facilitating positive and equitable teacher–student relationships. Throughout we illustrate important considerations in thinking about how these strategies might challenge and transform, rather than accept and reinscribe, narrow definitions of masculinity.

The Productive Pedagogies framework

The Productive Pedagogies (see Table 14.1 for a concise outline) is a comprehensive framework of quality teaching and learning which was developed in light of the Queensland School Reform Longitudinal Study (State of Queensland 2001), a three-year examination of the links between classroom practice and improved learning (Hayes et al. 2000). As a response to the findings of this study, principally the generally low levels of authentic or productive pedagogy characterising teaching and learning environments in Queensland, the Productive Pedagogies were presented as a way forward to improving the educational outcomes of all students (State of Queensland 2001; Lingard et al. 2002).

Table 14.1 Outline of the Productive Pedagogies framework

Intellectual quality	
Higher order thinking	Students are engaged in critical analysis and other forms of higher order thinking
Depth of knowledge	Central concepts and their complex relations are covered in depth and detail
Depth of understanding	Students' work and responses provide evidence of understanding of concepts or ideas and of the relationships between these concepts
Substantive conversation	Classroom talk breaks out of the initiation/response evaluation pattern and leads to sustained dialogue between students, and between teachers and students
Knowledge as problematic	Students critique and second-guess texts, ideas and knowledge
Meta-language	Aspects of language, grammar and technical vocabulary are foregrounded
Connectedness	
Knowledge integration	Teaching and learning ranges across diverse fields, disciplines and paradigms
Link to background knowledge	Teaching and learning is connected with students' background knowledge
Connection to the world beyond the classroom	Teaching and learning resembles or connects to real-life contexts
Problem-based curriculum	Teaching and learning focuses on identifying and solving intellectual and/or real-world problems

(continues)

Table 14.1 *continued*

Supportive classroom environment	
Students' direction of activities	Students have a say in the pace, direction or outcomes of the lesson
Social support for student achievement	Classroom is a socially supportive, positive environment where student success is valued and celebrated
Academic engagement	Students are engaged and on-task
Explicit quality performance criteria	Criteria for student performance, and how these criteria may be met, are made explicit
Student self-regulation	The direction of student behaviour is implicit and self-regulatory

Recognition of difference	
Cultural knowledge	Diverse cultural knowledges are brought into play and valued
Inclusive participation	Deliberate attempts are made to increase the participation of all students of different backgrounds, abilities and needs
Narrative	Teaching draws on a variety of others' stories and narratives, rather than relying on expository styles
Group identities	Teaching builds a sense of community and identity
Active citizenship	Active citizenship is fostered through opportunities for authentic action in context

Source: Adapted from State of Queensland (2001, p. 133). Used with permission.

The Productive Pedagogies framework comprises four dimensions, and all four should be drawn on in constructing, and reflecting on, quality teaching and learning, and thus should be seen as interconnected. However, given the relationships focus of this chapter, the following will focus on the Supportive Classroom Environment dimension only.

Facilitating a supportive classroom environment

Boys, Literacy and Schooling highlights the importance of teachers providing an environment that supports student agency, choice and autonomy. The Supportive Classroom Environment dimension of Productive Pedagogies explores the importance of relationships and, principally, student–teacher relationships in making this possible. As the stories and voices in this chapter have illuminated, this focus is critical. In determining positive learning outcomes, what matters here are teachers who are friendly, firm and relate well to their students (Lingard et al. 2002). Key here is facilitating an environment of mutual respect and support where students' behaviour is self-regulatory, where students have a say in what they do and how they do it, where students are academically engaged and where criteria for student performance are made explicit (State of Queensland 2001).

As mentioned earlier, issues of power, control and authoritarianism are key elements within the masculinities literature. These issues are positioned as particularly significant in understanding how mutually respectful and supportive teacher–student relationships might be facilitated with boys in the middle years (Lingard et al. 2002; Martino & Pallotta-Chiarolli 2003). In developing these sorts of relationships the importance of breaking down the power imbalances between teachers and students is central, particularly given many boys' resistances to being overpowered and controlled. In acknowledging issues of power and masculinity, research tells us that boys' social and behavioural outcomes are enhanced through democratic disciplinary approaches (Lingard et al. 2002; Martino & Pallotta-Chiarolli 2003). In considering these approaches, we can see how breaking down the power imbalances within the teacher–student relationship can work to challenge and transform (rather than reinscribe) boys' investments in dominant constructions of masculinity (mobilised around power and control) through disrupting, and offering alternative ways of being. In developing positive student–teacher relationships of mutual respect there are three important considerations.

A democratic classroom environment

The shift towards positive and (more) equitable teacher–student relationships will require teachers to share their power and authority to reflect a more democratic classroom environment (Alloway et al. 2002). The pedagogies of connectedness in relation to teachers tapping into boys' preferences, interests and learning styles are key issues here, in terms of shifting power relations of authority by offering boys positions of expertise, agency, autonomy and choice in the classroom at levels appropriate for the growing independence and decision-making sophistication of middle years students. Reflecting a (greater) valuing of student opinion and advice, this means teachers allowing students to have greater input in what, how and when they engage in particular tasks while maintaining high expectations that they will achieve successful outcomes. As well as the negotiation or choice of content and materials, this includes making transparent the criteria against which student performance is judged. Within a scaffold of clear instructions (Lingard et al. 2002), this may involve students defining their own goals and monitoring and documenting their progress on particular tasks. In shifting power relations in this way, students are more likely to take ownership of the task or activity which will facilitate self-regulatory rather than teacher-directed behaviour (Alloway et al. 2002). The point here is facilitating an environment where students are positioned with not only legitimacy and agency in terms of their everyday school lives, but also with responsibility for their own learning.

A classroom environment of mutual respect and dignity

Establishing positive teacher–student and student–student relations involves creating a 'safe' classroom environment of respect and dignity where students feel confident in sharing their knowledge, ideas and opinions. A negotiated, positive and socially just disciplinary approach is a key part of constructing this environment. Here the principal emphasis is on knowing and understanding rather than controlling and punishing, and on acknowledging boys' enactments of masculinity as located within broader cultural and social contexts (Gilbert & Gilbert 1998; Lingard et al. 2002). In this sense, for example, boys' threatening and harmful behaviours are recognised as associated with broader relations of, and investments in, power and masculinity (and their interplay with other identity relations such as femininity, sexuality, race and class) (Gilbert & Gilbert 1998). To these ends, generic and prescriptive policies and programs (on bullying and harassment, for example) must not ignore the wider social and cultural practices (often sexist, racist, homophobic or classist) that inform student behaviour. Often, for example, sex-based, racial or homophobic bullying or harassment occurs within, and is supported and rewarded by, broader social contexts. As Denborough (1996) argues, if we do not locate boys' problematic behaviours within broader social systems and dynamics, we run the risk of blaming relatively powerless boys or year levels for the problems of masculinity.

Facilitated through teachers' active interest in and concern for students, a connected and conciliatory approach will involve teachers listening and respecting students' points of view and involving students in negotiating and deciding a 'way forward' in terms of what might constitute preferred behaviours. In this regard, Martino and Pallotta-Chiarolli (2003) argue the importance of teachers using strategies that diffuse and deflect rather than confront and challenge. Teaching boys the social skills of effective and harmonious collaboration with others has been seen as helpful here. Skills-based approaches can also be effective in boys developing conflict resolution strategies through dialogue and negotiation and using experiential techniques such as role-play scenarios (Commonwealth of Australia 2003).

Building networks of connection, support and understanding

Supportive classroom relations can be facilitated through constructing situations that necessitate student sharing and collaboration, and encourage respectful relations, such as establishing small student discussion groups. In this context students' sharing of personal experiences and interpretations concerning identity issues, and their informed and critical reflection on their beliefs and values, have been effective in improving the quality of social relationships through a broader understanding of others' perspectives (Gilbert & Gilbert 1998; Alloway et al. 2002; Lingard et al. 2002).

In reference to the development of conflict resolution strategies and the sharing of personal experiences, an important issue, particularly for boys in the middle years, is facilitating capacities for expressing feelings and for expressing empathy and emotional connectedness with others (McLean 1996; Kenway & Fitzclarence 1997; Commonwealth of Australia 2003). In building a climate of social support and mutual respect, Kenway and Fitzclarence talk of developing a 'pedagogy of emotions'. They highlight the significance of teachers facilitating students' exploration and understanding of the powerful feelings that are implicated in some of their behaviours and interactions (such as suffering, fear, anger, rage, shame and humiliation, jealousy, revenge and remorse, as well as joy and pleasure). Certainly these explorations are conducive to disrupting traditional versions of masculinity as emotionally neutral or distant, and in this sense can work to broaden boys' modes of expression to encompass alternatives to dominant and dominating ways of being; such explorations could be facilitated within the supportive group contexts described above or through individual reflective exercises such as journal entries (Commonwealth of Australia 2003).

In sharing power in the middle school classroom, teachers may need to expand their existing expectations of what constitutes acceptable and unacceptable student behaviour. This may mean teachers increasing their latitude beyond the normal purview or tolerance of institutionalised schooling, in terms of allowing boys to experiment with 'a range of possibilities for (re)presenting themselves in the classroom, and with acceptable ways of conducting their presence and activity within the school' (Alloway et al. 2002, p. 128). To reiterate, much of this is made possible through teachers connecting with boys' interests, preferences and opinions with the aim being to affirm boys' sense of self and to increase their self-esteem and academic engagement through a closer alignment between boys' enactments of themselves and classroom or school culture (Alloway et al. 2002).

Conclusion

Facilitating relations of mutual respect and support, through the strategies outlined above, works to disrupt, and provide alternatives to, the traditional power inequities that continue to exist between teachers and students. While we acknowledge the broader sociopolitical contexts that support such practice, this chapter has presented these inequities, and particularly relations of authority and control, as constraining academic and social outcomes through suppressing boys' sense of legitimacy and agency. In articulating a way forward, we have argued the importance of teacher–student relationships characterised by mutual respect, support, dignity, connection and understanding. We see such relationships as central to teachers developing meaningful and productive pedagogies with boys in the middle years.

In presenting a way forward, we have also argued the importance of moving beyond essentialist assumptions about boys' behaviours to a location of these behaviours within the broader sociopolitical dimensions of masculinity and power. Here we must recognise that many boys' investments in dominant or hegemonic constructions of masculinity are implicated in shaping their disruptive behaviours. To these ends, the strategies presented in this chapter orientate around providing alternatives to dominating and controlling modes of being (Alloway et al. 2002). A principal aim here is to broaden boys' understandings and enactments of masculinity through an approach that teaches rather than preaches. We see positive and mutually respectful teacher–student relations as central to this process and as necessary for addressing disruptive or anti-school behaviours in sustainable and socially just ways (Kenway & Fitzclarence 1997).

Questions

1 Take a couple of minutes to think back over your own experiences as a student in the middle years. Who would you nominate as the best teacher you had during those years? What factors led you to name that particular teacher? How significant in your thinking were factors related to the teacher–student relationship? Now repeat the process, but this time thinking of your worst teacher.

2 Think about whether you agree or disagree with this statement:

(Most) boys are biologically very different from (most) girls. In the middle years this means that (most) boys will need more firm control than (most) girls.

If you agree, what are the implications for teachers' management of boys and girls in the middle years? What are the implications if you disagree? What are the implications if you are undecided or don't know?

3   It's common for things to get worse before they get better when teachers try new approaches to learning and classroom management. What professional risks might this entail for an individual teacher? How might whole-school approaches help to alleviate individual risks and encourage teachers to persist with new approaches to relationships and management?

15

Managing behaviour

Terry de Jong

Despite the contention that teachers in the middle years of schooling require specialist preparation, little exists in the way of specialist resources to facilitate their development in effectively managing the behaviour of middle school students. This chapter attempts to address this disparity. Informed by two recent research projects on good practice associated with the management of student behaviour in the Australian context, I propose a set of six principles and a comprehensive framework of the characteristics of good practice that focus specifically on the management of student behaviour in the middle years of schooling, and conclude with a case study and a series of questions.

I have often heard middle school teachers lament how challenging they find managing the behaviour of their students. I have witnessed on a number of occasions middle school teachers throwing up their arms in despair in response to the lively behaviour of their students. Conversely, I have been in middle school classrooms where teachers manage student behaviour with such finesse that I begin to wonder what all the fuss is about this age group. Before delusion overwhelms me, I remind myself that the anguish many middle school teachers experience when confronted with managing student behaviour is real and largely justified. Young adolescents pose behaviour management challenges for teachers more complex and demanding than those posed by any other age group (Bennett 1997; Jackson &

Davis 2000). We are reminded too by *Turning Points* (2004, p. 8) that 'between the ages of ten and fourteen, the young adolescent grows and develops more rapidly than during any other developmental stage except for infancy'. The combination of early adolescence and the transition from the primary to secondary phase of schooling presents multifaceted challenges for the middle school student, often manifested in behaviours that are more complex, pronounced and challenging than those generally exhibited during the primary and upper secondary school years. I have argued previously that 'the fundamentals of good student behaviour management practice appear to be common to all age groups' (de Jong 2003, p. 8). In view of the profound transitional nature of early adolescence, and the complexity of behaviour associated with this developmental phase, I also contend that middle school administrators and teachers have to go beyond the fundamentals of good behaviour management practice. What is it that they have to do to manage middle school student behaviour effectively so that learning outcomes are successfully achieved? In short, what are the principles and characteristics of good practice associated with the management of middle school student behaviour?

In this chapter I attempt to address the above questions. In doing so I have drawn liberally from two of my recent research projects. The first was a survey carried out in 2002 in which I endeavoured to find out from experienced school staff in nine Perth-based middle schools what they considered to be good behaviour management practice in middle schools. I synthesised their views with an analysis of the literature on the same topic, and constructed a framework of the characteristics of good practice (see de Jong 2003). The second project, conducted from March 2003 to June 2004, led to the development of a framework of principles and good practices that can be used to support the development of successful student behaviour management programs on a systemic, district, school, classroom and individual level in Australian education environments (de Jong 2004).

In the first section of this chapter I briefly explain my understanding of the main concepts related to the topic. I also present the organising framework that I used to classify and define the principles and characteristics of good practice. Section two discusses the six principles identified from the surveys and literature that underpin good practice associated with the behaviour management of middle school students. In section three I present a framework of the characteristics of good practice related to the effective behaviour management of middle school students. This framework is a synthesis of the two frameworks that emerged from the two surveys. Section four concludes the chapter with a series of questions based on a case study.

Key concepts

A number of key ideas and concepts pervade this chapter, namely: early adolescence; young adolescents; middle school students; behaviour; misbehaviour; discipline; behaviour management; and principles and characteristics of good practice. For the purposes of my discussion, I have elected to give a very brief explanation of my understanding of these ideas and concepts.

Early adolescence, young adolescents, middle school students

'Early adolescence', as opposed to 'late adolescence', is a specific human development period that spans approximately the 10–15 years age group. It is characterised by the onset of puberty and profound changes in the physical, cognitive, social, emotional and moral dimensions of a child's development. 'Young adolescents' refers to young people who are experiencing early adolescence, while 'middle school students' refers to students who are in the middle grades of their schooling, namely Years 6 to 10.

Behaviour, misbehaviour, discipline

In the context of this chapter, 'behaviour' is considered to be the observable actions that a middle school student exhibits. 'Misbehaviour' is defined as 'behaviour that is considered inappropriate for the setting or situation in which it occurs', encompassing in descending order of seriousness five broad types: aggression, immorality, defiance of authority, class disruptions and goofing off (Charles 1999, pp. 2–3). 'Discipline' refers to a repertoire of strategies that aim to help middle school students 'learn more effective responsible behaviours that enable themselves and others to learn' (Edwards & Watts 2004, p. 134). It is an educative process, and focuses on promoting responsibility and developing self-discipline.

Behaviour management

Taken literally, the idea of 'managing' a middle school student's behaviour could imply control and authoritarianism. In the context of this chapter, however, I see this notion as being inclusive of all different kinds of practices that aim to develop self-discipline in the student. In this sense, 'behaviour management' has a broad meaning. It refers to overseeing all aspects of a student's learning environment and learning experience so that conditions are created to promote appropriate behaviour and to maximise opportunities for the student to learn self-discipline.

Principles and characteristics of good practice

I have deliberately chosen to use the idea of 'good practice' rather than 'best practice' in this chapter. The notion of 'best practice' tends to imply that other approaches and methods are not as worthy of consideration.

It is useful to classify behaviour management practice according to five broad categories, namely, policy, culture, curriculum, pedagogy and classroom management. Underpinning these categories are the six principles which are discussed in the next section. I view alternative learning programs, which are sometimes considered narrowly as behaviour management strategies for students at educational risk, as part of the curriculum category. I see behaviour management practice as operating fundamentally at a system, district, school and classroom level within a typical education structure. Figure 15.1 illustrates these levels and highlights which categories of behaviour management practice operate most predominantly at each level. Table 15.1 presents a structure which was used to define, classify and organise the characteristics of good practice according to the five categories and different levels within the education system that they operate. The principles of good practice are placed at the top of the table. This serves to emphasise that the five categories of good practice are based on a rationale.

Figure 15.1 Levels in the education system at which the most predominant categories of behaviour management practice occur

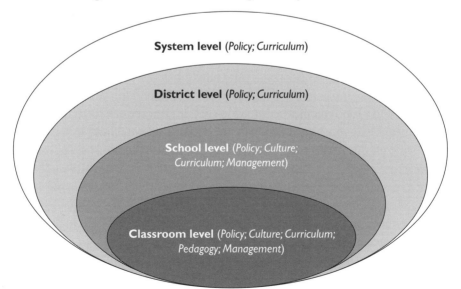

System level *(Policy; Curriculum)*

District level *(Policy; Curriculum)*

School level *(Policy; Culture; Curriculum; Management)*

Classroom level *(Policy; Culture; Curriculum; Pedagogy; Management)*

Table 15.1 Classification and definition of the characteristics of good practice

Principles	'Rules' that guide and determine the rationale of good behaviour management practice in the middle years of schooling	
Classification	*Levels*	*Characteristics (defining features)*
Policy	All levels of the system	A *broad-based plan* that focuses directly and indirectly on establishing good behaviour management practice
Culture	School and classroom	*Conditions* related to the school and classroom ethos and climate that facilitate and encourage appropriate student behaviour
Curriculum	All levels of the system	The *teaching and learning plan* that incorporates features which maximise student engagement and learning, and minimise behavioural issues
Pedagogy	Classroom	*Teaching and learning practices* that incorporate features which maximise student engagement and learning, and minimise behavioural issues
Management	School and classroom	*Specific management strategies* that focus on promoting appropriate behaviour, preventing misbehaviour, and correcting misbehaviour

Principles of good practice

Knowing which principles underpin your student behaviour management practice, and why you apply those particular principles, is essential for two reasons. Firstly, principles are like fundamental 'rules', which act as a framework to guide your practice and ensure that you have a rationale for doing what you chose to do. Secondly, having principles provide a source for critical reflection. Is my practice congruent with the principles that I uphold? If not, what do I need to do differently in my practice to ensure coherence with my principles? If my practice is working well, but contradicts some of my principles, do I need to modify or change some of my principles to ensure coherence? These are important questions to ask when reviewing and developing your approach to behaviour management.

The six principles that underpin good practice associated with the behaviour management of middle school students are:

1   Management of middle school student behaviour should be developmentally responsive.

2   Middle school student behaviour needs to be understood from an eco-systemic perspective.

3   Practices associated with behaviour management of middle school students must embrace a health-promoting approach to creating a safe, supportive and caring environment.

4   The management of middle school student behaviour must embrace inclusiveness, which caters for the different potentials, needs and resources of all middle school students.

5   The management of middle school student behaviour should incorporate a student-centred philosophy that places the student at the centre of the learning process and focuses on the whole student (personal, social and academic).

6   Developing positive relationships with middle school students is fundamental to maximising appropriate behaviour and achieving learning outcomes.

Each principle is now considered in turn.

Principle 1: Management of middle school student behaviour should be developmentally responsive
In the context of the middle years of schooling, this principle broadly means understanding, acknowledging and responding appropriately to the developmental needs of young adolescents. With reference to young Australian adolescents, Cummings (1988) has this to say:

> Like all students, young adolescents have a range of personal, intellectual and social needs. With the onset of puberty, however, there are particular physical, emotional and cultural needs that also need to be addressed. The middle years of schooling should provide opportunities for young people to learn and grow in ways that acknowledge and respect this unique and special phase of their development (p. 14).

Developmental responsiveness is vital to ensuring success for every middle school student (Jackson & Davis 2000). It underpins the breadth of middle schooling practice, including the culture and organisational structure of the school, and its curriculum and pedagogy. It is in fact an integral part of all the principles that underpin good practice in the behaviour management of middle school students.

Principle 2: Middle school student behaviour needs to be understood from an eco-systemic perspective

This principle is based on an integration of ecological theory and systems theory. It is based on the idea that systems such as eco-systems (rainforests, deserts), social systems (families, peer groups) and education systems (departments, districts, schools, classrooms) are made up of different sub-systems or groups where the functioning of the whole system is dependent on the interaction between all sub-systems.

What does this principle mean in terms of our understanding the behaviour of middle school students? Firstly, it requires us not to oversimplify our interpretation of behaviour by merely seeking to explain it in a linear fashion, where we look for a cause, assume that the behaviour we observe is the direct effect of this cause, and then endeavour to tackle the cause single-mindedly with the hope that the behaviour will change. It is possible that adopting this approach works occasionally. However, human behaviour is multifaceted and, as was pointed out earlier, the complex developmental and environmental transitions during early adolescence pose particular challenges for the middle school student and teacher alike. We need to view the behaviour of middle school students in relation to a range of inter-dependent environmental, interpersonal and intra-personal factors. Instead of using linear causality to explain behaviour, we should adopt circular causality, where behaviour is viewed as cycles of interaction. In other words, the behaviour of a student is understood to affect and be affected by context and the behaviour of others.

The seminal *Turning Points 2000* presents a school reform design that is based on systems theory. Integral to the successful implementation and management of middle schools is the concept of systems thinking (Jackson & Davis 2000). Jackson and Davis assert that to meet the needs of all young adolescents, and thus ensure success for all middle school students, it is critical to understand the complexity of change processes. They argue that when a systemic approach is used comprehensively and with fidelity in implementing the *Turning Points* model, there are significant improvements in student outcomes. However, they caution that 'half measures' in the establishment and development of middle schools is likely to make little difference in improving student outcomes. Structural change without reforming curriculum and pedagogy is unlikely to address the needs of middle school students adequately and will probably result in levels of student disengagement. This serves to emphasise the point I made above about the importance of adopting a comprehensive approach to the management of behaviour issues.

Principle 3: Practices associated with behaviour management of middle school students must embrace a health-promoting approach to creating a safe, supportive and caring environment

This principle asserts that the promotion of *both* health and learning is the core business of schools. Its basic rationale is that health and learning and behaviour are integral to each other, and a healthy learning environment will enhance appropriate student behaviour. Health is defined broadly in terms of physical, cognitive, social, emotional and spiritual dimensions.

The National Safe Schools Framework (MCEETYA 2003) clearly advocates that the promotion of a healthy school environment is the business of all Australian schools. Creating a safe, supportive and caring environment is obviously not exclusive to middle schools. However, the significance of highlighting this principle in relation to behaviour management and middle school students is related to the increased vulnerability that young adolescents may experience during this phase of their life. Developing a healthy self-esteem is probably the most important life task facing young adolescents. Being in a state of constant transition, they can be susceptible to feelings of anxiety, insecurity and poor self-worth.

Of all the changes experienced by middle school students, the increase in peer focus and involvement in peer-related activities is probably the most pronounced (Eccles & Wigfield 1997). Being socially accepted can become a priority at the expense of school activities. Harter (in Eccles & Wigfield 1997, p. 19) makes the point that 'young adolescents' confidence in their physical appearance and social acceptance is often a more important predictor of self-esteem than confidence in their cognitive/academic competence'. When transferring from primary to secondary school the challenge of developing a healthy self-esteem, especially in terms of establishing social relationships, becomes more prominent for young adolescents. At a time when relationships with peers are so important to them, their social networks are at risk of being disrupted (Mizelle & Mullins 1997).

Young adolescents desire to feel safe, supported and nurtured (Jackson & Davis 2000) and middle schools have a responsibility to ensure that these needs are adequately met in relation to developing a healthy psychosocial culture.

Principle 4: The management of middle school student behaviour must embrace inclusiveness, which caters for the different potentials, needs and resources of all middle school students

This principle celebrates diversity by emphasising the importance of accepting and accommodating middle school students as individuals rather than viewing them as a homogenous group where 'one size fits all'. Where schools tend to have a homogenised culture which pays little attention to the fact that young adolescents develop at different rates, seek recognition for their individuality and strive for autonomy, they are placing their students potentially at risk of identity confusion, particularly if the school culture reflects high levels of sex-role stereotyping and homophobic tendencies.

This principle constructs student behaviour as an integral component of student diversity and not primarily a 'deficit' concept which requires the teacher to 'fix' a student's behaviour. 'At risk' behaviour is not a constant. It is part of a continuum of life-factors, with middle school students' level of vulnerability being variable over time as they move in and out of 'risk'. This implies that all middle school students will at some point be at risk as a natural function of their development, and perhaps behave inappropriately at some time during early adolescence. This principle implicitly cautions middle school teachers to be realistic about their expectations of possibly striving for perfect behaviour, and accepting that misbehaviour *will occur* in their classrooms.

Principle 5: The management of middle school student behaviour should incorporate a student-centred philosophy that places the student at the centre of the learning process and focuses on the whole student (personal, social and academic)

The rationale for this principle is based on three key propositions. First, student behaviour is inextricably linked to the quality of the learning experience. Secondly, relevant curriculum and effective pedagogy are critical to student engagement. Thirdly, an engaged student is less likely to misbehave than the student who is disengaged from the learning process.

This principle, like the others, advocates developmental responsiveness by deeming the needs and interests of the middle school student to be of paramount importance. This means that the emphasis in the teaching and learning process should be placed on the student rather than subject. A learner-centred curriculum should be central to the middle years of schooling (Jackson & Davis 2000; Manning & Bucher 2005). In the Australian context, middle schooling philosophy constitutes principles associated with a learner-centred, collaboratively organised and flexibly constructed approach to teaching young adolescents (Cumming 1998).

Engaging young adolescents by being responsive to their needs is especially pertinent because of their increasing desire to experience learning activities that are relevant, connected to the real world and ultimately meaningful. In comparison to other age groups, young adolescents are more at risk of experiencing alienation disengagement, and exhibiting disruptive behaviour (Chadbourne 2001). If engagement is minimal, it is highly probable that the teacher will experience behaviour issues.

Principle 6: Developing positive relationships with middle school students is fundamental to maximising appropriate behaviour and achieving learning outcomes

The development of positive relationships between teachers and students, and between students themselves, in the middle years of schooling was highlighted in the two surveys on good practice (de Jong 2003, 2004) as being vital to the establishment of a healthy learning environment and sound foundation for effective behaviour management.

Clearly developmental responsiveness permeates this principle. In terms of social development, young adolescents have an intense need to belong, to be accepted and to have a sense of identity. Rigby (1998) emphasises that key to the health and well-being of young people is the quality of relations they experience with their peers at school. As suggested previously, this quest is considered to be the single most important feature of early adolescence. This places middle school teachers in a very influential position to facilitate healthy peer relationships. They can provide cooperative learning opportunities, raise social issues and topics of concern, and foster a sense of identity with the peer group (*Turning Points* 2004). However, this influence can only have real impact if it is embedded in socially healthy school and classroom cultures. Lipsitz's investigative study on the discipline practices of successful middle schools revealed that healthy relationships, along with an intimate and caring school culture, contribute substantially to positive outcomes (Bennett 1997).

Characteristics of good practice

This section presents the key characteristics of good practice associated with the effective behaviour management of middle school students as Table 15.2. The characteristics are based on two surveys (de Jong 2003, 2004) and synthesised into a comprehensive framework of five broad categories, namely, policy, culture, curriculum, pedagogy and management (see Table 15.1). This framework is certainly not meant to be definitive in the sense that these elements represent the *only* characteristics of good practice. There may be characteristics of good practice that you would like to add. Alternatively, there may be some characteristics that, in your context, may not be considered to be good practice. Further, the framework does not make any distinction as to which characteristics might be more or less relevant to the middle years of schooling. This does not imply that they are necessarily of equal importance or relevance. Within your particular context you may wish to argue that some characteristics are more important and relevant than others.

Table 15.2 Key characteristics of good practice associated with the behaviour management of middle school students

Policy
- Middle school adopts a whole-school approach to behaviour management.
- Embraces middle schooling philosophy (developmentally responsive, student-centred, constructivist, outcomes-based, inclusive, and community-focused).
- Takes into particular account the developmental needs of young adolescents and consequently has a strong focus on middle school students developing independence, self-discipline and self-regulation.
- Focuses explicitly on providing a middle school environment which is safe, supportive and caring, and is concerned with fostering the well-being of all its school community.
- Embraces the notion of rights, responsibilities and rules that every member of the middle school community is accountable for adhering to.
- Includes clear and reasonable consequences that are explicitly linked to rights, responsibilities and rules.
- Views the management of middle school student behaviour as an educative process where it is essentially a means to an end in supporting the student to behave appropriately, and not simply an end in itself (i.e. punishment).
- Encourages self-reflection as a middle school strategy to develop self-regulation and self-discipline.
- Reflects a commitment to positive reinforcement of appropriate behaviour.
- Includes, where appropriate, inter-agency collaboration in the development and implementation of the middle school's behaviour management programs and practices.

Culture
- The middle school has a health-promoting approach to creating a safe, supportive and caring environment that reflects a healthy psychosocial culture through the facilitation of positive peer relations and development of social skills among its middle school students.
- The middle school embraces inclusiveness and acknowledges student diversity, particularly in terms of adolescent gender differences, variability of development, multiplicity of interests, subcultures and Indigenous people.
- The middle school values flexibility and strives to be responsive to students' needs.
- Relationship-building between teachers and students is integral to the daily life of the middle school. This is demonstrated by a climate in which:
  - teachers make it their priority to develop positive relationships with their students;
  - teachers hold the view that 'I earn respect' rather than 'I deserve respect';
  - teachers endeavour to get to know their students in different contexts;
  - teachers demonstrate that they like young adolescents and that they can relate to this age group;
  - there is a strong focus on pastoral care.

- Collaboration and team work among all middle school staff are highly valued, especially in relation to a whole-school approach to behaviour management.
- Student 'connectedness' is central to the mission, culture and daily life of the middle school.
- The middle school incorporates a proactive, rather than reactive, approach to potential student behaviour issues and challenges.

Curriculum
- Is responsive to the needs of all its middle school students. It is inclusive, catering for all students. It is relevant and engaging, recognising that the risk of alienation is high during early adolescence.
- Reflects high expectations of its middle school students and upholds success for all. It promotes the intellectual development of its students and exhibits the belief that young adolescents have the capacity to develop higher order thinking and 'deep' knowledge.
- Embraces and makes explicit values associated with social justice, enterprise and citizenship.
- Is flexible, and might include the development of planned future pathways, which offer middle school students choice and increased access to alternative forms of education, work experience, training and employment.
- Is demonstrably connected with the wider community and global context.
- Literacy and numeracy are explicitly incorporated in the curriculum, and delivered where possible in authentic contexts (real-life situations).
- Includes challenging activities that build leadership skills, success and confidence (for boys in particular, physical endeavour-based activities).
- Incorporates resilience-building experiences and life-skills, particularly those that help middle school students manage conflict appropriately (problem-solving skills, conflict resolution).
- Develops critical, reflective, rational thinking skills, focusing especially on decision making, appraising conflict situations, and restorative justice.

Pedagogy
- Is fundamentally student-centred. It places the middle school student at the centre of the learning process rather than the content of the curriculum ('We teach students, not subjects').
- Aims to ensure success for all middle school students by using appropriate methods of engagement that are responsive to the social, emotional and cognitive needs of the students, taking into account prior learning, different learning styles, gender preferences, ability and personal interests.
- Reflects high degrees of intellectual qualities (e.g. higher order thinking, knowledge as problematic) and connectedness (e.g. knowledge integration, connectedness to the world).
- Incorporates activity-based methods of learning.
- Includes cooperative learning practices.
- Keeps students busy and on task, keeping 'down time' to a minimum.
- Encourages students to take responsibility for their own learning and behaviour.
- Involves, where appropriate, students in collaborative decision making.
- Enhances self-esteem.

Management
- The middle school teacher constructs his/her own approach to behaviour management, which is coherent with the school policy.

(continues)

Table 15.2 *continued*

- The middle school teacher negotiates with the students a classroom management plan (a whole-class statement that incorporates agreed values and acceptable behaviour).
- The middle school teacher endeavours to understand the function (goals) of behaviour. This is the basis upon which effective management and change strategies are applied.
- Ownership for the management and resolution of middle school student behaviour issues remains with the class teacher(s) for as long as is possible.
- Middle school student behaviour issues are dealt with as promptly as possible.
- Developing positive relationships with middle school students is critical for effective management. This should incorporate an underemphasis on power; modelling of trust; an emphasis on the positives, even under adversity; and de-escalation of conflict through humour.
- Middle school teachers model appropriate behaviour and attitudes.
- There is an emphasis on positive reinforcement of appropriate behaviour.
- Behaviour management strategies aim to develop responsibility (students take ownership for their behaviour), self-discipline and self-regulation in the middle school student.
- When misbehaviour occurs, the corrective and educative process must focus on the inappropriate behaviour and not the student as a whole.
- There is a focus on responsible thinking processes (encouraging students to do the thinking in managing their own behaviour) and restorative justice (emphasis on the impact of inappropriate behaviour on people, not just the consequences of breaking of school rules).
- There is evidence of a range of management strategies that maximise on-task behaviour, such as proximity, setting clear expectations, with-it-ness and planning student transitions.
- A mutual problem-solving approach is applied in conflict management and conflict resolution.
- Behaviour management is flexible, offering middle school students appropriate choice and taking into account the individual needs of the students.
- The middle school teacher recognises when it is appropriate to call upon the system for help.

Source: Adapted from de Jong (2003, 2004). Used with permission from the Middle Years of Schooling Association and the Ministerial Council on Education, Employment, Training and Youth Affairs.

Conclusion

Despite the contention that teachers in the middle years of schooling require specialist preparation, little exists in the way of specialist resources to facilitate their development in effectively managing the behaviour of middle school students. Hopefully this chapter has gone some way to address this disparity, in aiming to offer a broad Australian perspective on the general behaviour management practices that are claimed by many experienced teachers and administrators to work well in the middle years of schooling. The principles and framework of good practices are certainly not definitive or exhaustive. They are tendered as a possible 'tool' for reflection and review of practice, and are amenable to modification themselves.

Questions

Read this case study, and answer the questions that follow.

> Anne Jameson is a Year 9 teacher at Boab Middle School, which serves a low to middle income community in metropolitan Perth. The school has a culturally diverse population of approximately 800 students, many of whom are immigrants from South-East Asia, Eastern Europe and the Middle East. The school is structured into six learning communities. Ms Jameson teaches in the Kestrel Learning Community with a team of five teachers.
>
> It is Monday morning and Ms Jameson is standing at the door greeting each of her Year 9 students as they enter their classroom for the start of the day. Antonio saunters in, eyes to the ground, and grunts in response to Ms Jameson's greeting. He drops his schoolbag onto his table with a thud and in the process, knocks Christopher's pencil case onto the floor. Christopher mumbles something that sets Antonio off. 'Pick it up yourself, f—k face!' yells Antonio angrily, in a voice that stretches uncomfortably from a strained squeak to a crackling baritone. Christopher responds by flicking Antonio's cap off, and being physically smaller than Antonio, moves himself quickly behind Carol and retorts: 'Pizza face!'

Some background information . . .

This incident is an example of a pattern of behaviour that Ms Jameson has observed in Antonio over the past two weeks. At the beginning of the year Antonio appeared to be generally well adjusted. Almost six months into Year 9 it is apparent to Ms Jameson that many things have changed for him. For a start, his growth spurt leaves him looking and feeling uncomfortable in clothes that are ill-fitting. His acne doesn't help. His peaked cap is always at maximum tilt to hide his eyes. Peter and Rafiq, his two closest Year 8 mates, have been selected for the school's junior basketball team. Antonio rarely mixes with them now. Carol, who paid Antonio a lot of attention earlier in the year, and whom Antonio had fancied as a prospective girlfriend, has found a Year 10 boyfriend. Chris is still Antonio's mate, but increasingly Antonio appears irritated by his childish behaviour.

Academically, life has changed for Antonio too. In primary school he had always achieved very well in mathematics, science, and technology and enterprise. In Year 8 he experienced some difficulty in understanding certain concepts in maths and science. This year Ms Jameson is supporting him considerably in making conceptual connections in these learning areas. English remains a struggle for Antonio. He now openly displays a resistance towards this learning area, and other than reading soccer and computer magazines, he refuses to read any of the books offered to him at school. Antonio's oral communication skills are good. He expresses himself confidently in class. Of late though, he often manifests intolerance of views that are contrary to his own, and becomes quite agitated and argumentative when articulating his viewpoint. Antonio has always enjoyed projects, especially ones that required the use of computer technology for design purposes and desktop layout, but Antonio has contributed little in the way of his computer skills to his current group project on environmental issues.

Ms Jameson is aware that Antonio is experiencing some problems at home. It is rumoured that his father is unemployed and drinks heavily. She met Antonio's mother briefly a few weeks ago, and noted that English was not her first language.

Back to the incident . . .

Ms Jameson moves decisively to the scene of conflict. She indicates calmly and assertively to Antonio and Christopher that she does not approve of their behaviour and directs them to separate and sit quietly in their seats. She asks them both to see her at the beginning of recess and reminds them that they have a choice; either they settle down and focus on their projects or, if they behave in a disruptive manner again, they have chosen time-out with Mr Everatt, the Year 9 team leader. She then quips that it's far too early in the day to spend so much precious energy on conflict, and concludes by encouraging the boys to start the day on a more positive note and save their energy for their project work.

After greeting the class as a whole, and explaining the procedures for the morning, Ms Jameson instructs the students to spend the next 45 minutes on planning how they wish to present their integrative studies project on environmental issues.

Christopher finds it difficult to focus on his work, and tends to wander from his group, chatting with other students. Ms Jameson makes a point of regularly walking over to Christopher's group and monitoring their progress, praising them for what they have achieved and encouraging them to stay on task.

Antonio is slumped in a chair next to his group, gazing out the window. His group is having a lively discussion on how best to present their findings on global warming. Ms Jameson stands quietly behind the group, listening and observing. Dana suggests a PowerPoint presentation, which could include a clip from the movie *The Day After Tomorrow*. Her suggestion is met with enthusiasm, but dampened by comments which indicate that such a task is beyond the expertise of the group. Ms Jameson gently interrupts, and asks the group if they have checked whether or not this is really the case. She hints that in fact there is someone in their group who is highly skilled in ICT. Five minutes later she notes that Antonio is sitting with the group, making suggestions about how they could design a PowerPoint presentation.

At recess Ms Jameson speaks briefly with Christopher and Antonio. She commends them on their ability to behave appropriately in class most of the time, but emphasises that their behaviour at the start of the day was unacceptable. Making reference to their class charter on rights and responsibilities, Ms Jameson asks the boys what they think was unacceptable about their behaviour, and why. After some discussion, she asks them to consider how their behaviour might affect other people around them, and if such a situation arose again, what they could do differently to ensure a better outcome. She dismisses Christopher, and then chats privately with Antonio. Expressing concern for his well-being, she shares some of her observations about his behaviour and general progress. Antonio sits silently, and although he is not forthcoming, nods lightly in acknowledgment of what Ms Jameson is saying to him. Ms Jameson indicates that she understands that it may be difficult for Antonio to talk to her, and invites him to speak with her anytime he wishes to do so. She asks him if there is anyone else in Kestrel Learning Community or the school whom he thinks he would feel comfortable talking to. At first Antonio says 'No,' and then murmurs, 'Maybe Mr Pestano.' Their meeting concludes with Antonio cautiously agreeing to Ms Jameson letting Mr Pestano know that Antonio may wish to speak to him about some of the difficulties he is experiencing at school and at home.

1   What good practices of middle school behaviour management do you see evidence of in this case study? Why do you consider these practices 'good'?
2   Are there behaviour management practices in this case study that you feel are inappropriate or in need of modification? Are there other practices that you believe would have been more appropriate? Give reasons for your answers.
3   Are there additional principles that you would like to see evidence of in this case study? If so, what are they, and why do you feel they should be demonstrated in this case study?
4   How do you think this chapter could support you in your management of middle school student behaviour? Are there aspects of this chapter that you would modify or change? Why?

16

Digital literacies

Muriel A. Wells and Leanne J. Reynolds

Students in the middle years of schooling are facing increasingly sophisticated literacy demands from new technologies, demands that go well beyond those of the traditional printed page as they interact with information communicated through a range of digital media both inside and outside of school. At best, these new technologies can open doors to students for researching and accessing a world far beyond their own environment, empowering them to direct and control their own learning and produce quality work.

These technologies include computer software, CD-ROMs, DVDs, electronic games, email, chat programs and Internet chat rooms, websites and video conferencing, as well as the older technologies such as radio, television, video and movies. Added to this is the proliferation of mobile phones and messaging systems and a continuous stream of emerging new technologies.

This chapter explores new technologies used for communications and for retrieving and publishing information, in terms of students *reading digital texts*, *creating digital texts*, *searching, finding and using information*, and *being critical users of digital texts*. Each of theses perspectives suggests specific roles for students as they operate as navigators, transformers, interpreters and critics of digital texts (Green & Campbell 2003).

New technologies make new and different demands on teachers' pedagogical practices. The New London Group (2000) describe pedagogy as a 'complex integration of four factors: Situated Practice, Overt Instruction, Critical Framing and Transformed Practice' (p. 32). This view of effective pedagogy acknowledges the value of learning experiences that include immersion as a community of learners while engaged in authentic versions of such practice (situated practice), supplemented by overt instruction and enhanced by teaching approaches that give rise to critical understanding of the workings of power, politics, ideology, values (Fairclough 1992), and cultural sensitivity. As the New London Group explain, these four components of pedagogy do not constitute a linear hierarchy but rather are components that are related and interact in complex ways.

Some educators express concerns about the proliferation of new technologies and yearn for the literacies of the past. Glister (1997) disagrees. He explains that people worry about the survival of the text and reading when children spend a lot of time on computers but that 'sceptics may discover that the Internet is providing us with a way to use language again'. Glister uses the examples of students, as well as people who are long out of school, who had simply got out of the habit of writing but who now use email communications all the time.

Teachers may have other concerns about the incorporation of new technologies in teaching learning. Some are concerned about issues of safety on the Internet. Educators (and parents) express concern about the unsuitable material available. Some are concerned about how working on computers might isolate students and limit the development of social skills. This is countered by those who argue that the use of new technologies and computers can provide opportunities for students to work in pairs or small groups. The products of group work can also be combined to create whole-class publications as students work in a community of learners who utilise new technologies.

New technologies provide new teaching and learning possibilities as students engage in higher order thinking skills as they seek to transform information for their own purposes or conduct critical evaluations. Active learning requires the student to transform or customise the information to make it their own. Inactive learning is merely electronic cutting, pasting and rearranging.

It is also important for teachers to see the use of new technologies in the wider context of education and the development of young people who are able to analyse, synthesise and make informed judgments from their learning experiences. According to Lankshear and Snyder (2002):

> it is still common for teachers to think of technology in terms of tools and implements . . . concentrating only on the tools or implements aspect of technology

[that] can blind us to its important social and cultural dimensions . . . This is not to say that it is wrong to identify technology with tools and applications and gadgets—only that it can be limiting (p. 32).

Middle years learners and new technologies

Teachers in the middle years need to acknowledge not only the world of school and the world of textbooks but also the world outside of school; they cannot ignore the uses students make of new technologies outside the school curriculum. Adolescence has been described as a time of potential and promise, a time of enthusiasm, curiosity and eagerness to achieve; a time when young people are developing their ability to reflect and think abstractly; a time when they are developing a sense of social conscience, are willing to think critically about social issues, and have an interest in participation and decision making (Kruse 1998). Conversely, it is also a time when young people are at greatest risk of disengaging with school and becoming at risk of not completing their education (Fuller 1998). Fuller has identified some of the factors that help young people develop resilience, or coping strategies, in relation to schooling. These include: having a sense of belonging and connectedness to school, having positive achievements in the school setting, having someone who believes in them and having a positive relationship with an adult outside the family, who may or may not be a teacher.

The inclusion of new technologies in teaching and learning can lead to positive achievements in the school setting for some students who otherwise may not have their successes celebrated. Students who have difficulty with presentation of their work, due to poor fine-motor skills and accompanying handwriting difficulties, may find that publishing their work using a computer will overcome some of these difficulties as they are often more willing to edit their writing, repeatedly if necessary (including the use of the spell checker). With the removal of the stress associated with writing neatly, many of these students will demonstrate a greater willingness to take risks, greater creativity, more enhanced skills in composing, revising and editing, and more interesting text development (Glister 1997). Computers provide a means for the development of both independent and collaborative writing. Many students experience pride in the professional quality of the work they publish using computers.

The inclusion of new technologies in teaching practices can provide opportunities to challenge curiosity and critical thinking. Whether it be researching within the complex domain of the Internet, the decision making and intricacies of developing websites or the skills required to communicate effectively in chat rooms or with text messaging, new technologies provide, for many, a means of excitement and engagement that cannot be matched by any teacher or textbook. A teacher may, however, be the adult outside the family who believes in them and supports them toward positive achievements in the school setting, and technologies may be the key to that success for some students.

Teachers have an enormous responsibility to equip themselves and their students to operate effectively in this world of new technologies. 'Some children will have more constrained life chances if school literacies do not include learning and applying the available processes of reading and using information that are now more commonly available in digital form' (Green & Campbell 2003 p. 154). Experiences for some children beyond the classroom are vast; for example, playing electronic games or visiting a chat room. How can quietly reading a page in a book or magazine compare to playing an online game with 1500 other participants, at the same time sending and receiving text messages and listening to music on CD? Students in the middle years may be so used to multi-tasking outside school that they find it difficult to focus independently on one task within school. Others, of course, have little or no experience of electronic multi-tasking.

Even without new technologies, students in the middle years are faced with literacy experiences that are becoming ever more complex as the learning materials they are exposed to increase in length and level of abstractness, complexity of language and modes of delivery.

Language of new technologies

The development of new technologies brings with it evolving language forms and structures. These include new words and new uses of old words; for example, 'accessing' a website instead of 'gaining access'. There are new or modified ways of structuring text with the inclusion of hyperlinks. You will often hear students in the middle years using language associated with the use of computers, computer games and other new technologies. In recent research carried out with a cluster of students in the middle years this happened repeatedly (Wells 2004). The researchers had to ask the students to explain the meanings of certain terms they used in connection with computers. The students were talking about things such as the problem of firewalls in their school computers blocking access to their favourite online games. They spoke of wikis, viruses, trojans and blogging. This is not to say that teachers need to know or keep up with all the latest language of new technologies, but they need to have open and accepting minds. They need to have enough confidence with new technologies to have a go and learn about those terms they wish to use in their teaching. Often this learning can 'happen' with students in a real learning community where the expertise of others, not just the teacher, is valued.

How can students learn about new technologies?

The four pedagogies of multiliteracies described by the New London Group (2000) as immersion/situated practice, overt instruction, critical framing and transformative practice, can be used to assist students to learn about and with new technologies.

Immersion/situated practice

Often it is useful to start with a 'playing in the sandpit' approach which allows for immersion and trial-and-error learning. This approach requires a totally non-threatening environment where all learning is celebrated and problems are seen as learning opportunities as students work as a community of learners. Students should be aware that their efforts will not be assessed in any way and that risk-taking will be valued. Keeping a notebook with details about 'how' to do new things on a computer or when using a particular piece of software is a very useful strategy that students (and teachers) can refer to at a later date.

Overt instruction

Following an opportunity to 'play in the sandpit' with a new task, activity or piece of software, the class or teacher may identify particular aspects that require overt instruction. The teacher can then present a mini lesson for the whole class, or decide to target particular students who require specific support on a particular task rather than 'teaching' the whole class how to do something most already know how to do.

Critical framing

Lankshear and Snyder (2000) argue that the 'critical dimension of literacy is the basis for ensuring that individuals are not merely able to participate in an existing literacy and make meanings within it, but also that, in various ways, they are able to transform and actively produce it' (p. 31). Overt instruction lends itself well to the 'how', but critical framing is an important dimension that provides opportunities to address the 'why' and the 'why not'. This is particularly important when creating texts and when searching and finding.

Transformed practice

Transformative practice provides students with opportunities to apply their learning in new or slightly different contexts. This allows students to build on and practise previous skills and understandings, to revise and to apply what they have learned in other contexts or cultural sites (Lankshear & Snyder 2000). One of the strengths of new technologies is that it allows texts to be saved and remade in different formats at a later time. What was created in a Word document or as a PowerPoint presentation can be reused later incorporating more elements of colour or changes in design, or recreated as webpages with images, sound and/or animation. A PowerPoint presentation can become an animated cartoon by making duplicates of slides with minor changes to each one that are then run at high speed to simulate movement.

What can teachers do?

Teachers need a positive attitude and a willingness to engage and experiment with technology. Teachers need sufficient skills and confidence in the use of new technologies to be able to support students to develop the literacies required to interact effectively with both the more complex literacy demands across all areas of the curriculum (including the new technologies that will be part of these learning experiences) and the more traditional, flat print-based texts. Teachers need to be aware that there is an ever-evolving language associated with new technologies including the language of computer-mediated communications and the World Wide Web.

Students at this time need to be challenged and supported in their literacy learning. How can teachers include various digital media in their classroom practice, and what are the practical ways they can engage and challenge their students while supporting them to become effective readers of digital texts, critical users of digital texts and effective creators of digital texts?

Becoming familiar with the basics of a small number of new technologies and computer software so that you can help students who need extra support is a good place to begin. Conduct an audit of what is available in your school and start small. Using a small number of pieces of software effectively is a more effective teaching strategy than knowing a little about lots of different items. Decide on some basics. Learning how to use the basics of two pieces of software available in your school for word processing and for creating a spreadsheet might be a good starting point. You don't have to know it all. There will often be one or two skilled users in a class who can be a great resource—for the teacher and the other students.

Use the software you have available to its maximum potential rather than beginning by purchasing new, unfamiliar software. As teachers become more familiar with one piece of software and the teaching and learning opportunities it supports, they are better able to make informed decisions about future purchases.

When selecting computer software, a small number of open-ended pieces of software that can be used across grade levels and across curriculum areas makes sense financially. Basic word processing programs, spreadsheets, and mixed media programs such as MicroWorlds and HyperStudio meet these criteria. By starting small, teachers can experience a measure of success and a sense of achievement that will encourage them to continue the journey. It would be useful to trial various pieces of software, and a range of ways of using software with students, for various purposes. Teachers should reflect upon their experiences (maybe keeping a learning journal) and modify their choices and use of new technologies in light of their increased knowledge and understandings.

In creating digital texts, students will be making decisions about audience, structure, design elements, links and the various media to be included. Some teachers may decide to focus first on 'reading' digital texts and then work on 'creating' digital texts, but it is more likely that a mix of experiences will work best, with students and teachers learning from each experience and each other, which in turn will help them to be more effective in the other forms.

Reading digital texts

Any reading involves active engagement with a text. It is a complex process of creating, interpreting and analysing meaning from text as the sources of information are integrated (Green & Campbell 2003, p. 155). Reading digital texts places many additional demands on the learner. Students have to navigate and transform textual information rather than just predicting and interpreting it. They not only have to make meaning from letters, words, phrases and other key elements familiar from print-based texts, but they also have to deal with various visual and audio components and a structure that is rarely linear, or left-right, top-down in format. When students read digital texts they not only have to decode and make meaning of the 'marks on the page' but also have to make meaning out of the images, animations, sound and video snippets, and integrate this information with the words, sentences or paragraphs. Even the 'marks on the page' may be presented differently to the way they appear in traditional, flat print-based texts.

The 'marks on the page' in information published digitally has many similarities to factual instructional texts in organisation and presentation, in that digitally published texts tend to use lots of headings (which may or may not be images) and dot-points and lists are commonly used. They are usually more interactive than traditional print-based texts, in that some of the objects will be links or will cause 'something to happen', such as an animation or the opening of a new window. This non-linear aspect can confuse those inexperienced in the reading of digital texts, who may lose track of, or forget, where they have been and have difficulty finding their way back to the original piece of text.

Making meaning of images

In order to learn how to effectively decode digital texts, students should be given time for immersion/situated practice where they explore a digital text and identify aspects that cause them difficulty. This can be followed by overt instruction (explicit teaching), demonstrating how different components work. In a session the teacher could show a particular website and demonstrate how running a cursor over some images or pieces of text will cause a window to appear that explains about or describes an object. If the cursor changes its form from an arrow to a hand, this alerts the reader to the fact that this image (or text) is also a link that will take the user to another place. In a similar way, if the cursor is placed over a link, it will cause the site, or place it is linked to, to appear in the status bar at the bottom of most web browsers. This allows the reader to make a more informed decision about whether or not they wish to use that link. It is also useful for readers of digital texts, and websites in particular, to know that some links will move you to another webpage or site and others will open a new window while the previous window remains open behind. This is a particularly useful piece of knowledge when users are wishing to navigate back to a previous page. Teachers would also want to ensure that all their students understood and could use the navigation section of the web browser which is independent from the particular webpage or site. After overt instruction on aspects such as these, teachers should allow students an opportunity to apply and practise these strategies.

Sound files and animations are part of some digital texts. If the digital text is a CD-ROM the sound files commonly run seamlessly, but when they are part of a website it is not uncommon to find they require special software to be installed on individual computers. Some files require plug-ins such as Shockwave, for example; most will show a warning if this is the case. This can cause frustration for the inexperienced user, so overt instruction incorporating modelling and demonstrations can support students.

Creating digital texts

Writing is a complex process. Ideas, feelings and information are recorded in print according to conventions that assist the writer to record their message and the reader to interpret it appropriately. As a 'text creator' the nature of the writing process changes with the use of new technologies. The term 'creating' is used rather than 'writing' in reference to digital texts, to reflect the complexity and what is different about creating digital texts. For example, the use of hyperlinks encourages students to read and write in a non-linear fashion. In creating digital text, students may be involved in an inter-layered process where planning, drafting, editing and publishing are happening simultaneously rather than chronologically, as more commonly occurs in the creation of print-based texts. Creating webpages and using PowerPoint and HyperStudio are two examples of digital texts that will now be considered.

Creating webpages

When creating texts that will be published as webpages, the writer/creator will have to make a number of decisions. They will need to make decisions about the content: What content? How much content? Who might our audience be? What sort of language will be used? What else will be included—still images, animation, video, audio? What will they be linked to? What will be used for links? What colours will be used? How will colour be used? How will other media be used? How will the layout be managed? Where will non-textual items be placed? How many pages? Will it just be one page or an entire site? How will the files be managed? So it can be seen that this is not just a process of making marks on a page.

Added to this is the question as to what computer software might be used to create webpages. Although they could be created by writing the html (hypertext markup language) tags throughout a piece, this is not a very efficient use of time. Let us assume that students in the middle years will be using a software program that makes this task manageable. Macromedia DreamWeaver is widely used, but most word processing programs come with an option to create webpages or 'save as' html (for example, MS Word).

Since websites usually include images it may be useful to ensure students have some skill in basic image manipulation. This task, along with most tasks using new technologies, will have its own specific language for students and teachers to learn.

Creating PowerPoint and HyperStudio

It is not intended to promote any particular products in this chapter, rather to refer to what is widely available in schools in Australia. HyperStudio and PowerPoint both allow students to create presentations through the creation of slides that include other media, visual and sound, and allow them to make hyperlinks. They also allow students to animate text and/or objects in their presentations. These types of programs require the creator to be quite succinct in their use of language, so students may need to be assisted to identify the main ideas and supporting ideas in their texts.

These types of programs are commonly used for factual texts but could also be used to create narratives, especially ones with various pathways similar to the 'choose your own adventure' genre.

Searching, finding and using information

When students create and publish texts on a website it helps them read, understand further and critically evaluate the sites (critical framing) they find when searching on the web. Through the process of creating and publishing their own material students come to a better understanding of the content of the web. Once they know that material they have created can be published on the web just like any other material, they may develop a healthy scepticism about some of the material they find there.

Teachers often suggest that their students research the Internet to find information on a particular topic. But students need the necessary skills to do this effectively. If not, they can spend an enormous amount of time for very little value. For example, a search was carried out recently using the search engines Google and Yahooligans to identify websites that provide information about 'the environment'. Google provided 66 200 000 responses—which is at least 66 million more than anyone could want. Yahooligans, described as 'the web guide for kids', and directed more towards primary-age students, provided 266 responses. This sort of activity may be worth carrying out with students to help them to understand the differences between search engines. Following that, it would be advisable to use the advanced search feature in Google to support students in developing more efficient searching skills.

As students peruse the webpages they find as a consequence of their search it may be helpful to use the 'Find' function to scan an individual page to identify whether the particular information they require is actually on it. Internet Explorer allows the user to go to 'Edit, Find on this page' and to type in the word or words required. This can be a useful strategy to help identify which sites are the most useful.

Critical users of digital texts (critical framing)

We need our middle years students to be critical users of digital texts. We want them to be able to work independently to plan, research, evaluate and transform information and ideas using several texts, and to study and compare texts created in different forms and from a range of viewpoints.

To achieve this, teachers need to support students to develop skills and strategies to identify the source of information found in digital texts, particularly those accessed through the Internet. Students need to be supported to search in ways that provide them with the information they are seeking, to identify the source of the information on such sites and to critically analyse the information that is identified to ensure it meets their needs. Students need to be able to ask and answer questions such as: Who is the author of the material? What sources have they used to create the material? Where is the material published? Who finances the server or site? In whose interest is this material published? Is the site used to advertise anyone's products or to promote particular points of view? Which information on the page is most noticeable? How are multimedia objects used on the site? Where do links in the site take you to? Did you realise you had changed sites when you clicked on a link? What do other similar sites say about the same topic? How do you now feel about this material? Do you think it is reliable/ verifiable/correct?

Glister (1997) provides a tip for checking sources. If you find information that you want to use on a website and it sounds right, but you don't know much about the author or the organisation behind that page, he suggests you enter the name of the organisation on a search engine and see what you find out. Search engines are not just for concepts or keywords. If you find no name or organisation, Glister says, that's a red flag.

When students are creating digital texts they commonly include objects such as images they have found on other websites. Part of critical framing is being aware of the need to acknowledge and reference your source. Similarly, when students are using text materials, sources should be acknowledged appropriately. Students should also be supported to take notice of the source of materials they use in digital texts.

The opportunities of new technologies

New technologies provide teachers with opportunities for learning that reach far beyond the classroom. They provide the opportunity for students to contact experts online, or to participate in collaborative online projects in which they work with students from diverse cultures across the world, using email, online discussion boards, video conferencing or other new technologies to collaborate in cultural, humanitarian or environmental projects and, as a consequence of participation in relevant and meaningful tasks, develop tolerance and understanding of cultures different from their own. For examples see Trinity College Western Australia's site at http://library.trinity.wa.edu.au/teaching/collab.htm for a list of project sites; Oz Projects at http://ozprojects.edna.edu.au/; iEARN projects at http://www.iearn. org.au/gcpproj.htm or the Global SchoolNet Foundation at http://www.global schoolnet.org/. These projects provide real and meaningful uses for information and communication technologies.

Assessment

Including new technologies in teaching and learning allows for different forms and processes, particularly in relation to creating texts in digital formats. Alternative forms of assessment are required to reflect this change. Some teachers use scoring rubrics to identify the possible levels of quality of student work. One successful strategy is to work with the class to develop a rubric for a particular project or unit of work so that students know exactly what is required to achieve a particular level of success. In this way the assessment process can be demystified. It also addresses the issue of fairness, which students in the middle years are particularly sensitive about. Students in the middle years are quick to mention any case of a teacher who does not apply rules or mark work in a fair and equitable manner. Students at this age are becoming increasingly critical of adults, so developing scoring rubrics in conjunction with them is a particularly useful strategy to overcome this issue. Rubrics should acknowledge the role of new technologies in the learning process and application of learning. Teachers must then apply the rubric carefully in the assessment process.

Teaching activities

Suggested activities for students that incorporate new technologies:

- Publishing a narrative text using video snippets (iMovies).

- Publishing a factual text using animations to demonstrate 'how'.
- Using concept mapping software (e.g. Inspiration) to prepare a response to a text or to present visual representations of connecting concepts or ideas.
- Operating as digital text authors/designers.
- Creating electronic texts for younger students based on learning needs through knowing the audience/learner and tailoring to suit their needs, e.g. using PowerPoint books to help kids with particular aspects of reading.
- Collaborating with students who live remotely to involve them in an enquiry-based unit of work to solve an identified problem or a question.
- Drawing on prior knowledge of content of other digital texts or print-based texts of other forms of communication.
- Comparing the same narrative in different forms.
- Testing alternative ways of creating mood, e.g. colour, sound effects, music and words.
- Identifying and using the meta-language of new technologies, e.g. cropping, file size, jpeg, image size; participating in collaborative online projects, e.g. First People's Project, The Teddy Bear Project.
- Creating video snippets for use in digital text using software such as iMovies.
- Contacting experts in a particular field to gain their expert knowledge to help solve a problem.
- Combining material gathered from other curriculum areas such as drama, video clips, animations, art, scanning, still images, to incorporate into digitally published texts.

Conclusion

Students in the middle years are growing up in the digital age. Teachers need to encourage their students to be effective readers, innovative creators and effective and critical users of digital texts. To do this teachers must provide learning opportunities that include immersion/situated practice, overt instruction, critical framing and transformed practice where students create digital texts and use digital texts innovatively and effectively. Teachers need to think about assessment differently. They need to integrate new technologies into the teaching and learning environment where appropriate. Teachers need to make their choices wisely, aware that older forms of texts may be appropriate at some times and newer forms of texts more suitable at other times. They need to be open to opportunities to combine both the old and the new in complex and imaginative ways.

Questions

1   How is the reading of digital texts different from the reading of more traditional print-based texts?
2   What are some of the factors to be aware of for students using the Internet for research?
3   How can teachers support students to be innovative creators of digital texts?
4   How can students be supported to evaluate the source of Internet sites?

17

Community

Donna Pendergast and Peter Renshaw

The literature of the middle years of schooling is heavily sprinkled with terms such as 'family' and 'community partnerships'. Some theorists argue that one of the signature practices for effective teaching and learning in middle years schooling is the development of relevant curricula through meaningful family, school and community linkages and partnerships. There is no doubt that the middle years philosophical approach places particular emphasis on pastoral care, school and parent partnerships, seamless integration of school and community services, and authentic student and community experience. So what does this mean? What might family and community partnerships look like? How do families and communities work with middle years students to make learning meaningful? Why are the notions of family and community partnerships, and learning communities, particularly relevant for the middle years?

Perspectives on community

The notions of community and learning underpin much current educational thinking and, as noted in Chapter 2, creating a sense of community is a distinguishing feature of middle schooling. In this new century there has been a shift in emphasis, from learning focused on the individual to learning as part of a community. Educators are being urged to become members of professional learning communities as a strategy for enhancing student outcomes. Classrooms as organisational units are theorised as local communities of practice. Schools are conceived as learning communities with nodes and networks that extend into the immediate neighbourhood as well as nationally and internationally via the Web to create virtual communities that extend across the borders of time and space. For many schools, the concept of community is fundamental to their philosophical underpinnings.

This current shift to community is best considered by reflecting on the twentieth century, when educational theory and practice was dominated by modernist ideology. Modernity is typified by several general features, the most relevant to understanding the emergence of community being a focus on individualism, where each person was considered to be an emancipated individual who was self-determining and responsible for their successes and failures. Typical of this approach was educational theory such as that formulated by Piaget (1955), who constructed developmental theories based on the individual learner progressing through a series of stages. More recently, in our postmodern world, the approach of sociocultural theorists such as Vygotsky (1978), with a focus on social constructivism, is evidence of a shift from an individual focus to one that recognises learning as an ongoing engagement in community practices and ways of knowing. In addition to this paradigmatic shift, the changing nature of the world in which we live has been blamed for loss of the sense of community and belonging. Community as a lived experience in contemporary society is elusive and threatened by the interrelated and numerous forces of mobility, transitoriness, the pre-eminence of economic and commercial interests, growing mutual suspicion, increasing fear and insecurity in public places, and the loss of boundaries and enclosures. This loss of connectedness is part of the reason schools and educators have been called upon to aid in the rebuilding of a sense of community.

The focus in education on community is also about the new economy, and about preparing students to enter into a new way of working. Renshaw (2002) argues that the types of classrooms that are compatible with the new economy bear a striking resemblance to the ideal promoted under the banner of a community of learners. There is a need for new types of workers who can work flexibly, constantly adapting to the 'new times', and people who can work openly and in teams—as promoted in the idea of communitiy—are ideal for the new world of work (see also Gee et al. 1996). Theorists such as Grundy and Bonser (2000) describe the type of learning opportunities necessary to develop attitudes and abilities for the new work order, including shared decision making; participatory/flattened management structures; teamwork; decentralisation; networking; flexibility; cooperation; collaboration; and more democratic practices, many of which can be achieved by adopting a learning community and outreach-to-the-community approach to learning.

Renshaw (2002) further explains that a focus on learning through community and community participation is underpinned by sociocultural theory, which:

> . . . frames learning as an aspect of interrelated historical, cultural, institutional and communicative processes. To adopt this theory means to view social activities as constitutive of learning, not merely supportive or ancillary—over time the social comes to constitute the individual . . . larger-scale institutions such as the family, the school, the church, community centre, professional organisation and so on. Social interaction within these institutions and communities gives us the tools for making sense of the world; tools such as ways of speaking, conventions for representing experience, as well as beliefs and values. These social semiotic systems are both appropriated in communities and provide the resources to maintain and transform the communities in which we live (p. 7).

In this way, schools become the hub for reproducing our understandings of how society operates. Schools serve as critical learning spaces for developing ethically aware and engaged members of contemporary society. Leckey (2001) confirms this social imperative, proposing that there is a pedagogical urgency in education for citizenship. She suggests that by transforming classrooms into communities of philosophical inquiry, the skills and attributes essential for effective citizenship may be promoted. Students in the middle years are considered to deserve special attention because they are at the juncture of childhood and adulthood, a time when they are evolving as citizens with the critical capacities to act effectively in and on the world.

Related to this understanding is the idea of community as the sharing of ventures and collaboration. This concept is derived from the managerial concept of capacity building—working together for greater possible outcomes. The strengthening of social and institutional relationships is the focus for synergistic relationships, where benefits for all parties are the outcome. In this approach, the enhancement of individual learning is seen as creating the possibility of advancing whole communities, in whatever way they are defined. Typically, a community might be defined as a geographical location (such as a cluster of schools forming a learning community) or more likely, a common interest (such as a group of teachers with an interest in higher order thinking skills).

Gardner (1995) suggests that contemporary communities should be characterised by:

- wholeness, incorporating diversity;
- reasonable base of shared values;
- caring, trust and teamwork;
- participation in a two-way flow of influence and communication;
- reaffirming self and building morale; and
- institutional arrangements for community maintenance.

We agree with Gardner's normative view of communities, particularly his stance on communities as inclusive of diversity. The goal of inclusive communities is not easily achieved, however, because the notion of community itself sets boundaries and can be used to create an 'us and them' mentality. The term 'community' defines some individuals as members and others as non-members, some individuals as core or full members and others as peripheral or marginal. The implication in saying 'I'm a member of this or that community' is that I share a sense of belonging and a common identity with particular individuals, but also that community membership is limited and bounded to some extent. The notion of community always raises the question: 'Who is included and who isn't?' Our goal as educators should be to create learning communities where diversity of cultural resources and viewpoints is valued. At the heart of a 'reasonable base of shared values', we suggest, is the core value of appreciating difference by fostering a community for diversity. In practice, such a normative agenda can only be achieved by enabling the two-way flow of influence and communication identified by Gardner, where decisions are reached by participation and engagement by all community members. In a community for diversity, there has to be room for dissent and a tolerance for working and living with people with whom we might disagree. These values of respect and tolerance for diversity, paradoxically, are the key values which bind the community together.

Learning communities as curriculum organisers utilises the notion of organised structures to facilitate deeper learning for students (Kilpatrick et al. 2003). In essence, 'staff, students and administrators value learning, work to enhance curriculum and instruction, and focus on students' (Peterson 2002). Peterson and Deal (1998) have identified five recurring characteristics that describe schools that have become learning communities:

- Staff have a shared sense of purpose—that is, they pour their hearts into teaching and have a personal commitment to their students;
- Norms of collegiality, improvement and hard work underlie relationships, and students are involved in classroom decisions on a continuous basis;
- Rituals and traditions celebrate student accomplishments, teacher innovation and parental commitment;
- An informal network of storytellers, heroes and heroines provides a social web of information, support and history, extending the community beyond the walls of the classroom; and
- Success, joy and humour are characteristic of the school climate.

From these perspectives, two differing yet interrelated and compatible understandings of community emerge, both of which are anchored by the purpose of a community approach as a means of engaging indivduals actively within their everyday life-worlds as active contributors: community in the sense of connectedness and belonging, of shared venture and collaboration; and learning community, or community of learners, as a curriculum organiser.

Regardless of the understanding of community, there are some collective themes, including a common or shared purpose, interest or geography; collaboration, partnership and learning; respecting diversity; and enhanced potential and outcomes (Kilpatrick et al., 2003). There are also some clear benefits to developing effective school, family and community connections, such as those proposed by Epstein (1996), who suggests that such connections serve to: improve school programs and school climate; provide family services and support; increase parents' skills and leadership in school matters; connect families with others in the school and in the community; help teachers with their work; and increase ownership and commitment to the school by the community.

Community and middle schooling

The idea of developing learning communities, and of creating a sense of community, is particularly relevant for the middle years. In middle years literature there are many instances where a focus on community is deliberately fostered. Ruebel (2001) concurs, noting 'one of the overarching characteristics describing responsive middle level schools is the establishment of family and community partnerships' (p. 285). Let's consider some instances where relevant middle schooling reforms have included a focus on community.

The Australian Curriculum Studies Association (ACSA 1996), suggests the middle years of schooling should provide opportunities for all young learners to learn and grow in ways that acknowledge and respect this special phase in their development, and that in order to achieve this, effective middle schooling curriculum needs to be: learner-centred; collaboratively organised; outcome based; flexibly constructed; ethically aware; adequately resourced; strategically linked and, importantly, community-oriented. From this perspective, community orientation is seen as a key element in effective middle schooling, where it is taken to mean that parents and representatives from other community institutions and organisations beyond the school are involved in productive partnerships.

In the same vein, Hill and Russell (1999) have developed a set of strategic intentions, or guiding principles, for reform in the middle years, among which is the need for creating outward-looking learning communities. They argue that the middle years are characterised by less frequent contact between the school and the home and yet there is a need for parents to be better informed of what is going on, to be supportive of their children's learning, and to be partners in the learning process. Hill and Russell also extend the notion of community beyond parents to include the wider community, arguing that early adolescence is a time when young people need to interact with the wider community in a structured way and to make use of the rich opportunities for productive learning in society at large. Hill and Russell have developed a set of general design elements they believe collectively contribute to the quest for more effective models of schooling. These general design elements are the basis for approaching the task of developing specific programs and whole-school designs targeted at the middle years of schooling. The nine elements are highly interconnected and interdependent and, not surprisingly, include home, school and community partnerships. It is argued that these nine general design elements, when utilised collectively, are capable of bringing about significant improvement in the achievement of students, in their attitudes to schooling and learning, and in their behaviours. The nine elements are: leadership and coordination; standards and targets; monitoring and assessment; classroom teaching strategies; professional learning teams; school and class organisation; intervention and special assistance; and home, school and community partnerships. In considering the home, school and community partnerships element, Hill and Russell emphasise the importance of parents/guardians forming a better cooperative relationship with the teacher and school, and as a resource contributing to the school's programs. They also highlight the role of businesses, industry and community organisations in providing out-of-school learning experiences for students, as well as giving inputs into the school's programs. They argue that this results in a holistic, as opposed to a fragmented, approach to student learning.

When looking beyond Australian shores, the trend for aligning community and middle schooling is consistent with these frameworks. For example, the position paper 'This We Believe: Successful Schools for Young Adolescents', developed by the US National Middle School Association (NMSA), includes many references to community. With respect to the development of successful schools for young adolescents, the NMSA believes the character of the school should be composed of eight features, including two centred on community, viz:

- high expectations for every member of the learning community; and
- school-initiated family and community partnerships (NMSA 2003).

These elements are argued to facilitate stronger bonds within and extending beyond the school, and to aid in the creation of learning environments where students are motivated to take on challenging learning activities. It is rationalised that this leads to higher levels of achievement and improved student behaviour. Concomitant with these intellectual and engagement-related benefits is the utilisation of organisational structures that support and assist in the building of meaningful relationships. The NMSA specifies that there should be an 'interdisciplinary team of two to four teachers working with a common group of students' as this is 'the building block for a strong learning community with its sense of family, where students and teachers know one another well, feel safe and supported, and are encouraged to take intellectual risks' (NMSA 2003).

Family/school/community partnerships in middle schooling

The Australian literature around community and middle schooling produces multidimensional understandings of community. In some cases 'community' is constructed around geographical/proximity criterion, so it becomes: community within schools; and community extending beyond the boundaries of the school. This reconfiguring incorporates the two understandings of community previously explored; that is: community in the sense of connectedness and belonging, of shared venture and collaboration; and learning community or community of learners as a curriculum organiser.

Strategies that can be utilised to enhance community in the sense of connectedness and belonging, of shared venture and collaboration within a school might include those listed in Table 17.1.

Table 17.1 Strategies for enhancing a sense of connectedness within a school

Targeted community group	Examples of strategies
Parents: Promoting parental engagement and support	• encourage parents to participate in school events • utilise parent satisfaction surveys • engage parents in specific programs, e.g. reading, sport • establish parent training/education programs
Teachers: Facilitating teachers to work collegially	• establish middle-school teaching teams • utilise pedagogies such as collaborative teaching and cooperative learning • develop classrooms as communities of inquiry, with shared goals for learning • provide opportunities for celebration of achievements
Students: Engaging students as community members	• create shared interests and common purpose • establish a common territory such as defined learning spaces

An example of a school that has set out specifically to develop a strong sense of community and connectedness within the school environment is Calamvale Community College, a public Preschool–Year 12 school in an outlying suburb of Brisbane. The first year of operation was 2002 with a predicted enrolment of 2200 in 2006. The college operates in a culture of innovation, including developing a strong commitment to developing community. According to the School Planning Overview 2004–6, the school purpose is: '[A]s a community, we build success for all learners through a future-oriented curriculum.' This purpose is supported by valuing 'learning, teamwork, respect, and environment' and believing in 'maximising everyone's potential; developing positive partnerships; creating a sense of safety and belonging; and celebrating our achievements'. One specific strategy the school has implemented to achieve this sense of community, particularly in the middle years, includes a community structure. Middle years students are members of 'pods'. There are five pods, each with 120 students, ranging across Years 7–9. Year 7 students are identified as Phase 1, Year 8 as Phase 2, and Year 9 as Phase 3. Each pod has a purpose-built facility with access to computers, wet and dry areas, flexible teaching spaces. There is a head of department and four teachers for each pod, along with two specialist teachers known as integrating facilitators, and in some cases there are learning support teachers. Each pod operates according to the decisions made by the team of teachers. Hence, students work within a small community (120 students, 7 teachers) for three years. They participate with other students in their pod in various team structures, dependent upon the activity/topic being investigated. The purpose of the pod structure is to develop relationships:

- between teachers and students;
- between students and students;
- between teachers and parents; and
- through community involvement.

The pod structure is also used as the basis for implementing the curriculum. A three-year cyclic rotation of units across the five pods has been developed, with each depth study lasting for approximately a term. Students remain in the same pod for three years, with students progressing through the three phases. In the last two phases, students culminate their depth study by completing a rich task for statewide moderation. The day is broken into three sessions with the pod teaching team determining the timetable to meet the needs of their students and teachers within the depth study currently being implemented. Teachers remain with their pod over a period of years, and teacher looping is common (that is, teachers commence with a group of Year 7 students and stay in the same pod for three years, then might change to another pod).

The pod structure, which relies on and fosters interaction between teachers, students, parents and other community members, actually changes in important ways the concepts of 'leadership' and 'authorship' that have underpinned traditional teaching methods. Leadership in schools is typically seen as resting in teachers, due to their institutional role and professional status. Within the pod structure, however, leadership is distributed and enacted in a more complex manner. Leadership may reside in students who have specific expertise and experience to contribute to the whole team; parents and other community members may be included in specific activities to provide leadership based on their knowledge and skills. Rather than monopolising pedagogical leadership, teachers in the pod structure orchestrate learning activities by bringing together complementary types of experience and expertise whether it comes from students themselves or from other community participants. With regard to the 'authorship' of ideas, within traditional models of education, students are taught to assimilate and reconstitute the ideas of experts. Such a transmission approach to authorship places students in a receptive and largely passive role as learners. They are not being challenged to address local problems or seek creative and innovative solutions. With the pod structure, however, students are positioned as active contributors to solving authentic problems and addressing relevant issues in their communities. They may draw upon existing knowledge and use well-tried methods for collecting and processing information and data, but they are not merely receiving acquired wisdom. Rather, they are drawing on knowledge and skills in ways that are relevant to their interests and to the needs of the local community within which they live.

In addition to strategies for enhancing community within schools, there are at least three important strategies to establishing community that extends beyond the perimeter of the school. These can be categorised as full service schools; service learning; and vocational programs.

In Australian middle school settings currently, there is a focus on service learning and to a growing degree full service school models as forms of community partnerships. Vocational programs provide the opportunity for students to participate in paid and unpaid internships and to assume job responsibilities under the guidance of workplace mentors. Though aimed at the age group beyond middle schooling, this may have an impact on the later middle years.

Full service schools

The term 'full service school' is borrowed from America, where many such schools have been established over the last decade or more. In Australia they are a relatively recent phenomenon. There are several models of full service schools but most share the idea that schools are the centre for the development of community and the logical site for linking services needed by students and their families (Groundwater-Smith et al. 2001). The Commonwealth Government has latterly supported the trial of full service schools in Australia, which to date has typically occurred in centres where social problems are significant—though this is not a necessary precursor to establishing a full service school. An example of a full service school is Northland Secondary College in Melbourne, which has the highest secondary enrolment of Indigenous students in Victoria. Many of the students had a history of interrupted schooling, juvenile justice problems and homelessness. Activities undertaken as part of the project feature school-based:

· individual counselling and family support;
· specific curriculum development;
· a breakfast program;
· a recreation program;
· community projects, including the development of a code of practice about student use of the local shopping centre, negotiated with security guards;

- local agencies network for student referrals;
- a student housing submission, so Years 11 and 12 students who are homeless have a place to live that is administered by the school (Groundwater-Smith et al. 2001).

There are many issues to consider in the establishment and ongoing support of full service schools in Australia, including the important question of who benefits from the model, but they are seen as a trend for the future.

Currently, there are initiatives underway in Australia that sit somewhere between the idea of full service schools and service learning, in what are called community access schools. These schools engage in practices to establish dynamic relationships with their broader communities, so that parents, carers and wider members of the community can engage in school processes to enhance learning outcomes for students. The goal is to enhance community involvement and relationships that influence school policy and structures, curriculum, teaching and learning, assessment and student support. Specific benefits of community access schools might typically be expected in the following areas:

- Collaboration: where two or more people or groups of people create a shared understanding that could not have been achieved alone;
- Building community capacity: social development that enables sustainable benefits to suit local contexts;
- Social capital: improvements in the quality and quantity of social interactions;
- Community development: an increase in social capital by building community capacity;
- Curriculum reform: shaping the school curriculum to the context of the local school community, thereby focusing on the development of civic pride and responsibility;
- Sustainability: the capacity for learning projects to continue over time because of relevance to the unique local context (Education Queensland 2004).

An example of a community access school project is that operating at Cairns West Primary School in Queensland, which has a focus on establishing the school as a key access point for the delivery of a range of educational programs for community members, not all of which are directly related to the education of children. Education courses on offer have included: computer, first aid, nutrition, government and administration skills, with the aim of assisting participants to secure employment and/or to become valued school volunteers.

Service learning

Service learning is the introduction of directly linked community projects into the school context/curriculum. Mutual gains and developing a sense of belonging are direct benefits of this approach, along with enhancing relevance and authenticity. For students, the opportunity to participate in authentic learning experiences serves to increase their engagement and to develop transferable skills, along with the development of resilience and leadership traits. For teachers, new teaching approaches, ideas for professional development, and ready access to tools and resources to maximise learning outcomes can be achieved through school–community links. For communities, increased community commitment to young people and a revitalising of community building occurs. Service learning projects typically offer students the opportunity to practise citizenship while meeting community needs.

There are many excellent examples of service learning underway around Australia. The Education Foundation website at http://www.educationfoundation.org.au/curr.asp includes the branch Kids and Community. The website explains the benefits of service learning, along with current examples. The Kids and Community project provides a practical guide to school and community partnerships to enable schools and communities to work together to provide challenging, real-life learning experiences for young people. Included on the site are some examples of past and current service learning projects. One is the Gardening Connection project, facilitated by Rosewall Primary School in conjunction with Flinders Peak Secondary College, both located Victoria. The project aims to ease transition from primary to secondary school by providing vocational skills for those students who are not motivated by traditional classroom activities and thereby engaging students' interest so they are more likely to complete secondary education.

Conclusion

Developing a sense of community, and developing productive learning communities, are key elements in middle schooling philosophy. Without a focus on community, it would be difficult to argue that a school or system could implement reforms in middle schooling in a sustainable manner. Creating connections from which intellectual rigour can grow, providing opportunities for developing a sense of belonging and cohesion, are critical elements in the middle schooling ethos.

Questions

1   Reflect on your teaching experiences. Have there been any attempts to develop community, in the full sense of the word? What has it looked like, or alternatively, what might it have looked like? Who was responsible for the initiative?

2   There can be argued to be a range of interests being served in the incorporation of community as a signifying practice of middle schooling. Compile a list of those whose interests might be served by a focus on community in middle school reform.

3   Is middle school reform possible without a focus on community and learning community? Argue your position.

PART
4

ASSESSMENT
PRACTICES FOR
THE MIDDLE YEARS

18

Redesigning assessment

Claire M. Wyatt-Smith, J. Joy Cumming and John Elkins

Over the last decade, assessment and accountability have emerged as areas of significance in educational policy and practice, though this has been happening from two distinct perspectives. On the one hand, considerable investment has been made in strengthening the role of externally mandated and reported assessment for accountability purposes. Against this backdrop on the other hand, educators are focusing on improving student learning across the whole curriculum through policies and programs to improve practical knowledge and assessment expertise of teachers. The middle years of schooling are the years most under focus for accountability, with testing systems for national reporting in Years 3, 5 and 7, other systems mooted for Years 4, 6 and 9, and international comparative studies such as the Third International Mathematics and Science Studies (TIMSS) and the Program for International School Assessment (PISA) assessing English, mathematics and science achievement for 10- and 14-year-olds.

The focus on assessment stems from recognition that good assessment plays a significant role in education, and that the links between teaching, learning and assessment are inseparable. As a recent major report in the United States (NRC 2001) indicated, how do we know what students know? If we don't know what they know, how do we develop effective instruction? What is it that we value that they should know? Hence, effective assessment is seen as enhancing learning as well as allowing a means for providing information on student achievement and learning needs. The NRC report considered the impact of modern theories of learning and the need for modern techniques of assessment to reflect instructional philosophies such as constructivism—the recognition that we do not so much teach in a transmissive sense as provide situations that facilitate students making meaning in their own terms, based on their own prior experiences and knowledge—and emphases on students' development of effective learning processes, such as metacognition and reflection, and problem solving, as much as discipline content in the traditional sense.

The middle years of schooling are a critical time in the pathway of learning. Students have attained some of the basic curriculum knowledge and skills to embark on wider learning adventures. Both the nature of the learning and the diversity of expectations on students continue to increase in demand and volume. At the same time, students' lives outside school are becoming more complex and distracting. Family, friendships, extracurricular activities, sport, computers and other technology compete with the school for student attention. It is an easy time for students to become at risk and disengage from schooling. Effective pedagogy needs to ensure students in these critical years engage with their learning and become effective learners. Effective pedagogy requires effective assessment, assessment that provides the critical links between what is valued as learning, ways of learning, ways of identifying need and improvement, and perhaps most significantly, ways of bridging school and other communities of practice. The middle years of schooling encompass students at critical ages of learning, highly self-aware, needing to build confidence, needing to be recognised for their individuality and their strengths (Stevenson 1992), needing stimulation and opportunities to demonstrate their intellectual strengths and curiosity, and seeking autonomy and independence (VDEET 2000, p. 3). Nothing can be so dampening on learning by middle year students as narrowly-construed assessment that serves only to reinforce a sense of failure and diminish self-esteem. As the following discussion shows, effective instruction for the middle years not only needs to accommodate these characteristics of the learner, but also to recognise the rapidly changing environment in which schooling now takes place.

A general framing of assessment

In this section, we introduce some of the common concepts underlying assessment theory and practice, including terms you will frequently encounter in reading about assessment, to frame our discussion of effective practices. We contextualise the concepts here briefly in middle years practice.

Summative, formative and diagnostic assessment

Assessment of varying nature and significance occurs in schools. Research has estimated that teachers spend more than one-third to one-half of their class time engaged in one or another type of assessment activity (Stiggins & Conklin 1992). This proportion is most likely increased when we consider the amount of time teachers spend in questioning children individually in order to gauge their level of understanding and to provide effective feedback to move learning on. There is a sense in which we can ask, When are teachers *not* assessing? However, when teachers and others talk about assessment, the tendency is to focus on tasks and tests that report what a child is able to do at a certain point in time. This is generally referred to as *summative* assessment, the summing-up of student achievement at a single point, even though this might be drawn from a large amount of evidence collected over time. The ongoing activity of a teacher in gauging student knowledge and understanding, provision of feedback orally or in writing, in order to promote learning, is generally referred to as *formative* assessment. A specific use of formative assessments, both formal and informal, is to provide *diagnostic* information— either through summative forms and reporting where a student's achievement might lie in comparison with peers or on a learning continuum, in order to identify that the student might be experiencing difficulty, or in formative forms—in terms of identifying specific gaps in knowledge or processes or learning difficulties or disabilities that need to be addressed.

Recent research in assessment shows that the most powerful assessment that occurs for students is formative assessment—'rich questioning, comment-only marking (no grades), sharing criteria with learners, and student peer-assessment and self-assessment' (Wiliam et al. 2004, p. 54), assessment that in the end results in improved student achievement. The examples of effective formative assessment noted by Wiliam and colleagues demonstrate that formative assessment can include informal classroom observations as well as more formalised activities. The focus is on the nature of the feedback, the need for constructive feedback and the use to which feedback is put.

Summative assessments in classrooms can also be based on informal and formal activities. The most valuable sources of information for most teachers in the middle years will include ongoing observations made of student work and understanding. These can be recorded through anecdotal records or more formalised checklists (see, for example, Forster and Masters, 1996a, 1996b, for examples of different ways of recording student outcomes on observation records and checklists).

Validity and reliability

Recent accountability policies of federal and state governments have resulted in the introduction of external testing programs in the middle years. A major practical difference between classroom-based assessments and external assessments for summative purposes is that the former can be based on a range of activities and formats with recorded outcomes built up over a period of time, while the latter tend to be one-off, usually paper-and-pencil tests, although practices that incorporate external set tasks and standardised grading schemes, overseen by teachers, can also occur. The differences between teacher-derived classroom-based assessments and external tests are not only practical. Different theoretical models and philosophies underpin different types of assessment and, according to context, different assessments are more suitable for classroom contexts than others:

> We can describe assessment models [often referred to as paradigms of measurement and assessment] as being on a continuum that has psychometric and measurement models of testing at one end and interpretivist/constructivist models of assessment at the other (Gipps & Stobart 2003).

Most external tests are developed using psychometric or measurement principles. Consider the tests of literacy achievement that students undertake. Student performance is usually reported as a score on a dimension; while a student's score can be described in terms of what a typical student with that score can do, it can also be reported in terms of other children's scores in the school, across the state and even internationally. The descriptive interpretation is usually an inference to an overall rating of proficiency, based on the type of items the student has been able to do. So, for example, for the results for Reading Literacy for the international 2003 OECD, a 14-year-old student who achieved at Level 2, one of the lower levels, is described as being able to:

- cope with basic reading tasks such as locating straightforward information;
- make low-level inferences, using some outside knowledge to help understand a well-defined part of a text;
- apply their own experience and attitudes to help explain a feature of a text (OECD 2004, p. 8).

Psychometric measurement has derived from application of principles of scientific certainty to educational assessment. The focus is usually on inference from a test score of the degree to which a student has achieved on some underlying trait or ability, such as, in this case, reading literacy. In keeping with the scientific approach and a focus on comparability, psychometric test development and implementation focus on reliability and standardisation. Reliability is usually interpreted as consistency: over assessors, over time, over repetitions of a test. If two assessors are observing the same student outcome and rating or scoring it, the assessors will generate the same results. For psychometric purposes, the most reliable test that can be used is a multiple-choice test that can be machine-scored. However, most modern external tests allow open-ended items (where students have to supply a response of some type) to structured questions. Raters are given a range of possible student responses and appropriate scoring schema. The format and administration of the test are still sufficiently constrained to be highly standardised, and the nature of responses that can occur restricted by the question focus and structure. For good tests, validity is also necessary, that is, the extent to which the assessment is assessing what it is supposed to. Psychometric testing has to trade validity for reliability, by narrowing the scope of the dimensions being assessed.

The other theoretical end of the assessment continuum described by Stobart and Gipps (2003) reflects the type of summative assessment developed by the teacher that usually takes place in a classroom, assessment that is much more contextualised in the curriculum of the classroom, the achievements and standards of the students, and the general community contexts of schooling. The more closely and effectively such assessment is linked to the intended learning of the classroom, the higher its validity as assessing what it is intended that the students learn. Contextualising assessments, as well as providing more open-ended activities (as opposed to test items), and engaging students in peer- and self-assessments, reflects modern interactionist and constructive philosophies of teaching and learning. In classrooms, then, validity is usually more important than reliability.

Various procedures exist for moderating classroom assessment results; for example, Australian practices of teachers meeting and discussing student examples of work and standards to reach consensus of comparability—referred to in some situations as 'social moderation'. These processes allow diversity of assessment tasks to suit contexts, rather than standardisation, as long as statements of desired standards are available for consideration. Thus, in the classroom a teacher may determine a student's performance in terms of the demonstrated work in order to improve learning, and may also make reference to achievement of more generic statements, such as syllabus outcome statements, for comparability and reporting purposes. However, classroom assessments are not usually used to make inferences about underlying attributes or traits, such as writing skills, being more likely to focus on multiple contexts of performance such as writing in different genres, drafting and revision skills, even computer literacy, as elements that create the effective writer. Indeed, attempts to make international comparisons of writing skills have failed, as the nature of writing could not be decontextualised from cultural environments, nor could reliability of scoring procedures be established internationally (Cumming 1996).

Modern interpretations of validity encompass more than the match of an assessment activity or test to the curriculum being taught. Validity has been argued to extend to the interpretation of the outcomes of the assessments, and the purposes to which they are put (Messick 1989, 1994). Results obtained for one purpose should not be used for a purpose for which they were not intended and which they do not suit—for example, it is common for employers to look at the university entrance rankings of job applicants, even though these rankings have been developed to identify students' potential to study at university, not their capacity to undertake a range of workplace activities.

Principles of effective assessment practice in the constructivist framework abound. In general, these principles endorse contextualised activities, activities that engage students in meaningful tasks, and opportunities to demonstrate strengths rather than weaknesses. For example, the Australasian Curriculum Assessment and Certification Authorities (ACACA 1995) principles state that effective assessment in high-stakes certification 'in order to avoid being itself a barrier to students' demonstrating their command of [an area] . . . should involve a range and balance of types of assessment instruments and modes of response, including a balance and range of visual and linguistic material that involves a range and balance of conditions' (p. 3), echoing the American Educational Research Association (AERA 2000) principle of protection against high-stakes decisions based on a single test—that decisions that affect individual student's life chances or educational opportunities should not be made on the basis of test scores alone.

Reframing middle school assessment in a learning culture

In this section, we focus on ways to reframe middle school assessment in a learning culture so that it has positive consequences for learning. While much of the focus here will be on developing learning and assessment practices that contribute to summative assessment and reporting on a range of student achievement, you are asked to consider how the worth of assessment lies in its contribution to learning and the improvement of learning over time, extending to diagnosing difficulties and monitoring individual and whole cohort progress over time. In Australian schools, especially in the middle years and in the absence of formal certification, formative and summative assessments are not distinct entities. In general, a summative assessment becomes a point-in-time summary of evidence collected from a range of activities and forms. On occasions, summative assessments may result from specific tasks or activities introduced within a contained point of time (for example, a few days or a week, rather than an activity over a term) to gauge student learning against a framework with explicit outcomes and statements of standards. Different frameworks may be operating in different settings. For example, key learning area syllabuses in Queensland (see www.qsa.qld.edu.au) provide statements of outcomes across a number of levels intended to represent a developmental continuum. Other frameworks that originated have been the New Basics curriculum and associated rich tasks and assessment pro forma. Readers interested in more information about this curriculum and its approach to assessment are advised to visit http://education.qld.gov.au/corporate/newbasics/. Of note here is that schools may develop their own learning and assessment activities with associated criteria (the dimensions of performance that are important) and standards (the different levels of quality of performance on each criterion that a student may demonstrate). This use of the terms 'criteria' and 'standards' is common in Queensland secondary school practice and in general refers to a system of criteria-referenced or criteria-based assessment of performance with descriptive standards (rather than norm-based assessment against other students). The term 'rubric', often used in American writing on assessment, usually represents such a set of criteria and standards descriptors. All frameworks recognise that students learn and demonstrate achievement at different paces and that optimum learning environments will present appropriate learning activities for all students.

The diversity of student cohorts in today's classrooms is well recognised. The undeniable fact is that students come to school with existing knowledges and skills, as well as repertoires of practice in literacy and numeracy that cover a wide range, in terms of both how they are constituted and stages of development. By the middle years the range of students' repertoires has broadened, not narrowed—but what all students have in common is the need to progress, to learn.

A powerful factor shaping learning growth is assessment. Our starting position is that assessment is always and inevitably:

- **Historical:** enacted at particular times and in particular places;
- **Value-laden:** reflective of value systems that routinely work to shape the selection (inclusion/exclusion) of activities/tasks and resources involved in undertaking assessment; and
- **Constructive of student identity:** shaping student understandings about who they are, what their place in the world is, and even what their short- to mid-term futures might hold.

We identify the hallmarks of quality assessment in the middle years as assessment that makes provision for:

- **Connectedness and responsiveness:** taking account of students' interests, capabilities and repertoires of practice both inside and outside schooling, including the actual and virtual communities in which students live;
- **Explicit recognition of the increasing autonomy of middle year students as learners:** providing students with a role in negotiating selection of goals, timing and manner of reaching these, through to assessment;
- **A tailored, diverse and yet balanced range of learning and assessment options and modes:** ensuring students can extend their knowledge and existing strengths in working with particular combinations of knowledges, modes and resources, while encouraging risk-taking beyond this;
- **Room for teacher and student talk and other interactions around quality:** enabling students to engage productively in self-assessment as a means to improve learning; and
- **The deliberate integration of a mix of new, emerging and traditional technologies in assessment practices:** providing opportunities for students to use both to facilitate communication and learning between teacher and students and among peers.

Given this framing, some key considerations for middle school teachers in realising quality assessment are:

- What assessment helps you to see how your students are learning and where they are having difficulty?
- What is the link between the desired learning outcomes, the pedagogical practices, and the development of systematic (but not necessarily formal) assessment processes?
- What information might you expect or want to collect from what students do as they complete teacher-generated learning and assessment activities?

- What is the sufficiency of the range of assessment methods and modes used in the classroom and how are these presented to students?
- What challenges face assessment in the middle years in the future?

Formative assessments

What assessment helps you to see how your students are learning and where they are having difficulty?

Formative assessment is designed to support student learning and to help teachers improve their instruction. Black and Wiliam (1998) claim, following an extensive review of research and follow-up research with teachers, that formative assessment raises standards, that we can do better if we know how. Improved formative assessment is particularly helpful for low-achieving students. Teachers have to recognise that shifting focus to formative assessment may require a change in teaching, it demands time and may cause you to seek new ideas about teaching. In return, it enhances feedback to students, increases their active learning, motivation and self-esteem, and raises achievement. Effective formative assessment can take many forms, from simple to complex. We discuss a number of them, and the design of some tasks specifically for formative purposes, below.

Know your students

Getting to know students as people is important. Students are all different, and you need to have some idea of their interests and activities in and out of school. A core issue of engaging students in learning as their outside world becomes less restricted is finding a match between student interests and activities and schooling. Sometimes simple scales or structured interviews can be used to determine how students feel about the curriculum that is often imposed in the early middle years. Guidance staff may be able to assist you in choosing or constructing suitable instruments.

Referral

As a teacher of students in the middle years, you should increase your understanding of the needs of your students by working collaboratively with guidance and support staff. Difficulties in basic areas of learning such as literacy and numeracy need keen attention during these years of schooling. It is not necessary for most teachers to become familiar with diagnostic tools in literacy and numeracy, but you should know some of the indicators of learning difficulties so you can request advice and assistance. These often show up in students' written work as spelling, grammatical and organisational problems and in subjects where they need to use mathematical concepts, such as science, practical arts and geography. As a middle years teacher you may be working with multiple classes as a specialist teacher or subject specialist, and you may be tempted to assume that English or mathematics specialists will handle such learning difficulties. All teachers, however, must contribute to literacy and numeracy 'across the curriculum'.

Self- and other- assessment

If, as we hope, students are supported to become self-directed learners, then much assessment needs to be in their hands also:

> If formative assessment [by students] is to be effective, pupils should be trained . . .
> so that they can understand the main purposes of their learning and thereby grasp
> what they need to do to achieve (Black & Wiliam 1998).

Gibbons (2002) shows how teachers can provide scales and checklists that students can use to consider their progress.

A further way to widen the basis of assessments, formative and summative, and provide effective feedback, is to involve others in the judgement process. Peers can often offer critical insights into each other's work. Mentors, who might be more competent students or people who support student learning in community placements, bring fresh and sometimes more expert insights into student learning.

Effective feedback

Finally, as a teacher, you should ensure that comments on a student's work also offer guidance for improvement, tap deep knowledge, avoid comparisons with other students and counter the sometimes negative effects of external testing regimes. Conversely, research has also shown that false praise is not effective for students and has a negative impact on achievement. Students know when praise is not warranted and both they and parents are equally frustrated. Comment on the positive but also suggest where work can be improved.

Designing specific formative assessments

Open-ended tasks or items

Specific activities or tasks may be devised to assist in formative assessment drawing from a wide choice in items. In high stakes standardised tests, an item such as

'Simplify, if possible, $5x - 2y$' might be regarded as unfair, because it violates the assumption that tricks are not allowed (Wiliam 2000). However, if developed for diagnostic purposes and allowing students to provide an open-ended response with reasons for their answer, this item enables you to determine whether students can recognise the end of the process of simplification of algebraic expressions. Teaching then can target any identified weaknesses, which is the essence of formative assessment. If such a question is used for formative assessments, it does not need to be 'returned' with a 'mark'. The essential component of the feedback is to give learning guidance about the appropriateness of the student's response and where to go.

Dynamic assessment

A stronger form of formative assessment is dynamic assessment, which comes from the Vygotskian (1978) notion of teaching as support to enable performance of new skills or attainment of new knowledge. In dynamic assessment, the key indicator is the type and amount of support, rather than the success or failure of students on assessment tasks. Dynamic assessment takes time to prepare, but can inform not only you as a teacher, but also students, who should gain insight into why they have found tasks impossible. It is especially useful for students from different cultural backgrounds and students with disabilities. While most often used in one-to-one situations, it can be used in a class by numbering prompts and having students note when they are successful. An example of dynamic assessment in mathematics education in a classroom is given in Figure 18.1.

Figure 18.1 Example of dynamic assessment in mathematics

> **Prepare the following task on an OHT or PowerPoint:**
>   Solve $x^3 - x^2 = 2x$
>
> Prompt successively:
> 1.   Transfer all terms to the left of the equals sign.
> 2.   How? By subtracting $2x$ from both sides.
> 3.   Do all terms have a common factor?
> 4.   Divide by x (remember that x can't $= 0$).
> 5.   What is $x^2 - x - 2$?
> 6.   Express as a product of two terms in x.
> 7.   What values of x make the expression $= 0$?

Keeping anecdotal records

As part of assessment that is criteria-based and closely related to teaching and learning, anecdotal records can play an important part. Anecdotal records (or observation notes) can serve both formative and summative purposes. Their advantage is that they allow you to observe learning and 'record a wide range of actual . . . experiences' (Boyd-Batstone 2004, p. 230). The techniques are commonly practised by early years teachers but are gaining recognition for their usefulness for older students due to their effective ways of providing rich, contextualised information.

Some teachers find it useful to keep logs of their observations during the course of the term, using any convenient method, such as file cards or a tape recorder at the end of the lesson. Another useful opportunity for adding to the information is during student 'conferences', which are used frequently by English teachers, but could be helpful in all subject areas. The essential prerequisite for many of the assessment approaches described is having some time to talk with students individually. Through ongoing observation, you will be monitoring student understanding and development in a systematic way.

Observations must be recorded as soon as possible if they are to capture important qualitative and quantitative information, and impressions that may need to be confirmed later. To do this, target about a fifth of the students each lesson/day. By carrying a pen and some sticky labels (with the date and the students' initials), it becomes routine to obtain useful data. Boyd-Batstone (2004) describes a series of steps that can be easily implemented by teachers. Although Boyd-Batstone writes in terms of literacy, her method is easily extended across the curriculum to key learning areas and to integrated topics. Indeed, literacy will be evident in all of these, though the focus of note-making may vary. The following verbs are useful in note-making in English: spell, use alphabetical order, recognise, describe, link ideas. Others might apply in science, and practical content areas.

You may find it helpful to keep a notebook with a page for each student in which each completed adhesive label can be added, along with any longer notes you might make upon reflection. You may develop your own shorthand for recording, such as ID for 'identified'. (Another approach might be to use a handheld electronic device.) At the end of each term, a summary of the anecdotal records can be written, along with steps to be taken that can be used in planning, and for reporting to the students and their parents (Rose & Meyer 2002).

Think alouds

As a teacher, you will be constantly challenged to understand your students' thinking; unless there are observable elements such as reading aloud, writing or practical activities, windows into students' thinking can be scarce. Think alouds are opportunities for students to verbalise their thoughts as they carry out a task such as performing actions or reading. While they can be used in instruction, the focus here is on illuminating student understanding. The evidence obtained using think alouds is metacognitive, that is, it reveals strategies and misconceptions in a very immediate fashion.

It may be best to introduce students to think alouds by demonstrating the technique in a couple of situations, such as reading a section from a textbook and carrying out a task such as writing a letter, navigating a website (displayed on a large screen) or assembling some apparatus for an experiment. Another approach is to provide a list of probes, such as, 'What does that mean?', 'Why do you do this next?', 'I thought that would happen', 'I remember that from last week', and then ask students to verbalise or jot down thoughts as they carry out a task. If it is text-based, red dots can be placed strategically to prompt think alouds. Block and Israel (2004) suggest that metacognitive bookmarks can be used to help students assess their own understanding; by providing them with a list of strategies, they can note the page/paragraph where they used each strategy and later can write how the strategy used helped them. The same approach can be adapted to suit practical task completion, going beyond overall success, which might be mainly a memory activity to enable analysis of whether understanding has been achieved, thereby increasing the likelihood that the skills will transfer to new learning situations.

Computer assessments

Information and communication technologies are another developing means of assessment. While current computer forms of achievement tests are traditional in format, they may offer additional resources for diagnosis. In literacy and numeracy, important information such as speed of response, an indicator of learning difficulties, is easily measured using computer presentation (Singleton 1997). The Australian Council for Educational Research has been exploring a service whereby parents can purchase an online literacy assessment. Computer-based assessment programs are available to diagnose severe reading difficulties (Turner & Smith 2003) and mathematics difficulties (Butterworth 2003).

Linkages

What is the link between the desired learning outcomes, pedagogical practices and the development of systematic (but not necessarily formal) assessment processes?

This question points to the crucial relationship between curriculum, teaching, learning and assessment. It is widely recognised that some summative assessments can have a narrowing effect on teaching and learning. This is especially the case where teachers feel constrained in their practice to teach to '*the* test', spending considerable classroom time rehearsing students for test-taking. Clearly it is unfair to ask students to sit for tests or undertake any form of assessment without some preparation in the kinds of tasks and conditions (time, location, access to resources) in which they will be expected to perform. Teachers may also feel anxious about how their students will compare with other students and reflect on their teaching, even though the repertoires of practice different groups of students bring to the classroom may be quite varied. However, the potential for standardised external or school-derived tests to regulate, even shrink, learning possibilities needs to be avoided.

The converse of this undesired consequence of standardised testing is that, in a true learning culture, assessment activities become productively interwoven with learning and teaching. That is to say, assessment is taken to be continuous (rather than an end-point or terminal) in nature. This is not to suggest that the students are continually being assessed. Instead, it is to make clear that while you are expected to teach students what they need to know and be able to do to succeed at any assessment activities, teaching and learning occur as students undertake the activities, and vice versa, while you observe limitations as well as strengths in particular achievements.

Before assessment is planned and implemented, however, you need to establish goals that are realistically attainable for individual students. (When task demands exceed a student's current levels of knowledge, skills and strategies, then it is the task that sets the student up for failure from the beginning.) Optimally, in the middle years, goals should be collaboratively established, involving both you and the student in an assessment partnership. It is the learning goals, therefore, and your decisions about what counts as valued learning, that inform how you design and implement assessment activities. Further, in response to these goals, you with the students may well jointly decide upon a range of activities, with students able to exercise choice, selecting those they wish to engage with. In short, right through the middle years it is not necessarily the case that all students need to complete the same learning and assessment activities simultaneously. So, far from wholly regulating learning, assessment should strive to open up learning and teaching possibilities, providing options for engaging learners in suitably challenging activities.

Information

What information might you expect or want to collect from what students do as they complete teacher-generated learning and assessment activities?

Optimally, you will collect a robust body of evidence of different types to inform your assessment decision-making. This could include evidence from *observations*, both planned and incidental, with observations routinely occurring in the course of classroom interactions and recorded, as previously discussed. Also important are *consultations*, including those consultations that you have with students, individually and in small groups, as well as consultations with other teachers, parents, and education and health professionals, as appropriate. Given your position to make first-hand observations of students as they learn in a range of settings, it is you as a teacher who is best placed to identify the need to call on advice from others, or to share insights about a student's progress, especially where that progress is being impacted by variables that can be addressed directly by others.

Summative information derived from a *focused analysis* of work in progress or final versions of completed work can also be vital in developing a performance profile of student growth over time. Such focused analysis is best informed by external or teacher-generated statements of assessment expectations, sometimes written up as criteria and standards-grading specifications. The advantage of using these guides is that they can work not only to direct your attention to particular features of the work, but they also direct student attention to what they should attend to in undertaking the task. Optimally, teachers and students collaborate around the identification of features to be included in the assessment specifications, with this being integral to how learning occurs and is progressed. Andrade (2001) reported on the impact of such statements on the writing of Year 8 students and found that essay gradings improved where they were used, and that students learned the sorts of criteria that were characteristic of good writing. Such research builds on significant writing by Sadler (1989) that the essence of good assessment to inform student learning is to make explicit the implicit, that is, the expectations that you hold as a teacher for successful demonstration of learning.

The example given in Figure 18.2 of an assessment task and criteria/standards framework incorporates outcomes from the Queensland syllabuses for English, Mathematics, Science, Studies of Society and Environment and Technology Education, as well as cross-curriculum literacies (discussed later) (www.qsa.qld.edu.au). Your students may be working to lower or higher levels depending on their previous achievement, and demonstrating a transition between levels.

Figure 18.2 Example of an assessment task and outcomes-framework rating grid

Assessment task

After discussing and reviewing some causes for endangering animals and suitable survival strategies, the students will use various types of survival strategies to design an animal that can live in the school grounds without the threat of endangerment.

Outcomes	Emerging	Developing	Consolidating
1 Students are able to discuss and identify the needs of living things.	An attempt has been made to discuss	Can discuss with direction and some relevance	Can discuss with complete relevance
2 Students collect a range of information about diverse sources of food and shelter for animals in the community.	An attempt has been made to collect information	Can collect information with assistance	Can collect information accurately and independently
3 Students make relevant links between different features of their natural and built environment and the specific needs of living things, including animals.	Has attempted to make links	Can make links with assistance	Can independently make links
4 Students describe cause and effect relationships in known or familiar settings.	An attempt has been made to describe	Can describe with assistance	Can describe independently
5 Students make explicit connections between elements of simple ecosystems and can elaborate on these.	Can make connections with assistance	Can make connections as well as providing some elaborations	Can confidently make connections and provide complex elaborations
6 Students identify common needs of animals in natural and built environments.	Can identify needs with assistance	Can identify needs	Can confidently identify needs
7 Students design chosen animals and communicate using drawings, models and appropriate labels.	An attempt to design and communicate has been made	Can design and communicate with assistance	Can design and communicate using a range of means including detailed labelling
8 Students use non-standard measurements to measure and compare sizes.	An attempt to measure and compare has been made	Can measure and compare with assistance	Can measure and compare with accuracy

To design quality criteria and standards frameworks yourself, you need to go through two stages. First, what are the elements of learning that you are hoping to observe? Secondly, what type of demonstration is sufficient to show that the student has indeed learned? In developing the second, exploration of qualitative descriptors and use of informing words are important, rather than terms such as 'none', 'some' or 'good', or use of numbers such as '0 references', '< 5 references', '> 5 references'. Quality learning is distinguished by depth, not quantity. Here the distinctive qualitative standard is degree of independence.

The second assessment example (Figure 18.3) provides a point-in-time assessment for all students against a common expected goal and activity, and differentiation of quality of achievement against that goal. Again, you will see that considerable effort has been made to identify the criteria that are the important outcomes to be assessed and the quality descriptors for different standards of performance. Learning to develop these assessment frameworks and grading schema is like all of teaching, an art that develops with practice over time. Therefore you should persist with developing your own statements, for your classroom or groups of students, or preferably at a school level in collaboration with others. This will ensure maximum validity for the links between the assessment and the expected learning that you have contextualised within the needs of your own school community.

One of the critical factors in engaging students across the middle years of schooling is not just increased learner autonomy but the increased demand and authenticity of learning and assessment activities in order to create real and meaningful challenges for students (Cumming & Maxwell 1999). These learning and assessment activities are often transdisciplinary in the middle years, allowing students to connect knowledge from a range of key learning areas, and as much as possible with community and other practices. In some cases, students role-play problem solving in real-life types of activities. Singleton (1997) has noted that computers will increasingly enable the presentation of complex multimedia information to achieve more authentic items. Authentic types of performance assessments are key elements of assessing students in areas such as music and dance. They can also be valuable in any subject that involves real-life activities, and are probably underused because teachers' own experience of being assessed is dominated by 'academic' types of assessment.

It may seem difficult to set up criteria-based assessment for open-ended tasks, but by carefully stating the criteria in terms of providing evidence of understanding, it is possible to avoid assessment constraining teaching and learning. For

Figure 18.3 Example of an assessment task, criteria and standards rating grid for an investigation and report of an issue of local community relevance

Criterion	Standard			
	A	**B**	**C**	**D**
Forms a coherent piece of work relevant to intended audience	Adheres to conventional spelling, grammar and paragraphing. Uses concise, fluent language that is appropriate to a peer audience.	Adheres to conventional spelling, grammar and paragraphing with minor errors. Uses concise language most of the time that is appropriate to a peer audience.	Adheres to conventional spelling, grammar and paragraphing with reasonable accuracy. Uses concise language some of the time that is appropriate to a peer audience.	Has not adhered to conventional spelling, grammar and paragraphing. Language usage is not concise and is inappropriate to target peer audience.
Depth of research	Has selected relevant data from a wide variety of resources. Has included relevant documentation, sources across a range of modes and provides a comprehensive bibliography. Some attempt has been made to verify or cross check sources content.	Has selected relevant data from a variety of resources though print materials dominate. Has incorporated a restricted range of sources and bibliography.	Has selected reasonable variety of print resources. Basic sources used and noted though lacking currency and scope. Has attempted to include a bibliography.	Little evidence of attempts to use a variety of resources.
Linkages to contextual and cultural beliefs	Has clearly identified and indicated relevant cultural links to local community group/s.	Has identified and indicated cultural links to local community group/s.	Some evidence of cultural linkages to local community group/s.	No evidence of attempted cultural linkage whatsoever.
Oral presentation	• Clearly explains the process undertaken in completing the task. • Presents finished product using effective control of oral language to communicate gained understandings to peers. • Answers audience questions to a high degree of audience satisfaction.	• Explains the process undertaken in completing the task. • Uses good control of oral language to communicate understandings to peers. • Answers questions to satisfy audience requests for additional information.	• Has provided a reasonable explanation of the process of conducting a project. • Limited or uneven control of oral language to communicate ideas. • Satisfies audience questions some of the time.	• Unable to explain to a reasonable degree the process undertaken in creating the end product. • Poor oral language skills resulting in communication difficulties. • Unable to satisfy audience requests for clarification of information

example, in mathematics, a challenge question may be solvable in more than one way. This requires the teacher to consider various possible solutions, some of which may not have been thought of when the task was formulated. By asking students to formulate a similar problem, it may be easier to determine if they have a deep understanding of the topic. An extension of this reasoning is the need in today's technological world to allow for student-identified problems and responses that go beyond your own knowledge and experience. In establishing criteria and standard statements of expectations, always allow room for some surprise.

Complementing the assessment information generated from observation, consultation and focused analysis is the information that students themselves provide as they participate in self- and peer-assessment activities, discussed previously in our consideration of formative assessment. Taken together, this toolkit of assessment techniques not only sets you up with useful ways of collecting and interpreting assessment information, but provides a way for students to be active insiders, a part of the classroom assessment culture. It is through actively engaging students in reflecting on their learning that you can access key assessment insights not otherwise available, moving to putting in place responsive interventions where necessary.

We have suggested that you will have gathered with your students a comprehensive amount of varied evidence on student learning and achievement. A way to organise this and to demonstrate student learning over a semester or year is to have students amass and organise evidence of their learning outcomes into portfolios. While it is relatively easy for students to collect such evidence, much can be gained by having them develop their own frameworks for presenting the portfolio evidence.

While there is often a focus on 'best work', it can be helpful for students to sometimes use a developmental approach, so they can illustrate how their mastery has grown. This could be through inclusion of early plans, drafts and final 'published' writing, or through photographs or other records indicating activities along the way to completion of an activity or product. In some cases, students may wish to produce electronic portfolios, which can take the form of PowerPoint or other multimedia presentations. Where students have no previous experience of working with portfolios, they may need careful explanation and frequent feedback about their developing portfolios, as well as examples of finished products. George et al. (1998) and Stevenson (2002) give detailed steps for using portfolios with middle school students.

Many schools arrange a 'Learning Expo' for students to present their folios to parents and peers, and ideally to a wider community audience. If students are able to offer these outcomes on their own terms, further goals of self-directed learning and self-assessment are achieved. Finally, schools are also arranging for student work in portfolios to be scanned and stored digitally, a virtual portfolio that a student can take from year to year and that you could obtain from other teachers to see quickly what type of work your students have successfully demonstrated, as well as passing on such portfolios to others.

Sufficiency

What is the sufficiency of the range of assessment methods and modes used in the class-room and how are these presented to students?

We want to highlight your vital role as a middle school teacher in ensuring that in your assessment practice you take account of the impact of performance context and conditions on learner demonstrations of their capabilities. There are critical differences between performance modes, and for this reason you need to distinguish and identify with students the demands of written, spoken, visual, auditory and multimodal learning, and the demands of demonstrations of proficiencies. (A more detailed discussion of literacy demands and assessment follows.)

If students are to engage in learning for the twenty-first century and to develop the characteristics of the lifelong learner, then it is not only appropriate, but also necessary, for learning and assessment activities to involve a wide range of channels of communication and semiotic systems. In practice, for example, students in the middle years may be involved in learning how to search the Internet for project work, to evaluate what they find in terms of its suitability for their purposes and its credibility, and to construct websites for public audiences. In this project-related work, over time, the summative assessment interest may focus on students' demonstrations of their knowledge and skills in both locating and evaluating Internet resources, as well as on the quality of the websites as final projects. These examples serve to illustrate the need for assessment to take seriously the rapid changes that are occurring in information communication technologies, and the need for the inclusion of such technologies into assessment and reporting, where educationally relevant. Against this backdrop, we turn our attention to consider the relationship between assessment on the one hand, and on the other, literacy and curriculum.

Curriculum literacies and assessment

It is well recognised that literacy is a sharp focus in the early years, routinely giving particular emphasis to foundational skills and knowledge relating to coding-cracking (decoding and encoding). After this intensive focus, however, the pressure to fast-track through curriculum delivery seems to restrict opportunities for students to explore the multiple meanings that they may make of what they hear, do and see in the classroom.

There are at least two main reasons for this. The first concerns the sheer volume of content that teachers are expected to cover and students to be assessed on, all in relatively short timelines; the second is an apparent lack of pedagogical and assessment emphasis (and therefore value) given to knowledge integration, both within and across discipline areas. This can and often does result in a situation where, as students progress through the middle years, literacy demands can remain unclear to them because too little framing information is directly available to bring those demands into clear focus. A related point is that the intended (as distinct from the official) curriculum and how it is being assessed may seem perfectly obvious to you as the teacher, but the nature and point of activities and how students may succeed with them may not always be framed for students explicitly and in a way that motivates them.

All of this points to the value of building a classroom community in which you and your students share talk about the critical relationship between curriculum, teaching, learning and, of vital importance, assessment. Another hallmark of quality practice in middle schooling is a teacher–student relationship characterised by talk and other interactions intended to make literacy demands, learning expectations and assessment practices explicit. All too often middle school students can 'lose out' when these demands remain implicit and they are left to engage with assessment as though working in the dark (Wyatt-Smith & Cumming 2003).

At this point we put two propositions to you: first is the notion that literacy and curriculum in middle schooling are fundamentally interrelated. Given this, it is useful to reconceptualise this relationship in terms of *curriculum literacies* understood to be dynamic, contextualised, complex, and always underpinned by assumptions about the nature of knowledge within a discipline. The second proposition is the idea that curriculum literacies should be made explicit both in instruction and assessment. This reconceptualisation of curriculum literacies challenges current constructs of assessment in middle schooling and calls for the domains of assessment to be expanded to include both curriculum knowledge and epistemological domains that take account of diverse ways of working with and in semiotic systems. Student success across the years of schooling hinges on their increasing control of this combination of knowledges and ability to use these productively.

We use 'curriculum' deliberately as a noun in this discussion, rather than the adjectival 'curricular', in order to demonstrate that this conjunction represents the interface between a specific curriculum area, or integrated areas, and the related literacies. This is distinct from literacies related to curriculum in a generic sense, or a single literacy considered to be generic across the whole curriculum. The point is that traditional definitions that construe literacy as primarily reading and writing do not match the literacy environment of middle school classrooms in which students are typically expected to coordinate multiple literacies simultaneously, drawing on listening, viewing, reading, writing, speaking and critical thinking. Students are expected to use these various literacy modes in dynamically networked ways, thereby engaging in multiple literacies in the course of a lesson and a day.

Specifically, if as a middle school teacher you carry forward an interest in curriculum literacies through to assessment, what is necessary is a focus on the ways in which the various modes of representation and communication interact and are foregrounded in different curriculum areas.

What this means for formative assessment is that a key role of your day-to-day assessment of student learning will be to check how all students are managing the meta-language of a subject area: monitoring student understandings of specific terminology, checking fluency, and assisting students in the ways of gaining such fluency; checking how students are coping with the reading, writing and speaking demands of the current subject; and their control of:

- subject terminology and specific vocabulary;
- symbolic codes and other representational forms;
- relationships between common everyday language and subject-specific terminology;
- the language of the processes of the subject, such as scientific or mathematical processes;
- the match between the language of instruction and the language of formal assessment requirements; and
- the literacies of the classroom and the social interactions within which curricular learning is to occur.

As just one aspect of formative assessment, as a teacher you need to understand how well your middle years students are able to use resource materials. With textbooks, it is straightforward to devise a series of activities early in the school year that will show how students handle information location tasks, such as using the table of contents and the index, finding details, getting the gist of paragraph meaning, using a glossary, reading figures and tables. Thelen (1984) provides an example of a study skills inventory for a science textbook. This model could be expanded to include other sources of information, including using the Internet.

Challenges

What challenges face assessment in the middle years in the future?

We have already discussed the possible and important use of think alouds as one way of assessing student thinking formatively to identify effective and ineffective strategy use and misconceptions. However, think-aloud outcomes can also be summarised to provide information for reporting to children and parents. It is important for learning and assessment to encompass all important and desired outcomes of school learning, beyond the simple discipline knowledge bases. Every nation argues the expectation that schooling will develop lifelong learners, individuals who can make a positive contribution to society. One group of outcomes that is globally endorsed involves the development of *engagement* and *flexibility* such as effort, persistence, willingness to learn, interdependence, intuition (Cumming 2001); self-awareness in target-setting, capacity to choose rapidly between options, self-reliance or, more globally, intuition (Broadfoot 2000). These personal learnings relate to development of lifelong learning orientations as well as to effective personal and work habits.

All education systems worldwide endorse lifelong learning attributes as desired learning outcomes for students, outcomes that logically, therefore, are to be developed not just at home but also within school by you as a teacher. Queensland Studies Authority, for example, lists the following desirable characteristics (QSA 2002a, p. 1):

- a knowledgeable person with deep understanding;
- a complex thinker;
- a creative person;
- an active investigator;
- an effective communicator;
- a participant in an interdependent world;
- a reflective and self-directed learner.

Syllabus outcomes extend beyond traditional knowledge to description of a student's 'repertoire of knowledge, *practices* and *dispositions* for each key learning area, subject area and subject' (QSA 2002b, p. 1). While these are new, and certainly not easy, areas of learning and assessment, practices and suggestions are developing.

Marzano et al. (1993) included subject domain knowledge standards and lifelong learning standards in their five dimensions of learning. Their lifelong learning standards include: complex thinking standards; information processing standards; effective communication standards; collaboration/cooperation standards; and 'habits of mind' standards—self-regulation, critical thinking, creative thinking. Their five dimensions include use of the 'effective habits of mind'. Marzano et al. provided a four-level exemplar rubric for 'planning':

> Level 4: I set clear goals and describe each step I must take to achieve them. I make a detailed schedule for each step and closely follow the schedule.
>
> Level 3: I set clear goals and describe some steps I must take to achieve them. I make and use a schedule.
>
> Level 2: I begin working with only unclear goals. I describe few of the steps I must take to achieve my goals, and I make an incomplete schedule.
>
> Level 1: I begin working and just let things happen as they happen. I do not describe the steps I must take and I do not make a schedule (p. 126).

This example uses language appropriate for middle years students; a parallel format can be used by you for teacher rating. Students can use the rubric to assess their overall performance at a point in time, or the example can be embedded within specific learning and assessment activities as a dimension of student performance. One criticism of this set of statements is that it does imply one set desirable process of working, whereas not all effective people work in such a linear way, or at least not for every activity.

The following example from Wiggins (1998) demonstrates an integration of dispositional and engagement outcomes with more traditional aspects of performance in a rating descriptor for a specific learning and assessment activity, an oral presentation: 'There is strong evidence of preparation, organization, and enthusiasm for the topic' (p. 166).

In another rubric for listening and participation, leadership and conduct (in discussion seminars), Wiggins (1998) describes a 'high' level as:

> Demonstrates respect, enthusiasm, and skill for the purpose of the seminar: insight into important texts and ideas gained through the interplay of collaborative and personal inquiry into a text. Demonstrates in speech and manner a habitual respect for the text, reasoned discussion, and shared enquiry. Effectively contributes to deepening and broadening the conversation, revealing exemplary habits of mind.

and a 'fair' level as:

> Does not regularly listen very well and/or is not always attentive, as reflected in comments and body language. Verbal reactions reflect an earlier difficulty or failure to listen carefully to what was said. Behavior may signify either that the student lacks effective note-taking strategies and/or does not grasp the importance of listening to different points of view and reflecting on them (pp. 70–1).

The language here is clearly complex and could not be provided, nor even sufficiently explained, to middle class students. However, you could look at the essential concepts to develop your own middle schooling-appropriate statements to be embedded in specific activities. Ask students what criteria should be expected of performance in such areas and what the descriptors of good outcomes would be.

In general, for self-assessing growth in such areas, students should be able to handle simple grids, such as those in Figure 18.4, suggested ways of assessing dimensions of personal quality assurance and, engagement with task and others (Cumming 2004). These grids, again, are designed for use within specific assessment activities to promote self-reflection on important processes of learning, not as generic assessments of student approaches.

The examples in Figure 18.4 focus on learning processes and engagement with learning. Another evolving dimension of learning attracting assessment focus is 'values'. Many school systems already have in place statements of expectations of values and ways of reporting on these. If not, the above grids could provide templates for developing statements of learning of values that suit the community context of your school.

Possible legal challenges in assessment

Challenges to education law in Australia have primarily focused on duty of care for physical safety, staff union and employment issues, and staff and student discrimination issues. However, following trends overseas, it is likely that litigation and legal

Figure 18.4 Examples of self-assessment rating grids for extended learning outcomes

Personal quality assurance

	At this stage of the project, an example to demonstrate this is:	What I think I can do better here/ may do next:	Teacher/peer comment
Integrity (my own work, honesty, care for others)			
Attention to detail			
Effective time management			
Good organisational skills			

Engagement with task and others

	At this stage of the project, I would rate my:*	An example to demonstrate this is:	What I think I should try to do now is:	Teacher/peer comment
Effort (how hard I am trying)				
Persistence (when things get hard)				
Resilience (when things dont work)				
Collaboration with others				
Self-reliance (work by myself when necessary)				
Initiative (taking a lead, thinking of new ideas)				
Enthusiasm				
Self-discipline				

* 1. I really haven't got involved
   2. I'm working on it but not giving the task/others sufficient attention and priority
   3. I am working steadily on this
   4. I am putting in 100% so that the outcomes are the best I can achieve

Source: Adapted from Cumming (2004).

challenges in the area of educational assessment will be seen in the future. The accountability requirements for assessment and reporting, including the use of external system-wide tests and reporting, that we have discussed can lead to the threat of financial or other punitive measures always just around the corner. They can lead to student profiling, and to teacher, school and state-level identification. In Australia, accountability outcomes have so far led to increased financial access to assist in developing effective programs for low achievers. If, as overseas, punitive financial or other impacts do occur, legal reactions can be expected.

More generally for education assessment, increased competition between schools, both across the government and non-government sectors and within sectors, has led to schools operating in a semi-commercial environment, with school promotional material targeting parent and student expectations of student outcomes, including learning. Clearly, parents and students will come to have expectations that the schools will deliver the results promised. These expectations can translate into the types of assessments, and their outcomes, that a school puts in place.

To date, Australian courts do not intervene in what are seen as institutional responsibilities, such as education policy and practice. However, cases have been mounted in areas such as inappropriate assessment for students with special needs that have resulted in inappropriate placement, as well as general discrimination cases, and may emerge for inappropriate assessments for students without English as a first language. A recent challenge in New South Wales, reaching the Supreme Court, challenged the appropriateness of accommodations made for a student with mild Attention Deficit Disorder for the Higher School Certificate examinations [*BI* v *Board of Studies* [2000] NSWSC 921]. Advice to schools is that they should 'put in place appropriate documentation and protocols to ensure that there are systems in place to minimise the risk of . . . claims' (Stewart & Knott 2002, p. 162).

One major reason for the potential for increased legal challenge is that as policies of inclusivity in schools become more truly enacted, parent and child expectations will increase that schools should provide appropriate learning opportunities, and outcomes, for all students. Accompanying this is the expectation that systems will provide appropriate assessment forms to accommodate all types of learners. For example, this may be an area where computer use for communication by disabled learners will be important for assessment (Singleton 1997). Equity provides a core challenge to the enactment of fair assessment overall, but may most readily emerge in legal challenges on grounds of discrimination.

Fundamental to equity in assessment is the recognition that the construction of the knowledge and skills to be assessed should involve a critical evaluation of the extent to which the choice of a particular set of knowledge and skills is likely to privilege certain groups of students and exclude others by virtue of gender, socioeconomic, cultural or linguistic background. A concern with equity also leads to adopting a proactive stance on the appropriate representation in the curriculum of different kinds of cultural knowledge and experience as valued knowledge and skills (ACACA 1995, p. 1).

The sheer quantity of the current focus on assessment and accountability occurring for the middle years of schooling places teachers in these areas under more pressure to deliver not only good outcomes but also to ensure that appropriate assessment practices occur. Here we return to the recommendation that you work with professional colleagues such as learning assistance teachers, ESL instructors and guidance counsellors in assessing special needs of and provisions for students, especially during assessments. We also recommend that principals and teachers should undertake legal professional development regarding responsibility in this area.

Conclusion

Attention has turned to the middle years of schooling in recognition of the vital role they play in the transition from young learner to successful high school completion and beyond. Different ways of engaging students, developing curricula and pedagogical practices, as discussed throughout this book, are developing to ensure student progress and to enhance the quality of learning that occurs. As this chapter has demonstrated, effective assessment that is cognisant of the nature of learners, of implicit cultural and literate practices of the curriculum, and of demonstrated ways in which assessment can inform and report on learning, plays a very significant role in education. We can only provide a selection and brief overview of critical issues that you as a teacher need to consider. Hopefully we have provided sufficient intellectual stimulation to raise your awareness to engage with these issues as well as provided some further resources for your own continued self-learning in the area of educational assessment for the middle years of schooling.

Questions

1 What are some of the different types and purposes of assessment?

2 What are the main issues of reliability and validity of assessments for classroom teachers?

3 What do you see as the key advantages of focusing on formative assessment in your classroom?

4 What are some procedures you might undertake to practise formative assessment?

5 How would you identify key learning outcomes and the standards that you expect students to demonstrate in related assessment activities or projects?

6 How would you translate these into a form that students can understand and use to guide their work?

7 Why is literacy such a special factor in student learning and assessment?

8 What is your role in facilitating student learning and success in assessment in terms of literacy?

9 How should you monitor students' understanding of the literacy demands of a subject area?

10 What are some important areas of student learning to promote and assess that go beyond traditional notions of discipline content?

11 In what ways do you think you could assess these?

12 Why do you think students and parents might use the courts to challenge assessment practices and outcomes?

13 What activities will you undertake to increase your own understanding and expertise in educational assessment?

14 How do you think you can promote a healthy whole-school assessment climate as a middle years teacher?

References

Adams, C. and Walkerdine, V. (1986). *Investigating gender in the primary school.* London: Inner London Education Authority.

Allen, L. (1994). *Oral language resource book.* Melbourne: Longman.

Allison, B.N. and Schultz, B. (2004). Parent–adolescent conflict in early adolescence. *Adolescence. Spring, 39*(153), 101.

Alloway, N. (1995). *Foundation stones: The construction of gender in early childhood.* Carlton: Curriculum Corporation.

Alloway, N., Freebody, P., Gilbert, P. and Muspratt, S. (2002). *Boys, literacy and schooling: Expanding the repertoires of practice.* Canberra: Commonwealth Department of Education, Science and Training.

American Educational Research Association (AERA) (2000). *Position statement concerning high-stakes testing in preK–12 education.* Retrieved 20 October 2004, from www.aera.net/about/policy/stakes.htm

Ames, N. (2004). Lessons learned from comprehensive school reform models. In S.C. Thompson (ed.), *Reforming middle level education: Considerations for policymakers* (pp. 131–54). Greenwich, CT: Information Age Publishing.

Andersen, S.L. (2003). Trajectories of brain development: Point of vulnerability or window of opportunity? *Neuroscience and Behavioral Reviews, 27*(1), 3–18.

Andrade, H.G. (2001, April 17). The effects of instructional rubrics on learning to write. *Current Issues in Education [On-line]*, 4(4). Retrieved 20 October 2004, from http://cie.ed.asu/volume4/number4/

Anfara, V.A. (2004). Creating high-performance middle schools: Recommendations from research. In S.C. Thompson (ed.), *Reforming middle level education: Considerations for policymakers* (pp. 1–18). Greenwich, CT: Information Age Publishing.

Anfara, V.A., Andrews, G.P., Hough, D.L., Mertens, S.B., Mizelle, N.B. and White, G. (eds) (2003). *Research and resources in support of 'This we believe.'* Westerville, OH: National Middle School Association.

Anstey, M. and Bull, G. (2000). *Reading the visual: Written and illustrated children's literature.* Sydney: Harcourt Australia.

Argyris, C. (1970). *Intervention theory and method: A behavioural science view.* Reading: Addison-Wesley.

Armour, K. (1999). The case for a body-focus in education and physical education. *Sport, Education and Society*, 4(1), 5–17.

Armstrong, N. (2002). *Physical fitness, physical activity and physical education.* Keynote address at the AIESEP Conference, La Coruña, Spain, October.

Armstrong, N. and Biddle, S. (1992). Health-related physical activity in the national curriculum. In N. Armstrong (ed.), *New directions in physical education, Volume 2* (pp. 71–110). Champaign, IL: Human Kinetics.

Arnett, J.J. (2001). *Adolescence and emerging adulthood: A cultural approach.* New Jersey: Prentice Hall.

Arnsten, A.F.T. and Shansky, R.M. (2004). Adolescence: Vulnerable period for stress-induced prefrontal cortical function? Introduction to Part IV. *Annals of the New York Academy of Sciences*, 1021, 143–7.

Australian Association of Mathematics Teachers Inc. (AAMT) (1997). *Numeracy = everyone's business.* Report of the Numeracy Education Strategy Development Conference. Adelaide: AAMT.

Australian Curriculum and Certification Authorities (ACACA) (1995). *Guidelines for quality assessment and equity.* Retrieved on 20 October 2004, from http://www.acaca.org.au/guide.htm

Australian Curriculum Studies Association (1993). *In the middle or at the centre? A report of a national conference on middle schooling.* Belconnen, ACT: Australian Curriculum Studies Association.

——(1996). *From alienation to engagement: Opportunities for reform in the middle years of schooling.* (Vols 1–3). Belconnen, ACT: Australian Curriculum Studies Association.

Australian Education Council (1990). *A national statement on mathematics for Australian schools.* Carlton, Vic: Curriculum Corporation.

Ausubel, D.P. (1954). *Theory and problems of adolescent development.* New York: Grune & Stratton.

Baker, D. (1992, April). *Letting students speak: Triangulation of qualitative and quantitative assessments of attitude toward science.* Paper presented at the Annual Meeting of the American Educational Research Association, San Francisco.

Baker, R. (2003). Promoting a research agenda in education within and beyond policy and practice. *Educational Research for Policy and Practice, 2,* 171–86.

Ball, D. (2000). Bridging practices: Intertwining content and pedagogy in teaching and learning to teach. *Journal of Teacher Education, 51*(3), 241–7.

Balog, D. (ed.) (2001). *The Dana sourcebook of brain science.* New York: Dana Press.

Bandura, A. (1977). *Social learning theory.* Englewood Cliffs, NJ: Prentice-Hall.

——(1986). *Social foundations of thought and action: A social cognitive theory.* Englewood Cliffs, NJ: Prentice-Hall.

Barber, M. (1999). *Taking the tide at the flood: Transforming education in the middle years.* Paper presented at the Middle Years of Schooling Conference, Melbourne, March. Retrieved 10 November 2001, from http://www.sofweb. vic. edu.au/mys/other.htm

Barratt, R. (1997). *National Middle Schooling Project.* Australian Curriculum Studies Association Biennial Conference, Sydney.

——(1998a). *Shaping middle schooling in Australia: A report of the National Middle Schooling Project.* Canberra: Australian Curriculum Studies Association.

——(1998b). The future: The shape of middle schooling in Australia. *Curriculum Perspectives 18*(1), 53–5.

Batten, M. and Russell, J. (1995). *Students at risk: A review of Australian literature 1980–1994.* ACER Research Monograph No. 46. Melbourne: ACER.

Battista, M.T. (1999). The mathematics miseducation of America's youth: Ignoring research and scientific study in education. *Phi Delta Kappan, 80*(6), 424–33.

Beane, J. (1990). Rethinking the middle school curriculum. *Middle School Journal, May,* 1–4.

——(1991). The middle school: The natural home of the integrated curriculum. *Educational Leadership, 49,* 9–13.

——(1993). *A middle school curriculum: From rhetoric to reality* (2nd edn). Columbus, OH: National Middle Schooling Association.

——(1995). Myths, politics, and meaning in curriculum integration. In Y. Siu-

Runyan and V. Faircloth (eds), *Beyond separate subjects: Integrative learning at the middle level.* Norwood, MA: Christopher-Gordon Publishers, Inc.

——(1996). On the shoulders of giants! The case for curriculum integration. *Middle School Journal, 28,* 6–19.

——(1997a). Curriculum for what? The search for curriculum purposes for middle level students. In J.L. Irvin (ed.) *What current research says to the middle level practitioner* (pp. 203–7). Westerville, OH: National Middle School Association.

——(1997b). *Curriculum integration. Designing the core of democratic education.* New York: Teachers College Press.

——(1999). Middle schools under siege: Points of attack. *Middle School Journal,* March, 3–9.

——(2004a). Creating quality in the middle school curriculum. In S.C. Thompson (ed.), *Reforming middle level education: Considerations for policymakers* (pp. 49–64). Westerville, OH: National Middle School Association.

——(2004b). *No progressive idea left alone: A middle school curriculum ten years later.* Paper presented at the National Middle School Association annual conference, Minneapolis.

Beane, J. and Apple, M. (1995). The case for democratic schools. In M. Apple and J. Beane (eds), *Democratic Schools.* Alexandria, VA: Association for Supervision and Curriculum Development.

Beane, J.A. and Brodhagen, B. (1995). *Strategies for improving the schools, Exploring middle school curriculum options: Part 2. The middle years kit.* Ryde, NSW: National Schools Network.

Beck, C. (1999). *The role of the teacher in today's world.* Paper presented at Kobe Women's University, 11 June.

Beck, C. and Kosnik, C. (2001). From cohort to community in a preservice teacher education program. *Teaching and Teacher Education, 17*(8), 925–48.

Beck, U. (1992). *Risk society: Towards a new modernity.* London: Sage Publications.

Begg, S. (2001). *Teaching writers in the classroom years 3 and 4.* South Melbourne: Longman.

Behets, D. (1997). Comparison of more and less effective teaching behaviors in secondary physical education. *Teacher and Teacher Education, 13*(2), 215–24.

Benard, B. (1991). *Fostering resilience in kids: Protective factors in the family, school and community* (pp. 1–36). Western Regional Center Drug-free schools and communities. Retrieved 17 November 2004, from http://nwrac.org/pub/library/f/f_foster.pdf

Bennett, B.J. (1997). Middle level discipline and young adolescents: Making the Connection. In J. Irvin (ed.), *What current research says to the middle level practitioner*. Columbus, OH: National Middle School Association.

Benson, P.L. (1997). *All kids are our kids: What communities must do to raise caring and responsible children and adolescents*. San Francisco: Jossey-Bass.

Bereiter, C. (1994). Implications of postmodernism for science, or, science as progressive discourse. *Educational Psychologist, 29*(1), 3–12.

Berger, B. and Pargman, D. (2002). *Foundations of exercise psychology*. Morgantown, WV: Fitness Information Technology Inc.

Berninger, V.W. and Richards, T.L. (2002). *Brain literacy for educators and psychologists*. San Diego: Elsevier Science.

Berridge, K.C. (2003). Comparing the emotional brains of humans and other animals. In R.J. Davidson, K.R. Scherer and H. Hill Goldsmith (eds), *Handbook of affective sciences* (pp. 25–52). Oxford: Oxford University Press.

Bessant, B. and Holbrook, A. (1995). *Reflections on educational research in Australia: A history of the Australian Association for Research in Education*. Coldstream, Vic: Australian Association for Research in Education Inc.

Bessant, J., Sercombe, H. and Watts, R. (1998). *Youth studies: An Australian perspective*. (pp. 132–46), Melbourne: Longman.

Black, P. and Wiliam, D. (1998). Inside the black box: Raising standards through classroom assessment. *Phi Delta Kappan*. London: School of Education, Kings College.

Blanksby, B., Anderson, M. and Douglas, G. (1996). Recreational patterns, body composition and socioeconomic status of Western Australian secondary school students. *Annals of Human Biology, 23*(2), 101–12.

Block, K.C. and Israel, S.E. (2004). The ABCs of performing highly effective think-alouds. *The Reading Teacher, 58*, 154–167.

Bloom, B. (1956). *Taxonomy of educational objectives*. New York: Longman.

Blum, D. (1997). *Sex on the brain: The biological differences between men and women*. New York: Penguin Putnam Inc.

Boomer, G. (ed.) (1982). *Negotiating the curriculum: A teacher–student partnership*. London: The Falmer Press.

Boomer, G., Lester, N., Onore, C. and Cook, J. (1992). *Negotiating the curriculum*. London: The Falmer Press.

Bourdieu, P. (1977). *Outline of a theory of practice*. Cambridge: Cambridge University Press.

Boyd-Batstone, P. (2004). Focussed anecdotal records assessment: A tool for standards-based, authentic assessment. *The Reading Teacher, 58*, 230–9.

Bradley, M.J. (2003). *Yes, your teen is crazy: Loving your kid without losing your mind.* Gig Harbor, Wash: Harbor Press.

Braggett, E. (1997). *The middle years of schooling: An Australian perspective.* Australia: Hawker Brownlow Education.

Brandt, R. (1999). Educators need to know about the human brain. *Phi Delta Kappan, 81*(3), 235–9.

Bransford, J.D., Brown, A.L. and Cocking, R.R. (eds) (1999). *How people learn: Brain, mind, experience and school.* Washington, DC: National Academy Press.

Brendtro L. and Larson, S. (2004). The resilience code: Finding greatness in youth. *Reclaiming Children and Youth: Cultivating Resilience, 12*(4). Retrieved 20 November 2004, from www.cyc-net.org/Journals/rcy–12–4.html

Brendtro, L., Brokenleg, M. and Van Bockern, S. (1990). *Reclaiming youth at risk: Our hope for the future.* Bloomington, IN: National Education Service.

Brennan, M. and Sachs, J. (1998). Integrated curriculum for the middle years. In J. Cumming (ed.), *Extending reform in the middle years of schooling: Challenges and responses* (pp. 18–24). Deakin West, ACT: Australian Curriculum Studies Association (ACSA).

Bronfenbrenner, U. (1979). *The ecology of human development: Experiments by nature and design.* Cambridge, MA: Harvard University Press.

Brown, D.F. (2001). Flexible scheduling and young adolescent development. A perfect match. In. V.A. Anfara (ed.), *The handbook of research in middle level education* (pp. 125–42). Greenwich, CT: Information Age Publishing.

Brown, H. and Cambourne, B. (1988). *Read and retell: A strategy for the whole-language/natural learning classroom.* Melbourne: Nelson.

Brown, R.A.J. (1998). 'Where do you people get your ideas from?': Negotiating zones of collaborative learning within an upper primary classroom. In B. Baker, M. Tucker and C. Ng (eds), *Education's new timespace: Visions from the present* (pp. 107–12). Brisbane: Post Pressed.

——(2001). *A sociocultural study of the emergence of a classroom community of practice.* Unpublished doctoral thesis, University of Queensland, Brisbane.

Brown, R.A.J. and Renshaw, P.D. (2000). Collective argumentation: A sociocultural approach to reframing classroom teaching and learning. In H. Cowie and G. van der Aalsvoort (eds), *Social interaction in learning and instruction: The meaning of discourse for the construction of knowledge* (pp. 52–66). Amsterdam: Pergamon Press.

——(2004). Integrating everyday scientific ways of knowing mathematics through forms of participation in classroom talk. In I. Putt, R. Faraghar and

M. McLearn (eds), *Mathematics Education for the third millenium: Towards 2010. Proceedings of the 27th Annual Conference of the Mathematics Education Research Group of Australasia*, pp. 135–42. Townsville: Mathematics Education Research Group of Australasia (MERGA).

Brown, W., Macdonald, D., Trost, S., Miller, Y., Braiuka, S. and Hornsey, A. (2001). *Final report to the Australian Sports Commission: Young people's participation in physical activity*. Brisbane: The University of Queensland.

Bruer, J.T. (1999). Neural connections: Some you use, some you lose. *Phi Delta Kappan, 81*(4), 264–78.

Buckingham, J. (2003). Class size and teacher quality. *Educational Research for Policy and Practice, 2,* 71–86.

Bunton, R. and Burrows, R. (1995). Consumption and health in the 'epidemiological' clinic of late modern medicine. In R. Bunton, S. Nettleton and R. Burrows (eds), *The sociology of health promotion*. London: Routledge.

Butterworth, B. (2003). *Dyscalculia screener*. London: Nelson.

Buzan, T. (2000). *The mind map book*. London: BBC.

Caine, G. and Caine, R.N. (2001). *The brain, education, and the competitive edge*. Lanham, MD: Scarecrow Press Inc.

Cam, P. (1995). *Thinking together: Philosophical inquiry for the classroom*. Sydney: PETA/Hale & Iremonger.

Cameron, A. (2004). I'll never grow up, not me! *Macleans, 117*(31), 56–7.

Campbell, D. (1997). *The Mozart effect: Tapping the power of music to heal the body, strengthen the mind and unlock the creative spirit*. New York: Avon Books.

Carlson, N.R. (2000). *Physiology of behavior* (7th edn). Boston: Allyn & Bacon.

Carnegie Council on Adolescent Development (1989). *Turning points: Preparing American youth for the 21st century: The report of the Task Force on Education of Young Adolescents*. New York: Carnegie Corporation.

Carr, E.G., Dunlap, G., Horner, R.H., Koegel, R.L., Turnbull, A.P., Sailor, W., Anderson, J.L., Albin, R.W., Koegel, L.K. and Fox, L. (2002). Positive behavior support: Evolution of an applied science. *Journal of Positive Behaviour Interventions, 4*(1), 4–16.

Carrington, V. (2002). *The middle years of schooling in Queensland: A way forward*. Discussion paper prepared for Education Queensland.

——(2004). Mid-term review: The middle years of schooling. *Curriculum Perspectives, 24*(1), 30–41.

Carrington, V., Pendergast, D., Bahr, N., Mayer, D. and Mitchell, J. (2002). *Education futures: Transforming teacher education (re-framing teacher education for the middle years)*. *Proceedings of the 2001 National Biennial Conference of the Australian Curriculum Studies Association*. Canberra: ACSA.

Casey, B.J., Giedd, J.N. and Thomas, K.M. (2000). Structural and functional brain development and its relation to cognitive development. *Biological Psychology, 54*, 241–57.

Caskey, M.M. (in press). *Action research at the middle level: Teachers and administrators in action*. Westerville, OH: National Middle School Association.

Caskey, M.M. and Ruben, B. (2003). Research for awakening adolescent learning. *The Education Digest, 69*(4), 36–8.

Catholic Education Archdiocese of Brisbane (2004). *Pathways for middle schooling: Walking the talk. A position paper and self-audit process*. Brisbane: Catholic Education Archdiocese of Brisbane.

Cavill, N., Biddle, S. and Sallis, J.F. (2001). Health enhancing physical activity for young people: Statement of the United Kingdom Expert Consensus Conference. *Paediatric Exercise Science, 13*, 12–25.

Cefai, C. (2004). Pupil resilience in the classroom: A teacher's framework, *Emotional Behavioural Difficulties, 9*(3), 149–70.

Centre for Collaborative Education (2000). *At the turning point: The young adolescent*. Boston: Retrieved 23 March 2004, from http://www.turningpts.org

Chadbourne, R. (2001). *Middle schooling for the middle years: What might the jury be considering?* Victoria: Australian Education Union.

——(2003). Middle schooling and academic rigour. *International Journal of Learning, 10*, 541–50.

Charles, C.M. (1999). *Building classroom discipline*. New York: Longman.

Chi, M.T.H. and Ceci, S.J. (1987). Content knowledge: Its role, representation, and restructuring in memory development. *Advances in Child Development and Behaviour, 20*, 91–142.

Chi, M.T.H., Glaser, R. and Rees, E. (1982). Expertise in problem solving. In R. Sternberg (ed.), *Advances in the psychology of human intelligence* (Vol. 1). Hillsdale, NJ: Lawrence Erlbaum.

Clark, B. (2001). Some principles of brain research for challenging gifted learners. *Gifted Education International, 16*, 4–10.

Clark, M. (1993). *The great divide*. Carlton: Curriculum Corporation.

Coil, C. (2003). *Surviving the middle years: Strategies for student engagement, growth and learning*. Cheltenham, Vic: Hawker Brownlow Education.

Cole, M. (2004). Howard vows to make fat kids run. *The Courier Mail*. 1 June, p. 3.

Commonwealth of Australia (2003). *Educating boys: Issues and information.* Canberra: Commonwealth of Australia.

Conlan, R. (ed.) (2001). *States of mind: Discoveries about how our brains make us who we are.* New York: John Wiley & Sons, Inc.

Corbett, D. and Wilson, B. (1995). Make a difference with, not for students: A plea to researchers and reformers. *Educational Researcher, 24*(5), 12–17.

Cormack, P. (1991). *The nature of adolescence: A review of literature and other selected papers.* Adelaide: Education Department of South Australia.

——(1998). Middle schooling: For which adolescent? *Curriculum Perspectives 18*(1), 56–60.

Cormack, P. and Cumming, J. (1995). *From alienation to engagement: Opportunities for reform in the middle years.* Canberra: Australian Curriculum Studies Association.

Costa, A. (ed.) (1985). *Developing minds.* Alexandria, VA: Association for Supervision and Curriculum Development.

Côté, J. (2000). *Arrested adulthood: The changing nature of maturity and identity.* New York: New York University Press.

Cothran, D. and Ennis, C. (1997). Students' and teachers' perceptions of conflict and power. *Teaching and Teacher Education, 13*(5), 541–53.

——(1998). Curricula of mutual worth: Comparisons of students' and teachers' curricular goals. *Journal of Teaching in Physical Education, 17*, 307–26.

Creenaune, T. and Rowles, L. (1996). *What's your purpose: Reading strategies for non-fiction texts.* Marrickville: Primary English Teaching Association.

Csikszentmihalyi, M. (1997). *Living well: The psychology of every day life.* London: Weidenfeld & Nicolson.

Cumming, J. (1996). *From alienation to engagement: Opportunities for reform in the middle years of schooling,* Volumes 1, 2, 3. Belconnen, ACT: Australian Curriculum Studies Association.

——(ed.) (1998). *Extending reform in the middle years of schooling: Challenges and responses.* Canberra: Australian Curriculum Studies Association.

Cumming, J.J. and Maxwell, G.S. (1999). Contextualising authentic assessment. *Assessment in Education: Principles, Policy and Practice, 6*(2), 177–94.

Cumming, J.J. (1996). The IEA studies of reading and writing literacy: A 1996 perspective. *Assessment in Education: Principles, Policy and Practice, 3*(2), 161–78.

——(2004). *Assessing and reporting all learning.* Paper presented at Conference of the Association for Commonwealth Examination and Accreditation Boards, Fiji, March.

Curriculum Corporation (2000). *The national numeracy benchmarks.* Carlton South, Vic: Curriculum Corporation.

Daiman, S. (1995). Women in sport in Islam. *Journal of the International Council for Health, Physical Education, Recreation, Sport and Dance, 32*(1), 18–21.

Damasio, A.R. (1995). *Descartes' error: Emotion, reason and the human brain.* New York: G.P. Putnam Books.

——(1999). *The feeling of what happens: Body and emotion in the making of consciousness.* New York: Avon Books.

Damon, W. (1988). *The social world of the child.* San Francisco: Jossey-Bass.

Daniels, D., Bizaz, M. and Zemelman, S. (2001). *Rethinking high school: Best practice in teaching, learning and leadership.* Portsmouth, NH: Heinemann.

Daniels, H. (2002). *Literature circles: Voice and choice in book clubs and reading groups* (2nd edn). Portland, Me: Stenhouse Publishers.

Darling-Hammond, L. (1997). *The right to learn: A blueprint for creating schools that work.* San Francisco: Jossey-Bass.

Davies, B. (1993). *Shards of glass.* Sydney: Allen & Unwin.

——(2000). *A body of writing 1990–1999.* New York: Alta Mira Press.

Davis, B., Sumara, D. and Luce-Kapler, R. (2000). *Engaging minds: Learning and teaching in a complex world.* Mahwah, NJ: Lawrence Erlbaum Associates.

Davis, P. and Florian, L. (2004). *Teaching strategies and approaches for pupils with special educational needs: A scoping study* (Research Report No. 516). Norwich, UK: Department for Education and Skills.

de Bono, E. (1995). *Six thinking hats.* Melbourne: Hawker Brownlow Education.

de Jong, T. (2003). Behaviour management in the middle years of schooling: What is good practice? *Australian Journal of Middle Schooling, 3*(1), 1–8.

——(2004). *Best practice in addressing student behaviour issues in Australia.* Report submitted to the Ministerial Council on Education, Employment, Training and Youth Affairs (MCEETYA): Perth, Western Australia.

De Pauw, K. and Doll-Tepper, D. (2000). Toward progressive inclusion and acceptance: myth or reality? The inclusion debate and the bandwagon discourse. *Adapted Physical Activity Quarterly, 17*(2), 135–43.

Dellu, F., Piazza, P.V., Mayo, W., Le Moal, M. and Simon, H. (1996). Novelty seeking in rats: Biobehavioral characteristics and possible relationship with the sensation-seeking trait in man. *Neuropsychobiology, 34,* 136–45.

Denborough (1996). Step by step: Developing respectful and effective ways of working with young men to reduce violence. In C. McLean, M. Carey and C. White (eds), *Men's ways of being.* Boulder: Westview Press.

Department of Education and Training Victoria (2002). *Middle years of schooling—thinking curriculum*. Retrieved 10 October 2002, from http://www.sofweb.vic.edu.au/mys/Thinking/index.htm

Department of Education, Tasmania (2002). *Essential learnings framework 1*. Hobart: Department of Education, Tasmania.

Department of Education, Training and Youth Affairs (DETYA) (2000). *Numeracy, a priority for all: Challenges for Australian schools*. Canberra: J.S. McMillan Printing Group.

——(2001). *Doing it well. Case studies of innovation and best practice in working with at risk young people*. Canberra: Department of Education, Training and Youth Affairs.

DETYA—Peter Cuttance and the Innovation and Best Practice Consortium (2001). *School innovation: Pathway to the knowledge society*. Canberra: DETYA.

Diamond, M. and Hopson, J. (1999). *Magic trees of the mind: How to nurture your child's intelligence, creativity, and healthy emotions from birth through adolescence*. New York: Penguin Putnam, Inc.

Dickenson, T.J. (ed.) (2001). *Reinventing the middle school*. London: Routledge Falmer.

Doda, N. (2002). It all adds up. In N. Doda and C. Thompson (eds), *Transforming ourselves transforming schools: Middle school change* (pp. 349–55). Westerville, OH: National Middle School Association.

Dodge, B. (1998). *The webquest page*. Retrieved 25 March 2004, from http://webquest.sdsu.edu/

Doig, B. (2001). *Summing up: Australian numeracy performances, practices, programs and possibilities*. Camberwell, Vic: ACER.

Dole, S. (2003). Questioning numeracy programs for at-risk students in the middle years of schooling. In L. Bragg, C. Campbell, G. Herbert and J. Mousley, *MERINO: Mathematics education research: Innovation, networking, opportunity. Proceedings of the twenty-sixth annual conference of the Mathematics Education Research Group of Australasia* (pp. 278–85). Geelong: Deakin University.

Donald, D., Lazarus, S. and Lolwana, P. (2002). *Educational psychology in social context* (2nd edn). Cape Town: Oxford University Press.

Dossel, S. (1993). Maths anxiety. *The Australian Mathematics Teacher*, 49(1), 4–8.

Dryfoos, J.G. (1990). *Adolescents at risk: prevalence and prevention*. New York: Oxford University Press.

——(1993). Common components of successful interventions with high-risk youth. In, N.J. Bell & R.W. Bell, *Adolescent risk taking* (pp. 131–47). London: Sage.

——(1998). *Safe passage: Making it through adolescence in a risky society.* New York: Oxford University Press.

Dumbleton, M. and Lountain, K. (1999a). *Addressing literacy in science: A middle years resource.* Carlton South, Vic: Curriculum Corporation.

——(1999b). *Addressing literacy in society and environment: A middle years resource.* Carlton South, Vic: Curriculum Corporation.

——(1999c). *Addressing literacy in the arts: A middle years resource.* Carlton South, Vic: Curriculum Corporation.

Dyson, A.H. (2003). *The brothers and sisters learn to write: Popular literacies in childhood and school cultures.* New York: Teachers College Press.

Dyson, B. (2002). The implementation of cooperative learning in an elementary physical education program. *Journal of Teaching in Physical Education, 22*(1), 69–85.

Eccles, J. and Wigfield, A. (1997). Young adolescent development. In J. Irvin (ed.), *What current research says to the middle level practitioner.* Columbus, OH: National Middle School Association.

Education Department of Western Australia (1997). *Writing resource book.* Port Melbourne, Vic: Rigby Heinemann.

——(2000). *New Basics Project—Technical Paper,* Version: 3 April. Brisbane. Education Queensland.

——(2001a). *Make their heads spin! Improving learning in the middle years.* Carlton South, Vic: Curriculum Corporation.

——(2001b). *Years 1–10 curriculum framework for Education Queensland schools.* Brisbane, Australia: Education Queensland.

——(2002). *A guide to productive pedagogies. Classroom reflection manual.* Brisbane, Australia: Education Queensland Curriculum Implementation Unit.

——(2003). *The middle phase of learning: State school action plan.* Brisbane. Education Queensland.

——(2004). *New Basics Branch.* Retrieved 20 November 2004, from http://www.education.qld.gov.au/corporate/newbasics

Edwards, C.H. and Watts, V. (2004). *Classroom discipline and management: An Australasian perspective.* Brisbane: John Wiley & Sons Ltd.

Edwards-Groves, C. (2003). *On task: Focused literacy teaching.* Newtown, NSW: Primary English Teaching Association.

Egeland, B., Carlson, E. and Sroufe, L.A. (1993). Resilience as a process. *Development and Psychopathology, 5,* 517–28.

Eisner, E.W. (2003). Preparing for today and tomorrow. *Educational Leadership, 61*(4), 6–10.

Elmore, R. F. (1996). Getting to scale with good educational practice. *Harvard Educational Review*, *66*(1), 1–27.

Engels, R.C.M.E., Vitaro, F., Blokland, E.D.E., de Kemp, R. and Scholte R.H.J. (2004). Influence and selection processes in friendships and adolescent smoking behaviour: The role of parental smoking, *Journal of Adolescence*, *27*(5), October, 531–44.

Epstein, J. (1995). School/family/community partnerships. *Phi Delta Kappan*, *7*(9), 701–12.

——(1996). Advances in family, community and school partnerships. *New Schools: New Communities*, *12*(3), 5–13.

Epstein, J., Coates, L., Salinas, K. and Simon, B. (eds) (1997). *School, family and community partnerships: Your handbook for action*. Thousand Oaks, CA: Corwin Press.

Erikson, E. (1959). Identity and the life cycle. *Psychological Issues*, *1*, 50–100.

——(1963). *Childhood and society.* New York: W.W. Norton.

Ernest, P. (2000). Empowerment in mathematics education. In M.A. Clements, H.H. Tairab and W.K. Yoong (eds), *Energising science, mathematics, and technical education for all, Proceedings of the Conference Brunei* (pp. 79–93). Universiti Brunei Darussalam.

Evans, L. (2002). *Reflective practice in educational research.* New York: Continuum.

Eyers, V. (1992). *Report of the junior secondary review.* Adelaide: Education Department of South Australia.

Fairclough, N. (1992). Discourse and text: Linguistic and intertextual analysis within discourse analysis, *Discourse and Society*, 3(2), 193–17.

Feltovich, P.J., Spiro, R.J., Coulson, R.L and Feltovich, J. (1996). Collaboration within and among minds: Mastering complexity, individually and in groups. In T. Koschmann (ed.), *CSCL: Theory and practice of an emerging paradigm* (pp. 25–44). Mahwah, NJ: Lawrence Erlbaum Associates.

Fitzclarence, L. (2000). Learning and teaching in education's shadowland: Violence, gender relations and pedagogic possibilities, *The Review of Education/ Pedagogy/Cultural Studies*, *22*(2), 147–73.

Fitzgerald, H. and Jobling, A. (2004). Student-centred research: Working with disabled students. In J. Wright, D. Macdonald and L. Burrows (eds), *Critical inquiry and problem-solving in physical education* (pp. 74–91). London: Routledge.

Fleckenstein, K. (2003). Writing bodies: Somatic mind in composition studies. *College English*, *61*(3), 281–306.

Fletcher, S., Hope, S. and Wagner, S. (2001). Making maths meaningful and manageable at the middle years. Paper presented at Middle Years Conference Melbourne, March. Retrieved 13 November 2001, from: http://www./sofweb.vic.edu.au/mys/conf/papers01/b6.htm

Forster, M. and Masters, G. (1996a). *Performances*. Melbourne: Australian Council for Educational Research.

——(1996b). *Portfolios*. Melbourne: Australian Council for Educational Research.

Forte, I. and Schurr, S. (1997). *The middle years of schooling: A handbook for success*. Australia: Hawker Brownlow Education.

Fountas, I. and Pinnell, G.S. (2001). *Guiding readers and writers, grades 3–6*. Portsmouth, NH: Heinemann.

Frankenberger, K.D (2004). Adolescent egocentrism, risk perceptions, and sensation seeking among smoking and nonsmoking youth. *Journal of Adolescent Research*, 19(5), September, 576–90.

Freire, P. (1996). *Letters to Cristina: Reflections on my life and work*. London: Routledge.

Freud, A. (1968). Instinctual anxiety during puberty. In A. Freud, *The ego and the mechanisms of defence*. London: the Hogarth Press and the Institute of Psycho-Analysis.

Frydenberg, E. (2002). *Adolescent coping: Theoretical and research perspectives*. London: Routledge.

Fullan, M. (2001). *The new meaning of educational change* (3rd edn). New York: Teachers College Press.

——(2003). *Change forces with a vengeance*. London: Routledge Falmer.

Fullan, M. and Hargreaves, A. (1991). *Working together for your school: Strategies for developing interactive professionalism in your school*. Hawthorn, Vic: Australian Council for Education Administration Inc.

Fullan, M. and Miles, M. (1992). Getting reform right: what works and what doesn't. *Phi Delta Kappan*, 73(10), 744–52.

Fuller, A. (1998). *From surviving to thriving: Promoting mental health in young people*. Melbourne: Australian Council of Educational Research (ACER).

——(2002). *Raising real people: Creating a resilient family* (2nd edn). Melbourne: Australian Council of Educational Research (ACER).

——(2003). *Don't waste your breath: An introduction to the mysterious world of the adolescent brain*. Retrieved 1 November 2004, from http://www.andrewfuller.com.au/research/wasteBreathe.pdf

Garcia, J., Spalding, E. and Powell, R. (2001). *Contexts of teaching: Methods for middle and high school instruction*. New Jersey: Merrill Prentice-Hall.

Gard, M. (2004). An elephant in the room and a bridge too far, or physical education and the 'obesity epidemic'. In J. Evans, B. Davies and J. Wright (eds), *Body
knowledge and control: Studies in the sociology of physical education and health*
(pp. 68–82). New York: Routledge.

Gard, M. and Wright, J. (2001). Managing uncertainty: Obesity discourse and physical education in a risk society. *Studies in Philosophy and Education, 20*(6),
535–49.

Gardner, H. (1983). *Frames of mind: The theory of multiple intelligences.* New York:
Basic Books.

——(1993). *Multiple intelligences: The theory in practice.* New York: Basic Books.

Garmezy, N. (1987). *The role of competence in the study of risk and protective factors
in childhood and adolescence.* Paper presented at IX Biennial International
Society for the Study of Behavioural Development meetings, Tokyo.

Gaskins, I.W., Satlow, E., Hyson, D., Ostertag, J. and Six, L. (1994). Classroom talk
about text: Learning in science class. *Journal of Reading, 37*(7), 558–65.

Geake, J.G. (2003). Adapting middle level educational practices to current research
on brain functioning. *Journal of the New England League of Middle Schools,
15*(2), 6–12.

Gearge, P., Lawrence, G. and Bushnell, D. (1998). *Handbook for middle school teaching* (2nd edn). New York: Addison Wesley Longman.

Gee, J.P., Hull, G. and Lankshear, C. (1996). *The new work order: Behind the
language of the new capitalism.* Sydney: Allen & Unwin.

Geertsen, H.R. (2003). Rethinking thinking about higher level thinking. *Teaching
Sociology, 31*(1), 1–19.

George, P., Stevenson, C., Thomason, J. and Beane, J. (1992). *The middle school—
and beyond* (pp. 81–103). Alexandria, VA: Association for Supervision and
Curriculum Development.

George, P.S. and Alexander, W.M. (1993). *The Exemplary Middle School* (2nd edn).
Fort Worth, TX: Harcourt Brace Jovanovich College Publishers.

Gerard, J.M. and Buehler, C. (2004). Cumulative environmental risk and youth
maladjustment: The role of youth attributes. *Child Development, 75*(6),
Nov–Dec, 1832–49.

Gibbons, M. (2002). *The self-directed learning handbook: Challenging adolescent
students to excel.* San Francisco: Jossey-Bass.

Giedd, J. (2004). Structural magnetic resonance imaging of the adolescent brain.
Annals of the New York Academy of Sciences, 1021, 77–85.

Giedd, J.N., Blumenthal, J., Jeffries, N.O., Castellanos, F.X., Liu, H., Zijdenbos, A.,

Paus, T., Evans, C. and Rapoport, J.L. (1999). Brain development during childhood and adolescence: A longitudinal MRI study. *Nature Neuroscience, 2*(10), 861–3.

Giedd, J.N., Vaituzis, C., Hamburger, S.D., Lange, N., Rajapakse, J.C., Kaysen, D., Vauss, Y.C. and Rapoport, J.L. (1996). Quantitative MRI of the temporal lobe, amygdala and hippocampus in normal human development: Ages 4–18 years. *Journal of Comparative Neurology, 366*, 223–30.

Gilbert, R. and Gilbert, P. (1998). *Masculinity goes to school.* Sydney: Allen & Unwin.

Glenn, R.E. (2002). Using brain research in your classroom. *The Education Digest, 67*(7), 27–30.

Glister, P. (1997). A new digital literacy: A conversation with Paul Gilster by Claire Pool, *Educational Leadership: Integrating Technology into Teaching, 55*(3), 6–11.

Glover, S., Burns, J., Butler, H. and Patton, G. (1998). Social environments and the emotional wellbeing of young people. *Family Matters, 49* (Autumn), 11–16.

Gogtay, N., Giedd, J.N., Lusk, L., Hayashi, K.M., Greenstein, D. and Vaituzis, A.C. (2004). Dynamic mapping of human cortical development during childhood through early adulthood. *Proceedings of the National Academy of Sciences of the United States of America, 101*, 8174–9. Retrieved 7 October 2004, from http://www.pnas.org/cgi/content/full/

Goleman, D. (1995). *Emotional intelligence: Why it can matter more than IQ.* New York: Bantam Books.

——(1998). *Working with emotional intelligence.* New York: Bantam Books.

Goswami, U. (2004). Annual review: Neuroscience and education. *British Journal of Educational Psychology, 74*, 1–14.

Graber, J.A., Brooks-Gunn, J. and Petersen, A.C. (1996). *Transitions through adolescence: Interpersonal domains and contexts.* Mahwah, NJ: Erlbaum.

Green, D. and Campbell, R. (eds) (2003). *Literacies and Learners: Current perspectives.* Frenchs Forest, NSW: Prentice Hall.

Green, P. (1998). The journey from primary to secondary school: The Literacy-related demands in transition. *Australian Journal of Language and Literacy, 21*(2), 118–34.

Gross, P. (1997). *Joint curriculum design: Facilitating learner ownership and active participation in secondary classrooms.* New Jersey: Lawrence Erlbaum Associates

Grosz, E. (1994). *Volatile bodies: Toward a corporeal feminism.* Sydney, NSW: Allen & Unwin.

Groundwater-Smith, S., Brennan, M., McFadden, M. and Mitchell, J. (2001). *Secondary schooling in a changing world.* Sydney: Harcourt.

Grundy, S. and Bonser, S. (2000). The new work order and Australian schools. In Day, C., Fernandez, A., Hange, T. and Moller, J. (eds), *The life and work of teachers: International perspectives in changing times.* London: Falmer Press.

Gump, P.V. (1980). The school as a social situation. *Annual Review of Psychology, 31,* 553–82.

Gurian, M. (2001). *Boys and girls learn differently.* San Francisco: Jossey-Bass.

——(2003). *Boys and girls learn differently: Action guide for teachers.* San Francisco: Jossey-Bass.

Habermas, J. (1971). *Knowledge and human interests* (J. Shapiro, Trans.). Boston, MA: Beacon Press.

Haeckel, E. (1868). *Naturliche Schopfungsgeschichte [Natural history of creation].* Berlin: George Reimer.

Hall, G.S. (1904). *Adolescence* (Vols 1 & 2). Englewood Cliffs, NJ: Prentice Hall.

Hamburg, B. (1974). Early adolescence: A specific and stressful stage of the life cycle. In G. Coelho, D.A. Hamburg and J.E. Adams (eds), *Coping and adaptation* (pp. 101–25). New York: Basic Books.

Hardiman, M.M. (2003). *Connecting brain research with effective teaching: The brain-targeted teaching model.* Lanham, MD: Scarecrow Press Inc.

Hargreaves, A. and Earl, L. (1990). *Rights of passage: A review of selected research about schooling in the transition years.* Toronto: Queen's Printer.

Hargreaves, A., Earl, L. and Ryan, J. (1996). *Schooling for change: Reinventing education for early adolescents.* London: Falmer Press.

Hargreaves, D. (1997). In defence of research for evidence-based teaching: A rejoinder to Martin Hammersley. *British Educational Research Journal, 24*(4), 405–19.

Harper, D. (2001). *Online etymology dictionary.* Retrieved 20 July 2004, from http://www.etymonline.com

Harrison, L. (1995). African-Americans: Race as a self-schema affecting physical activity choices. *Quest, 47,* 7–18.

Harvey, S. (1998). *Nonfiction matters: Reading writing and research in grades 3–8.* Portland, Me: Stenhouse.

Harvey, S. and Goudvis, A. (2000). *Strategies that work: Teaching comprehension to enhance understanding.* York, Me: Stenhouse.

Hatano, G. and Inagaki, K. (1991). Sharing cognition through collective comprehension activity. In L.R. Resnick, J.M. Levine, and S.D. Teasley (eds), *Perspectives on socially shared cognition* (pp. 331–48). Washington, DC: American Psychological Association.

Havinghurst, R.J. (1972). *Developmental tasks and education* (3rd edn). New York: David McKay.

Hayes, D., Lingard, B. and Mills, M. (2000). Productive pedagogies. *Education Links, 60*, 10–13.

Hellison, D. (1995). *Teaching responsibility through physical activity.* Champaign, IL.: Human Kinetics.

Hembree, R. (1990). The nature, effects and relief of mathematics anxiety. *Journal for Research in Mathematics Education, 21*(1), 33–46.

Hepburn, M. (1983). *Democratic education in schools and classrooms.* Washington, DC: National Council for the Social Studies.

Hidi, S. and Harackiewicz, J.M. (2000). Motivating the academically unmotivated: A critical issue for the 21st century. *Review of Educational Research, 70*, 151–79.

Hill, B. (1995). What's open about open education? In D. Nyberg (ed.), *The philosophy of open education* (pp. 3–13). London: Routledge & Kegan Paul.

Hill, P. (1995). *The middle years of schooling.* Melbourne: Centre of Applied Research, The University of Melbourne.

Hill, P. & Russell, V. (1999). Systemic, whole-school reform of the middle-years of schooling. In R.J. Bosker, B.P.M. Creemers and S. Stringfield (eds), *Enhancing educational excellence, equity and efficiency: Evidence from evaluations of systems and schools in change* (pp. 167–96). Dortrecht: Kluwer Academic Publishers.

Hill, P.W., Mackay, A.D., Russell, V.J. and Zbar, V. (2001). *The middle years, school innovation: Pathway to the knowledge society.* Retrieved 22 November 2001, from http://www.detya.gov.au/schools/Publications/2001/innovation/chapter 5.htm:

Hoffman, J. (2002). Flexible grouping strategies in the multi-age classroom. *Theory into Practice, 41*(1), 47–52.

Holdsworth, R. (1998). Two challenges. *Connect, 110*, 15–17.

——(1999). Enhancing effective student participation: 33 curriculum approaches. *Connect, 116*, 6–9.

Hopkins, D., Ainscow, M. and West, M. (1994). *School improvement in an era of change.* New York: Teachers College Press.

Hopson, M.H., Simms, R.L. and Knezek, G.A. (2001/2002). Using a technology-enriched environment to improve higher-order thinking skills. *Journal of Research on Computing in Education, 34*(2), 109–19.

Howard, P.J. (2000). *The owner's manual for the brain.* Atlanta: Bard Press.

Hoyt, L. (1999). *Revisit, reflect, retell: Strategies for improving reading comprehension.* Portsmouth, NH: Heinemann.

Hubscher-Younger, T. and Hari Narayanan, N. (2003). Authority and convergence in collaborative learning. *Computers & Education, 41*, 313–34.

Hunt, G., Wiseman, D. and Bowden, S. (1998). *The middle school teachers' handbook*. Springfield, IL: Charles C. Thomas.

Hunter, L. (2002). *Young people, physical education, and transition: Understanding practices in the middle years of schooling*. Unpublished doctorate thesis. School of Human Movement Studies. Brisbane: The University of Queensland, 374.

——(2004). Who gets to play? Kids, bodies, and schooled subjectivities. In J.A. Vadenboncour and L.P. Stevens (eds), *Re/Constructing 'the adolescent': Sign, symbol and body* (pp. 182–210). New York: Peter Lang.

Hunter, L., Patel Stevens, L., Pendergast, D., Carrington, V., Kapitzke, C., Bahr, N. and Mitchell, J. (2004). *Finding sustainable spaces for young people in middle schooling: An historical and theoretical enquiry into adolescence*. Bathurst: Australian Association of Teacher Education.

Hurd, P. (2000). *Transforming middle school science education*. New York: Teachers College Press.

Hurley, G. and Weldon, E. (2004). A culture for thinking and learning. *Education Views, 13*, 8.

Inhelder, B. and Piaget, J. (1958). *The growth of logical reasoning from childhood to adolescence*. New York: Basic Books.

Jackson, A.W. and Davis, G.A. (2000). *Turning points 2000: Educating adolescents in the 21st century*. Columbus, OH: National Middle Schools Association.

Jacobs, H.H. (1997). *Mapping the big picture: Integrating curriculum and assessment K–12*. Alexandria, VA: Association for Supervision and Curriculum Development.

Jaggar, A.M. and Rothenberg, P.S. (1993). *Feminist frameworks: Alternative theoretical accounts of the relations between women and men*. (3rd edn). New York: McGraw-Hill.

Jalongo, M.R. (2003). The child's right to creative thought and expression. *Childhood Education, 79*, 218–28.

Jensen, E. (1998). *Teaching with the brain in mind*. Alexandria, VA: ASCD.

Johnson, D., Johnson, R., Holubec, E. and Roy, P. (1984). *Cooperation in the classroom*. Edina, MN: Interaction Books.

Johnston, P.H. (1997). *Knowing literacy: Constructive literacy assessment*. York, Me: Stenhouse.

Kahan, D. (2003). Religious boundaries in public school physical-activity settings. *The Journal of Physical Education, Recreation and Dance, 74*(1), 11–14.

Kalivas, P.W., Churchill, L. and Klitenick, M.A. (1993). The circuitry mediating the translation of motivational stimuli into adaptive motor responses. In P.W. Kalivas and C.D. Barnes (eds), *Limbic motor circuits and neuropsychiatry* (pp. 237–87). Boca Raton, FA: CRC Press.

Kamler, B., Maclean, R., Reid, J. and Simpson, A. (1994) *Shaping up nicely: The formation of schoolgirls and schoolboys in the first month of school.* Canberra: Department of Employment, Education and Training.

Karvelas, P. and Tobler, H. (2004). Fat lot of good that'll do. *The Australian*, 30 June, p. 13.

Keddie, A. (2003) Little boys: Tomorrow's macho lads. *Discourse: Studies in the Cultural Politics of Education, 24*(3), 289–306.

——(2004). Working with boys' peer cultures: Productive pedagogies . . . productive boys. *Curriculum Perspectives, 24*(1), 20–9.

——(*forthcoming*). Pedagogies and critical reflection: Key understandings for transformative gender justice. *Gender and Education.*

Keddie, A. and Churchill, R. (2004). Power, control and authority: Issues at the centre of boys' relationships with their teachers. *Queensland Journal of Teacher Education, 19*(1), 13–27.

Keith, J. (1985). Age in anthropological research. In R.H. Binstock and E. Shanus (eds), *Handbook of aging and the social sciences* (2nd edn). New York: Van Nostrand Reinhold.

Kellet, Mand Nind, M. (2003). *Implementing intensive interaction in schools: Guidance for practitioners, managers, and coordinators.* London: David Fulton.

Kenway, Jand Fitzclarence, L. (1997). Masculinity, violence and schooling: Challenging 'poisonous' pedagogies'. *Gender and Education, 9*(1), 117–33.

Keogh, J., Rohner, C., Pendergast, D., Bahr, N., Carrington, V., Hunter, L., Kapitzke, K., Mitchell, J., Stevens, L. and Wright, T. (2004) *Three years on: Growing teachers for the middle years.* Paper presented at the Australian Association for Research in Education Conference, Melbourne.

Kett, J. (1977). *Rites of passage: Adolescence in America, 1790 to the present.* New York: Basic Books.

Kiddey, P. and Robson, G. (2001a). *Make their heads spin! Improving learning in the middle years.* Carlton, Vic: Curriculum Corporation.

——(2001b). *Success for all: Selecting appropriate learning strategies.* Carlton, Vic: Curriculum Corporation.

Kiesner, J., Kerr, M. and and Stattin, H. (2004). 'Very Important Persons' in adolescence: Going beyond in-school, single friendships in the study of peer homophily. *Journal of Adolescence, 27*(5), October, 545–60.

Killen, R. (2002). Outcomes-based education: Principles and possibilities. *Interpretations, 35*(2), 1–18.

Kilpatrick, S., Barrett, M. and Jones, T. (2003). *Defining learning communities.* Paper presented at the Australian Association for Research in Education Conference.

Kimmel, D.C. and Weiner, I.B. (1985). *Adolescence: A developmental transition.* New Jersey: Lawrence Erlbaum.

Kincheloe, J. and Steinberg, S. (1998a). Students as researchers: Critical visions, emancipatory insights. In S.R. Steinberg and J.L. Kincheloe (eds), *Students as researchers: Creating classrooms that matter* (pp. 2–19). London: Falmer Press.

——(1998b). Making meaning and analysing experience: Student researchers as transformative agents. In S.R. Steinberg and J.L. Kincheloe (eds), *Students as researchers: creating classrooms that matter* (pp. 228–44). London: Falmer Press.

Kirk, D. (1997). Schooling bodies in new times. In J.M. Fernandez-Balboa (ed.), *Critical postmodernism in human movement, physical education and sport* (pp. 39–63). Albany: State University of New York Press.

——(1998). *Schooling bodies: School practice and public discourse, 1880–1950.* London: Leicester University Press.

Kirk, D. and Macdonald, D. (1998). Situated learning in physical education. *Journal of Teaching in Physical Education, 17*(3), 376–87.

Klap, J. (1999). Students evaluating teachers. *Connect, 115,* 5–8.

Kochanska, G. and Murray, K.T. (2000). Mother–child mutually responsive orientation and conscience development: From toddler to early school age. *Child Development, 71,* 417–31.

Koepp, M.J., Gunn, R.N., Lawrence, A.D., Cunningham, V.J., Dagher, A., Jones, T., Brooks, C.J., Bench, C.J. and Grasby, P.M. (1998). Evidence for striatal dopamine release during a video game. *Nature, 393,* 266–8.

Kohlberg, L. (1986). A current statement on some theoretical issues. In S. Modgil and C. Modgil (eds), *Lawrence Kohlberg: Consensus and controversy.* Philadelphia: Falmer.

Komesaroff, L. and Morrison, F. (2002). Shifting to more authentic language and literacy. *Practically Primary, 7*(1), 18–21.

Krause, K., Bochner, S. and Duchesne, S. (2003). *Educational psychology for learning and teaching.* Southbank, Vic: Thomson.

Kress, G. and Van Leeuwen, T. (1996). *Reading images: The grammar of visual design.* London: Routledge.

Kuther, T.L. and McDonald, E. (2004). Early adolescents' experiences with, and views of, Barbie. *Adolescence, Spring, 39*(53) 39–51.

Kvernmo, S. and Heyerdahl, S. (2004). Ethnic identity and acculturation attitudes among indigenous Norwegian Sami and ethnocultural Kven adolescents. *Journal of Adolescent Research, 19*(5), 512–32.

Lampert, M. (1990). When the problem is not the question and the solution is not the answer: Mathematical knowing and teaching. *American Educational Research Journal, 27* (1), 29–63.

——(1998). Introduction. In M. Lampert and M.L. Blunk (eds), *Talking mathematics in school: Studies of teaching and learning* (pp. 1–14). Cambridge: Cambridge University Press.

Lankshear, C. and Snyder, I. (2000). *Teachers and techno-literacy: Managing literacy, technology and learning in schools.* Sydney: Allen & Unwin.

Lawton, D. (1975). *Class, culture and the curriculum.* London: Routledge & Kegan Paul.

Lazear, D. (1991). *Seven ways of knowing: Teaching for multiple intelligences.* Melbourne: Hawker Brownlow Education.

Leahy, D. and Harrison, L. (2001). *Mind your own body: Regulating gendered and sexual subjectivities within the secondary health and physical education curriculum.* Paper presented at the annual meeting of the Australian Association for Educational Research, Fremantle, Perth.

Leckey, M. (2001). *Towards citizenship: The untapped potential of students in the middle years of schooling.* Retrieved on 20 October 2004, from http://www.acsa.edu.au/2001conf/Leckey%20–20Towards%20Citizenship.doc

LeDoux, J. (1996). *The emotional brain: The mysterious underpinnings of emotional life.* New York: Simon & Schuster Inc.

——(1998). Fear and the brain: Where have we been, and where are we going? *Biological Psychiatry, 44,* 1229–38.

Lee Manning, M. (2002). *Developmentally appropriate middle level schools.* Olney, MD: Association for Childhood Education International.

Lefrancois, G.R. (1976). *Adolescents.* California: Wadsworth.

Lemke, J.L. (1998). Metamedia literacy: transforming meanings and media. In D. Reinking, M.C. McKenna, L.D. Labbo and R.D. Kieffer (eds), *Handbook of literacy and technology: Transformations in a post-typographic world.* Mahwah, NJ: Lawrence Erlbaum Associates.

Lemos, M. (1996). Students' and teachers' goals in the classroom. *Learning and Instruction, 6*(2), 151–71.

Lerner, R.M. and Benson, P.L. (2003). *Developmental assets and asset building communities: Implications for research, policy, and practice.* Norwell, MA: Kluwer Academic.

Letendre, G.K. (2000). *Learning to be adolescent.* New Haven: Yale University Press.

Levitt, P. (2003). Structural and functional maturation of the developing primate brain. *The Journal of Pediatrics, 143*(4), 35–45.

Lewis, D.A. (1997). Development of the prefrontal cortex during adolescence: Insights into vulnerable neural circuits in schizophrenia. *Neuropsychopharmacology, 16,* 385–98.

Lingard, B. (2003). Where to in gender policy in education after recuperative masculinity politics? *International Journal of Inclusive Education, 7*(1), 33–56.

Lingard, B., Ladwig, J.A., Mills, M., Bahr, M., Chant, D. and Warry, M. (2001). *Queensland school reform longitudinal study.* Brisbane: Education Queensland.

Lingard, B., Martino, W., Mills, M. and Bahr, M. (2002) *Addressing the educational needs of boy: Strategies for schools.* Canberra: Commonwealth Department of Education, Science and Training.

Lipsitz, J., Jackson, A.W. and Austin, L.M. (1997). What works in middle-grades school reform. *Phi Delta Kappan, 78*(7), 517.

Lloyd, D. and Wallace, J. (2004). Imaging the future of science education: The case for making futures studies explicit in student learning. *Studies in Science Education, 39,* 139–77.

Lopata, C., Miller, K.A. and Miller, R.H. (2003). Survey of actual and preferred use of cooperative learning among exemplar teachers. *The Journal of Educational Research, 96*(4), 232–9.

Louis, K. and Marks, H. (1998). Does professional community affect the classroom? Teachers' work and student experiences in restructuring schools. *American Journal of Education, 106*(4), 532–75.

Lounsbury, J.H. (1997). Foreword. In J.L. Irvin (ed.), *What current research says to the middle level practitioner* (p. x1). Columbus, OH: National Middle School Association.

Luke, A., Elkins, J., Weir, K., Land, R., Carrington, V., Dole, S., Pendergast, D., Kapitzke, C., van Kraayenoord, C., Moni, K., McIntosh, A., Mayer, D., Bahr, M., Hunter, L., Chadbourne, R., Bean, T., Alverman, D. and Stevens, L. (2003). *Beyond the middle: A report about literacy and numeracy development of target group students in the middle years of schooling* (Vols 1 and 20). Brisbane: J.S. McMillan Printing Group.

Luke, A., Matters, G., Herschell, P., Grace, N., Barrett, R. and Land, R. (2000). *New Basics Project: Technical Paper.* Brisbane: Education Queensland.

Luke, M. and Sinclair, G. (1991). Gender differences in adolescents' attitudes toward school physical education. *Journal of Teaching in Physical Education, 11,* 31–46.

Luthar, S.S., Cicchetti, D. and Becker, B. (1997). The construct of resilience: A critical evaluation and guidelines for future work. *Child Development, 71*(3), 543–62.

Macdonald, D. (2004) Rich tasks, rich learning. In J. Wright, D. Macdonald and L. Burrows (eds), *Critical inquiry in health and physical education* (pp. 120–32). Sydney: Routledge Falmer.

Macdonald, D. and Hunter, L. (2003a). *Report 3: Rich task case studies from a health and physical education perspective.* Brisbane: School of Human Movement Studies, The University of Queensland.

——(2003b). *Slip, slid'n across fields: An analysis of EQ rich tasks.* Paper presented at the 10th Australian Curriculum Studies Association Inc. Biennial National Conference, Adelaide.

Macdonald, D., Tinning, R., Glasby, P.M. and Hunter, L. (2002). *Rich tasks and citizenship: A critique of health discourses.* Australian Association for Research in Education conference, Brisbane.

Mackay, H. (1993). *Generations.* Sydney: Macmillan.

McCabe, M.P. and Ricciardelli, L.A. (2004). A longitudinal study of pubertal timing and extreme body change behaviors among adolescent boys and girls. *Adolescence, Spring, 39*(153), 145–66.

McCandless, B.R. (1970). *Adolescents.* Hinsdale: Dryden.

McEwen, B.S. and Seeman, T. (2003). Stress and affect: Applicability of the concepts of allostasis and allostatic load. In R.J. Davidson, K.R. Scherer and H. Hill Goldsmith (eds), *Handbook of affective sciences* (pp. 1117–37). Oxford: Oxford University Press.

McGeehan, J. (2001). Brain-compatible learning. *Green Teacher, 64*(7), 7–12.

McInerny, D.M. and McInerny, V. (1998). *Educational psychology: Constructing learning* (2nd edn). Sydney: Prentice Hall.

McIntosh, A., Reys, R. and Reys, B. (1992). A proposed framework for examining basic number sense. *For the Learning of Mathematics, 12*(3), 2–8.

McKinney, M., Sexton, T. and Meyerson, M.J. (1999). Validating the efficacy-based change model. *Teaching and Teacher Education, 115,* 471–85.

McLean, D. (1996). Men, masculinity and heterosexuality. In L. Laskey and C. Beavis (eds), *Schooling and sexualities.* Geelong: Deakin Centre for Education and Change, Deakin University.

McMillan, R. and Hagan, J. (2004). Violence in the transition to adulthood: Adolescent victimization education, and socioeconomic attainment in later life. *Journal of Research on Adolescence, 14*(2), 127.

Mahony, P. (1999). Girls will be girls and boys will be first. In D. Epstein, J. Elwood, V. Hey and J. Maws (eds), *Failing boys: Issues in gender and achievement.* London: Open University Press.

Main, K. (2003). *A study of teachers' perceptions of their effectiveness as educators working within a middle schooling framework.* Unpublished honours' thesis, Griffith University, Brisbane.

Maloney, S. (1993). *Reciprocal teaching: Extending reading strategies* (video). Wellington, NZ: Parallax Communications for the Ministry of Education.

Mann, J.J. (1997). Serotonin and judgement. *Brain Briefing.* Retrieved 19 October 2004, from http://apu.sfn.org/content/Publications/BrainBriefings/serotonin.html

Manning, L. (1993). *Developmentally appropriate middle level schools.* Olney, MD; Association for Childhood Education International.

Manning, M.L. and Bucher, K.T. (2005). *Teaching in the middle school* (2nd edn). New Jersey: Pearson Education, Inc.

Marcia, J.E. (1980). Identity in adolescence. In J. Adelson (ed.), *Handbook of adolescent psychology* (pp. 159–87). New York: John Wiley.

Marshall, J. (1999). Explicitly teaching the reading of nonfiction texts. In J. Hancock (ed.), *The explicit teaching of reading* (pp. 97–111). Newark, Del: International Reading Association.

Martino, W. and Mellor, B. (1995). *Gendered fictions.* Chalkface Press: Cottesloe.

Martino, W. and Pallotta-Chiarolli, M. (2003). *So what's a boy?* Sydney: Allen & Unwin.

Marzano, R.J., Pickering, D. and McTighe, J. (1993). *Assessing student outcomes: Performance assessment using the dimensions of learning model.* Alexandria, VA: Association for Supervision and Curriculum Development.

Masten, A.S. and Coatsworth, J.D. (1998). The development of competence in favorable and unfavorable environments: Lessons from research on successful children. *American Psychologist, 53*(2), 205–20.

Matter, R.M. (1982). Elkind's theory of adolescent egocentrism as expressed in selected characters of M.E. Kerr, *Adolescence, 17*(67), 657–66.

Matters, G. (2004). Variations on a theme by Paganini. *Curriculum Perspectives, 24*(1), 58–60.

Matthews, L.S. and Conger, R.D. (2004). 'He did it on purpose!' Family correlates of negative attributions about an adolescent sibling. *Journal of Research on Adolescence, 14*(3), 257.

Maxwell, J. (1983). Failures in mathematics: Causes and remedies. *Mathematics in School, 12*(2), 8–11.

Mead, M. (1935). *Sex and temperament in three primitive societies.* New York: William Morrow.

Meece, J.L. (2003). Applying learner-centred principles to middle school education. *Theory into Practice, 42*(2), 109–16.

Mellor, S. (1998). Student cynicism about political participation: 'What's the point?' *Connect, 11*, 3–7.

Messick, S. (1989). Validity. In: R.L. Linn (ed.), *Educational measurement* (3rd edn) New York: Macmillan.

——(1994). The interplay of evidence and consequences in the validation of performance assessment. *Educational Researcher, 23*(2), 13–23.

Meyer, M. and Fennema, E. (1992). Girls, boys and mathematics. In T.R. Post (ed.), *Teaching mathematics in grades K–8: Research-based methods* (pp. 443–64). Boxton: Allyn and Bacon.

Meyers, S.A. and Miller, C. (2004). Direct, mediated, moderated, and cumulative relations between neighborhood characteristics and adolescent outcomes. *Adolescence, Spring, 39*(153), 121–44.

Miller, J. and Pelham, D. (1983). *The human body: A three-dimensional study.* London: Cape.

Ministerial Council on Education, Employment, Training and Youth Affairs (MCEETYA), Student Learning and Support Services Taskforce (2003). *National Safe Schools Framework.* Carlton South, Vic: Curriculum Corporation.

Mizelle, N.B. and Mullins, E. (1997). Transition into and out of middle school. In J. Irvin (ed.), *What current research says to the middle level practitioner.* Columbus, OH: National Middle School Association.

Moline, S. (1995). *I see what you mean: Children at work with visual information.* Melbourne: Longman.

Money, J. and Ehrhardt, A. (1972). *Man and woman, boy and girl.* Baltimore: Johns Hopkins University Press.

Morris, A. and Stewart-Dore, N. (1984). *Learning to learn from text: Effective reading in the content areas.* North Ryde, NSW: Addison-Wesley.

Mosston, M. and Ashworth, S. (2002) *Teaching physical education* (5th edn). Cummings: London.

Muth, D.M. and Alvermann, D.E. (1999). *Teaching and learning in the middle grades.* Needham Heights, MA: Allyn & Bacon.

Myers, J. and Beach, R. (2001). *Hypermedia authoring as critical literacy.* Retrieved

16 January 2004, from http://www.readingonline.org/electronic/jaal/3–01_ Column/index.html

Nagel, M. (2003). Connecting teachers, boys and learning: How understanding the brain can enhance pedagogy in the middle school. *Australian Journal of Middle Schooling*, *3*(2), 20–3.

——(2004). Lend them an ear: the significance of listening to children's experiences of environmental education. *International Research in Geographical and Environmental Education*, *13*(2) (in press).

National Middle School Association (1995). *This we believe: Developmentally responsive middle level schools.* Columbus, OH: National Middle School Association.

——(2001). *This we believe—and now we must act.* Westerville, OH: National Middle School Association.

——(2003a). *This we believe: Successful schools for young adolescents.* Westerville, OH: National Middle School Association.

——(2003b). *Research and resources in support of 'This we believe'.* Westerville, OH: National Middle School Association.

National Research Council (NRC) (2001). *Knowing what students know: The science and design of educational assessment.* Washington, DC: National Academy Press.

National Schools Network (1995). *The middle years kit booklet: Beane/Brodhagen methodology for negotiating an integrated curriculum unit of study with students.* Ryde, NSW: National Schools Network.

New London Group, The (1996). A pedagogy of multiliteracies: Designing social futures. *Harvard Educational Review*, *66*(1), 60–92.

——(2000). A pedagogy of multiliteracies: Designing social futures. In B. Cope and M. Kalantzis (eds), *Multiliteracies: Literacy learning and the design of social futures* (pp. 9–38). Melbourne: Macmillan.

Newhouse-Maiden, L.P. (2002). *Hearing their voices: Building a career development model for women in engineering.* Unpublished doctoral thesis. Perth, Western Australia: Curtin University of Technology.

Newman, F. and Associates (1996). *Authentic achievement: Restructuring schools for intellectual quality.* San Francisco: Jossey-Bass.

Newmann, F. (1988). Higher-order thinking in high schools. *The Education Digest*, *54*(4), 23–7.

Nicoll, V. and Roberts, V. (1993). *Taking a closer look at literature-based programs.* Newtown, NSW: Primary English Teaching Association.

Norton, J. (2003). *Important developments in middle grades reform.* Retrieved June 24 2004, from http://www.pdkintl.org/kappan/klew0006.htm

Noss, R. (1998). New numeracies of a technological culture. *For the Learning of Mathematics, 18*(2), 2–12.

Novak, J.D. (1977). *A theory of education.* Ithaca, NY: Cornell University Press.

O'Brien, T.C. (1999). Parrot math. *Phi Delta Kappan, 80*(6), 434–8.

O'Connor, M.C. and Michaels, S. (1996). Shifting participant frameworks: Orchestrating thinking practices in group discussions. In D. Hicks (ed.), *Discourse, learning and schooling* (pp. 63–103). Cambridge: Cambridge University Press.

OECD PISA (2004). *PISA in brief from Australia's perspective.* Retrieved 20 October 2004, from www.oecd.org

Ogle, D. (1983). K-W-L-Plus: A strategy for comprehension and summarisation. *Journal of Reading, 30*, 626–63.

Onosko, J.J. (1992). Exploring the thinking of thoughtful teachers. *Educational Leadership, 49*(7), 40–3.

Organisation for Economic Cooperation and Development (OECD) (1999). *Measuring student knowledge and skills: A new framework for assessment.* Paris: OECD.

Osborn, A.F. (1963). *Applied imagination: Principles and procedures of creative problem-solving* (3rd edn). New York: Charles Scribner's Sons.

Osborne, B. and Wilson, E. (2003). Multiliteracies in Torres Strait: A Mabuiag Island state school diabetes project. *Australian Journal of Language and Literacy, 26*(1), 23–38.

O'Tuel, F. S. and Bullard, R.K. (1995). *Developing higher order thinking in the content areas K–12.* Australia: Hawker Brownlow Education.

Palincsar, A.S. and Brown, A.L. (1984). Reciprocal teaching of comprehension-fostering and comprehension-monitoring activities. *Cognition and Instruction, 1*, 117–75.

——(1985). Reciprocal teaching: A means to a meaningful end. In J. Osborn, P.T. Wilson and R.C. Anderson (eds), *Reading education: Foundations for a literate America.* Lexington, MA: Lexington Books.

Palincsar, A.S. and Herrenkohl, L.R. (2002). Designing collaborative learning contexts. *Theory and Practice, 41*(1), 26–32.

Pallotta-Chiarolli, M. (1997). We want to address boys' education but . . . In J. Kenway (ed.), *Will boys be boys?* Deakin West, ACT: Australian Curriculum Studies Association.

Parker, F.J. (1996). *Teacher and student beliefs: A case study of a high school.* Doctoral thesis: The University of Massachusetts.

Paul, R.W. (1992). *Critical thinking.* Santa Rosa, CA: Foundation for Critical Thinking.

Pearl, A. and Knight, T. (1999). *The democratic classroom: Theory to inform practice.* New Jersey: Hampton Press.

Pendergast, D. (2001). *Virginal mothers, groovy chicks and blokey blokes: Rethinking home economics (and) teaching bodies.* Brisbane: Australian Academic Press.

——(2002). Teaching in the middle years: Perceptions of real versus ideal teachers. *The Australian Journal of Middle Schooling,* 2(1), 1–6.

Pendergast, D. and Wilks, J. (2005) *Sustaining the supply of hospitality teachers: Some issues.* Paper presented at the Home Economics Institute of Australia Biennial Conference, Tasmania.

Pendergast, D., Flanagan, R., Land, R., Bahr, M., Mitchell, J., Weir, K., Noblett, G., Cain, M., Misich, T., Carrington, V. and Smith, J. (2005). Developing lifelong learners in the middle years of schooling. Unpublished MCEETYA Report.

Penney, D. (ed.) (2002). *Gender and physical education.* London: Routledge.

Perkins, D. and Swartz, R. (1992). The nine basics of teaching thinking. In A. Costa, J. Bellanca and R. Fogarty (eds), *If minds matter: A forward to the future* (pp. 53–69). Australia: Hawker Brownlow Education.

Perry, B. and Fulcher, J. (2003). A whole school approach to the provision of mathematics for low-achieving girls in a secondary school. In L. Bragg, C. Campbell, G. Herbert and J. Mousley (eds), *MERINO: Mathematics Education Research: Innovation, Networking, Opportunity, Proceedings of the twenty-sixth annual conference of the Mathematics Education Research Group of Australasia* (pp. 570–8). Geelong: Deakin University.

Perry, B. and Howard, P. (2000). *Evaluation of the impact of the Counting On program: Final report.* Sydney: NSW Department of Education and Training.

Petersen, A. (1997). Risk, governance and the new public health. In A. Petersen and R. Bunton (eds), *Foucault, health and medicine.* London: Routledge.

Petersen, A. and Lupton, D. (1996). *The new public health: Health and self in the age of risk.* Sydney: Allen & Unwin.

Petersen, K. (2002). Positive or negative? *Journal of Staff Development,* 23(3), 1–6.

Petersen, K. and Deal, T. (1998). How leaders influence the culture of schools. *Educational Leadership,* 56(3), 58–60.

Peterson, C. (2004). *Looking forward through childhood and adolescence.* Sydney: Prentice-Hall.

Piaget, J. (1955). *The construction of reality in the child* (trans. M. Cook). London: Routledge & Kegan Paul.

Pianta, R.C. and Walsh, D.J. (1996). High-risk children in schools: constructing sustaining relationships. New York: Routledge.

Pinquart, M. and Silbereisen, R.K. (2004). Transmission of values from adolescents to their parents: The role of value content and authoritative parenting. *Adolescence, Spring, 39*(153), 83–100.

Ponton, L.E. (1997). *The romance of risk: Why teenagers do the things they do.* New York: Basic Books.

Porter, M.K. (2000). Integrating resilient youth into strong communities through festivals, fairs and feasts. In S.J. Danish and T.P. Gullotta (eds), *Developing competent youth and strong communities through after-school programming* (pp. 183–237). Washington, DC: Child Welfare League of America Press.

Portman, P. (1995). Who is having fun in physical education classes? Experiences of sixth-grade students in elementary and middle schools. *Journal of Teaching in Physical Education, 14*(4), 445–53.

Pullela, T. (1993). Reciprocal teaching. *Reading Around, 1,* 1–4.

Queensland Board of Teacher Registration (1996). *Teachers working with young adolescents.* Report of the Working Party on the Preparation of Teachers for the Education of Young Adolescents. Toowong: Queensland Board of Teacher Registration.

Queensland Government (2003). *See the future: The middle phase of learning state school action plan.* Brisbane: Queensland Government.

Queensland School Reform Longitudinal Study (2001). *Final Report, Volumes 1 & 2.* Brisbane: The University of Queensland.

Queensland Studies Authority (QSA) and Queensland School Curriculum Council (QSCC) (2002a). *Overall learning outcomes and the valued attributes of a lifelong learner.* Brisbane: QSA. Retrieved 20 October 2004, from www.qsa.qld.edu.au/ publications/1to10/index.html

——(2002b). *Characteristics of the 'best practice' of an outcomes approach.* Retrieved 20 October 2004, from www.qsa.qld.edu.au/publications/1to10/index.html

Rabone, M. and Wilson, S. (1997). 'Stepping out of the box: The beginning of one teacher's journey into negotiating with students. *Connect, 106–107,* 10–16.

Raphael, T.E. and Hiebert, E.H. (1996). *Creating an integrated approach to literacy instruction.* Fort Worth, TX: Harcourt Brace College Publishers.

Raviv, A. and Raviv, A. (1990). Teachers and students: Two different perspectives? Measuring social climate in the classroom. *American Educational Research Journal, 27*(1), 141–57.

Reay, D. (2001). 'Spice girls', 'nice girls', 'girlies', and 'tomboys': Gender discourses, girls' cultures and femininities in the primary classroom. *Gender and Education*, *13*(2), 153–66.

Reid, J., Kamler, B. and Maclean, R. (1994). Discipline and cherish. *Education Links*, *48*, 19–23.

Reis, S.M. (1998). Underachievement for some—dropping out with dignity for others. *ITAG News*, Iowa Talented and Gifted Association Newsletter, *23*(4), 1, 12–15.

Reising, B. (2002). Middle school models. *The Clearing House*, *76*(2), 60–2.

Renshaw, P. (2002). *Community and learning*, Professorial Lecture Series, Griffith University, Brisbane.

Renshaw, P.D. and Brown, R.A.J. (1997). Learning partnerships: The role of teachers in a community of learners. In L. Logan and J. Sachs (eds), *Meeting the challenges of primary schools* (pp. 200–11). London: Routledge.

Renzulli, J.S. (2000). Raising the ceiling for all students: School improvement from a high-end perspective. In A.L. Costa (ed.), *Teaching for intelligence: A collection of 11 articles* (pp. 151–77). Frenchs Forest, NSW: Skylight-Hawker Brownlow.

Resnick, M.D., Bearman, P.S., Blum, R.W., Bauman, K.E., Harris, K.M., Jones, J., Tabor, J., Beuhring, T., Sievingr, E., Shew, M., Ireland, M., Bearinger, L.H. and Udry, J.R. (1997). Protecting adolescents from harm: Findings from the national longitudinal study on adolescent health. *Journal of the American Medical Association*, *278*(10), 823–32.

Reys, B. (1994). Promoting number sense in the middle grades. *Mathematics Teaching in the Middle School*, *1*(2), 114–20.

Rice, F.P. and Dolgin, K.G. (2005). *The adolescent: Development, relationships, and culture* (11th edn). Boston, MA: Allyn & Bacon.

Rigby, K. (1998). Peer relations at school and the health of adolescents. *Youth Studies Australia*, *17*(1), 2–5.

Roberts, J. (1998). Student questions leading middle years reform. *Curriculum Perspectives*, *18*(1), 71–5.

Rogoff, B. (1998). Cognition as a collaborative process. In W. Damon (ed.), *Handbook of child psychology* (5th edn, Vol. 2). New York: Wiley.

Rose, D.H. and Meyer, A. (2002). *Teaching every student in the digital age: Universal design for learning*. Washington, DC: ASCD.

Roth, W-M. (1995). Inventors, copycats, and everyone else: The emergence of shared resources and practices as defining aspects of classroom communities. *Science Education*, *79*(5), 475–502.

Ruebel, K. (2001). Coming together to raise our children: Community and the reinvented middle school. In T. Dickinson (ed.), *Reinventing the middle school* (pp. 269–87). New York: Routledge Falmer.

Sadler, D.R. (1989). Formative assessment and the design of instructional systems. *Instructional Science*, *18*(2), 119–44.

Samway, K.D. (1996). *Literature study circles in a multicultural classroom*. York: Stenhouse.

Santrock, J.W. (2003). *Adolescence* (9th edn). Boston: McGraw-Hill.

Sapolsky, R. (1999). Stress and your shrinking brain. *Discover*, *20*(3), 116–22.

Sarason, S. (1996). *Revisiting 'The culture of the school and the problem of change.'* New York: Teachers College Press.

Scales, P. (1991). *A portrait of young adolescents in the 1990s: Implications for promoting healthy growth and development.* Minneapolis: Search Institute Center for Early Adolescence.

Scardamalia, M. and Bereiter, C. (1991). Higher levels of agency for children in knowledge building: A challenge for the design of new knowledge media. *Journal of the Learning Sciences*, *1*(1), 37–68.

——(1994). Computer support for knowledge-building communities. *Journal of the Learning Sciences*, *3*(3), 265–83.

Schacter, D.L. (1996). *Searching for memory.* New York: Basic Books.

Schaffer, D.R. (2002). *Developmental psychology: Childhood and adolescence* (6th edn). California: Wadsworth.

Schettini Evans, A. and Frank, S.J. (2004). Adolescent depression and externalizing problems: Testing two models of comorbidity in an inpatient sample. *Adolescence*, *Spring*, *39*(153), 1–17.

Schoen, H.L., Fey, J.T., Hirsch, C.R. and Coxford, A.F. (1999). Issues and options in the math wars. *Phi Delta Kappan*, *80*(6), 444–53.

Schoenfeld, A.H. (1988). When good teaching leads to bad results: The disasters of 'well-taught' mathematics courses. *Educational Psychologist*, *23*(2), 145–66.

Schunk, D. (1992). Theory and research on student perceptions in the classroom. In D.H. Schunk and J.L. Meece (eds), *Student perceptions in the classroom* (pp. 3–23). New Jersey: Lawrence Erlbaum Associates.

Scott, L. (1997). Six principles for the middle years. *EQ Australia* (1), 12–13.

Seifert, K. and Hoffnung, R. (2000). *Child and adolescent development.* Boston, MA: Houghton Mifflin.

Seixas, P. (1993). The community of inquiry as a basis for knowledge and learning: The case of history. *American Educational Research Journal*, *30*(2), 305–24.

Selman, R. (1980). *The growth of interpersonal understanding*. New York: Academic Press.

Shilling, C. (1993). The body, class and social inequalities. In J. Evans (ed.), *Equality, education, and physical education* (pp. 55–73). London: Falmer Press.

Shulman, L. (1986). Those who understand: Knowledge growth in teaching. *Educational Researcher, February*, 4–14.

Shulman, L.S. and Sherin, M.G. (2004). Fostering communities of teachers as learners: Disciplinary perspectives. *Journal of Curriculum Studies, 36*(2), 135–40.

Siemon, D., Virgona, J. and Corneille, K. (2001). *The middle years numeracy project (MYNRP) 5–9, successful interventions numeracy research project—Final Report, May*. Bundoora, Vic: Royal Melbourne Institute of Technology (RMIT).

Sigelman, C.K. and Waitzman, K.A. (1991). The development of distributive justice orientations: Contextual influences on children's resource allocations. *Child Development, 62*, 1367–78.

Silver, E.A. and Metzger, W. (1989). In D.B. McLeod and V.M. Adams (eds), *Affect and mathematical problem solving: A new perspective* (pp. 59–74). New York: Springer-Verlag.

Singleton, C. (1997). Computer-based assessment of reading. In J.R. Beech and C. Singleton (eds), *The psychological assessment of reading*. London: Routledge.

Sisk, C.L. and Foster, D.L. (2004). The neural basis of puberty and adolescence. *Nature Neuroscience, 7*(10), 1040–7.

Slavin, R.E. (2004). Built to last: Long-term maintenance of success for all. *Remedial and Special Education, 25*(1), 61–7.

Smith, J.M. (2004). Adolescent males' view on the use of mental health counseling services. *Adolescence, Spring, 39*(153), 77–82.

Society for Neuroscience, The (2002). *Brain facts: A primer on the brain and nervous system*. Hong Kong: Society for Neuroscience.

Sowell, E.R., Thompson, P.M., Holmes, C.J., Jernigan, T.I. and Toga, A.W. (1999). In vivo evidence for post-adolescent brain maturation in frontal and striatal regions. *Nature Neuroscience, 2*(10), 859–61.

Spady, W. (1994). *Outcome-based education: Critical issues and answers*. Arlington, VA: American Association of School Administrators.

Sparapani, E.F. (1998). Encouraging thinking in high school and middle school: Constraints and possibilities. *The Clearing House, 71*, 274–6.

Sparks, W. and Verner, M. (1995). Intervention strategies in multicultural education: A comparison of pre-service models. *The Physical Educator, 52*, 170–80.

Spear, L.P. (2000a). The adolescent brain and age-related behavioral manifestations. *Neuroscience and Behavioral Reviews*, 24(4), 417–63.

——(2000b). Neurobehavioral changes in adolescence. *Current Directions in Psychological Science*, 9(4), 111–14.

Stacey, R.D. (1996). *Complexity and change in organizations*. San Francisco: Berrett-Koehler.

State of Queensland, Department of Education (2001). *The Queensland School Reform Longitudinal Study*. Brisbane: State of Queensland, Department of Education.

Steen, L.A. (1999). Numeracy: The new literacy for a data-drenched society. *Educational Leadership*, October, 8–13.

Steinberg, L. (2005). *Adolescence* (7th edn), New York: McGraw-Hill.

Steinberg, L. and Lerner, R.M. (2004). The scientific study of adolescence: A brief history. *Journal of Early Adolescence*, 24(1), February, 45–54.

Steinberg, S.R. and Kincheloe, J.L. (1998). *Students as researchers: Creating classrooms that matter*. London: Falmer Press.

Stevens, L., Hunter, L., Pendergast, D., Carrington, V., Kapitzke, C., Bahr, N. and Mitchell, J. (under review). Reconfiguring 'adolescence': Ambiguous bodies in ambivalent settings. *Harvard Educational Review*.

Stevenson, C. (1992). *Teaching ten to fourteen year olds*. New York: Longman.

Stiggins, R.J. and Conklin, N.F. (1992). *In teachers' hands: Investigating the practices of classroom assessment*. Albany, NY: SUNY Press.

Stowell, L. (2000). Building alliances, building community, building bridges through literacy. In K.D. Wood and T.S. Dickinson (eds), *Promoting literacy in grades 4–9: A handbook for teachers and administrators* (pp. 77–96). Boston, MA: Allyn & Bacon.

Strauch, B. (2003). *The primal teen: What the new discoveries about the teenage brain tell us about our kids*. New York: Doubleday.

Stringer, B. (1997). Better connections. *EQ Australia* (1), 21–3.

Stringer, P. (1998). Middle schooling in a P–12 context. *IARTV Seminar Series*, No. 79. Jolimont, Vic: Incorporated Association of Registered Teachers of Victoria.

Super, D.E. (1980). A life-span, life-space approach to career development. *Journal of Vocational Behavior*, 16(30), 282–98.

——(1983). The history and development of vocational psychology: A personal perspective (pp. 5–37). In W.B. Walsh and S.H. Osipow (eds), *Handbook of vocational psychology, Vol. 1: Foundations*. Hillsdale, NJ: Lawrence Erlbaum Associates.

——(1990). A life span, life space approach to career development. In D. Brown and L. Brooks (eds), *Career choice and development: Applying contemporary theories to practice* (pp. 197–261). San Francisco: Jossey-Bass.

Swain, S. (2004). Strength in the middle. *Education Week, XXIII*(32), 4–6.

Swanson, D.P., Beale Spencer, M. and Petersen, A. (1998). *The adolescent years: Social influences and educational challenges.* Chicago: The University of Chicago Press.

Sykes, H. (2001). Understanding and overstanding: Feminist-poststructural life histories of physical education teachers. *Qualitative Studies in Education, 14*(1), 13–31.

Sylwester, R. (1994). How emotions affect learning. *Educational Leadership, 52*(2), 60–5.

——(1995). *A celebration of neurons: An educator's guide to the human brain.* Alexandria, VA: The Association for Supervision and Curriculum Development.

——(1997). The neurobiology of self-esteem and aggression. *Educational Leadership, 54*(5), 75–9.

——(2000). On teaching brains to think: A conversation with Robert Sylwester. *Educational Leadership, 57*(7), 72–5.

——(2003). *A biological brain in a cultural classroom: Enhancing cognitive and social development through collaborative classroom management* (2nd edn). Thousand Oaks, CA: Corwin Press Inc.

Sytsma, S.E. (2004). *What about choice for a change?* Unpublished manuscript: University of Queensland.

Szymusiak, K. and Sibberson, F. (2001). *Beyond leveled books: Supporting transitional readers in grades 2–5.* Portland, Me: Stenhouse.

Thelen, J. (1984). *Improving reading in science.* Newark, DE: International Reading Association.

Thorsborne, M. and Vinegrad, D. (2004). *Restorative practices in classrooms: Rethinking behaviour management.* Brisbane.

Tinning, R. (1990). *Ideology and physical education: Opening Pandora's box.* Geelong, Vic: Deakin University.

Tinning, R. and Fitzclarence, L. (1992). Postmodern youth culture and the crisis in Australian secondary school physical education. *Quest, 44*, 287–303.

Tinning, R. and Glasby, P. (2002). Pedagogical work and the 'cult of the body': Considering the role of HPE in the context of the 'new public health'. *Sport, Education & Society, 7*(2), 109–19.

Tomlinson, C.A. and Kalbfleish, M.L. (1998). Teach me, teach my brain: A call for differentiated classrooms. *Educational Leadership, 56*(3), 52–5.

Torff, B. (2003). Developmental changes in teachers' use of higher order thinking and content knowledge. *Journal of Educational Psychology, 95*, 563–9.

Tovani, C. (2000). *I read it, but I don't get it: Comprehension strategies for adolescent readers*. Portland, Me: Stenhouse.

Trost, S. (2003). *Discussion paper for the development of recommendations for children's and youths' participation in health promoting physical activity*. Canberra: Commonwealth of Australia.

Turner, M. and Smith, P. (2003). *Dyslexia screener*. London: Nelson.

Turning Points (2004). At the Turning Point the young adolescents learned. Retrieved on 2 November 2004, from www.turningpts.org

Venville, G., Wallace, J., Rennie, L. and Malone, J. (1999). *Science, mathematics and technology: Case studies of integrated teaching*. Perth: Curtin University of Technology & Education Department of Western Australia.

——(2000). Bridging the boundaries of compartmentalised knowledge: Student learning in an integrated environment. *Research in Science and Technological Education, 18*(1), 23–35.

——(2002). Curriculum integration: Eroding the high ground of science as a school subject? *Studies in Science Education, 37*, 43–84.

Vervoorn, J. and van Haren, R. (2002). *MyRead: Strategies for teaching reading in the middle years*. Retrieved 29 March 2004, from http://www.myread.org/

Victorian Department of Education, Employment and Training (VDEET) (2000). *Middle years matters: Young adolescents and middle years curriculum*. Victoria: VDEET.

Vygotsky, L.S. (1962). *Thought and language*. Cambridge: MIT Press (original work published 1934).

Vygotsky, L.S. (ed.) (1978). *Mind in society: The development of higher psychological Processes*. Cambridge, MA: Harvard University.

Watson, J.B. (1913). Psychology as the behaviorist views it. *Psychological Review, 20*, 158–77.

——(1925). *Behaviorism*. New York: Norton.

Waxman, H. and Huang, S.Y. (1998). Classroom learning environments in urban elementary, middle, and high schools. *Learning Environments Research, 1*(1), 95–113.

Weller Jnr, L.D. (2004). *Quality middle school leadership* (2nd edn). Lanham, MD: Scarecrow Education.

Wells, M. (2004). *Middle years of schooling cluster research report*, Deakin University, unpublished.

Weymouth, A., Cole, J. and Grasso, R. (2001). *Younger readers' webquest.* Retrieved 25 March 2004, from http://www.internal.schools.net.au/edu/webquests/young_readers/

White, S.H. (1968). The learning–maturation controversy: Hall to Hull. *Merrill-Palmer Quarterly, 14,* 187–96.

——(1994). G. Stanley Hall: From philosophy to developmental psychology. In R.D. Parke, P.A.J. Ornstein, J. Relser and C. Zahn-Waxler (eds), *A century of developmental psychology* (pp. 204–25). Washington, DC: American Psychological Association.

Wiggins, G. (1998). *Educative assessment: Designing assessments to inform and improve student performance.* San Francisco: Jossey-Bass.

Wilhelm, J.D. (2001). *Improving comprehension with think-aloud strategies.* New York: Scholastic Professional Books.

Wiliam, D. (2000). Integrating formative and summative functions of assessment. Paper at the International Congress on Mathematics Education Tokyo, August. Retrieved 20 October 2004, from http://www.kcl.ac.uk/depsta/education/publications/ICME9%3DWGA10.pdf

Wiliam, D., Lee., C., Harrison, C. and Black, P. (2004). Teachers developing assessment for learning: Impact on student achievement. *Assessment in Education: Principles, Policy and Practice, 11*(3), 49–65.

Wilkins, J.L. (2000). Preparing for the 21st century: The status of quantitative literacy in the United States. *School Science and Mathematics, 100*(8), 405–19.

Williams, W.V. (1988). Answers to questions about math anxiety. *School Science and Mathematics, 88*(2), 95–103.

Williamson, R.D. and Johnston, J.H. (1998). The fate of middle schooling. *School Administrator, 55*(7), 7–13.

Wilson, E.O. (1998). *Consilience: The unity of knowledge.* New York: Vintage.

Wilson, S. (1998). Curriculum theorising amongst secondary school students. *Curriculum Perspectives, 18*(3), 23–32.

Winch, C. (2002). Accountability and relevance in educational research. In M. McNamee and D. Bridges (eds), *The ethics of educational research* (pp. 151–69). Oxford, UK: Blackwell Publishers.

Wing Jan, L. (2001). *Write ways: Modelling writing forms* (2nd edn). Melbourne: Oxford University Press.

Withers, G. and Batten, M. (1995). *Programs for at-risk youth: A review of American, Canadian and British literature since 1984.* ACER Research Monograph Number 47. Melbourne: ACER.

Withers, G. and Russell, J. (2001). *Educating for resilience: Prevention and intervention strategies for young people at risk.* Camberwell, Vic: ACER Press.

Wolfe, P. and Brandt, R. (1998). What do we know from brain research? *Educational Leadership, 56*(3), 8–13.

Wolfe, P. (2001). *Brain matters: Translating research into classroom practice.* Alexandria, VA: Association for Supervision and Curriculum Development.

——(2003). *The adolescent brain: A work in progress.* Retrieved 10 November 2004, from http://www.patwolfe.com/index.php?pid=100

Wright, J., Macdonald, D. and Groom, L. (2003). Beyond participation: Physical culture and young people. *Sport, Education and Society, 8*(1), 17–34.

Wright, P. (2001). Violence prevention: What can coaches and sport educators do? In B.J. Lombardo, T.J. Caravella-Nadeau, H.S. Castagno and V.H. Mancini (eds), *Sport in the twenty-first century: Alternatives for the new millennium.* Boston: Routledge.

Wyatt-Smith, C.M. and Cumming, J.J. (2003) Curriculum literacies: Expanding domains of assessment. *Assessment in Education: Principles, Policy and Practice, 10*(1), 47–60.

Yecke, C. (2003). *The war against excellence: The rising tide of mediocrity in America's middle schools.* Westport, CT: Praeger.

Young, M.F.D. (1971). *Knowledge and control: New directions for the sociology of education.* London: Collier-Macmillan.

——(1998). *The curriculum of the future: From the 'new sociology of education' to a critical theory of learning.* London: Falmer Press.

Young, R. (1992). *Critical theory and classroom talk.* Adelaide: Multilingual Matters.

Zaman, H. (1997). Islam, well-being and physical activity: Perceptions of Muslim young women. In G. Clarke and B. Humberstone (eds), *Researching women and sport* (pp. 50–67). London: Macmillan.

Zemelman, S., Daniels, H. and Hyde, A. (1998). *Best practice: New standards for teaching and learning in America's schools.* Portsmouth, NH: Heinemann.

Zevenbergen, R. (2003a). Keynote address. *Nineteenth Biennial Conference of the Australian Association of Mathematics Teachers (AAMT)*, Brisbane, 13–17 January 2003.

——(2003b). Reforming mathematics education: A case study within the context of new times. In L. Bragg, C. Campbell, G. Herbert and J. Mousley, *MERINO: Mathematics education research: Innovation, networking, opportunity, Proceedings of the twenty-sixth annual conference of the Mathematics*

Education Research Group of Australasia (pp. 791–8). Geelong: Deakin University.

——(in press). Teaching numeracy in new times. In R. Zevenbergen (ed.), *Teaching numeracy across the middle years*. Canberra: ACSA.

Index